The

Earthmover Encyclopedia

The Complete Guide to Heavy Equipment of the World

Keith Haddock

MOTORBOOKS

The Earthmover Encyclopedia

The Complete Guide to Heavy Equipment of the World

Keith Haddock

First published in 2002 by Motorbooks, an imprint of MBI Publishing Company, Galtier Plaza, Suite 200, 380 Jackson Street, St. Paul, MN 55101 USA

MBI Publishing Company titles are also available at discounts in bulk quanity for industrial or sales-promotional use. For details write to Special Sales Manager at MBI Publishing Company, Galtier Plaza, Suite 200, 380 Jackson Street, St. Paul, MN 55101 USA.

To find out more about our books, join us online at www.motorbooks.com.

Library of Congress Cataloging-in-Publication Data

Haddock, Keith, 1943-
  The earthmover encyclopedia / by Keith Haddock.
    p. cm.
  Includes index.
  ISBN-13: 978-0-7603-2964-1
  ISBN-10: 0-7603-2964-8 (hc. : alk. paper)
    1. Earthmoving machinery—North America—Encyclopedias. I. Title

TA725 .H328 2003
629.225—dc21

Front cover: Clockwise from upper left: Bucyrus-Erie 1950-B, Caterpillar D11R, LeTourneau L-1800, Liebherr T-282

Back cover: Bucyrus-Monighan 7-W and O&K Sch Rs 70/.05 6.5

Edited by Amy Glaser
Designed by Kou Lor

Printed in the United States of America

About the Author:
Keith Haddock, P.Eng., is one of the world's leading experts on earthmoving and surface mining equipment. His articles appear regularly in industrial and equipment magazines in Canada, the United States, and the United Kingdom. He often appears as a commentator on the History, Discovery and Learning Channels. Born in Sheffield, England, and graduating as a professional engineer in that city, he worked for major earthmoving contractors in the U.K. In 1974, he moved to Canada where he worked 24 years for a large surface coal mining company, becoming manager of engineering. Of his six books published by MBI Publishing Company, Keith considers *The Earthmover Encyclopedia* his greatest writing achievement and the most comprehensive ever written on earthmoving equipment. He currently lives in Edmonton, Alberta, Canada.

CONTENTS

ACKNOWLEDGMENTS

This comprehensive encyclopedia would not have been possible without the assistance from the individuals listed below. To each of you, whether you provided a single image or helped extensively, I give you my utmost thanks and appreciation. I hope you find the book is worth your efforts. I am again honored to include a significant number of images from acclaimed author and friend, Eric Orlemann. His professional advice and great images are an asset to any book. Thanks again, Eric! A special thank you goes to my wife, Barbara, for her patience and understanding during the past 12 months of intense research and writing. She has meticulously edited all my text, and supported me all the way.

Alvin E. Nus; Hendersonville, North Carolina
Andrew Gaudielle; Holland Loader Company
Arthur McNae; Queensland, Australia
Arthur Henuset; Henuset Pipeline Services, Ltd.
Audrey Faulkner; Fermec International, Ltd., England
Becky West; Galloway-Wallace
Bill Seidel; Case Corporation
Cindy Turner; Bell Equipment Co., South Africa
Claire Weslaski; Image Management LLC
Darin McCoy; CMI Corporation
David R. Wootton; Hednesford, England
David Lang; Bucyrus International, Inc.
David Maginnis; Seattle, Washington
Debbie Campbell; Terex Mining, Scotland
Denis Gaspe; Fording Coal, Ltd.
Dennis Medina; RAHCO International
Don Frantz; Historical Construction Equipment Association
Eric C. Orlemann; ECO Communications
Francis Pierre; ATM, Malakoff, France
Gary Middlebrook; Syncrude Canada, Ltd.
Gordon Morris; Wajax Industries, Ltd.
Heinz Herbert Cohrs; Holstein, Germany
Jan Miller; Guntert & Zimmerman, Construction Division

Jim Strobush; Terex Lifting
Jodi Bosscher; Vermeer Manufacturing Company
Joe Hanneman; Malcolm Marketing Communications
John Nichols; Finning Canada, Ltd.
Johnny Campos; Caterpillar, Inc.
Kelly J. Ralls; Trench-Tech
Kent Henschen; Bucyrus International, Inc.
Larry Anderson; The Charles Machine Works, Inc.
Lee Haak; Komatsu America International Co.
Linda Frederick; Krupp Canada, Inc.
Mark Dietz; P&H Mining Equipment
Merilee Hunt; Liebherr Mining Equipment
Nigel Chell; JCB Sales, Ltd., England
P. Aydin; Cleveland Trencher Co.
Peter A. Cottam; Bucyrus Europe, Ltd.
Peter Grimshaw; PNG Communications
Peter Ahrenkiel; Terex Mining
Peter Gilewicz; Parker Bay Company
Randall Nelson; Deere & Company
Richard Fielder; Tesmec
Richard Yaremko; Cobble Hill, British Columbia
Robert Jelinek; Bucyrus International, Inc.
Roland Witte; Case Corporation
Sharon L. Holling; Caterpillar, Inc.
Stan Banovac; Liebherr-Canada, Ltd.
Steen Ahlberg; Wajax Industries, Ltd.
Susan Maldonado; Rimpull Corporation
Terra Peters; Trencor, Inc.
Tina Eckeroth; Moxy Trucks AS
Tom Berry; Historical Construction Equipment Association
Tonya Creasman; Link-Belt Construction Equipment
Urs Peyer; Brunnen, Switzerland
Vince Frantz; Lakewood, Ohio
Walter Baertsh; Uter, Switzerland
Winston Leonard; Volvo Construction Equipment
Walter Baertsh; Uster, Switzerland
Yvon LeCadre; Trignac, France

INTRODUCTION

This book is a tribute to the machines that move the earth. Almost every activity we perform today, either in business or pleasure, has been made possible by the use of some form of earthmoving machine. Today, earthmoving equipment manufacturing has evolved into a truly global industry. Gone are the days when one brand name was made by one company in its country of origin. Through a series of company mergers, acquisitions, and inter-country manufacturing agreements over the past 25 years, it is no longer immediately obvious where a brand name originates, which is its parent company, or what other brands originate from the same manufacturer. The big manufacturing conglomerates have plants in many countries, and may make a certain machine type in one country for export to the rest of the world.

Other manufacturers may make a certain machine type in one factory and export it under several different brand names to various markets. If you are familiar with popular manufacturer's brand names, you may be surprised to find those familiar names on equipment types not traditionally associated with that company. Now we have Case rigid-frame off-highway haulers, articulated dump trucks and motor graders, Link-Belt articulated dump trucks and wheel loaders, Fiat-Allis articulated dump trucks, Hitachi articulated dump trucks, Terex tractor-backhoes, and Volvo motor graders. The list could go on and on. These familiar names now belong to parent companies with families of products that allow access to the other brands owned by the same parent company. For instance, the articulated dump truck in the Case New Holland group originated in the United Kingdom as the DDT and is now sold in different parts of the world under no less than seven brand names. In other examples the parent company has chosen to brand its own name on former product lines it now owns (examples: Volvo, Hitachi, and Terex). Or, machines are made under license from another company and badged with a familiar name (examples: Deere-branded loaders and dozers made by Liebherr, and New Holland-branded dozers made by Orenstein & Koppel (O&K).

Over the past quarter-century, the greatest advancement in machine design has been in the area of health and safety. The early machines offered no consideration for the operator. Gone are the large machines with non-power-assisted levers and open cabs exposed to the elements. Contrast these with today's air-conditioned, heated, radio-equipped cabs with power-assisted controls. Machines no longer damage the hearing of those who operate them, or disturb the peace of those nearby. Rollover protection is mandatory, and even the paint finish must meet non-toxic standards. The cab exterior is more than just plain functional. Stylish designs of excavators consistent with styling standards of the automobile industry bring aesthetics into play in each new model series. Paint schemes add distinctive character to each brand.

You are holding probably the most comprehensive book ever written on earthmoving equipment in North America, but even a book of this size could not cover all manufacturers on a worldwide basis. It is regrettable that many hundreds of European manufacturers in such countries as Germany, Italy, and France, as well as manufacturers on other continents that contribute their part to the worldwide earthmoving industry, had to be omitted due to space restrictions. The book therefore focuses on those machines built in North America and those with a strong presence there, either through importation or with global company connections as noted above. Foreign machines are described where they have major significance in the industry, or because a certain type of machine originated in a country other than the United States.

The first chapter describes the evolution of earthmoving from manpower to animal power, and then machine power. It covers the development of the primary energy sources from steam to electricity, and to the modern diesel engine. The very first earthmoving machines are described in this chapter. The rest of the book consists of a chapter on each type of earthmoving machine. Each chapter commences with a short introduction describing the machine type, its development, and significant innovations over the years that have resulted in today's modern marvels. The rest of each chapter contains a wide variety of photographic images covering each manufacturer arranged in alphabetical order for ease of reference.

The machines illustrated have been selected for their importance in a company's product line, or because of their overall significance in product development in the earthmoving industry. A brief company history, as well as each machine's description, is included in the captions. Emphasis has been placed on selecting images not previously published. It was not possible to include representative photographs of each era, of companies with extensive product lines spanning many decades.

CHAPTER 1

EARLY EARTHMOVING MACHINES

The need to reshape Mother Earth goes back almost as far as civilization itself. For thousands of years man toiled, without any form of mechanized assistance, to complete projects large and small, some counting among the Wonders of the World. Using primitive hand tools, armies of men assisted by animal power achieved immense undertakings such as the pyramids of Egypt, the Great Wall of China, and the Roman network of highways across Europe. The early constructors dreamed of moving earth by mechanical means. Famous Italian painter and man of science Leonardo da Vinci (1452–1519) sketched many types of earth-moving contrivances. The technology required to build these machines was simply not available until after the advent of steam power some three centuries later.

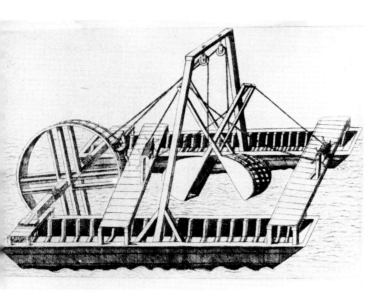

Early Clamshell Dredge. Before the machine age, massive earthmoving projects were carried out using manual labor assisted only by animals. As the centuries passed, the idea of moving material by mechanized equipment began to crystallize in some of the creative minds of the day. Leonardo da Vinci (1452–1519) sketched many types of earthmoving and other contrivances, but lack of technology prevented them from being built. The picture shows an early floating clamshell excavator from an illustration in a book by Verantius in 1591. Similar drawings of excavating machines appeared in certain ancient documents, but there is no record of them actually being built. *Keith Haddock collection*

The earliest types of excavating machines were floating dredges of the bucket chain or ladder type. Driven by animals, manpower, or even windmills, they were used in the eighteenth century to lift mud from shipping channels. One of the earliest recorded steam-powered dredges was one recorded working in 1796 for the Port of Sunderland, England. In the early nineteenth century, large ladder dredgers initially constructed and later dredged present-day ports.

On land, early earthmoving projects arose from the need to transport men and materials. First came primitive roads used by horse-drawn buggies and wagons. Then a network of transportation canals was constructed in Europe. These were operated by horse-drawn barges pulled by the animals walking along a towpath. The invention of steam power and the Industrial Revolution of the eighteenth century brought massive expansion to industry, and the need for mined resources like coal for heating and iron ore for steel making. Railway development in the early nineteenth century was crucial to industrial expansion. Not only did the raw materials need transporting to the factories, but also manufactured goods had to be moved from the factories to their markets. Canals were slow, and roads were crude and almost impassable in wet weather, leaving rail transportation as the only alternative.

Railway construction was the most significant factor leading to the development of the first land excavator and first earthmoving machine. The 1835 steam-powered shovel designed by William S. Otis is the earliest known single-bucket excavator used on land. It was designed out of a need to lower excavating costs on railroad construction projects done by the firm of contractors in which Otis was a partner. The Otis family contracting business retained the shovel patent for over 40 years and benefited from this advantage, but such strictly held patents and the availability of inexpensive labor caused mechanized excavation to evolve very slowly. The Otis shovels were built in very small numbers but remained in production by manufacturer John Souther & Company until about 1913, surprisingly without major design changes.

When the Otis patents finally expired in the 1870s, several other companies began building steam shovels.

8

Otis Steam Shovel. The steam shovel, designed by William S. Otis in 1835 and patented in 1839, is the earliest known single-bucket excavator for use on land. This drawing, made in 1841 by S. Rufus Mason, is the earliest illustration of an Otis steam shovel, although it does not depict Otis' first machine. Otis was a partner in the contracting firm of Carmichael, Fairbanks and Otis, which used its own machines for railroad construction. Eastwick and Harrison of Philadelphia, Pennsylvania, built the illustrated machine. When William Otis died of typhoid fever in 1839 at the early age of 26, the shovel patents were strictly held by the family contracting business for over 40 years, but the machines were only built in small numbers. *Keith Haddock collection*

Priestman Steam Clamshells. Probably the earliest project to utilize large fleets of earthmoving machines was the Manchester Ship Canal in England. The canal connects the inland city of Manchester with the ocean, some 35 miles away. The project employed 97 steam excavators, including 58 Ruston steam shovels, 18 Priestman steam clamshell excavators (illustrated), and several bucket chain excavators built in Germany. These were teamed with 173 steam locomotives and 6,300 rail wagons to move material at rates up to 1.2 million cubic yards per month. In all, 54 million cubic yards, including 12 million cubic yards of rock, were excavated over a six-year period starting in 1887. *Keith Haddock collection*

Hand Excavation. Although the steam shovel was invented in 1835, its use was extremely limited during the next 50 years, when most of the world's railways were built using hand labor. The Otis family held the patents tightly, and the abundance of plentiful, cheap, hand labor did not promote the use of the steam shovel. The laborers, called "navvies," worked long hours for minimal pay. They lived in makeshift timber or mud huts and moved from job to job, often without any permanent residence. It was not until the start of the really massive earthmoving ventures that the capability of the steam shovel was fully appreciated. *Keith Haddock collection*

In the United States, these included the Osgood Dredge Company, Troy, New York (1875); the Bucyrus Foundry & Manufacturing Company, Bucyrus, Ohio (1882); Vulcan Iron Works Company, Toledo, Ohio (1882); and Marion Steam Shovel Company, Marion, Ohio (1884). In the same period several others in the United Kingdom, including Ruston, Proctor & Company (1874), also designed and built steam shovels. All these shovels were rail mounted and built on principles similar to the original Otis design. They consisted of a steel or wooden house mounted on a frame that supported the draw works, boiler, and swinging boom. The boom was capable of swinging approximately 180 degrees. To Otis' credit, this design configuration remained current for almost 100 years, and since most of the work performed by steam shovels during the nineteenth century was in connection with railroad construction, these half-swing machines became known as "railroad shovels."

While mechanized excavation slowly progressed, most of the world's railways were built using hand labor, even after the invention of the steam excavator. However, a few early projects involved moving earth and rock in such vast quantities that they would dwarf

Bucyrus Ladder Dredger. Most of the early earthmoving projects arose from the need to transport men and materials across land and sea. The desire to move people and materials from place to place spawned the earliest forms of mechanized equipment. Because ships were one of the first means of transportation over long distances, it was only natural that the first self-powered excavators were dredges. The earliest forms of waterborne machines excavated harbors and deepened waterways to make them navigable by the world's ships. The ladder or placer dredge shown here was built in Russia to Bucyrus designs. About a dozen similar dredgers, as well as a number of steam shovels, were built in Russia under an agreement established in 1900 by the Bucyrus Company and the Poutilov Works. *Keith Haddock collection*

Dunbar & Ruston Steam Navvy. In 1874, Ruston, Proctor & Company of Lincoln, England, developed a machine known as the Dunbar & Ruston Steam Navvy. Its name was taken from the laborers known as navvies. The Ruston company had purchased the patents from engineer James Dunbar. For its day, the Dunbar Navvy was built strongly and with many improvements over the earlier Otis design. It was built entirely of steel and employed a double-cylinder engine in place of the single-cylinder type on the Otis. It also used friction clutches to swing the boom instead of the sliding positive pinions used on the Otis. The ground crew pauses for the photographer to capture this Dunbar & Ruston Navvy busy in railway construction.
Keith Haddock collection

most of today's earthmoving jobs. In fact, they would have been impossible to complete without huge fleets of steam shovels.

The earliest recorded project to use a large concentration of railroad shovels was the Manchester Ship Canal in England, starting in 1887. Here, 58 Ruston steam shovels, 18 Priestman revolving clamshell excavators, and numerous other excavators worked with 173 steam locomotives and 6,300 rail wagons to move 54 million cubic yards over a six-year period. The Chicago Main Drainage Canal, which started construction in 1894, employed over 60 railroad shovels. The largest and most famous of the early projects, the Panama Canal, was completed in 1914 following an intermittent construction period spanning some three decades. The French utilized well over 100 steam-powered excavators and dredges in the first attempt from 1883 to 1889. Even though this effort was aborted, the French did succeed in moving a significant portion of the project's total volume. The American-led Isthmian Canal Commission took over the project in 1904 and completed the massive digging operation with 102 steam shovels (48 of which were the largest available), 379 steam locomotives, and about 6,000 railcars. This equipment replaced the obsolete machines used by the French.

After the steam shovel was established, steam power gradually progressed to other types of earthmoving

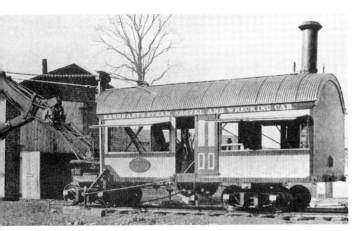

Barnhart Steam Shovel. As one of the pioneering steam shovel manufacturers, Marion Power Shovel Company was established in 1884 as the Marion Steam Shovel Company in Marion, Ohio, to manufacture "Barnhart's Steam Shovel and Wrecking Car" shown here. Like all railroad shovels, the Barnhart was mounted on standard railroad trucks, and its boom swung just over 90 degrees to each side. Marion grew into one of the foremost manufacturers of excavating machines and, in competition with its archrival Bucyrus, made similar products such as railroad shovels, dredges, cranes, walking draglines, and drills. Marion's excavator range extended from the smallest .5-cubic-yard shovel to the largest shovel ever put to work, the 180-cubic-yard Model 6360. *Keith Haddock collection*

equipment formerly powered by teams of horses and mules. The big steam-wheeled tractors of the late nineteenth century were used to pull scrapers and graders. The first crawler tractors appeared just after the turn of the century, but the idea of mounting a vehicle on crawler tracks to improve traction and decrease ground pressure actually dates back over two centuries. In 1770, Richard Edgeworth patented a track system in England that clearly employed the principles of the modern crawler, but no records exist to show that it was actually put into practice.

Holt's now-famous first crawler tractor of 1904 was a steam tractor converted from wheels to tracks. The following year saw crawler tracks fitted to an oil tractor built by R. Hornsby & Sons of Grantham, England. These pioneering experiments proved milestones on the way to more reliable and efficient machines. As the twentieth century progressed, steam power was gradually replaced—first by oil and gasoline engines, and later by the diesel engine. The Monighan Machine Company built a dragline in 1910. It was the first excavator powered by an internal-combustion engine. Caterpillar introduced its first diesel-powered tractor in 1931.

Prior to the 1930s, off-highway road vehicle technology seriously lagged behind the development of

Vulcan Steam Backhoe. The Vulcan Iron Works of Toledo, Ohio, was established in 1870. The first steam shovels built by the company were to the design of H. T. Stock, a long-standing figure in the steam shovel world, who worked for William Otis in the early days. By 1889, the company was building steam shovels to its own designs, and changed its name to the Vulcan Steam Shovel Company in 1908. The machine in the picture is Vulcan's version of a backhoe, one of the first ever built. It was introduced in 1896, but was not a success for obvious reasons. Vulcan's other shovels were of conventional construction and superior design. Their success attracted the attention of the Bucyrus Company, and in 1910, Vulcan and Bucyrus merged to form the Bucyrus-Vulcan Company. The following year this company was consolidated into the Bucyrus Company. *Keith Haddock collection*

Bucyrus 85-Ton Steam Shovel. The Bucyrus Foundry & Manufacturing Company was established in 1880. It started building shovels when it took over manufacture of the Thompson railroad shovel in 1882. The machine shown was introduced in 1899 and is working for Biwabik Mining Company. It's a typical railroad shovel of the turn of the century, with a boom swinging a little more than a halfcircle. Since nearly all shovels sold in the 1800s were employed in railroad construction, shovels of this type became known as "railroad shovels." The modern Bucyrus giant mining shovels can trace their ancestry back to this machine. *Keith Haddock collection*

This is the crawler tractor that started an industry! In 1904, after several unsuccessful attempts by other manufacturers, the Holt Manufacturing Company of Stockton, California, tested the crawler idea by removing the driving wheels from one of its three-wheeled steam traction engines, and replacing them with a pair of crawler tracks. The front steering, or tiller, wheel was retained. The idea was to allow the tractor to work in relatively soft ground by increasing its bearing area. The experiment was a success, and after further testing, the first production steam crawler was sold in 1906. The first Holt crawler machine is shown on test in 1905. *Caterpillar, Inc. Corporate Archives*

Wilson Steam Shovel. John H. Wilson & Company of Liverpool, England, built one of the first full-circle shovels in 1887. (The very first was built by Whitaker & Sons, Leeds, England, in 1884.) The crowding arrangement on the Wilson machine consisted of a direct-acting steam cylinder fitted between the dipper arms. The machine shown is working on the Manchester Ship Canal, where it joined 96 other steam shovels to complete this mammoth task by 1893. Another Wilson shovel carried the distinction of being the first long-boom fully revolving stripping shovel. The 78-ton rail-mounted outfit was built in 1900 to uncover iron ore for Lloyds Ironstone Company. *Keith Haddock collection*

power shovels. The heavily built shovels with dipper capacities up to 2 cubic yards were totally unsuited to the light-duty vehicles of the day. Rail transport worked well when the shovels were rail mounted, but as the shovels left their restrictive rails and began to move on wheels or crawler tracks, more mobile vehicles became essential. Wooden wagons drawn by horses were used at first. Then large-capacity steel trailers pulled by crawler tractors achieved some measure of success, but their slow speed was a major disadvantage. The only trucks available were the highway type, built with light-duty frames, wooden bodies, and narrow wheels. The heavy shovels pounded the flimsy truck bodies with rocks, and the trucks frequently became stuck in muddy conditions. Obviously a new kind of off-highway vehicle was needed, and it took a project the magnitude of the Boulder Dam (now the Hoover Dam) to provide the answer. Mack supplied a fleet of specially built Model AC and AP Bulldog trucks in 1931 for use at Boulder Dam. The Euclid Road Machinery Company followed in 1934 with its first Trac-Truk, and was the first company to specialize in off-road haulers.

Wheeled earthmoving equipment took a giant leap forward when the pneumatic tire was invented. Reliable tires opened the door to high-speed earthmoving with self-propelled scrapers introduced by LeTourneau in

Hornsby Steam Tractor. Simultaneous development of the crawler track was taking place in England. David Roberts, chief engineer with R. Hornsby & Sons of Grantham, patented a crawler track design in 1904. The following year, a Roberts "chain track" was fitted to a Hornsby oil tractor. Several Hornsby steam- and oil-powered tractors were completed with crawler tracks, but despite energetic promotion, including the first film ever made for commercial purposes (1908), very little interest ensued. Hornsby eventually sold its patent rights of the "chain track" to Holt in 1914. The Hornsby steam tractor in the picture was sold to the Northern Light Power & Coal Company for hauling coal to the Klondike goldfields in northern Canada. Built in 1910, it was the only Hornsby crawler tractor sold for civilian use, and the world's first fully tracked (no tiller wheel) steam crawler. The undercarriage of this tractor still exists on Vancouver Island, British Columbia. *Keith Haddock collection*

1938. Wheeled dozers were in use a decade later, and the capacity of off-road haulers began a seemingly endless upward spiral.

During times of war, use of earthmoving equipment has been an essential part of any military operation. And the needs of war often spawned advances in machine design that benefited post-war machine use. World War I gave Winston Churchill the idea of developing the tank when he saw a crawler tractor demonstration. During World War II, thousands of airfields were built around the world in record time using fleets of the latest equipment. In addition, the well-known triumphs of the Sea Bees, with their large fleets of mobile earthmovers, are legendary.

The use of hydraulically powered equipment, first tried just after World War II, has now become universally accepted. And in the case of excavators, hydraulic power has all but eliminated cable-operated machines, except for the giant shovels and draglines found in surface mines. As projects increased in size, so did the machines. But at the other end of the scale, smaller and smaller machines also became economical as labor became more expensive. Today, in an age where hand excavation is almost extinct, we observe even the smallest jobs being performed by mini excavators. Just a few decades ago, laborers would no doubt have done this work.

Horse Transportation. The earliest form of earth haulage was performed by horse-drawn wagon. These wagons, built mostly of iron-reinforced wood, moved millions of cubic yards of earth on early highway, drainage, and dam construction projects. Shovel technology advanced at a faster pace than haulage vehicles as evidenced by this Model 30-B steam shovel, built by the Bucyrus Company, about to drop a loaded dipper into the wagon, much to the apprehension of the two horses! Although the 30-B, produced from 1920 to 1928, came equipped with a standard dipper holding 1 cubic yard, the one illustrated wields a special .75-cubic-yard dipper with an extra long handle designed for digging trenches. These long-stick front ends, known as sewer shovels, were soon outmoded when efficient backhoes appeared on the scene. *Keith Haddock collection*

Holt 60 Crawler Tractor. Holt crawler tractors kept things moving when roads were in an atrocious condition. In the early days of mechanized haulage over unpaved public roads, contractors and short-haul freight companies turned to the crawler tractor, the only off-road vehicle capable of negotiating soft, muddy roads. The going was slow but the big tractor made up for its slow speed by hauling a train of six or more fully loaded wagons. Here, a Holt 60 gasoline-powered tractor hauls a road train in Michigan in 1911. The steerable tiller wheel, as shown at the front of this crawler tractor, was typical of early crawler models. Crawler tractors began to appear without tiller wheels in 1913, and steered quite successfully without them. *Caterpillar, Inc. Corporate Archives*

Rail Transportation. In the era before off-road haulers had been developed, rail haulage was the preferred method to transport large quantities of earth and rock over long distances. In fact, rail haulage on excavation projects dates back to the very first steam-powered railroad shovels of the mid-1800s. Rail haulage reached its zenith in the excavation of the Panama Canal during the first decade of the twentieth century, but rock quarries and construction projects continued to utilize rail for their bulk haulage needs. This New York Trap Rock operation at Verplanks Point, New York, ran a rail system for many years. The picture shows a 5-cubic-yard Bucyrus 120-B shovel at work in the 1920s. Some quarries were known to be still operating rail systems into the early 1980s. *Bucyrus International*

Bucyrus 50-B Steam Shovel. Shovel development outpaced haul truck development by several years. This 1920s action shot at Jersey Limestone Quarries, Hamburg, New Jersey, shows a heavy-duty Bucyrus 50-B steam shovel with its 2-cubic-yard dipper loading quarry rock into an obviously under-designed truck. The light frame and narrow solid-tired wheels were entirely unsuitable for site duties, especially in wet weather, but that's all they had in the 1920s. Operators had to wait until the early 1930s before rugged off-highway trucks came on the scene. *Keith Haddock collection*

Western Wheeled Scraper. Horses and mules originally pulled scrapers for earthmoving. The earliest form consisted of a small scoop with handles, which was controlled by a man walking behind. These became known as slip scrapers or the Fresno type, named after the town in California where blacksmith Abijah McCall patented a very successful early type. By the 1870s, pull-type scrapers with wheels began to appear. The one shown was made by the Western Wheeled Scraper Company of Mount Pleasant, Iowa. Railroad contractor C.H. Smith & Company, which previously had designed and built pull scrapers for use on its private contracts, founded this company in 1879. *Keith Haddock*

Richardson Rotary Scraper. The power of wheeled and crawler tractors increased in the early part of the twentieth century, and many manufacturers developed varieties of pull-type scrapers to work with them. Few of these manufacturers survive today. The rotary scraper was popular, consisting of a cylindrical bowl designed to rotate into the carry position after collecting its load. An operator-controlled release mechanism caused the bowl to dump its load by rotating a full 360 degrees and then return to the carry position. The type shown was made by Richardson Road Machinery Co., Ltd. It has no wheels, but runs on circular skids that rotate the bowl through dig, carry, and dump positions. The positions are set by a complicated system of latches and linkages worked by the operator through ropes connected to the levers shown on top. *Keith Haddock*

Cable Loader on Fordson Tractor. Front-end loaders first appeared in the 1920s. Early models were mounted on standard farm wheel tractors, and a winch operated the loader hoist. The only bucket crowding action was provided by the tractor's own propulsion. The bucket was dumped by gravity through a latch release mechanism. The arrangement shown is an early cable loader mounted on a Fordson tractor equipped with solid rubber tires for industrial use. *Keith Haddock collection*

Galion Standard 14 Grader. Like the first scrapers, the first graders were pulled behind horse teams, and later behind tractors. They required their own operator, separate from the tractor driver, who stood on a platform at the rear of the grader. He wrestled with hand controls for all the blade movements, and developed strong muscles in doing so. It was not until 1919 that the first motor (self-propelled) grader appeared, and powered controls did not appear until the mid-1920s. The Galion Ironworks was famous for building big pull-type graders like the one shown being pulled by a crawler tractor. Galion continued selling its range of pull-type graders until 1945. The largest graders were capable of being pulled by the most powerful traction engines and crawler tractors up to that time. *Historical Construction Equipment Association*

CRAWLER TRACTORS AND BULLDOZERS

Of all the different types of earthmoving machines, the bulldozer is the most frequently used on construction projects today. From the quarrying of building materials and the mining of precious metals or coal, to the construction of roads, houses, and factories, bulldozers can be seen doing a multitude of tasks on every project. Access roads need construction and maintenance. Holes must be dug and filled in; dump areas must be leveled; vehicles must be pulled or pushed out when stuck; gravel has to be spread. Then, when the job is nearly finished, the bulldozer works on the final landscaping and reclamation, which usually includes a layer of topsoil neatly spread over the site prior to seeding. The bulldozer is expert in all these tasks.

The needs of agriculture at the turn of the twentieth century sparked the development of the crawler tractor. Vast areas of the California delta soil needed big, powerful tractors, but only wheel tractors were available, and the wheels caused severe problems when working on soft ground. The problem was partly solved by the Holt Manufacturing Company of Stockton, California. The company fitted larger and larger wheels on its tractors. Some of these multi-wheel behemoths measured over 45 feet wide, and ran on wheels up to 12 feet in diameter. However, these tractors were not entirely successful because they were extremely cumbersome to maneuver.

The crawler track principle did eventually solve the flotation problem. In 1904, Holt tested the idea by removing the driving wheels from one of its three-wheeled steam traction engines, and replacing them with a pair of crawler tracks. The front steering, or tiller, wheel was retained. After further tests, Holt sold the first production steam crawler in 1906. The Holt company prospered and, almost two decades later, merged with the C.L. Best Tractor Company to form the familiar Caterpillar Tractor Company.

The bulldozer had its origins in crude, horse-pushed contraptions in the last century. As crawler

ACCO Bulldozer. The largest crawler tractor of all time heads this chapter of crawler tractors and bulldozers. It was built in the early 1980s by Italian contractor Umberto ACCO for an earthmoving contract in Libya. Two engines mounted side by side under the hood, developing a total of 1,300 horsepower, transmit the power to the crawler tracks through both upper and lower drive sprockets. Equipped with Caterpillar engines and transmissions, the giant dozer is two stories high, weighs 183 tons, and measures almost 40 feet from blade to ripper. *Yvon LeCadre*

Allis-Chalmers Model L. Industrial giant Allis-Chalmers Manufacturing Company expanded its tractor division in 1928 when it purchased Monarch Tractor Corporation of Springfield, Illinois. Two tractors from the Monarch line, the 6-ton Model H and the 10-ton Model F, were initially manufactured by Allis-Chalmers. They were renumbered as the Models 50 and 75, but still bore the Monarch name. Allis-Chalmers introduced a new line of crawler tractors beginning in 1929 with the 48-drawbar-horsepower gasoline Model K. This was followed in 1931 with the 75-drawbar-horsepower Model L gasoline tractor. It was one of the largest crawler tractors built up to that time, and tipped the scales at 22,000 pounds. The fine example in the picture was restored by C.J. Moyna & Sons, Inc. *Keith Haddock*

Allis-Chalmers HD-14. The largest of the trio of diesel crawlers introduced by Allis-Chalmers in 1938 was the HD-14. At 132 drawbar-horsepower, it was the most powerful crawler tractor available on the market at that time. The original model was updated in 1945 to the HD-14C, the first crawler tractor to be offered with a torque converter. The tractor's gauge was 68 inches, and its shipping weight was 28,880 pounds. The HD-14C was discontinued in 1947. *Keith Haddock*

Allis-Chalmers HD-10. Allis-Chalmers started developing its diesel-powered tractor line in 1938 using General Motors engines. Three models were added to production in 1940 to replace the previous oil tractors; the HD-7, HD-10, and HD-14. The HD-10 was equipped with a General Motors two-cycle engine rated at 87 drawbar-horsepower, and was available in 62- and 74-inch gauges. It remained in the A-C production line until 1951. The HD-10 shown here has had its Baker dozer blade removed, possibly for agricultural work. *Keith Haddock*

tractors grew more robust and reliable, they were found to be ideal for carrying a bulldozer blade. The early tractor-mounted blades, however, did not have power control. It was left to the operator to crank the blade up and down by means of hand wheels.

Several companies, not associated with the tractor manufacturers, began to offer power-controlled blades in the 1920s. Crude cable winches with jaw clutches were attached to the tractors. The clutches were unreliable and prone to jamming. LaPlant-Choate Manufacturing Company of Cedar Rapids, Iowa, came out with a hydraulically operated dozer blade as early as 1925. In 1928, R.G. LeTourneau invented a reliable cable-operated power control unit (PCU). This unit employed individual clutches and brakes, and could operate not only a dozer blade, but also pull-type scrapers, rippers, and other attachments.

At the time when bulldozers first became recognized as an earthmoving tool, manufacturers other than those building the tractors supplied bulldozer blades. As time went on, the major builders of tractor attachments aligned themselves with a particular tractor manufacturer. Notable examples were Baker with Allis-Chalmers, Bucyrus-Erie with International, and LaPlant-Choate and LeTourneau with Caterpillar. It was not until well into the 1940s that the main tractor builders started to manufacture their own blades and other attachments.

Allis-Chalmers HD-19. Breaking the world record for size in 1947 was the Allis-Chalmers HD-19. It weighed 40,000 pounds without blade or attachments. At 163 flywheel-horsepower, it was equipped with torque converter drive. In 1951, the HD-19 was upgraded to the 175-horsepower HD-20, which was later replaced in 1954 by the HD-21, with power increased to 204 horsepower. These big tractors were a common sight on the largest earthmoving projects of the 1950s. *Keith Haddock*

The contribution the bulldozer made to the World War II effort is well documented. Thousands of crawler tractors, most carrying LeTourneau blades or pulling LeTourneau scrapers, made their way overseas, or to Alaska to prepare the ground for fighting forces. The Alaska Highway was built, as well as chains of bases across the Aleutian Islands. Chains of island air bases were built across the South Pacific. Adm. William F. Halsey stated, "The four machines that won the war in the Pacific were the submarine, the radar, the airplane, and the bulldozer."

By the mid-1950s, bulldozers were no longer considered a tractor with an attachment. They were an integrated unit, designed for production from the ground up. Bulldozers from the major manufacturers, such as International, Allis-Chalmers, Caterpillar, and Euclid appeared with equal frequency on big jobs, and manufacturers competed with each other to produce the biggest machine.

Crawler tractor development continued unabated in the 1960s. International Harvester brought out its

Allis-Chalmers HD-41. The Allis-Chalmers HD-41 made headlines at the 1963 Road Show in Chicago. With an operating weight of 70 tons and 524-horsepower engine, it broke the world crawler tractor-size record. A lengthy testing program with prototypes followed, and customers had to wait until 1970 before it was put into full production. In 1974, Fiat S.p.A. of Italy purchased the majority of Allis-Chalmers shares, and the Fiat-Allis joint venture was born. The crawler tractors were continued as Fiat-Allis machines, but the HD prefix was dropped. The upgraded 41-B model appeared in 1974, and further revisions brought the Fiat-Allis FD-50 in 1982. *Francis Pierre*

Best 60. Originally established as the C.L. Best Gas Traction Company in 1910 at Elmhurst, California, the Best company was founded by the son of an earlier tractor producer, Daniel Best, who sold his business to Holt in 1908. Undoubtedly the most successful tractor in the Best company's history was the C.L. Best 60 Tracklayer, launched in 1919. Some of its outstanding features were its oscillating crawler frames, the use of some 36 bearings at critical points throughout the machine, multiple-disc enclosed steering clutches, and a strong frame capable of withstanding much abuse. Power came from a four-cylinder overhead-valve Best gas engine of 35 drawbar-horsepower and 60 belt-horsepower. This engine ran at a slow 650 rpm, one of the slowest engines fitted to an early crawler tractor. The Best 60 would become the legendary Caterpillar Sixty, after the formation of the new Caterpillar Tractor Company in 1925. *Caterpillar, Inc.*

largest tractor to date, the TD-30, in 1962. Allis-Chalmers gave the industry a preview of its giant HD-41, the world's largest crawler tractor, at the 1963 Chicago Road Show, and all tractors received upgrades to comply with the latest technology. One example was Caterpillar's patented sealed and lubricated tracks that extended the life of pins and bushings by up to 30 percent, and is still a main feature today.

The first widespread use of hydrostatic-drive crawler tractors, pioneered by JCB in 1971, and Liebherr debuted in 1974. Probably the most significant tractor development in the 1970s was Caterpillar's "high drive" undercarriage design. Launched with the introduction of the D10 in 1978, this raised-sprocket design has since been adopted by Caterpillar on every size and class of tractor down to the D4. The push for larger tractors has continued to the present day with introductions of Caterpillar's D11N and D11R, and Komatsu's D475A and D575A-2, the latter model achieving power ratings of almost three times that of the largest crawlers built in the 1950s, and holding the title of the world's largest crawler tractor.

Unlike the earlier tractor designs, today's bulldozers and crawler tractors feature operator comfort as one of their main selling points. Contrast these machines with the cab-less machines of the 1950s, with controls that

Best 30. In 1921, Best added a smaller tractor to its product line, the Best 30 Tracklayer. It was designed on similar lines to the popular 60 model and replaced the earlier Best 25. At approximately half the size of its big brother, the Best 30 carried a four-cylinder Best motor rated at 20 drawbar-horsepower and 30 belt-horsepower when running at the rated 800 rpm. Like its larger brother, the Best 30 gained an enviable reputation for reliability, and was also carried forward into the new Caterpillar Tractor Company line after 1925, when it was named the Caterpillar Thirty. *Keith Haddock*

Case 450B. Case established its basic range of crawler models in 1957 after it purchased the American Tractor Corporation (Ateco). The machines received several upgrades until the mid-1960s when three new models appeared. These were the 57-horsepower 450 and 92-horsepower 1150 in 1965, followed by the 66-horsepower 850 in 1967. The new machines spotlighted Case engines with torque converters and power-shift transmissions. The 450 was an extremely successful small tractor; it enjoyed a long production run until 1978. It was then replaced by the 53-horsepower 450B (illustrated), which in turn was replaced by the 450C in 1983. *Keith Haddock*

kept the operator active throughout his shift and his muscles in top shape. Today's operators expect enclosed cabs with heaters, air conditioners, power-assisted ergonomically placed controls, and multi-position seats with state-of-the-art support. Added extras like radios and cupholders have now become the norm. Built-in diagnostics that inform the operator of any abnormal temperature or pressure have brought maintenance into the technology age. When repairs are necessary, modular components can be quickly removed and replaced in a couple of hours, instead of the day or two it took on the old machines.

Case Terratrac 1000. In 1957, J.I. Case Company purchased the American Tractor Corporation (Ateco) of Churubusco, Indiana, and entered the crawler tractor business. At that time, Ateco offered a line of small crawler tractors known as "Terratracs." Case launched a new line in 1957 consisting of four size ranges from the 40-horsepower Model 310 up to the 100-horsepower Model 1000. The two largest models (800 and 1000) featured a unique steering system that provided two speeds and reverse for each track. This system required four steering levers: a forward/reverse lever and a two-speed lever for each track. There were also two foot pedals to operate brakes for spin turns. With this arrangement, three types of steering could be effected: power turns using high and low speeds, spin-turns with counter-rotating tracks, or pivot turns using the brakes. *Case Corporation*

Case 1150B. Case introduced three new tractor models in the mid-1960s: the 450, 850, and 1150. The two smaller models featured an independent two-speed drive to each track, allowing turns with power to both tracks. The 1150 boasted the additional feature of track counter-rotation, allowing spin turns. This arrangement was the same as featured in the former 1000 model. When Case replaced the 1150 with the 100-horsepower 1150B in 1972, it broke the 100-horsepower barrier for the first time. The 1150 has since survived its C, D, E, and G upgrades to the present 1150H machine of 119 horsepower. *Keith Haddock*

Case 550E. Case released its first version of the 550 in 1989. The 67-horsepower dozer was replaced by the 550E in 1992 with minor changes, and soon after became the smallest crawler tractor in the Case line when the previous smallest 450C model was phased out. The 550E was followed by the 550G in 1994 and the 550H in 2000, featuring improved operator comfort and minor upgrades. As shown in the picture, the 550 Series is available in a rubber track version. Steel cords are integrated into the seamless rubber track to eliminate stretch. This option was designed to minimize surface disturbance on asphalt or in landscaping work. *Keith Haddock*

Case 1550. Case dabbled in hydrostatic drive for its largest crawler dozer of the twentieth century, the 1550. Launched in 1987, it replaced the previous top-of-the-line Case crawler, the 140-horsepower 1450B, which had regular power-shift transmission. The 1550 developed 150-horsepower from its Case 6T-830 engine, and its operating weight was 33,100 pounds when equipped with dozer blade. Case phased out its only hydrostatic model in 1993. *Case Corporation*

Case 650H. In 1999, Case announced its new line of five H Series crawler tractors. These ranged from the 67-horsepower 550H to the 119-horsepower 1150H. With three track choices: long track for improved stability and ease of transport, wide track to enhance stability on slopes, and extra-wide track providing low ground pressure to maximize flotation, the H Series incorporates fully rotating track bushings that increase track life. The H Series offers power-shift transmissions with improved operator visibility over the former models. The 650H tips the scales at 17,400 pounds and is equipped with a Case 4T-390 turbocharged diesel engine developing 75 flywheel-horsepower. *Case Corporation*

Case 1850K. In 2002, Case added to its line the largest crawler tractors ever marketed by the company. The 1650K and 1850K deliver 145 and 205 horsepower. They are derived from similar-sized tractors built in Italy by Fiat-Hitachi, which, along with Case, is a member of the CNH Global organization. They feature a torque converter and power-shift transmission with an "Auto-Shift" mode that automatically downshifts when the load increases, and selects first speed for forward and second speed for reverse when making direction changes. The tractors also feature differential steering driven by a hydrostatic motor. This allows full power to both tracks, while steering and counter-rotation capability is controlled by a single lever. *Case Corporation*

Caterpillar Sixty. In one of the most important mergers in equipment history, Holt Manufacturing Company merged with C.L. Best Tractor Company in 1925 to form Caterpillar Tractor Company. (The Best company had changed its name from the C.L. Best Gas Traction Company in 1920.) The Caterpillar name was formerly used by Holt as the trade name for its tractors. The Sixty was one of two former Best models brought forward to comprise the first Caterpillar product line.
It had already gained a reputation for ruggedness and reliability, and continued in production until 1931. The Sixty shown is equipped with probably the first hydraulically powered dozer blade. Built by the LaPlant-Choate Manufacturing Company of Cedar Rapids, Iowa, in 1925, the blade is mounted on a rectangular frame, pivoted on the crawler frames, and operated by a hydraulic cylinder at the rear. *Caterpillar, Inc.*

Caterpillar Twenty. In 1927, the Caterpillar Twenty was launched as the first of a new series of tractors. It was also the first machine to be designed entirely by the Caterpillar Tractor Company, and not derived from any former Best or Holt models. Its advanced design with enclosed engine and substantial operator's seat turned out to be the forerunner of a new era in tractor appearance. The Twenty was powered by a Caterpillar gasoline engine rated at 31.16 belt-horsepower. Built in Caterpillar's plants at San Leandro, California, and Peoria, Illinois, it stayed in production until 1932. The restored Twenty in the picture is putting a Caterpillar No. 10 pull grader through its paces at a Historical Construction Equipment Association annual convention. *Keith Haddock*

Caterpillar Ten. In late 1928, Caterpillar released the Model Ten. Caterpillar ads announced it as "a smaller size of the Caterpillar tractor...eagerly awaited by all small power users." It replaced the earlier Two-Ton model, which was the smallest of the Holt models included in the original Caterpillar line in 1925. Its engine was a side-valve, four-cylinder gasoline engine rated at 18.72 belt-horsepower. Some 900 pounds lighter than the Two-Ton, the Ten's weight of 4,420 pounds qualified it as Caterpillar's smallest tractor. It stayed in production until 1932. *Keith Haddock*

Caterpillar Twenty-Eight. In 1933 Caterpillar released the Twenty-Eight gasoline tractor to replace the Twenty-Five, which enjoyed a disappointingly short production run that had begun in 1931.
The improved tractor was considered a very well-designed tractor, and Caterpillar had high hopes for its success. With a shipping weight of 7,830 pounds, it carried a four-cylinder gasoline engine rated at 37.47 belt-horsepower. But sales once again proved disappointing, and the Twenty-Eight was withdrawn from production in 1935. The slow sales were probably due to the upsurge of diesel-powered tractors just entering the market and the generally depressed economy. *Keith Haddock*

Caterpillar Diesel Fifty. Following the diesel tractor's debut in 1931, gasoline tractors continued to sell. In an effort to capture both markets, Caterpillar offered its larger tractors in diesel and gasoline versions. The 55-belt-horsepower Fifty gasoline tractor was released in 1931. The picture shows the diesel counterpart, the Diesel Fifty, which followed in 1933. This came equipped with a Caterpillar four-cylinder diesel engine producing 65.6 belt-horsepower. Both Fifty versions were offered with either standard 60-inch or wide-gauge 74-inch track widths. The Diesel Fifty ended its production run in 1936, and the gas-powered Fifty held on for one more year. *Keith Haddock*

Caterpillar Thirty-Five. Another model to boast diesel and gasoline versions was the Thirty-Five model. Caterpillar launched the Thirty-Five in 1932, and the Diesel Thirty-Five the following year. The Thirty-Five replaced the former Thirty and carried a Caterpillar four-cylinder gasoline engine rated at 41 belt-horsepower. The Diesel Thirty-Five was fitted with a 46.08-belt-horsepower engine. Shipping weights were 12,480 pounds and 13,900 pounds, respectively. The Thirty-Five Series tractors were designed on similar lines to the Fifty Series tractors, with sheet-metal work covering the engine, and substantial sheeting around the operator's seat area. *Keith Haddock*

Caterpillar Diesel Forty. The Diesel Forty and Forty gasoline models were introduced in 1934 as replacements for the Diesel Thirty-Five and Thirty-Five models, which had very short production lives. Both the 48-belt-horsepower Forty and the 49-belt-horsepower Diesel Forty (shown) were built with a 56-inch track gauge as standard, and a 74-inch wide-gauge option. Apart from the engines, the outward appearance of both tractors was identical. The Diesel Forty and Forty weighed 14,700 pounds and 13,310 pounds respectively. Both models were discontinued in 1936. *Keith Haddock*

Caterpillar R-5. Caterpillar launched the first three of a new line of gas tractors in 1934. These were the R-2, R-3, and R-5, and they got their start in a substantial government order for tractors unavailable in Caterpillar's current lineup. These tractors were purchased for work on New Deal construction projects initiated by President Theodore Roosevelt, and the R designation was chosen to commemorate the president's name. After completing the government orders, Caterpillar retained the R Series designation for all subsequent gasoline tractor models. The R-5 in the picture is an example from a second series of R-5s that began production in 1936. *Keith Haddock*

Caterpillar Diesel Seventy-Five. Caterpillar's first diesel-powered tractor, the Diesel Sixty, was launched in 1931. Sales were slow at first, and there were many problems to overcome, such as inconsistent fuel quality and erratic fuel distribution. But with extraordinary sales efforts by Caterpillar and quick solutions to machine problems, sales picked up by the late 1930s, and diesels began to outsell their gasoline counterparts. Caterpillar brought out the larger Diesel Seventy in 1933 and upgraded it with the new D11000 engine almost immediately. Caterpillar introduced the 98-belt-horsepower Diesel Seventy-Five that same year. The top-of-the-line Diesel Seventy-Five was the forerunner of the famous D-8 Series beginning with the 110 belt-horsepower RD8 in 1935. *Keith Haddock collection*

Caterpillar RD-6. In 1935, Caterpillar adopted a new numbering system for its tractors, abandoning the cumbersome fully written numbers in favor of one or two single letters to describe the models. The gasoline tractors were given the prefix R, and diesel tractors were given the prefix RD, but the R was dropped in 1937. The RD-6 (2H Series) of 1935, an example of which is shown with cable-operated blade, was the forerunner of the famous D-6 Series, which is still in production today in a revised form. The RD-6 featured the Caterpillar D6600, three-cylinder diesel rated at 50 belt-horsepower, and 56-inch or 74-inch track gauge options. In 1937, the RD6 became the D6, and this same 2H version was continued until 1941. *Keith Haddock collection*

Caterpillar RD7. This model was also released in 1935, along with the RD6 and RD8 tractors. The RD7 (9G Series) progressed in a manner similar to the other two models. It featured the Caterpillar D8800 four-cylinder diesel rated at 70 belt-horsepower, and 60-inch or 74-inch track gauge options. In late 1937, the RD7 nomenclature was changed to D7, as with the other RD Series models, but the tractor remained the same. The 9G Series D7 continued in production until 1940, when it was replaced by the D7 7M Series. *Keith Haddock collection*

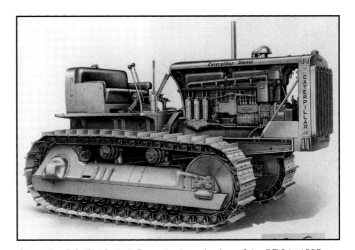

Caterpillar D8, (2U Series). From the introduction of the RD8 in 1935, Caterpillar's D8 Series tractors have been in continual development to the present day. Each major technical breakthrough was marked by a new model and given a different serial number prefix. In late 1937, the 1H Series RD8 became the D8 and continued until 1941 when it was replaced by the D8 8R Series. This tractor, along with the D7, spearheaded the war effort for the United States and its allies during World War II. The 8R progressed to the 2U Series (illustrated) in 1945, and then to the 13A in 1953. Caterpillar's outstanding D13000 engine was installed in all D8 models up to the 13A (1H, 8R, 2U, and 13A). Over this period, Caterpillar increased the power of the 1,000-rpm engine from 110 to 185 belt-horsepower. *Keith Haddock collection*

Caterpillar D4 (2T Series). Caterpillar launched the 2T Series D4 in 1943, and sold many to the U.S. armed forces. The 2T was a direct descendent of the RD4/D4 4G Series (1936–1938), and 7J Series (1939–1942). All these tractors were powered by the four-cylinder Caterpillar D4400 diesel engine rated at 41 belt-horsepower. All were offered with either 44- or 60-inch track gauges. The restored military D4 2T tractor shown is equipped with a LeTourneau bulldozer blade and cable-operated power control unit. *Keith Haddock*

Caterpillar D9D (19A Series). The legendary D9 was officially announced for sale in mid-1955, but its development had been ongoing since 1946. Caterpillar engineers experimented with many different designs and extensively tested several prototype tractors before the first commercial version, known as the D9D, was launched. It was offered in two versions, both with a 90-inch track gauge. The 18A Series had a direct drive transmission, and the 19A Series (shown) was equipped with a torque converter. The D353 turbocharged engine was initially rated at 286 flywheel-horsepower, and then increased to 320 flywheel-horsepower the following year. *Keith Haddock*

Caterpillar D9G (66A Series). Caterpillar announced a major upgrade to its D9 tractor in 1961 with the launch of the D9G. It replaced the former 335-horsepower D9E model, which had replaced the earlier D9D in 1959. Caterpillar's largest tractor now boasted 385 horsepower, and a most successful tractor was born, lasting in production until 1974. The D9G equipped with dozer blade weighed approximately 85,000 pounds, and soon became the backbone of many contractors' equipment fleets. *Keith Haddock collection*

Caterpillar D7C (17A Series). This model fits into a long series of D7 tractors beginning with the RD7 in 1935. Caterpillar introduced the 17A Series D7C in 1955, replacing the former 3T Series (1944–1955), and 7M Series (1940–1944). The D7-size tractor was a favorite among military circles, so several special military and armored versions were also produced during and immediately after World War II. Prior to the 17A Series, the D7 models carried the Caterpillar D8800 diesel engine, latterly rated at 108 belt-horsepower. The redesigned 17A Series D7 tractor incorporated several improvements, most important being its new D339 diesel engine rated at 128 belt-horsepower. *Keith Haddock*

Caterpillar D4D. This model had a long production run from 1963 to 1977. It replaced the earlier D4C, which originally appeared in 1959. Powered by a Caterpillar D330 diesel engine, the D4D received a power increase from 65 to 75 drawbar-horsepower in 1972. Shipping weight of the tractor equipped with dozer blade was around 16,100 pounds. The tractor shown is equipped with a Balderson hydraulic three-way blade with power angle and tilt. *Keith Haddock collection*

Caterpillar DD9H. Another double-tractor configuration was the DD9G, with one tractor behind the other. It was designed to get scrapers loaded and on the haul road in record time. Known also as the Quad Nine, the double tractor with four tracks on the ground could muster up 770 horsepower. When the DD9H appeared in 1974 (illustrated), power went up to 820 horsepower. The front push blade is cushioned (spring-mounted) so that the tractor could contact the scraper with a differential speed of up to 3 miles-per-hour. There was no seat on the rear tractor, but the single operator on the front tractor sat high and proud, and his seat was angled so that he could easily see what the rear tractor was doing. The twin-dozer concept continued until 1978, when it was eclipsed by the D10, which offered similar horsepower from a single tractor. *David Maginnis*

Caterpillar SxS D9H. When the largest tractor available wasn't big enough, high-volume dirt-moving contractors started joining two together like Siamese twins. This concept, initially tried in the 1950s and continued by Caterpillar in the 1960s, was necessary because the demand for large bulldozers exceeded the state-of-the-art capability of engines and transmissions at that time. Caterpillar's SxS D9G placed two tractors side by side under the control of one operator. With double the power of the big D9G (total 770 horsepower), the outfit could handle a 24-foot dozer blade. The picture shows the last model of this concept, the twin D9H outfit with a combined 820 horsepower. *Keith Haddock*

Caterpillar D10. Caterpillar's big breakthrough came in 1977 with the unveiling of the high-drive tractor, the first D10. Caterpillar's elevated sprocket design had a long development period going back as far as 1969. Engineers tested many ideas and concepts before building the first prototype in 1973. The D10, at 700 horsepower and weighing 88 tons with blade, was by far Caterpillar's heaviest and most powerful tractor built up to that time. The D10 shown carries a special 15-foot single-shank ripper used for deep ripping coal. It also is equipped with a Rivinius hydraulically powered step to assist the operator's climb to such heights. *Keith Haddock*

Caterpillar D9L. In 1980, Caterpillar added a second "high-drive" tractor to join the already successful D10. The high-drive D9L replaced the former D9H, and boasted a horsepower of 460, as opposed to the 410 horsepower of the former model. The two main advantages of Caterpillar's elevated sprocket design were that a cushioned undercarriage (instead of the drive axle) absorbed uneven ground shocks, and the drive train was raised out of the mud. These advantages translated into operator comfort, ease of servicing, and lower repair costs. The D9L shown is ripping coal prior to loading at a surface mine. *Keith Haddock collection*

Caterpillar D8N. The 285-horsepower D8N, unveiled in 1987, represented another technical breakthrough for Caterpillar. The tractor was Caterpillar's first to be equipped with a differential steering system. With this system, a double differential arrangement allowed the machine to be steered by speeding up one track and equally slowing down the other, while maintaining full power to both tracks at all times. In the time period from 1986 to 1987, Caterpillar totally revamped its large-tractor line by adding the D9N, D10N, and D11N. The N Series provided four tractors in Caterpillar's line, ranging from 285 to 770 horsepower. *Keith Haddock*

Caterpillar D8R. Continuing the long tradition of D8 crawler tractor models, Caterpillar launched the D8R in 1995. Current today in its Series II form, the D8R maintains the differential steer of the former D9N but with horsepower increased to 305. The D8R offers a choice of standard suspended undercarriage with bogie-mounted rollers, or a non-suspended option without bogies. The latter is intended for grading applications where the operator must be aware of critical grade angles. *Keith Haddock*

Caterpillar D5H LGP. Caterpillar's line of low ground pressure (LGP) models is represented here by the D5H LGP. These tractors are designed to work in soft ground conditions, and minimize ground pressure by utilizing long undercarriages, wider gauges, and wide track shoes. LGP versions of the Caterpillar tractor are available for the D3 up to the D8 sizes. The standard D5H tractor was powered by a 120-horsepower diesel engine, a descendent of the first D5 Series tractors originally launched in 1967. It was superseded by the D5M in 1996. *Keith Haddock*

Caterpillar D4H XL. Following the success of the original high-drive tractor, the D10 in 1977, Caterpillar expanded its high-drive design to all tractors down to the 105-horsepower D4-size shown here. In addition to the low ground pressure (LGP) versions, Caterpillar also offered XL versions on its tractors from the D3 up to the D6 sizes. The XL was an intermediate undercarriage, not as wide as the LGP model, but with a wider gauge and longer track on the ground than the standard version, giving stability for finish grading and slope work. *Keith Haddock*

Caterpillar D3C LGP. In 1997, Caterpillar began offering hydrostatic-drive versions on its D3C, D4C, and D5C models rated at 70, 80, and 90 flywheel-horsepower, respectively. Known by the name Hystat, these models are controlled by only two joysticks. The lever on the left controls speed, direction, and steering of the tractor; the lever on the right controls blade movements. The tractor shown is the LGP version of the D3C Series III Hystat model, equipped with three-way hydraulic angle and tilt blade. *Keith Haddock*

Caterpillar D11R CD. Mightiest of all current Caterpillar tractors is the D11R CD, which is the Carry Dozer version of the D11R. It replaced the 770-horsepower D11N in 1996, but retained the same engine and horsepower. In 1997, both the standard D11R and CD versions had their horsepower increased to the present 850 horsepower. The Carry Dozer has a special curved blade that is 22 feet wide to carry more material than the standard blade. Because it takes considerably less power to carry a load than to push it, the Carry Dozer moves 20 to 30 percent more material than the standard dozer. The massive D11R CD weighs 248,600 pounds when equipped with dozer and ripper. *Keith Haddock*

Caterpillar G Series. Caterpillar announced upgraded versions of its three smallest crawler tractors to the G Series in 2001. These hydrostatic models with conventional crawler drive comprise the D3G, D4G, and D5G of 70, 80, and 90 flywheel-horsepower. New features include a redesigned, more spacious operator's station with 13 percent more glass area than the former C Series models. A new, narrow engine hood provides the operator with an unobstructed view of both sides of the blade. And, with one hand and a single joystick lever, the operator controls speed, direction, and steering with counter-rotation capabilities. Another joystick lever is used to control all blade lift, angle, and tilt functions. *Caterpillar, Inc.*

Clark CA1. The small Clark Airborne was a military crawler tractor, which as its name suggests, could be carried by air freighter and dropped by parachute into remote areas. Starting in 1942, Clark Equipment Company built the tractor in accordance with military orders. It weighed 4,196 pounds, and was powered by a Waukesha four-cylinder gasoline engine developing 28 horsepower. Many of these tractors were taken to the South Pacific during World War II, but few were returned to the United States, and none were built after 1944. *Keith Haddock*

Cletrac F. The Cleveland Tractor Company was organized in 1916 and built the brand-name Cletrac crawler tractors. The company made extensive use of letters to distinguish its models. The small Model F appeared in 1920, and although utilizing a different design to the current Caterpillar models, it bears the distinction of being one of the first tractors to feature an elevated sprocket drive. Notice how the tracks run on a live roller belt instead of fixed rollers. The Model F weighed 1,920 pounds and was powered by a Cleveland 16-horsepower gasoline engine. *Keith Haddock*

Cletrac 25. Initially, the Cleveland Tractor Company built lightweight crawler tractors for farming, but during the 1930s, tractors for construction work were promoted. In 1932, the Cletrac Models 15, 25, 35, 55, and 80 were offered, with the numbers approximating the respective tractor's drawbar-horsepower. The Model 80 could be purchased with gasoline or diesel power, the 80 diesel being the company's first diesel-powered tractor. The Model 25 (shown) was built in 1934, and is powered by a six-cylinder Hercules gasoline engine. *Keith Haddock*

Cletrac BGS. Cleveland introduced this model Cletrac in 1944 and kept it in production for four years. It was equipped with a six-cylinder gasoline engine of 38 drawbar-horsepower. The Cletrac BGS in the picture has an interesting cable-operated backhoe attachment built by Maine Steel, Inc. The backhoe has no swing mechanism, so the operator must maneuver the tractor each time the bucket is filled in order to dump its load. The same pulley and winch arrangement can also be used to operate a loader on the front end of the tractor. *Keith Haddock*

Cletrac DDH. The Cleveland Tractor Company made some vital contributions to crawler tractor development. One of these was the differential steering mechanism whereby both tracks maintained power during turning. This patented system was based on a planetary arrangement allowing the tracks to be driven at different speeds. The Cletrac DD was manufactured in various versions from 1936 to 1958. The options included four-cylinder or six-cylinder Hercules diesel engines providing 61 drawbar-horsepower, and various track gauges. The example shown is a restored model pulling a LeTourneau scraper on an Alberta, Canada, road contract in 1985. *Keith Haddock*

Cletrac FDE. In 1944, the Cleveland Tractor Company was acquired by the Oliver Corporation, a farm tractor and equipment builder with roots going back to the 1850s. After the takeover, the machines were known as Oliver Cletracs. In 1945, the company upgraded its biggest crawler, the FD diesel tractor, and brought out the FDE, rated at 100 drawbar-horsepower. The example shown is a restored unit being demonstrated in 2001 at a meeting of the Historical Construction Equipment Association in Canandaigua, New York. *Keith Haddock*

Oliver-Cletrac OC-18. Beginning in the early 1950s, Oliver crawlers were updated and renumbered with OC as a prefix, signifying their Cletrac connections. The largest tractor in this series was the OC-18, at 161 horsepower and 32,800 pounds of operating weight. It retained the Cletrac tradition of differential steering, and remained in production until 1959. The example shown is equipped with a Heil cable-operated bulldozer blade. The White Motor Corporation purchased the Oliver Corporation in 1960. After this date, Oliver crawler tractors were sold only in limited numbers, the last ones shipped in 1965. *Keith Haddock*

Deere 1010. Well-known farm equipment manufacturer John Deere entered the crawler tractor business in 1947 when it bought the rights to the Lindeman tractors. After launching several small crawlers geared to the agricultural markets, Deere introduced two industrial crawlers in 1960, the 1010 and 2010 of 40 and 52 flywheel-horsepower. Diesel and gasoline options were available. The 1010 (shown) had an operating weight of 8,265 pounds including hydraulic dozer blade. Both the 1010 and 2010 remained in production until 1965. *Keith Haddock*

Deere 350D. John Deere replaced the 1010 and 2010 crawler tractors with the first Series JD350 and JD450 models in 1965. Gaining a modest increase in power to 42 and 57 flywheel-horsepower, the new tractors were very similar in appearance to the earlier models. The 350 went through revisions to the B model in 1970 and the C model in 1974. The 350D model shown was released in 1986, and was the last of the 350 Series tractors from Deere. *Keith Haddock*

Deere 550B. In 1975, John Deere introduced its largest crawler tractor yet, the 550 at 80 flywheel-horsepower. Its operating weight was 15,420 pounds with dozer blade, and was equipped with a power-shift transmission with three speeds forward and reverse. The 550 was upgraded to the 550A in 1983. Then, two years later, the 83-flywheel-horsepower 550B replaced the 550A. Apart from the slight increase in power, the new model featured a patented DuraTrax undercarriage with deep heat-treated sealed rollers and track links. *Keith Haddock*

Deere 550G. The 550G replaced the former 550B in 1988. A power-shift transmission provided four speeds forward and reverse from the 83-flywheel-horsepower John Deere engine. The picture shows the long-track (LT) version, with the track length on the ground measuring 85.4 inches. On this model a standard-track version was not available. But there was an optional low ground-pressure model with track shoes increased from the standard 18 inches to 24 inches. The 550G was replaced by the 550H in 1999. *Keith Haddock*

Deere 850C. John Deere served the smaller end of the crawler tractor market up to 1975, when the company announced it would make a major expansion into larger earthmoving equipment. It announced nine new machines in five equipment categories. Most of these were larger than any previously built by Deere, and included two crawler tractors, the JD750 and JD850 of 122 and 165 flywheel-horsepower. As well as being the largest crawlers built by Deere, they were equipped with hydrostatic drive, a bold concept at that time. These hydrostatic tractors remain in Deere's line today, with B Series and C Series upgrades, and power increases to 148 and 192 flywheel-horsepower. *Keith Haddock*

Deere 1050C. Deere introduced new additions to its crawler tractor line in 2000. In a joint venture with Germany's Liebherr, Deere began manufacturing Liebherr hydrostatic crawler tractors and loaders under license, and marketing them as Deere products. The top-of-the-line 1050C is based on the Liebherr PR752. It is equipped with a Liebherr engine developing 324 horsepower, and is by far the largest crawler tractor ever to carry the Deere name. The operating weight is in the 75,000-pound class, depending on blade and ripper combinations. *Keith Haddock*

Daewoo DD80L. Daewoo Heavy Industries, Ltd. was established in Korea in 1976, following the merger of Choson Machine Works with Korea Machinery Industries, Ltd. Daewoo commenced manufacturing hydraulic excavators the following year under a joint venture with Japan's Hitachi. In 1984, Daewoo began designing its own excavators to import into North America. The 90-horsepower DD80L bulldozer joined the product line in 1998. It has an operating weight of 18,519 pounds and comes complete with a Daewoo DB58 diesel engine and hydrostatic transmission. *Keith Haddock*

Doerr XDE 80. In 1962, Alberta Coal, Ltd. of Calgary, Alberta, Canada, built the 90-ton XDE 80, the largest crawler tractor produced up to that time. Designed by vice-president, Chuck Doerr, the machine only reached the experimental stage, but it did some good work for the surface coal mining company that built it. Based on two Euclid TC-12 tractors converted to electric drive, the four-crawler machine was powered by twin Cummins NVH-525-B engines totaling 1,050 horsepower. Two 500-horsepower generators provided power to an electric motor in each crawler assembly, and a third generator powered the blade. *Eric C. Orlemann collection*

Dresser TD40B. In 1982, Dresser Industries, Inc. purchased the Construction Machinery Division of International Harvester. The tractors became part of the International Hough Division of Dresser. Under this ownership, the biggest International crawler tractor, the TD-40, was tested in prototype form as early as 1978, but not marketed until 1985. Initially built at the Libertyville, Illinois, plant, it weighed over 67 tons outfitted for dozer work, and came with a 460-horsepower Cummins engine. Power was increased to 520 horsepower with the revised TD-40B in 1989. Today, the same tractor, upgraded to the TD-40C, is only built in Poland by Huta Stalowa Wola. *Komatsu America International Company*

Dressta TD25H. After Dresser purchased the International products in 1982, a manufacturing agreement was established with Huta Stalowa Wola (HSW) in Poland. HSW was established in 1937, and today is Poland's largest manufacturer of construction equipment. Under the brand-name Dressta, HSW manufactures a full line of crawler tractors, wheel loaders, and motor graders from former Dresser designs. These machines are exported worldwide, including certain models that are exported to the United States under the Komatsu brand name. The TD25H at 320 horsepower is a direct descendent of the former TD25 tractors built at Libertyville, Illinois, by Dresser and the former International Harvester Company. *Keith Haddock*

Eimco 103. The Tractor Division of the Eimco Corporation was located in Salt Lake City, Utah. The parent company, with roots going back to 1884, was famous for its underground rock loading machines, air locomotives, and other underground mining equipment. The company built crawler tractors and crawler loaders from 1952 to 1965 in relatively small numbers, but they were of advanced and radical design. Eimco tractors boasted torque converters and independent power-shift transmissions to each track. This allowed steering with full power to both tracks at all times, or spin turns when the tracks were counter-rotated. The operator was located in front of the machine, to give a full view of the dozer blade. Introduced in 1958, the Model 103 was rated at 158 horsepower with a Cummins engine, and weighed 27,800 pounds. *Urs Peyer*

Euclid TC-12. The Euclid Division of General Motors entered the crawler tractor industry in 1955 with the world's largest tractor, the TC-12. Equipped with twin GM 6-71 engines of 402 combined flywheel-horsepower, and mounted on each side of a split frame, the two halves of the tractor could oscillate independently over uneven ground. Since each engine drove one track through its own power-shift transmission, the 40-ton tractor was remarkably nimble. It could be steered by simply adjusting the speed or direction of one track, or making spin turns by putting one track in forward and the other in reverse. In 1959, the TC-12 power ratings were increased to 425 flywheel-horsepower. *Keith Haddock collection*

Euclid C-6. Euclid's second crawler was the C-6, a tractor half the size of the TC-12. It was presented to the market in 1958, following a test period that lasted more than three years. Its rounded appearance, similar to the TC-12, gave it a distinctly modern look. With a single GM 6-71 engine developing 202 flywheel-horsepower, the C-6 weighed approximately 42,500 pounds without the dozer blade. The C-6 in the picture is equipped with a cable-operated push block for push-loading scrapers. *Keith Haddock collection*

Euclid 82-30. In 1966, Euclid renumbered its models: the C-6 became the 82-30, and the TC-12 became the 82-80. That same year, an intermediate-sized crawler was introduced, the 275-flywheel-horsepower 82-40, carrying a GM 8V-71N two-cycle diesel engine. The 82-30 illustrated carries a special U-shaped dozer blade for coal stockpiling work. After 1968, all 82 Series Euclid crawler tractors were continued under the Terex name, following a Justice Department ruling that GM must discontinue making off-highway trucks in the United States for five years, and divest itself of the Euclid name. *Keith Haddock collection*

35

Fiat-Allis 14C. In 1974, Fiat S.p.A. of Italy purchased the majority of Allis-Chalmers shares, and the Fiat-Allis joint venture was born. The crawler tractors were continued with the HD prefix dropped, and models were upgraded to the B and C Series machines through the 1970s. The intermediate-sized 14C crawler tractor at 150 horsepower was introduced in 1977. Variations were offered, such as a forestry special with extensive machine and operator guarding, and a sanitary landfill special with anti-debris sealing of the engine compartment and a radiator resistant to plugging. *Keith Haddock*

Fiat-Allis 31. This model was launched in 1976 to fit in between Fiat-Allis' other two big tractors, the 21-B and 41-B. These two models were updates on the former Allis-Chalmers HD-21 and HD-41 models. The new 31 was a substantially designed heavy crawler tractor using undercarriage components from the larger 41-B, and a Cummins KT-1150-C engine that was capable of 425 flywheel-horsepower. Operating weight was just under 70 tons when it was equipped with a dozer blade, ripper, and cab. The 31 was replaced by the 455-horsepower FD-40 in 1982. *Keith Haddock*

Fiat-Allis FD-50. Beginning in 1980, Fiat-Allis began to upgrade its crawler line with the FD Series. The 16B became the 223-horsepower FD20; the 21-C which replaced the 21-B in 1976, became the 300-horsepower FD-30; the 31 became the 455-horsepower FD-40, and the top-of-the-line 41-B became the 550-horsepower FD-50. In 1982, the company's name changed slightly to Fiatallis. Market conditions softened for Fiatallis in the 1980s, and by 1989 the company was no longer manufacturing earthmoving products in North America. However, Fiatallis maintained a sales and parts organization to market machines imported from Italy. *Keith Haddock*

Fiat-Hitachi D180. In 1986, Japan's Hitachi and Fiat of Italy formed the joint venture Fiat-Hitachi to manufacture excavators and the former Fiatallis products. The new name was branded on some of the company's product lines, including crawler tractors sold in Europe. Fiatallis was retained for machines exported to North America. The D180 shown has a 180-flywheel-horsepower engine and falls into the 20-ton weight class. In 1991, Fiat acquired tractor builder Ford New Holland and, in 1999, Case Corporation and New Holland merged to form CNH Global. With other acquisitions, CNH brought several well-known construction equipment brands under its control. Crawler tractors from the former Fiatallis line were subsequently marketed under several brand names within the CNH group. They are sold as New Holland in North America. *Keith Haddock*

Hanomag K8. This 80-horsepower tractor was made by Rheinstahl Hanomag of Hannover, Germany. It was one of an extensive line manufactured by this company, in business since 1835. In 1974, Hanomag and its factory was purchased by Massey-Ferguson, and its crawler tractors merged into the M-F line. The K8, with revisions, became the MF400 dozer. In 1980, Germany's IBH group purchased Massey-Ferguson. When this group failed in 1983, Hanomag re-appeared under independent ownership and continued with its line of crawler tractors, wheel loaders, and hydraulic excavators. Komatsu took control of Hanomag in 1990, and the Hanomag name soon disappeared. *Francis Pierre*

Fowler VF. The Fowler organization was established in 1860 and produced crawler tractors from 1927. This small Fowler produced 40 horsepower from a single-cylinder Marshall diesel engine. Started by a cartridge, the tractor made a loud popping sound when in operation. The VF was made from 1947, updated to the VFA in 1952, and then discontinued in 1957. During the 1950s, large numbers of these tractors were exported to North America, especially to Canada. *Keith Haddock*

Holt 45. The Holt Manufacturing Company was one of the first to apply crawler tracks to a tractor (see chapter 1). In 1915, Holt's new 45 was one of the first crawler tractors to operate without a front tiller wheel to aid steering. It passed a rigorous testing program by the U.S. Army with flying colors, and was sent in large numbers to the battlefields of Europe during World War I. Some of the Holt 45s shipped to the army in 1917 and 1918 were special versions completely covered in armor plating. After the Holt 10-Ton was launched in 1918, the 45 was discontinued in 1920. *Keith Haddock*

Holt 75. The most popular of all the Holt tiller-wheel tractors was the 75. This heavyweight was first produced at the Stockton plant in 1913 and labeled the Holt 60-75 (A-NVS). A four-cylinder Holt valve-in-head gas engine powered it. In 1915, the Holt 75 was upgraded to a new model known as the T8 Series, and its production commenced at the Peoria plant. Production of the Holt 75 continued until 1921 at Stockton and until 1924 at Peoria, where Holt made the last tiller wheel tractors. *Keith Haddock*

Holt 10-Ton. This model was derived from an armor-plated tractor Holt built in 1917 as the 10-Ton Model 55 Artillery Tractor (Series T-16), and powered by a four-cylinder Holt gasoline engine rated at 55 brake-horsepower. The success of this military tractor prompted the company to introduce a similar-sized tractor for civilian use after the war. Full production commenced in 1919 at the Peoria plant. The 40 drawbar-horsepower tractor was listed with a shipping weight of 20,500 pounds. In 1924, some minor modifications were made to the 10-Ton, and this is the tractor that would continue as the Caterpillar 10-Ton tractor following the formation of Caterpillar Tractor Company in 1925. *Keith Haddock collection*

Holt 5-Ton. A smaller tractor, the Holt 5-Ton (Series T-11), had a similar military background to its larger brother. First introduced in 1917 as the 5-Ton Artillery Tractor, and later in 1919 in a civilian version, it was powered by a Holt gas engine rated at 40 brake-horsepower. This tractor lasted in production until 1923, when it was discontinued in favor of a revised 5-Ton (T-29) tractor of 40 brake-horsepower built in Stockton. In 1924, the 5-Ton was revised yet again to a model built in Peoria known as the new 5-Ton Caterpillar Tractor (T-29). This 5-Ton model was carried forward into Caterpillar Tractor Company's new line after 1925. *Keith Haddock*

Holt 2-Ton. Holt brought out a small tractor, the 2-Ton Model T-35, in 1921. It featured a unique overhead-camshaft Holt four-cylinder gasoline engine producing 25-belt-horsepower. Its riveted undercarriage and the Holt name on the radiator in stencil cutout form distinguished this initial 2-Ton model. In 1924, Holt introduced a new 2-Ton tractor boasting a much stronger undercarriage of cast-steel construction, and the Holt name cast on the radiator. This tractor would join the 5-Ton and 10-Ton models as Holt's three model contribution to the new tractor lineup after Caterpillar Tractor Company was formed in 1925. *Keith Haddock*

International T-20. As one of the leading builders of trucks and farm equipment, International Harvester Company (IHC) announced its entry into the crawler tractor business in 1929. Its first crawler tractor was the 10-20, which was based on the McCormick-Deering wheeled 10-20. In 1931, the T-20 crawler appeared, the first of several new tractor models known as TracTracTors. These models were denoted with a T for gasoline, and TD for diesel. The T-20 was listed as having 27.73 belt-horsepower with a shipping weight of 6,385 pounds. The first International diesel crawler was the 50-belt-horsepower TD-40, produced from 1933 to 1939. *Keith Haddock*

International TD-14A. Beginning in 1938, International redesigned its crawler tractors, and came out with a line consisting of four sizes. The diesel tractors were the 36-flywheel-horsepower TD-6, the 49.5-flywheel-horsepower TD-9, the 68.5-flywheel-horsepower TD-14, and the 88 flywheel-horsepower TD-18. Gasoline T Series models were also available on the two smallest sizes. In 1949, the intermediate-sized TD-14 was upgraded to the TD-14A, which remained current until 1956. The machine shown is equipped with a Bucyrus-Erie hydraulic angle dozer. *Keith Haddock*

International TD-24. International crawlers were a significant force in the earthmoving equipment business in the 1950s and 1960s. In 1947, the company launched its flagship tractor, the big TD-24, claiming that it was the world's largest crawler tractor. At 180 flywheel-horsepower, it clipped the title from the Allis-Chalmers HD-19 (163 horsepower), which had appeared earlier the same year. The TD-24 boasted planet power steering, which provided two speeds independently for each track and was hydraulically controlled. It remained in production until 1959; by this time its power had increased to 202 flywheel-horsepower. *Keith Haddock*

International TD-20. This model was unveiled in 1958 to replace the TD-18, which by then had received several upgrades since its introduction in 1938. In fact, the new TD-20 at 134 flywheel-horsepower was the same power as listed for the TD-18 in its final form. The TD-20 initially weighed 35,000 pounds, including the hydraulic dozer blade. This very successful model was revised to the TD-20B in 1963, the TD-20C in 1970, and the TD-20E in 1974. The TD-20E became a Dresser product when that company took over the line in 1982. It later passed into the hands of HSW, which still offers it today as the TD-20H. *Keith Haddock*

International TD-25C. The first version of the TD-25 appeared in 1959 with options of gear drive or torque converter drive, and an engine capable of developing 230 flywheel-horsepower. Following a similar development pattern as the TD-20, the TD-25 progressed through the B model in 1962, the C model in 1974, the E model in 1979, and the G model in 1984, by which time its power had increased to 320 flywheel-horsepower. The TD-25 was sold as a Dresser product after 1982, and today it is solely made by HSW in Poland as the TD-25H (see Dressta). *Keith Haddock*

Komatsu G40. Komatsu built its first crawler tractor, the G25, in 1931. Looking a lot like the Caterpillar 2-Ton, it had similar power and dimensions to its competitor. The initial orders were for the Japanese army and agricultural ministries. Komatsu's second model was this G40, possessing many mechanical and cosmetic features of the Caterpillar Thirty, but equipped with a 50-horsepower gasoline engine. The first of these was completed in 1935. Subsequent machines were sold for agriculture, and some special-purpose machines were sold to the Japanese navy. *Komatsu America International Co.*

Komatsu D65A. The first series D50 bulldozer made its debut in 1944, and Komatsu established a stable base and reputation with this model during the post–World War II period. By 1962, production of the D50 Series bulldozers had exceeded 10,000 units. The introduction of Komatsu tractors in the United States was assisted by LeTourneau-Westinghouse (Wabco), which became Komatsu's distributor in 1967. The first orders were for numbers of the 125-horsepower D60A and the 250-horsepower D125A crawler tractors, which were sold in California. The mid-sized 140-horsepower D65A followed in 1973 in the 34,680-pound weight class. *Keith Haddock*

Komatsu D155A. The crawler line expanded rapidly throughout the 1960s, and by 1972 Komatsu offered 12 models of crawlertractors ranging from 35 to 300 horsepower. The smallest was the D20A, weighing 6,460 pounds, while the top-of-the-line 300-horsepower machines were the D155A with torque converter and the direct-drive D150A. These tractors were in the 70,000-pound weight class. This D155A keeps a dump in order at a surface coal mine. *David Wootton*

Komatsu D355A. Komatsu introduced the 53-ton D355A and 82-ton D455A tractors in 1974 and 1977 to compete with the largest tractors on the market at that time. The D355A carried a Komatsu six-cylinder diesel engine of 410 flywheel-horsepower, while a Cummins VTA1710 12-cylinder motor of 620 flywheel-horsepower powered the massive D455A. By 1977, Komatsu had expanded its crawler lineup to an amazing 31 models, including swamp bulldozers and several special-purpose machines. Komatsu had introduced the world's first radio-controlled amphibious bulldozer in 1969, and the following year introduced the world's first underwater bulldozer. *Keith Haddock*

Komatsu D475A-2. In 1987, Komatsu bolstered its large tractor lineup by adding two new models to its line, the 508-flywheel-horsepower D375A-1, and the 740-flywheel-horsepower D475A-1. They were designed on the modular principle, allowing major components to be exchanged without dismantling the tractor. Until the early 1990s, Komatsu retained the older-designed D355A and D455A when introducing the two new modular tractors. The larger model was revised to the D475A-2 (shown) with horsepower increased to 770 in 1989. In 1996, the D375A was upgraded to the Dash-3 Series with a horsepower gain to 525. This model was further upgraded in 2002 to the D-375A-5 GALEO model, featuring a new fuel-efficient, emission-compliant engine, electronic power control, and joystick controls. GALEO stands for Genuine Answers for Land and Environment Optimization. *Keith Haddock*

Komatsu D575A-3 SD. In 1981, Komatsu presented the D555A at the Conexpo equipment exhibition in Houston, Texas. Hailed as the world's largest bulldozer, it boasted 1,000 horsepower and 133 tons of operating weight. Economic conditions of the 1980s delayed further development of this prototype, but a successor, the D575A-2 SR (Super Ripper) was launched on the market in 1991 as the largest production dozer available. The 145-ton monster was rated at 1,050 flywheel-horsepower. This machine was joined in 1995 by the D575A-2 SD (Super Dozer) at 1,150 horsepower, designed for dozer applications. It was revised in 2001 to the D575A-3 SD with a weight of 168 tons, consolidating its position as the largest bulldozer available. *Komatsu America International Co.*

Komatsu D65PX. In keeping with Komatsu's continual program of updating its machines, the company introduced a newly designed crawler in 1992. Available in two versions, a standard D65EX-12, and a low ground pressure D65PX-12 (illustrated), the 190-horsepower machine boasts several changes from Komatsu's previous designs. Apart from its distinctive appearance with sloping hood and fuel tank, the D65AX-12 features a hydrostatic steering system which retains power to both crawler tracks while turning, and allows counter-rotation for spin turns. Control of all tractor movements, including steering, is through a single joystick lever. Another joystick lever controls all dozer blade movements. *Keith Haddock*

Komatsu D155AX-3. Komatsu released a larger crawler of similar design to the D65AX in 1994. Like its smaller brother, the D155AX-3 features a hydrostatic steering system with independent drive to each crawler, retaining power to both tracks while turning and allowing counter-rotation for spin turns. Other features included a resilient equalized undercarriage, hydro mechanical transmission, and distinctive sloping hood and fuel tank. The D155AX-3 carries a Komatsu diesel of 302 flywheel-horsepower and has an operating weight of 85,160 pounds when equipped with a 20-foot, 8-inch-wide semi-U blade and single-shank ripper. *Keith Haddock*

Komatsu D32P. In 1988, Komatsu and Dresser Industries entered a joint venture to form Komatsu Dresser Company. Under this arrangement, in 1997 Komatsu began to import certain small crawler tractors from the former International line made by HSW in Poland, and market these under both the Dressta and Komatsu brand names. These include the Komatsu D32E, D38E, D39E, and D87E crawlers. The handy D32P-1 (low ground pressure) and D32E-1 (standard) tractors are derived from the 70-horsepower Dresser TD-7H, with the enhancement of joystick controls for all tractor and blade movements. *Keith Haddock*

Liebherr PR722. Germany's Liebherr entered the crawler tractor market in 1974 with the pioneering hydrostatic-drive PR731. Weighing 14 tons, the 120-horsepower crawler was one of the first to be controlled by a single joystick lever for direction, speed, and steering. After the success of this machine, Liebherr stayed with hydrostatic transmission as it expanded its crawler tractor line to larger and smaller bulldozers as well as crawler loaders. The PR722 shown is in the 128-horsepower class, and has an operating weight of 15 tons. Long-track and low ground pressure versions are also available. *Keith Haddock*

Liebherr PR752. By the early 1980s Liebherr offered a broad range of hydrostatic crawler tractors ranging up to the PR751. With 330 horsepower under the hood and an operating weight of 40 tons with the dozer blade, the PR751 was the world's largest hydrostatic crawler tractor. With the advent of its patented Litronic control, Liebherr brought out the PR752 in the same size class as the PR751. Litronic control adjusts and monitors the tractor's operating functions and results in efficient power transmission. All Liebherr crawler tractors are powered by Liebherr diesel engines. *Liebherr Construction Equipment*

Lindeman MC. The purchase of Lindeman Power Equipment Company by John Deere in 1947 brought crawler tractors to the well-established Deere line of wheeled tractors. Starting out as Holt tractor dealers in 1922, and later selling Cletracs, Lindeman began building crawler conversions for John Deere tractors. These sold extremely well, and prompted Deere to purchase the family business. The first fully John Deere–designed crawler was the MC, which came out in 1949. *Keith Haddock*

Massey-Ferguson 3366. Well-known agricultural group Massey-Ferguson came into the crawler tractor business after it took over the Italian firm of Landini in 1960. Established in 1884, Landini was Italy's oldest tractor builder. Massey-Ferguson's first crawler tractor was the Super 44 powered by a Perkins 40-horsepower engine. At that time, Perkins Engines was also owned by Massey-Ferguson. The 3366 model was introduced in 1965 and remained current for five years. It was powered by a Perkins 76-horsepower diesel engine. In 1968, Massey-Ferguson announced the opening of a new factory in Aprilia, Italy, and the manufacture of an expansive line of construction equipment. The first of these was the MF500, a Perkins-powered dozer of 136 flywheel-horsepower. It boasted an advanced power-shift transmission providing independent speed and direction of each track controlled by two levers at the operator's left hand. *Keith Haddock*

Massey-Ferguson MF700C. Massey-Ferguson purchased German tractor builder Hanomag in 1974, and the two ranges of tractor models were consolidated into one line. The largest crawler tractor was the former 180-horsepower Hanomag K-16E, which became the MF700C. The new nomenclature matched M-F's existing crawler line, first announced in 1968. Due to adverse business conditions, M-F sold its Italian plant in 1978 and transferred tractor production to the Hanomag plant. At the same time it discontinued marketing its products in North America. Germany's IBH group purchased the company in 1980. After IBH failed in 1983, Hanomag reverted to independent ownership and continued manufacturing the Hanomag crawler loaders and dozers.

New Holland DC180. The New Holland brand name on crawler tractors resulted from the merger of Case Corporation and equipment builder Ford New Holland to form CNH Global in 1999. Ford had acquired New Holland in 1986, and Fiat acquired Ford New Holland in 1991. With other acquisitions, CNH brought several well-known construction equipment brands under its control. Crawler tractors from the former Fiatallis line were subsequently marketed under several brand names within the CNH group. In North America they are badged as New Holland machines. An example is the DC180, powered by a 180-horsepower Cummins engine and weighing 44,500 pounds. *Keith Haddock*

Monarch 75. The industrial giant Allis-Chalmers Manufacturing Company expanded its tractor division in 1928 when it purchased Monarch Tractor Corporation of Springfield, Illinois. Monarch had been organized in 1913 as the Monarch Tractor Company of Watertown, Wisconsin, to build crawler tractors. Two tractors from the Monarch line, the 6-ton Model H and the 10-ton Model F, were initially manufactured by Allis-Chalmers, renumbered as Models 50 and 75, but still bearing the Monarch name. The Allis-Chalmers Monarch 75 produced 60 drawbar-horsepower from a Beaver-LeRoi four-cylinder gasoline engine. The Allis-Chalmers L replaced it in 1931. *Keith Haddock*

Terex 82-20. In 1968, the Euclid Division of General Motors came under a ruling by the U.S. Justice Department that GM must discontinue making off-highway trucks in the United States for five years and divest itself of the Euclid name. At that time, the Terex name was born to represent the remaining GM earthmoving products, including crawler tractors. The 82-20 was an addition to the Terex 82 Series crawler tractors started by Euclid in 1966. Released in 1973, the 82-20 was the smallest of the line, and was powered by a Detroit Diesel 6V-71-T engine rated at 180 flywheel-horsepower. *Keith Haddock*

Vickers Vigor VR-180. Billed as the world's fastest crawler tractor, the VR-180 was built by Vickers-Armstrong of the United Kingdom beginning in 1952. The unique undercarriage employed the high-speed characteristics of the military tanks formerly produced by the company. It consisted of large-diameter idlers and drive sprockets mounted in pairs on resilient bogies. This flexible undercarriage, with sealed and lubricated tracks, allowed the tractor to attain a top speed of just under 10 miles-per-hour. Power came from a Rolls-Royce six-cylinder diesel engine developing 190 flywheel-horsepower with torque converter. A smaller 142-horsepower Vikon model of similar design was introduced in 1956, but the high cost of manufacture caused Vickers to discontinue its tractors in 1961.

Terratrac GT-30. In 1951 the American Tractor Corporation (Ateco) of Churubusco, Indiana, commenced marketing a range of small crawler tractors known as Terratracs. The first machine was the GT-25 at 25 belt-horsepower. This was shortly followed by the GT-30 at 30 belt-horsepower. Both these models were fitted with Continental four-cylinder gasoline engines. In 1957, J.I. Case Company purchased Ateco, and the Terratrac crawler tractors became the foundation for future Case crawlers. *Keith Haddock*

Terex D800. German equipment group IBH acquired Terex in 1980, and the Terex crawler line was merged with the German Hanomag crawlers, also acquired by IBH. In 1982 the former Terex models were renumbered to match the Hanomag 100 Series designations. The D800 shown was derived from the former Terex 82-50. Its 12V-71T engine was rated at 350 flywheel-horsepower. When IBH failed in 1983, GM returned to Terex ownership. Three years later, Terex was sold again to Northwest Engineering Company, and at that time the Terex crawler tractors were discontinued. The last Terex crawler tractor built was a Model D800 in 1986. *Keith Haddock collection*

WHEEL BULLDOZERS

A wheel dozer can be made from any rubber-tired tractor by fitting a bulldozer blade on the front. These wheeled bulldozers range from light-duty attachments on farm tractors, to some of the very largest bulldozer-type machines ever constructed. It is the latter type, usually found in major earthmoving projects and surface mines, that are referred to as wheel dozers. Their obvious advantage over crawler machines is superior mobility and higher travel speed. Used as clean-up machines around large shovels, the wheel dozer can serve several units at the same time, scooting between them at high speed, cleaning the road as it goes. A wheel dozer can run to the dump, sweeping rocks off the haul road along the way; tidy up the dump while maintaining a safety berm; and then return to the shovels, all in a couple of hours. Wheel dozers are favorites on scraper jobs, working as push tractors. They can keep in pace with the fastest of scrapers, and boost their loads to maximum ratings during loading. When the dirt starts boiling over the scraper sides, the wheel pusher makes a hasty retreat in reverse and positions itself in a few seconds so it is ready to push the next scraper. Other wheel dozers are found in coal stockpile maintenance work, and in

heavy bulldozing such as reclamation work. Their perpetual advantage over their crawler cousins is that they don't damage paved roads, a definite asset when working around stockpiles in plants.

Cables from a tractor-mounted winch first operated the early wheel dozers, like the early wheel loaders. Some attempts to operate dozers and loaders by hydraulic power were made in the 1920s, but cable-operated machines were still being sold into the 1950s. By the 1960s, the transition to hydraulically operated dozer blades and loaders was complete.

Many wheel dozers were developed from wheel loaders by fitting a dozer blade in place of the loader arms and bucket. This adaptation was only a success where the machine was used for light-duty tasks. For the heavy work, manufacturers now realize that wheel dozers must be designed as wheel dozers from the ground up, and built with proper transmissions, gear ratios, and strong frames for mounting the dozer arms. These essential features provide maximum reliability in adverse conditions.

The first large rubber-tired dozers suitable for earthmoving applications were those produced by none other than earthmoving pioneer R.G. LeTourneau, beginning

Allis-Chalmers 555. Ranking as one of the largest wheel dozers ever built, the 75-ton Allis-Chalmers Model 555 wheel dozer was designed on an unusual concept. Launched in 1962, it was part of a mix-and-match combination of prime movers and scrapers, which included the Allis-Chalmers 562 twin-engined scraper. The 555 was simply a two-wheeled prime mover coupled through an articulated joint to a rear-powered push unit—in effect, a twin-powered scraper without its bowl. Front and rear engines were identical A-C 25000 diesels giving a total of 774 flywheel-horsepower. In 1963, Allis-Chalmers released the smaller D-30 and D-40 dozers, rated at 184 and 310 horsepower.

Caterpillar DW2. Some of the earliest Caterpillar wheeled dozers were conversions of its standard crawler tractors. They were initially developed by certain Caterpillar dealers, and found a niche market in special applications. Before long, Caterpillar was offering them as its own products. The DW2 shown is based on the 5U Series D2 of 50 flywheel-horsepower made in the 1950s. Equipped with tire chains, Balderson dozer blade, and rear winch, it is being used as a log skidder. *Keith Haddock collection*

in 1947. He developed four sizes known as the Models A, B, C, and D Tournadozers. The huge 750-horsepower Model A Tournadozers never really reached beyond the experimental stage. The 300-horsepower Model B, and 143-horsepower Model D had limited success, but the Model C and its successor the Super C became a big seller for the company and lasted in production until 1972, by which time it belonged to the LeTourneau-Westinghouse (Wabco) line. All Tournadozers had mechanical drive to all four wheels, and electrically operated blade controls. Tournadozers were steered by braking or slowing the wheels on one side, one of the first applications of the skid steer principle applied to a wheeled machine.

R.G. LeTourneau also built some world record-beating wheel dozers after the sale of his earthmoving equipment business to Wabco in 1953. The two 600-horsepower "Crash Pushers" built in 1955 for the U. S. Air Force were developed from an earlier "Tree Crasher" of similar six-wheel design. Starting in 1960, LeTourneau launched the intriguing K Series dozers. These included models with three, four, and five

Caterpillar DW6. Caterpillar also offered its D4 and D6 tractors as wheeled options. The DW6 was offered as far back as 1952 when about 100 of the then-current 9U D6 were built for sugar cane operations. Beginning in 1962, up to 200 DW6 tractors were produced based on the 44A Series D6, which replaced the 9U Series in 1959. The engine in those machines was rated at 115 flywheel-horsepower. The example is shown fitted with a push block and double-drum rear winch for pulling scrapers. *Keith Haddock*

Caterpillar 668C. Another type of Caterpillar wheeled dozer was based on a scraper prime mover. The 668C was based on the DW20 tractor but equipped with four-wheel drive. Produced only from 1956 to 1957, the 668C was a civilian version of a similar military unit previously built in 1954. It came equipped with the turbocharged D337F engine rated at 300 horsepower. *Eric C. Orlemann collection*

driving wheels, ranging from 420 to 1,260 horsepower. The massive K-205, with its power provided by three Cummins 420-horsepower engines, dwarfed any other bulldozer on the market. It was designed to push load scrapers, and the K-205 passed the test with flying colors. Literature published at the time boasted, "How to swap three tractors for one, and still load 45 scrapers an hour." The tractors being replaced in this example were none other than three of the world's largest crawler dozer, the Euclid TC-12.

By the 1960s, improved hydraulic power technology had convinced senior staff members and engineers at LeTourneau that hydraulics should be applied to LeTourneau machines. But they could not sway Mr. R.G. LeTourneau from his rack-and-pinion-drive fixation until he retired as president in 1966. Immediately after his retirement, engineers went to work to develop a new line of diesel-electric wheel loaders with motions controlled by state-of-the-art hydraulics. Although the first wheel dozer with hydraulic operation, the 475-flywheel-horsepower D-450B, never went into production, it was shown at the 1969 Conexpo show in Chicago. It paved the way for larger state-of-the-art LeTourneau wheel dozers launched in the 1970s.

Caterpillar 834. In 1963, Caterpillar launched two new articulated wheel dozers, the 824 and 834. Initially rated at 250 and 360 flywheel-horsepower, their power was boosted to 300 and 400 flywheel-horsepower by the end of the decade. This 834 is a push-loading scrapers, and carries a spring-loaded push block when assistance from a second tractor is needed. The 834 was discontinued in 1974, but returned as the larger 834B in 1982 with 450 flywheel-horsepower. Compactor versions, with steel tamping-foot wheels replacing the rubber tires, became available in the late 1960s. A smaller 170-horsepower model, the 814, came out in 1970. *Caterpillar, Inc.*

Caterpillar 844. In 1997, Caterpillar took over the designs and manufacturing rights of two large wheel dozers made by Tiger Engineering Proprietary, Ltd. of Australia. Tiger had been building wheel dozers since 1981, and its machines had found a niche market in surface mining with sizes larger than those offered by Caterpillar. The machines were based on standard Caterpillar wheel loaders, but with modified drive trains and frames strengthened for dozing applications. The Tiger Models 590B and 790G became the Caterpillar Models 844 and 854G with 625 and 800 flywheel-horsepower. The 854G is the largest and most powerful wheel dozer currently on the market. *Keith Haddock*

Not all large wheel dozers were built by well-known companies with a full line of earthmoving machines. Relatively small companies built some huge rubber-tired dozers. The Multi-Wheel 70 of 1970, designed and manufactured by CF & I Engineers, Inc. of Denver, Colorado, was an eight-wheel, 670-horsepower dozer that steered using the skid steer principle. The experimental V-Con V250, also of 1970 and designed by the Peerless Manufacturing Company of Dallas, Texas, was a diesel-electric wheel dozer of 1,000 horsepower. The larger V-Con V220

1,500-horsepower giant, unveiled in 1975, followed this up. The largest bulldozer of all time was the out-sized wheeled machine known as the Western 2000, built in 1963. Western Contracting Corporation desired power far exceeding anything on the market. They wanted to push load scrapers and load them in record time. So, using an associate company and building in-house, they produced a wheel dozer of superlative dimensions and 1,850 horsepower under the hood. No bulldozer of any type built since then has exceeded this monster's power.

Euclid 9FPM. Euclid was not known for its wheel dozers, but it did build several experimental models beginning with the Model 1FPM in 1949. Over the next decade, testing continued on several redesigned models. The prototype 9FPM was built in December 1955 as a redesigned version of the 6FPM, built a year earlier. The 9FPM shown was built in 1956. The non-articulated unit is steered by its rear wheels and powered by a GM 6-71 diesel engine. *Keith Haddock*

FWD-Wagner WI-30. This large wheel dozer was produced by FWD-Wagner, Inc., of Portland, Oregon, a company formed when FWD took over Wagner Tractor, Inc., in 1961. Wagner was associated with Mixermobile, the famous pioneer of the Scoopmobile articulated loaders of the mid-1950s. The 50-ton Model WI-30 utilized Scoopmobile articulated-steering technology, and featured dual controls with swivel seat for the operator. It could be fitted with a dozer blade on one end, and a push block for scraper loading on the other. Two Cummins 350-horsepower diesel engines powered the big dozer through dual torque converters.

Harris Tractor. The Harris Manufacturing Company of Stockton, California, built a skidsteer, four-wheel-drive tractor that was available with bulldozer or front-end loader attachments. A selection of different models was offered with choice of transmissions, front or rear operator's seat positions, and Chrysler or GM engines. All these models were based on the same tractor, rated around 62 brake-horsepower, with an operating weight of approximately 5 tons. Although the Harris Tractor Company had been established a number of years prior to introducing the tractor in 1953, the company had ceased production by the end of 1954. *Keith Haddock*

International D-500. International started at the top when it decided to build its first wheel dozer. Starting in 1959 as a prototype model, the D-500 was developed as a purpose-built wheel dozer of 600 horsepower and 64 tons of operating weight. When officially launched in 1961, it was claimed to be the first articulated wheel dozer. It was certainly the largest ever built by International. The D-500 was developed into the H-400, an articulated loader in the 10-cubic-yard class launched in 1964. That same year, International added two more models to its dozer line, the Models D-100 and D-120 of 220 and 300 flywheel-horsepower. *State Historical Society of Wisconsin*

Komatsu WD900-3. Komatsu's big wheel dozer is the WD900-3. Its Komatsu SA12V-140 engine puts 853 flywheel-horsepower behind its heavy-duty dozer blade, measuring 7 feet high by 21 feet, 3 inches-wide. Operating weight is just over 110 tons, and speeds up to 17.6 miles per hour are attained through its three-speed power-shift transmission with torque converter. The WD900-3 is the dozer version of Komatsu's WA900-3 wheel loader, which replaced the former WA900-1 in 2000. *Komatsu America International Co.*

LeTourneau Super C Tournadozer. Earthmoving equipment pioneer R.G. LeTourneau began developing rubber-tired dozers as early as 1943, but wartime production priorities resulted in delayed development. Four sizes of dozers were eventually released into production during 1947, the first in January as the C Tournadozer. This model and its successor, the Super C, were by far the most popular Tournadozers, and remained in production after 1953 as a LeTourneau-Westinghouse (Wabco) product until 1972. A Buda 160-horsepower engine powered the C Tournadozer. The upgraded Super C Tournadozer appeared in 1949 with a Detroit 6-71 engine capable of developing 186 horsepower. *Keith Haddock collection*

LeTourneau A Tournadozer. The largest of the Tournadozers was the huge 750-horsepower Model A released in 1947, and introduced at the 1948 Chicago Road Show as the largest bulldozer ever built. It was powered by a Packard marine engine set up to run on butane fuel, carried a 16-foot-wide dozer blade, and was capable of a top speed of 14 miles-per-hour. After proving unreliable in the field—transmissions kept failing—the Model A had its engine downgraded to 500 horsepower. But even after further testing, the Model A was withdrawn from production in 1950. All Tournadozers had mechanical drive and electrically operated blade controls, and the models utilized the skidsteer principle for steering. *Keith Haddock collection*

LeTourneau K-104 Pacemaker. After selling his earthmoving equipment business to Wabco in 1953, R.G. LeTourneau expanded into other types of equipment before returning to earthmovers in 1958. At that time, LeTourneau unveiled the first of many models of diesel-electric machines with electric motors in each wheel hub. A new line of wheel dozers, known as the K Series, was commenced in 1960. These electrically powered dozers comprised the 420-horsepower Models K-53 and K-54, 840-horsepower Models K-103 and K-104, and the K-205 fitted with three 420-horsepower Cummins engines. The last digit in the model numbers signified the number of wheels. *Keith Haddock collection*

LeTourneau K-205 Pacemaker. Designed to push-load scrapers, the colossal five-wheeled K-205 weighed 160 tons when ballasted for traction. All five wheels were powered, and the single rear wheel provided steering. As with all Pacemaker machines, power for steering, blade movements, and other attachments was transmitted from high-torque AC electric motors through rack-and-pinion drives. This largest of the Pacemaker electric dozer line was built with a 20-foot-wide dozer blade, and was powered with a battery of three Cummins V12 diesel engines capable of providing 1,260 horsepower. *Keith Haddock collection*

LeTourneau D-450B. After R.G. LeTourneau's retirement in 1966, engineers were finally free to work on a new line of diesel-electric wheel loaders with motions controlled by state-of-the-art hydraulics, something R.G. detested. Two new loaders, the L-500 and L-700, and a D-450B wheel dozer were simultaneously developed and shown to the public during the 1969 Conexpo show in Chicago. The D-450B was the dozer version of the L-500 loader. It was powered by a Detroit 12V-71N engine rated at 475 flywheel-horsepower. Unfortunately, due to lack of financing, D-450B and L-500 machines never went into commercial production. But the L-700 loader, the first LeTourneau production machine to use hydraulics, was a great success (see chapter 5). *LeTourneau, Inc.*

LeTourneau D-800. The big D-800 LeTro-Dozer came on the market in 1978 as the dozer version of the 15-cubic-yard L-800 loader, which itself was an upgrade from the earlier L-700 machines. Powered by either Detroit or Cummins diesel engines of 800 flywheel-horsepower, the D-800 weighed approximately 100 tons in operating condition. The standard 19-foot-wide blade could be exchanged for a special blade 9 feet high and 22 feet, 5 inches wide for coal stockpile dozing. *LeTourneau, Inc.*

Michigan 280. The Clark Equipment Company started its Construction Machinery Division in 1952, and the following year purchased the Michigan Power Shovel Company, a builder of excavators and cranes at Benton Harbor, Michigan. In 1954 the company introduced three rugged wheel loaders at a public demonstration. These were the Michigan 75A, 125A, and 175A. The following year, the first Michigan wheel dozer appeared, the 162-horsepower 180. In 1957 the range was expanded with the Models 275A and 375A, together with wheel dozer versions designated Models 280 and 380. These machines had engines of 262 and 375 maximum horsepower, and operating weights of 28 tons and 37 tons. The 280 in the picture efficiently loads a Euclid TS-14 scraper at a surface coal mine. *Keith Haddock*

Michigan 480. Clark boosted its wheel dozer line again in 1958 with the giant 52-ton Model 480 dozer. It was offered with either GM or Cummins diesels in the 600-maximum-horsepower class, and a 14-foot-wide dozer blade. This machine was targeted for heavy-duty reclamation work, push-loading scrapers, and general surface mining duties, and placed the Michigan name in a league among the largest wheeled equipment yet built. The 480 remained in production until 1965, by which time an articulated version had replaced the earlier rigid-frame model. *Eric C. Orlemann Collection*

Michigan 280 (Articulated). By the mid-1960s, Clark had expanded its Michigan wheel loader line to cover a broad range from .5 to 12-cubic-yards capacity. In 1965, the company began to introduce articulated loaders and dozers to replace all of its previous models. Some confusion arose in the model designations because the same model numbers were used as for the old rigid models. In 1967, the 33-ton articulated 280 was initially offered with either GM or Cummins engines of 318 or 210 maximum horsepower. Power was increased to 335 horsepower as the upgraded 280B and 280C models were introduced in 1982 and 1984. *Keith Haddock*

Melroe M-880. CF & I Engineers, Inc. of Denver, Colorado, designed and built a large dozer in 1970 called the Multi-Wheel 70. The machine consisted of a rigid frame and four in-line driving wheels on each side, connected by chains. Two 335-horsepower engines, each driving one side through its own transmission, allowed the operator to steer by varying the speed and direction of each drive train. This machine was acquired by Melroe, of Bobcat loader fame, which sold it from 1978 to 1982. Then the machine lay dormant until 1996, when a new company, Innovative Mining & Equipment of Gillette, Wyoming, started to rebuild the original machines. The picture shows the upgraded machine with twin 425-horsepower engines known as the M-880. *Innovative Mining & Equipment, Inc.*

Michigan 380 (Articulated). The 380 appeared in its articulated form in 1968 with a Cummins V1710 diesel rated at 500 maximum horsepower and an operating weight of 54 tons. It was a favorite in large surface mining operations where its 20-miles-per-hour road speed allowed it to handle assignments at widely spaced locations in a single shift. The 380 was upgraded to the B Model in 1980, by which time maximum horsepower had increased to 635. After the Clark Michigan Company became a subsidiary of VME Group (Volvo-Michigan-Euclid) in 1985, the popular 380B was carried forward into the new VME line as the W380. *Keith Haddock*

RayGo Wagner CHD-15-28. This rubber-tired coal dozer was made by RayGo Wagner of Portland, Oregon, after it became a subsidiary of RayGo, Inc. RayGo was established in 1964 and made its name in self-propelled compactors and the Giant grader in 1969. The CHD-15-28 came with a special carry-dozer blade, which stacked the coal on the "shelf" part of the blade as it dozed forward. To dump its load, hydraulic rams pivoted the blade forward. A Cummins 335-horsepower diesel ran under the hood, and the entire outfit weighed 27 tons. Raygo products were discontinued in 1985, when CMI Corporation purchased the company.

Terex WD3000. This wheel dozer was a Terex product for only the three years that Germany's IBH owned the company. Formerly, it belonged to the construction equipment line produced by the Zettelmeyer organization in Germany, which got its start building road rollers in 1910. Zettelmeyer was the company that kicked off the IBH empire in 1975. Its products were imported into North America as Terex products from 1981. Then, after the collapse of IBH in 1983, Zettelmeyer reverted back to independent ownership, and the products, including the wheel dozer, continued under the Zettelmeyer banner. The WD3000 had an operating weight of 50,700 pounds and was powered by a Deutz 280-flywheel-horsepower engine. It boasted a top speed of 40 miles-per-hour. *Eric C. Orlemann Collection*

Tiger 690D. In 1981, Tiger Engineering Proprietary, Ltd. of Australia began making dozer versions of Caterpillar's 690-flywheel-horsepower 992C wheel loader at the request of BHP Iron Ore for use at their Mount Whaleback Mine in western Australia. Known as the Tiger 690, units were sold around Australia to various surface mines. The first unit was exported to the United States in 1987. The 690D, based on the upgraded Caterpillar 992D, appeared in 1993. The Model 590, based on the Caterpillar 990 loader, was launched in 1994. In 1997, Caterpillar purchased the designs and manufacturing rights of Tiger's then current models, the 590B and 790G, and marketed them as the Caterpillar 844 and 854G. *Keith Haddock*

V-Con V250. Another large wheel dozer was the V-Con that first went to work in 1970. Designed by the Peerless Manufacturing Company of Dallas, Texas, it was a diesel-electric machine with planetary wheel motors in each wheel, and fitted with a 1,000-horsepower diesel engine. Designed as a reclamation dozer for surface mining operations, its operating weight was 125 tons. Only one prototype machine (illustrated) had been built by 1973, when the Marion Power Shovel Company acquired rights to purchase the V-Con Division from Peerless. However, Marion developed a larger V220 model with 1,500 horsepower and an operating weight of 150 tons. But after only two V220s were built and tested at various sites, the V-Con program was dropped in 1977. *Eric C. Orlemann collection*

Western 2000. The largest bulldozer-type machine of any kind was this behemoth designed and built by Western Contracting Corporation. First used on the 17-million-cubic-yard Milford Dam job near Junction City, Kansas, the diesel-electric machine derived a total of 1,850 horsepower from two engines, and weighed 170 tons in operation. The main engine, a 16-cylinder GM diesel of 1,650 horsepower, drove a 1,400-kilowatt DC generator providing power to a 400-horsepower electric motor in each of its four wheels. A second 200-horsepower GM engine ran a 75-kilowatt AC generator. The 15.5-foot-wide Western 2000 was articulated at both ends, and ran on 44.5x45 tires, the largest made at that time. The one and only machine served its owners well from 1963 until it was scrapped in 1981. *Eric C. Orlemann collection*

CHAPTER 4

CRAWLER LOADERS

The crawler loader is one of those machines that originated as an attachment to a crawler tractor and developed into an integrated production machine in its own right. The very first models consisted of a bucket mounted on a simple pivoting beam, raised and lowered by a cable winch driven by the tractor power take-off. To dump, the bucket was released by a simple latch mechanism, because there was no power provided to crowd (rotate) the bucket. To obtain a full bucket, the operator had to rely on the momentum of the machine to ram into the bank or earth pile.

The crawler loader reached its peak of popularity in the late 1960s. Since then, the hydraulic excavator has become more reliable and sophisticated, and has taken over much of the work formerly done by crawler loaders. But the crawler loader is far from obsolete. It is still the preferred tool for contractors who need a mobile digging and loading machine, offering more stability and breakout force than an equivalent-sized wheel loader. With its wide bucket, the crawler loader is ideal for cleaning up construction sites. And because its traveling speed is faster than that of an excavator, it is able to perform a multitude of tasks that may be scattered over a large construction site without wasting time traveling between them. When equipped with a clamshell-type loader bucket, the crawler loader is a favorite with demolition contractors who use the machines. Not only does it load debris into highway trucks, it can also pick out different materials such as steel and timber and sort them into piles. Sharp objects such as old reinforcing steel don't cause costly tire failures as they would with wheel loaders.

Because of the experience gained from the use of early crawler loaders, today's manufacturers realize that crawler loaders must be fully designed from the ground up. It is not sufficient simply to mount the loader arms and bucket on a standard crawler tractor. The entire machine must be designed with correct balance, and a frame to withstand the rigors of heavy excavating. And there is a lot more steering involved with the operation of a wheel loader compared with a crawler bulldozer, putting extra strain on the steering system. For each bucket cycle, the machine must be

Allis-Chalmers HD-5/TS5. In 1948 the Tractomotive Corporation introduced a new hydraulic loader attachment designed to fit the Allis-Chalmers HD-5 tractor. The loader, called a TS5, was the first to incorporate a hydraulically powered bucket crowd, permitting bucket rollback during digging and controlled dumping. The HD-5/TS5 combination carried a 1-cubic-yard bucket and weighed 16,500 pounds. Power came from a GM two-cycle diesel rated at 37.4 drawbar-horsepower. When sold by Allis-Chalmers, it became the HD-5G crawler loader. Tractomotive eventually supplied a loader for every Allis-Chalmers tractor model until 1959, when Allis-Chalmers purchased Tractomotive Corporation. These loaders included the record-beating 4-cubic-yard models, HD-19G, HD-20G, and HD-21G. *Keith Haddock*

maneuvered back from the digging face, turned to face the dumping position, then backed again, and turned to face the digging position.

The Trackson Company developed one of the first loading shovels, and designed it for mounting on standard Caterpillar tractors. Organized in 1922, the Milwaukee firm started making tractor equipment for Caterpillar in 1936, and the following year began supplying Caterpillar with vertical-lift cable-operated loader attachments for mounting on its tractors. The first of these was mounted on a Caterpillar Thirty tractor. Subsequently, the company developed a line of loaders specifically matched to the Caterpillar D2, D4, D6, and D7 crawler tractors and called them Traxcavators. The Trackson attachment consisted of a heavy

Allis-Chalmers H-3. Allis-Chalmers purchased the Tractomotive company in 1959, and continued to produce a long line of crawler loaders, offering the smaller models with either diesel or gasoline power. The first models to appear after the takeover were the 40-drawbar-horsepower crawlers H-3 (gasoline powered), and HD-3 (diesel powered). Loader versions of these models were fitted with a .75-cubic-yard standard bucket, and the entire outfits weighed 10,300 pounds. Allis-Chalmers continued to offer a full line of crawler loaders up to the formation of Fiat-Allis in 1974. After this, the crawler loader heritage carried forward into the new company, and new models were introduced. *Keith Haddock*

ASV 4810. A very modern concept is the rubber-tracked crawler loader like those made since 1988 by ASV (All-Season Vehicles, Inc.) of Marcell, Minnesota. These machines boast a patented flexible undercarriage of oversize dimensions. This results in very low ground pressure, down to less than 2 psi, enabling the machines to keep working in soft, marshy ground where other loaders would bog down. The first model, known as the Posi-Track MD70 came equipped with a 70-horsepower Isuzu diesel engine. The 4810 model shown here is the largest in the ASV line. Its operating weight is 8,640 pounds, and power comes from a Caterpillar diesel engine of 105 horsepower. In 2002, Caterpillar, Inc., held a 50 percent equity in ASV. *Keith Haddock*

Case 750 Loader. J.I. Case purchased the American Tractor Corporation (Ateco) in 1957, providing Case with a line of crawler tractors and loaders. Later that same year, Case launched a redesigned and expanded line consisting of four size ranges from the 40-horsepower Model 310 up to the 100-horsepower Model 1000. Each size was available in dozer or loader versions. Further upgrades brought the Model 750 in 1961. This machine featured the patented Terramatic steering system that was introduced on the former 800 and 1000 models. This system provided two forward speeds and reverse for each track, allowing turns with power to both tracks as well as counter-rotating spin turns. *Keith Haddock*

frame mounted over and above the tractor hood. The frame supported the hoisting sheaves and bucket arms as well as a cable winch driven from the tractor front power take-off. Traxcavator models were the T2, T4, T6, and T7 and matched their respective tractor models with bucket capacities ranging from .5 cubic yards for the T2 to 2 cubic yards for the T7.

By 1950, hydraulics had been incorporated into the Trackson loaders; the first was mounted on a modified D4 and known as the Model HT4. This hydraulic loader design was a real breakthrough. Gone were the complicated cables, winches, and mechanical linkages. In their place was a neat, two-motion hydraulically powered linkage, and two levers controlling hoist and bucket crowd. Most importantly, the heavy frame and top-heavy draw works previously mounted high above the engine hood had been eliminated. The result was a nimble, lighter, and more productive machine with vastly enhanced stability. Caterpillar favored this new design so much that it purchased the Trackson Company in December 1951, and adopted the Traxcavator name for its crawler loaders.

Initially, Trackson's former loader models were incorporated into Caterpillar's product line. But, with

Case 850B Loader. The Case 750 was replaced by the 66-flywheel-horsepower 850 in 1967. This popular model of dozer and loader remained in production a full decade, with power increases along the way. In 1977, Case presented the 75-flywheel-horsepower 850B model. The machine featured modular design enabling major components to be easily removed for maintenance. Although power steering, with power to both tracks while turning, was retained on the 850 and 850B models, the spin-turn capability of the former 750 model was dropped. All Case crawler loaders and dozers are powered by Case diesel engines. *Keith Haddock*

the exception of the well-liked 1.25-cubic-yard HT4, which continued in Caterpillar's product line until 1955, they were short-lived. Within a year, Caterpillar redesigned the former Trackson machines as crawler loaders from the ground up, and introduced its first integrated hydraulic crawler loader, the No. 6 Traxcavator, in 1953. This machine was the forerunner of all Caterpillar's subsequent crawler loader models. The present series began in 1955 with the launch of the first 933, 955, and 977 Traxcavators.

The collaboration between attachment supplier Trackson and tractor builder Caterpillar, culminating in the latter taking over Trackson, was not an isolated case in the crawler loader industry. In a parallel development, Tractomotive Corporation designed a loader attachment to fit the Allis-Chalmers Model HD-5 tractor in 1946. The loader was the first to include a hydraulically powered bucket crowd, permitting bucket rollback during digging and controlled dumping. Tractomotive became a major supplier to Allis-Chalmers over the subsequent decade, and offered some of the largest crawler loaders ever built. These were the giant crawler loader versions of the Allis-Chalmers tractors, the 4-cubic-yard-capacity HD-19G, HD-20G, and HD-21G models that were released from the late 1940s. In 1959, Allis-Chalmers finally purchased its main supplier of tractor equipment, Tractomotive Corporation.

Case 1150B Loader. Case pushed the limits on size when it unveiled the 1150B in 1972, reaching the 100-horsepower mark for the first time. It replaced the earlier 95-horsepower model 1150, introduced in 1965, but retained the same 1.75-cubic-yard bucket capacity as the earlier model. Unlike the smaller 850-size loaders, the 1150 and 1150B models retained the steering system from the earlier 1000 model. This system provided two forward speeds and reverse for each track, allowing turns with power to both tracks as well as counter-rotating spin turns. In 1978, the 1150B loader was replaced by the 1150C at 105 flywheel-horsepower. *Keith Haddock*

Case 1155E. This model was introduced as a replacement for the 110-horsepower 1155D loader, which was produced from 1983 to 1986. The 1155E was introduced in 1985 with increased power to 118 flywheel-horsepower and a bucket of 2-cubic-yards capacity. It still featured independent four-speed power-shift transmission to each crawler with counter-rotation steering. The 1155E turned out to be the last crawler loader made by Case, which phased out all its crawler loader models in 1993. *Keith Haddock*

Caterpillar Fifteen/Drott Loader. The early crawler loaders utilized loader attachments made by specialist manufacturers. This picture from 1930 shows one of the very first fitted to a crawler tractor. A Caterpillar gasoline engine of 26 belt-horsepower powers the Caterpillar Fifteen model shown. The loader is built by the Drott Manufacturing Company and carries about 1 cubic yard. Notice how the vertical hydraulic cylinder actuates the cable hoist. The bucket is dumped by gravity when the operator pulls the rope to release the latch. *Caterpillar, Inc.*

Caterpillar D2/T2 Traxcavator. In 1937, the Trackson Company began building cable-operated loader attachments for mounting on standard Caterpillar tractors. The vertical-lift loaders were available on all Caterpillar tractors up to the D7 size. Known as Traxcavators, the models were the T2, T4, T6, and T7; they matched their respective tractor models with bucket capacities ranging from .5 cubic yards for the T2 to 2 cubic yards for the T7. Notice the heavy frame over the engine hood that supports the hoisting sheaves, bucket arms, and cable winch driven from the tractor's front power take-off. All this made the machine rather unstable, especially when a loaded bucket was hoisted high. *Keith Haddock*

Caterpillar No.6 Traxcavator. Caterpillar introduced its first integrated hydraulic crawler loader, the No.6 Traxcavator, in 1953. Based on the D6 9U tractor, but with a modified frame and longer seven-roller undercarriage, the No.6 carried a 2-yard bucket. It replaced the earlier Trackson models, which were basically attachments to standard crawler tractors. Two years later, the No.6 was phased out to make way for Caterpillar's new line of Traxcavators. The first of these, the 955C with bucket capacity of 1-1/2 cubic yards, was announced early in 1955. *Keith Haddock*

Caterpillar D6/Hoover Loader. This was one of many overloaders or overshot loaders available in the 1940s and 1950s. In this type of loader, the bucket was hoisted right over the top of the cab, and dumped at the rear. Its main advantage was that the tractor did not have to turn to dump its load. Several companies manufacturing this type of loader offered both cable and hydraulic models. The manufacturers also supplied the heavy-duty protection package for the operator. Without this safety feature, operation could become hazardous, to say the least. Most suitable tractors were the wide-gauge variety like the D6 9U Series in the picture. It is equipped with an Overhead Dozer-Loader made by the Hoover Machine Co., Ltd. of Edmonton, Alberta. *Keith Haddock collection*

Another company collaboration was Bucyrus-Erie Company (B-E) and International Harvester (I-H). B-E manufactured tractor equipment from 1938 to 1954, and during the 1940s made a line of loader attachments that were hydraulically hoisted and gravity dumped. They were specifically designed for International crawler tractors, and sold exclusively through I-H dealers. In 1950, I-H and the Drott Manufacturing Company reached an agreement for I-H to sell crawler loaders fitted with Drott loaders under the International-Drott name. Drott had previously supplied tractor attachments and was the pioneer of the four-in-one clamshell-type bucket. With the additional clamshell action, the bucket could be used for loader,

scraper, dozer, or clamshell duties. From the Drott line, I-H developed its own line of crawler loaders.

Hydrostatically driven crawler loaders began to appear in the 1970s. By adding a hydrostatic motor for each crawler, the steering clutches, brakes, transmissions, and drive trains are eliminated. Control of speed, direction, and steering can be accomplished through one joystick lever. Another joystick lever controls all bucket movements. JCB of the United Kingdom produced a prototype hydrostatic loader in 1968, and officially released the JCB 110 crawler loader in 1971. This pioneering machine was the world's first rear-engined hydrostatic crawler loader, and its design configuration and appearance would set the standard for future crawler loaders. Liebherr introduced its first hydrostatic crawler tractor, the PR732, in 1975. By the end of the decade, Liebherr had added hydrostatic crawler loaders to its product line. Others followed the JCB lead, including Caterpillar with the introduction of its first hydrostatic-drive crawler loaders, the 943 and 953, in 1980.

Sales for crawler loaders have dropped significantly over the past 30 years. In the 1970s, manufacturers began dropping them from their product lines. Now, only 7 brands are available in the United States, down from a peak of over 20 in their heyday. But those still offering these jack-of-all-trades machines command respectable sales from niche-market contractors.

Caterpillar 977L. The first of Caterpillar's 900 Series crawler loaders appeared in 1955. In that year, three models, the 933C (1 yard), 955C (1.5 cubic yards), and 977D (2.25 cubic yards) were added to Caterpillar's product line. These models were all integrated crawler loaders that were greatly modified from their original crawler tractor format. The 977, like Caterpillar's other loaders, was periodically upgraded as new models were released. The 977E came out in 1958, the 977H in 1960, the 977K in 1966, and the 977L (illustrated) in 1978. The 977L wielded a standard bucket of 3.25 cubic yards, weighed 48,330 pounds, and came with a Caterpillar engine of 190 flywheel-horsepower. *Keith Haddock*

Caterpillar 931. Moving down in size, Caterpillar announced a trio of smaller machines in 1972, the D3 crawler tractor, the 910 wheel loader, and the 931 crawler loader. All three machines carried the same Caterpillar engine, which was rated at 62 flywheel-horsepower for the 931. The standard bucket of the 931 could carry 1 cubic yard, and the operating weight was 14,800 pounds. A low ground pressure model was also offered with ground pressures down to 4.2 psi, about half that of the standard machine. This smallest of the Caterpillar crawler loaders progressed through the 931B in 1979, the 931C in 1988, and the Series II 931C in 1990. The same engine was retained, but flywheel power increased to 70 in the last model, which ceased production in 1993. *Keith Haddock*

Caterpillar 983. In 1969, at the peak of crawler loader popularity in the industry, Caterpillar announced the 983, the biggest crawler loader it would ever make. Standard bucket capacity was initially 4.5 cubic yards, but this increased to 5 cubic yards by 1972. A Caterpillar engine of 275 flywheel-horsepower powered it. In 1978, the 983 became the 983B, with an improved operator's cab and a strengthened main frame. Capacity and horsepower remained the same, but operating weight increased to 78,530 pounds, about a ton heavier than the former model. Caterpillar discontinued the 983B in 1982 in favor of its modern hydrostatic models. *Keith Haddock*

Caterpillar 943. The first hydrostatically driven crawler loader from Caterpillar was the 943, which was unveiled in 1980. This 1.5-cubic-yard machine differed from Caterpillar's earlier designs, not only in its drive system, but also in its entire design. The operator now sat at the front with full view of the bucket, and the engine was at the rear. This configuration would set the standard for all of Caterpillar's future crawler loaders this size and larger. Hydrostatic drive allows steering clutches and brakes, transmissions, and drive trains to be eliminated. Independent motors control the tracks, and control of speed, direction, and steering can be accomplished through one joystick lever. The 943 remained current until 1992. *Keith Haddock*

Caterpillar 953C. Since 1980, when Caterpillar unveiled its first hydrostatic crawler loader, the company gradually replaced its entire line of conventional crawler loaders in favor of hydrostatically driven models. Today, the range covers five sizes from the 933C at 70 flywheel-horsepower, to the 973C at 210 flywheel-horsepower. The mid-sized 953C replaced the earlier 953B in 1996. Its standard bucket holds 2 cubic yards, operating weight tips the scales at 33,200 pounds, and its engine develops 121 flywheel-horsepower. There is also a wide-track option for soft ground operation. *Caterpillar, Inc.*

Cletrac BGS/Sargent. In 1944, the Cleveland Tractor Company introduced this Cletrac model with a six-cylinder gasoline engine of 38 drawbar-horsepower. Like other tractor builders of the day, Cletrac did not build attachments for its machines, so a lucrative market existed for others to supply a wide variety of tractor attachments. The Cletrac BGS in the picture is equipped with an Overhead loader built by Maine Steel, Inc. This cable-operated loader digs at the front and discharges at the rear. A similar hydraulically operated type is the Caterpillar D6 tractor and Hoover loader, also illustrated in this chapter. *Keith Haddock*

Deere JD440. The purchase of Lindeman Power Equipment Company by John Deere in 1947 brought crawler tractors to the well-established Deere line of wheeled tractors. In the 1950s, Deere introduced several small crawler tractors geared to agricultural markets, and some were offered with loader attachments, like this 440 tractor shown equipped with a model 831 loader. The 30-horsepower 440 was made from 1958 to 1961, but soon disappeared after Deere launched its two industrial crawlers, the 1010 and 2010, in 1960. *Keith Haddock*

Deere JD555. In 1974, John Deere introduced its largest crawler loader yet, the JD555 at 80 flywheel-horsepower. Its operating weight was 18,255 pounds with a standard 1.25-cubic-yard bucket. It featured a power-shift transmission with three speeds forward and reverse. The machine shown is attached to the Deere 9300 backhoe, which makes a versatile multi-purpose machine for trenching jobs. The 555 was upgraded through the 555A in 1983, the 555B in 1985, and the 555G in 1987. The latter model had its power increased to 90 flywheel-horsepower, and bucket capacity to 1.5 cubic yards. *Keith Haddock*

Deere JD 755. At the 1975 Conexpo equipment show in Chicago, John Deere announced a major expansion into larger earthmoving equipment. It announced several new machines that were larger than any previously built by Deere, including two crawler loaders, the JD755 and JD855 of 122 and 220 flywheel-horsepower. These models featured hydrostatic drive, a first for John Deere. The JD755 weighed 16 tons when equipped with its standard bucket of 2 cubic yards. In 1981, it was upgraded to the JD755A of similar capacity. *Keith Haddock*

Deere 455G. Like the larger JD555, John Deere's smallest crawler loader, the JD455, had a similar chain of development. Originating from the JD450C loader, the model was upgraded to the 455G in 1988. This model is offered with a choice of torque converter or direct-drive transmission. A John Deere engine rated at 70 flywheel-horsepower provides the power. With its bucket of 1.3 cubic yards, it weighs in at 19,400 pounds. A wide-track version, with track shoes increased from the standard 14 inches to 21 inches and ground pressure lowered some 40 percent, allowed the machine to work on soft ground. *Keith Haddock*

Deere 755C. The newest crawler loaders from Deere are derived from a partnership announced in 2001 with Germany's Liebherr company. Based on Liebherr's rear-engine design and hydrostatic technology, which has been utilized in all Liebherr crawler loaders since the first in 1980, the current Deere models in 2002 are the 655C and 755C. The larger model has a standard bucket capacity of 2.25 cubic yards and weighs in at 46,300 pounds. Its Liebherr engine puts out 177 flywheel-horsepower and drives a load-sensing hydrostatic system that automatically adjusts speed and power to match changing load conditions. *Deere & Co.*

Eimco 136RO. The Tractor Division of the Eimco Corporation built crawler tractors and crawler loaders from 1952 to 1965 in relatively small numbers. Eimco's dual power-shift transmissions for independent track control allowed full-power turns or spin turns when the tracks were counter-rotated—a major advantage for its loaders. Largest in Eimco's line was the 136RO (Rear Operator) heavy-duty crawler loader, designed for steel mill slag removal and furnace cleanout, but also used for general rock loading in quarries. The high-position seat kept the operator away from heat and dirt. The big 136RO weighed 57,800 pounds with a standard 3-cubic-yard bucket. It measured 11 feet to the top of the cab. *Keith Haddock*

Fiat-Allis FL-10C. After the Fiat-Allis joint venture was born in 1974, the former Allis-Chalmers crawler loaders were continued using the FL prefix used for Fiat's former crawler loaders. The intermediate-sized 110-horsepower FL10-B carried a bucket of 1.875 cubic yards. It was upgraded to the FL10-C in 1978 with a standard bucket capacity of 2 cubic yards and power up to 122 flywheel-horsepower. This model, popular in Europe, grew into the FL10E, and then the current FL145 at 128 flywheel-horsepower, with its bucket capacity remaining at 2 cubic yards. Today it is sold under the Fiat-Hitachi banner. *Keith Haddock collection*

Fiat-Allis FL-14E. A larger crawler loader offered by Fiat-Allis was the FL-14B. Initially rated at 143 flywheel-horsepower with a bucket capacity of 2.5 cubic yards, this machine was upgraded to the 150-horsepower FL14-C in 1978, then again to the 168-horsepower FL14E in 1986. Bucket capacity increased to 2.75 cubic yards. The FL14-E became the Fiatallis FL175, sold latterly as the Fiat-Hitachi FL175, currently rated at 170 flywheel-horsepower. *Keith Haddock*

International Hough H-12. The Frank G. Hough Company, subsidiary of International Harvester Company, marketed a crawler loader of advanced design for its day from 1955 to 1960. Ahead of its time, the sleek-lined H-12 featured a rear-mounted engine, a design not adopted by others until the 1970s. Also, its entire body could be raised at the rear by the hydraulic loader arms, exposing drive train, transmission, and final drives for quick service or inspection. The 1.75-cubic-yard H-12 was in the 11-ton weight class. *Historical Construction Equipment Association*

International TD-9. This International TD-9 crawler tractor is fitted with a Bucyrus-Erie Dozer-Shovel designed specially for this tractor. Bucyrus-Erie Company (B-E) began making tractor equipment designed for International tractors in 1938. In the late 1940s, B-E introduced its first loader attachments, which were hydraulically hoisted and gravity-dumped by a spring-loaded latch mechanism. The TD-9 illustrated is the improved version released in 1951, featuring a hydraulically controlled bucket crowd. Note the unusual arrangement of a sliding linkage on the bucket arms. The bucket on the machine shown has a rating of 1 cubic yard. *Keith Haddock collection*

International 175. Under a 1950 agreement, Drott Manufacturing Company began manufacturing a line of crawler loaders for International TD Series tractors. Drott was the pioneer of the four-in-one or clamshell-type bucket. They were initially known as Bullclams, and the loaders sold under the International-Drott name. From the Drott line, International developed its own line of crawler loaders, and launched them in the 1962–1963 time period. The Model 175 crawler loader in the 2-cubic-yard class grew out of the 120-flywheel-horsepower TD-15 tractor. Today this model survives as the 175C, upgraded through the 175B to 2.25 cubic yards and 142 flywheel-horsepower. It is the only former International crawler loader offered in the current Komatsu Dresser line, and manufactured by HSW in Poland. *Keith Haddock*

International Dresser 200. International construction products, including the crawler loaders, were known as Dresser products after the latter took over the line in 1982. In 1988, under the Dresser name, the hydrostatically driven, 2.5-cubic-yard Model 200 was announced. This modern-design loader, with rear-mounted engine, was controlled by a single joystick lever for speed, steering, and direction. However, this model only remained in the product line until 1991 and was Dresser's only hydrostatic loader. *Komatsu America International Company*

JCB 114. Hydrostatically driven crawler loaders began to appear in the 1970s. First came JCB, with a prototype as far back as 1968, and the public release of its 1.25-cubic-yard Model 110 crawler loader in 1971. This pioneering machine not only featured hydrostatic transmission with independent control of each crawler, but the engine was rear-mounted for excellent balance and superb operator visibility. This was the world's first rear-engined hydrostatic crawler loader, and its design configuration became the standard for crawler loaders in the 1990s. The 114 was the largest JCB crawler loader. In the 2-cubic-yard class, it made an appearance in 1976, but by 1979, JCB had phased out all its crawler loaders. *JCB Sales, Ltd.*

Komatsu D60S. Beginning in 1963, Komatsu began production of a new line of crawler loaders and tractors. The first loader was the 86-horsepower D50S with a capacity of 1.7 cubic yards. Komatsu used an S suffix to denote a crawler loader version of a particular tractor. The D60S followed, and this along with the 125-flywheel-horsepower D60A dozer version, were the first Komatsu machines to enter the United States. They were first exhibited at the San Francisco International Trade Fair in September 1964, and subsequently tested by contractor Guy F. Atkinson. *Keith Haddock*

Komatsu D95S. Komatsu rapidly expanded its crawler line throughout the 1960s, introducing smaller and larger models to suit all applications. In 1967, LeTourneau-Westinghouse (Wabco) became Komatsu's distributor in the United States. By 1972, Komatsu offered five sizes of crawler loaders with buckets ranging from the .5-cubic-yard D20S, to the 2.6-cubic-yard D75S. The larger D95S was added in 1974, with a bucket size of 4.2 cubic yards and powered with a Komatsu diesel engine developing 240 flywheel-horsepower. The D95S was only topped in the Komatsu line by the world's largest crawler loader, the massive 350-horsepower, 5.9-cubic-yard D155S. *Keith Haddock*

Komatsu D31S-15. Komatsu marketed this small crawler loader from 1974 until the mid-1990s, when most of Komatsu's crawler loaders were phased out. The 63-flywheel-horsepower D31S-15 carried a standard bucket of 1 cubic yard. Upgrades of this machine proceeded through the D31S-16, -17, -18, and -20 by 1992. By this time, the power of the D31S had increased to 71 flywheel-horsepower, but its bucket remained at 1 cubic yard. Komatsu offered low ground pressure or swamp dozer versions of some of its loaders. These had the suffix "Q" after the tractor model. The D31Q-20 boasted a ground pressure of 4.4 psi, some 40 percent less than the standard model. *Keith Haddock*

Komatsu D66S. This was the only Komatsu crawler loader to feature rear-mounted engine and hydrostatic transmission. With 160 flywheel-horsepower, a standard bucket of 2.6 cubic yards, and an operating weight of 41,180 pounds, the machine featured full-power steering, including counter-rotation turning capability through a single joystick lever. It was shown at the 1989 Bauma Exhibition in Germany, and marketed up to 1997, when all remaining Komatsu crawler loaders were discontinued except the 2.9-cubic-yard D75S-5, which remains current at the time of this writing. *Keith Haddock*

Liebherr LR641. Since Liebherr introduced its first crawler tractor in 1974, all its crawler dozers and loaders, without exception, have been hydrostatically driven. Controlling direction, speed, and steering with one hand on a single joystick lever is a major advantage in loader operation. After the success of Liebherr's initial tractor models, the first crawler loader, the 631, was added in 1980. By 1986, three more loaders were added to total a range of four sizes from the 1.6-cubic-yard LR611 to the 3.8-cubic-yard LR641. The top-of-the-line LR641 comes with a Mercedes-Benz engine of 219 horsepower. This machine and Caterpillar's 973C in the same size class are the two largest crawler loaders available today. *Keith Haddock*

Liebherr LR632. In 1997, Liebherr began upgrading its crawler loaders to the 2 Series. These featured Liebherr's patented Litronic electronic control system, which automatically balances hydraulic power applied to each bucket movement for maximum fuel efficiency. First came the LR622, which replaced the LR621C with slight increases in power and capacity to 2.3 cubic yards. This was followed in 1968 by the 3-cubic-yard LR632, which replaced the LR631C. The LR632 is powered by a Liebherr 180-horsepower diesel engine and has an operating weight of 46,000 pounds, depending on bucket options. *Keith Haddock*

Massey-Ferguson MF 600C. In 1974, Massey-Ferguson (M-F) purchased the German Hanomag company, and the former crawler dozer and crawler ranges of the two companies were consolidated into one line. The former Hanomag K-12C graduated into the 144-horsepower MF 600C crawler loader with a 2-cubic-yard standard bucket. The new nomenclature matched M-F's existing crawler line, first announced in 1968. Due to adverse business conditions, M-F discontinued marketing its products in North America in 1978, and two years later the company was purchased by Germany's IBH group. The 600C crawler loader resurfaced as the Terex L600C. After IBH's collapse in 1983, Hanomag once again became independent, and the same machines, including the L600C, were marketed as Hanomag products.

Massey-Ferguson 244. Massey-Ferguson came into the crawler tractor business when it took over the Italian firm of Landini in 1960. One of the first Massey-Ferguson crawler loaders was the 244 of the early 1960s. It was powered by a Perkins 45-horsepower diesel engine and weighed just over 5 tons. Massey-Ferguson had acquired Perkins Engines in 1959; consequently, all Massey-Ferguson equipment at this time was powered with these engines. The 244 remained in production until 1966, when it was replaced by the MF200.

Oliver OC-46. In 1944, the Oliver Corporation acquired the Cleveland Tractor Company, builder of the Cletrac line of tractors. The machines then took on the Oliver-Cletrac name. In the 1950s, the Cletrac name was dropped, and the Oliver crawlers were updated and re-numbered with "OC" as a prefix, signifying their Cletrac connections. The White Motor Corporation purchased the Oliver Corporation in 1960. After this date, Oliver crawler tractors were sold only in limited numbers. One of the last models was this small OC-46 loader produced from 1962 to 1965. It was based on the 28-flywheel-horsepower OC-4 tractor, and carried a .625-cubic-yard bucket. *Keith Haddock*

Oliver OC-96. Beginning in 1960, the Oliver line of crawler tractors and loaders did not flourish under the White Motor Corporation. Shipments declined until 1965, when they were phased out. The last model was the OC-96 crawler loader, which had been in production since 1959. Its bucket size was 1.625 cubic yards, and power came from a Hercules engine of 54 flywheel-horsepower. All the Oliver models retained the former Cletrac tradition of controlled differential steering, which provided power to both crawlers while turning. *Keith Haddock*

Terex L600D. This was another machine that had its ancestry in the German Hanomag line prior to becoming the Massey-Ferguson 600C in 1974. It lived through the IBH fiasco as the Terex L600C, and the L600D, then reverted back to a Hanomag product as the L600D in 1984 when that company became independent following the failure of IBH. As the Terex L600D, the crawler loader carried a 2.5-cubic-yard standard bucket and a Hanomag diesel engine of 144 flywheel-horsepower. Operating weight was 35,275 pounds.

CHAPTER 5

WHEEL LOADERS

The heritage of today's modern wheel loader can be traced back to the 1920s when small agricultural-type tractors were fitted with a loader bucket. The equipment was initially designed to re-handle light materials where the cost of a heavy crawler-mounted shovel, the only type available at that time, could not be justified. But over the years, the loader has graduated into a reliable machine of robust design, suited not only for light-duty re-handling work, but also able to perform heavier earthmoving assignments. Because of its greater capabilities and superior mobility, the wheel loader has become one of the most popular machines seen on construction sites, in sand and gravel pits, and surface mining. With the exception of large electric mining shovels, wheel loaders have largely taken over the work previously done by crawler-mounted cable shovels. Operators have found that even hard material can be moved profitably with wheel loaders if assisted by drilling and blasting, or if the material is previously ripped with large dozers. In surface mines, some of today's largest wheel loaders are performing duties once thought to be the exclusive domain of the cable excavator.

The earliest wheel loaders consisted of a pivoting bucket and lift arms mounted on a farm-type tractor. The bucket was hoisted by wire ropes via a clutch-operated winch, and then dumped by gravity through a trip release mechanism. When the bucket returned to the ground, it locked in a fixed position and consequently could not be crowded or tilted to obtain a load. Only the wheel traction or the momentum of the machine running into the bank could obtain a full bucket. E. Boydell & Company of Manchester, England, was one of the first recorded makers of this type with their Muir-Hill loader in 1929. It had a .5-cubic-yard cable-controlled bucket mounted on a 28-horsepower Fordson tractor. Other small wheel loaders began to appear by the late 1930s, including the Hough Model HS in 1939, which was one of the first integrated machines built specifically as a wheel loader.

After World War II, established manufacturers began to produce wheel loaders in larger sizes, and several new manufacturers joined the competition.

The Tractomotive Corporation, founded by engineer Van Dobeus, was the first company to introduce a hydraulic loader mechanism with hydraulic power to the bucket crowd. This breakthrough changed the wheel loader from a re-handling machine to a digging machine. By the early 1950s, the cable-operated loader was totally obsolete.

A common safety hazard on the larger wheel loaders of the 1950s resulted from the positioning of the loader arm pivot behind the operator, so that the loader arms came close to the operator as they moved up and down. In addition to the obvious possibility of injury from the moving parts, the operator's visibility to the side was nonexistent when the arms were in the raised position. Toward the end of the 1950s, manufacturers began working with the National Safety Council in the United States to relocate the arm pivot in front of the operator. One of the first manufacturers to adopt a

Allis-Chalmers TL-30. After almost a decade of building loader attachments for Allis-Chalmers tractors, the Tractomotive Corporation of Findlay, Ohio, was purchased by Allis-Chalmers Manufacturing Company in 1959. The former Tractomotive wheel loaders became Allis-Chalmers products, and the TL Series nomenclature was retained. The range of Allis-Chalmers loaders was expanded through the early 1960s with the two largest models, the TL-30 and TL-40, which were introduced in 1961 and 1962. The larger TL-40 had a standard excavating bucket of 5 cubic yards, while the TL-30 (illustrated) carried a 4-cubic-yard bucket. Both models were powered by Allis-Chalmers diesel engines rated at 310 and 184 horsepower. *Keith Haddock*

Allis-Chalmers TL-545. This 1.75-cubic-yard loader, along with the Model TL-645 (3 cubic yards), were both unveiled in 1965 as the first loaders from Allis-Chalmers to feature articulated steering. These models heralded the 45 Series loader range, which expanded to include smaller and larger machines and replaced the earlier TL Series. In 1972, Allis-Chalmers released its largest wheel loader to date, the Model 945, with an operating weight of 34 tons and a 6-cubic-yard general-purpose bucket. Fiat S.p.A. of Italy purchased the majority of Allis-Chalmers shares in 1974, and the Fiat-Allis joint venture was born. The wheel loader line continued under the Fiat-Allis name, with the upgraded FR Series gradually replacing the former TL models. *Keith Haddock collection*

Aveling-Barford TS-185. The British company, better known for its rollers and off-highway haulers, began building wheel loaders in 1962, and exported them into North America through dealers. The four-wheel-drive TS-185 represents one of the company's last rigid-frame models, which were produced into the early 1970s. It carries a standard bucket of 2 cubic yards capacity and is powered by a Ford diesel engine developing 120 horsepower. The Aveling-Barford wheel loader line, which ranged up to 5-cubic-yards capacity, included articulated models from 1970, when it purchased the pioneer of articulated loader builders, Matbro, Ltd. *Keith Haddock*

new, safer design was Hough with its Model HO. Soon, all manufacturers followed suit, including Allis-Chalmers in 1961 and Michigan in 1962. Case and Caterpillar both adopted the front-mounted arm pivot on their first wheel loaders introduced in 1958 and 1959.

Another significant step in wheel loader development was the introduction of the articulated frame. Mixermobile Manufacturers of Portland, Oregon, pioneered this concept in 1953 with its Scoopmobile Model LD-5. The second company to adopt loader articulation was Matbro, Ltd. in the United Kingdom. This company introduced articulation in its wheel loaders beginning in 1957. Subsequently, when North American and other manufacturers converted to articulation in their machines, the patented Matbro system was utilized under license.

Like so many other brilliant innovations, articulation was slow to be appreciated. Eventually, the entire loader industry recognized its greater maneuverability, which resulted in a shorter cycle time. Leading makers began introducing articulated models into their lines: Caterpillar in 1963, International Hough in 1964, Michigan and Allis-Chalmers in 1965, and Trojan in 1966. Today, all large wheel loaders and most small units have an articulated frame.

All-wheel steer was another alternative offered by select manufacturers to gain some advantages of the articulated machines while maintaining the simplicity of a single rigid frame. Michigan introduced all-wheel steer on some of its models in 1968.

Over the decades, manufacturers have differed in their opinions regarding where to locate the operator on articulated machines. Some chose the front section, in line with the bucket, while others chose placement on the rear section. Those from the "front-mounted" school point to better visibility, and compare the application to the cable shovel operator, who always faces his work. Those placing the operator on the rear section maintain there is great advantage in being able to "steer" the bucket, including for safety reasons. For example, it is safer if the operator always knows the position of the rear section of the machine in relation to the front section. Also, he is mounted further away from any material that may fall from the back of the raised bucket. Today, the general consensus appears to favor the rear-mounted operator, so some of the leading makers have recently changed the operator's position from front to rear in their latest designs.

Throughout the 1960s, the trend was moving toward larger wheel loaders. Following Caterpillar's introduction of the 6-cubic-yard Model 988 in 1963, industry surveys showed a need for loaders much bigger

Case W9B. In 1958, Case introduced the 1.25-cubic-yard W-9, the company's first integrated four-wheel-drive loader. It was joined the following year by three more models: the four-wheel-drive Models W-10 (2-cubic-yards), and the W-12 (2.5-cubic-yards), and the front-wheel-drive 1-cubic-yard Model W-5. These loaders were of the rigid-frame (non-articulating) type, common with all wheel loaders of that era. The W-9 was upgraded to the W-9A in 1960, and the W-9B in 1964. The 1966 W9B shown carries a 1.75-cubic-yard standard bucket and a Case diesel of 105 horsepower. *Keith Haddock*

Case W26B. Case expanded its W Series loaders with many models throughout the 1960s and 1970s. Articulated loaders first appeared with the introduction of the W-26 in 1968. This machine worked with a 3-cubic-yard standard bucket and it was the company's largest machine when it was introduced. It was upgraded to the W-26B in 1970, receiving a slight boost in power to 165 flywheel-horsepower from its Case engine. The W-26B was replaced with the larger 4-cubic-yard W36 in 1977. A distinguishing feature of the Case W Series loader is that the cab is mounted on the front half of the machine, unlike most of the competition. *Keith Haddock*

than the 5- to 6-cubic-yard standard machines then available. The Hough Division of International Harvester responded with a 10-cubic-yard loader in 1964. The company had already produced the large articulated D-500 wheel dozer of similar size, and many of the features of the basic D-500 tractor were transposed into the new loader, which surfaced as the H-400. Other loaders in the 10-cubic-yard class soon followed: the Michigan 475 in 1965, the Scoopmobile 1200 released in 1967, and the Caterpillar 992 in 1968.

Pushing the size envelope even further were International Hough's 21-cubic-yard 580 Payloader, and Clark-Michigan's massive 675 loader, at a 24-cubic-yard capacity. Both of these machines were developed in the early 1970s and displayed at the 1975 Conexpo as production machines. Ever larger machines were to follow. Japan's Surface Mining Equipment for Coal Technology Research Association (SMEC) developed the world's largest wheel loader sized at 25 cubic yards and had it built by Kawasaki Heavy Industries, Ltd. in 1986. Since then, Caterpillar, Komatsu, and LeTourneau have each made loaders with capacities of over 20 cubic yards available. LeTourneau seems to specialize in building the world's largest wheel loaders, since it has broken the world's record in 1990 (L-1400, 28 cubic yards), again in 1993 (L-1800, 33 cubic yards), and finally with the current record-beater announced in October 2000, the L-2350 at 57 cubic yards.

Case 921. Starting in 1987 with the introduction of the Model 621, Case's loader line graduated to the 21 Series of modern design, featuring the rear-mounted operator's cab. The 921 was the largest of the four Model range, covering sizes from 2 to 4.75 cubic yards. The 921 received refinements and a new Cummins engine when it was upgraded to the 921B in 1995. The 921C appeared in 1999 with further refinements, but retained the same 248-horsepower Cummins engine and standard bucket capacity of 4.75 cubic yards. *Keith Haddock*

Case 621D. Case introduced its new D Series loaders with this model in 2001. Technologically advanced over its predecessor 621C model, the 621D included features such as a cooling cube, where the radiator and the other system coolers are mounted around a cube-shaped frame. A hydraulically driven fan on one side of the cube draws cool air across these components. The cube is located behind the cab, and the engine has been moved further to the rear for improved balance. Bucket capacity on the 621D is 2.5 cubic yards, and power comes from a 110-horsepower turbocharged engine. *Case Corporation*

Caterpillar 922. Caterpillar entered the front-end loader market in 1959 with the Model 944. The following year two more loaders appeared, the 922 and 966 Series A machines. Buckets of these three models spanned from 1.25 to 2.75 cubic yards, and engines from 80 to 140 flywheel-horsepower. The loaders featured four-wheel-drive with power-shift transmission, torque converter, and a walk-through unobstructed operator's compartment, made possible by the front-mounted bucket arm pivot. The 922 was upgraded to the 922B in 1962, and it remained in production until 1969. The four loaders mentioned here were Caterpillar's only non-articulated models. *Keith Haddock*

Wheel loaders can be equipped with many sizes of buckets, depending on the density of material to be moved. For comparison purposes, the machines described in this chapter are rated according to the manufacturer's quoted standard bucket size for general excavation. Often, sizes up to double the standard size are offered for coal, wood chips, or other light materials.

One reason why wheel loaders have become so popular is their adaptability. The newly developed integrated tool carrier appeared in the 1980s. This is

Caterpillar 988B. Caterpillar's first articulated loader was the 988, introduced in 1963. It was also the company's largest wheel loader up to that time, carrying a 6-cubic-yard standard bucket and a 325-horsepower Caterpillar diesel engine. The 988 became the 988B in 1976, with its standard bucket gaining an extra yard, and its engine increasing to 375 flywheel-horsepower. The one shown is equipped with the patented Dystred cushion-track wheels for rocky conditions. Like its predecessor, the 988B had a long production run that lasted until 1993, when the updated 988F made an appearance with bucket capacity nudging up to 8 cubic yards. The current 988G, launched in 2000, features the single-arm box-section boom arrangement first seen on the 992G. *Keith Haddock*

Caterpillar 966B. Caterpillar's old faithful 966 model holds the distinction in Caterpillar's loader line for going through every suffix upgrade, from the original 966A in 1960 to the current 966G. From the 2.75-cubic-yard bucket size and 140 flywheel-horsepower of the original model, capacity and power increased over the years to 4.75-cubic-yards and 235 flywheel-horsepower of the current 966G. The 966B illustrated was Caterpillar's second loader to feature articulated steering. The 150-flywheel-horsepower loader was in production from 1963 to 1968 and carried a standard bucket of 2.75 cubic yards. *Keith Haddock*

Caterpillar 910. Caterpillar announced a trio of smaller machines in 1972: the D3 crawler tractor, the 931 crawler loader, and the 910 wheel loader. All three machines carried the same Caterpillar engine, rated at 65 flywheel-horsepower for the 910. The nimble, articulated 910 loader found a wide variety of uses, from farming to street cleanup. Its standard bucket was rated at 1.25 cubic yards, and it had a machine operating weight of 13,400 pounds. The 910, with its upgrades 910E in 1989 and 910F in 1992, reigned as Caterpillar's smallest loader until the company announced a new range of smaller, compact loaders in 1998. *Keith Haddock collection*

basically a loader, but the standard bucket is replaced with a frame that carries power hooks for the machine to attach itself to a host of available attachments such as brooms, hooks, forks, cutters, snow blowers, as well as buckets. In most cases, the operator can add or change these attachments without assistance and without leaving his cab.

Over the past decade, manufacturers have placed their number-one priority on operator comfort and ease of control. One of the many modern features found in today's loaders is joystick control. A single lever replaces the steering wheel, and from this same lever, machine direction and speed are also controlled. A second joystick lever held by the operator's other hand controls all bucket functions. Other modern refinements include computerized diagnostics that allow the operator to monitor many machine operating systems, computerized load-sensing controls, and fuel-efficient engines. Cabs equipped with everything from cup holders, air conditioning, stereos, and ergonomically positioned controls to a fully adjustable and superbly comfortable seat, make many of today's supervisors wish they could go back to operating!

Caterpillar 992. A big jump in size occurred in 1968 when Caterpillar introduced the 10-cubic-yard 992 wheel loader. Productivity almost doubled that of Caterpillar's next smaller loader, the 988, so the 992 was ready to tackle excavating and loading jobs formerly reserved for crawler shovels. Power for the 992 came from a big V-12 Caterpillar D348 diesel engine, capable of developing 550 flywheel-horsepower. The successful 992 was upgraded to the 992B in 1973, but power and capacity remained the same. This model continued in production until 1977. *Keith Haddock*

Caterpillar 992C. Caterpillar's biggest wheel loader, the 992, was totally redesigned and launched as the 992C in 1977. Now sporting Caterpillar's 3412 engine rated at 690 flywheel-horsepower, Z-type bucket linkage providing greater breakout force, and a bucket capacity increase of 25 percent, pundits expected this machine to be designated as a new model rather than an upgrade from the former model. Bucket capacity reached 12.5 cubic yards. Depending on bucket selection, operating weight touched the 100-ton mark, some 30 tons heavier than the former 992B. The 992C was a very successful loader, staying in production until replaced by the 14-cubic-yard 992D in 1992. *David Maginnis*

Caterpillar 992G. The latest version of Caterpillar's long-running 992 Series is the G model, first announced at the 1996 Minexpo mining equipment show in Las Vegas, Nevada. The most noticeable feature is its radical boom design, now a single box-section steel casting instead of the usual twin steel-plate lift arms. This provides improved operator visibility and overall weight reduction when compared with conventional loaders with twin lift arms. Standard bucket capacity on the 992G is 15 cubic yards, and power comes from a Caterpillar 3508B diesel of 800 flywheel-horsepower. *Keith Haddock*

Caterpillar 924F. In 1994, Caterpillar introduced the 924F wheel loader as a new model designation. It actually replaced the 918F model with improved operator's cab, larger torque converter, and pilot-operated controls. In the 2-cubic-yard class, the 924F was also available as an integrated tool carrier version known as the IT24F, with an array of hook-on attachments. Engine power was 105 flywheel-horsepower. In 1999, the 924G replaced the 924F, with increased bucket capacity to 2.2 cubic yards and engine power to 114 flywheel-horsepower. *Keith Haddock*

Daewoo Mega 500-V. Daewoo Heavy Industries, Ltd. was established in Korea in 1976 following the merger of Choson Machine Works with Korea Machinery Industries, Ltd. The new company began excavator manufacture in 1978, built up a line of wheel loaders during the 1990s, and introduced crawler tractors in 1998. In 2002, Daewoo announced its expanded "Mega-V" Series of wheel loaders, which consisted of six models including the company's largest to date. This is the Mega 500-V, a loader with an operating weight of 65,700 pounds and supporting a standard bucket of 6.3 cubic yards. It carries a Cummins N14-C diesel engine rated at 335 horsepower. *Daewoo Heavy Industries*

Caterpillar 994D. This massive machine is Caterpillar's flagship loader, and one of the largest front-end loaders currently produced. The standard bucket is 23 cubic yards for earth excavation or rock loading, but optional buckets with capacities up to 40 cubic yards are available for coal loading. Operating weight is approximately 210 tons. Caterpillar ventured into this size class of loader when it introduced the similar-sized 994 in 1990. This model was then refined and upgraded to the 994D in 1998. It is powered by a single Caterpillar 3516B engine with 1,250 flywheel-horsepower. *Eric C. Orlemann*

Dart D600. The Dart Truck Company entered the front-end loader market in 1966 with the largest production loader available up to that time, the 15-cubic-yard capacity D600. Equipped with a Cummins VT12 700-horsepower engine, the huge mechanical-drive articulated loader had a distinctive appearance with its isolated cab overhanging one side. It boasted a balanced boom, which incorporates two cylinders filled with nitrogen that are pulled with enough force to counterbalance the weight of the boom and empty bucket. This feature saves engine power during lifting. Dart only made one loader model, but it received upgrades through the D600B and 600C until 1995. At that point, production ceased after hundreds of models had been sold. *Keith Haddock*

Deere JD544-B. John Deere's 1967 entrance into the four-wheel-drive loader market was relatively recent. Its first model was the JD544, a modern-looking articulated loader with a 94-horsepower engine and standard buckets of 1.5 cubic yards. This model was joined by the larger JD-644 the following year, and then both received upgrades to the A Series in 1971. In 1974, further refinements and upgrades brought the B Series, which remained current until 1981. The JD544-B was powered by a Deere 105-flywheel-horsepower diesel engine and worked with a standard bucket of 1.75 cubic yards. *Keith Haddock*

Deere JD544-D. John Deere's continuing progression of wheel loader upgrades resulted in the JD544-D in 1985. Replacing the former JD544-C, the new loader gained additional power to 115 flywheel-horsepower, and standard bucket capacity to 2 cubic yards. An integrated tool carrier version was available with hook-on attachments, including a crane hook, pallet forks, and buckets. The hook-on buckets usually ran at about a .5 cubic yard less than the standard machine to allow for the extra support bracket and clamping arrangement. The JD544-D was replaced by the JD544-E in 1987. *Keith Haddock*

Deere JD644G. The G Series followed John Deere's E Series loaders in 1993. The JD644G came with a standard bucket of 3.25 cubic yards of capacity and a John Deere engine of 170 horsepower. Refinements of the G Series included a microprocessor system that monitored the status of 15 critical conditions throughout the machine, extended maintenance intervals, and eliminated daily greasing. By 1997, John Deere's entire loader line had been upgraded again to the H Series, which comprised of seven models from the 1-cubic-yard 244H to the 4.5-cubic-yard 744H. *Keith Haddock*

Deere 844. John Deere launched its biggest loader in 1977 following one of the most extensive development projects ever taken on by the company. The four-wheel-drive articulated loader featured a newly developed John Deere V-8 diesel engine of 260 flywheel-horsepower and a new John Deere power-shift transmission specifically designed for the 844. Special attention to the cab design resulted in operator comfort that was advanced for its day. The loader's weight was 51,820 pounds and its standard bucket held 5 cubic yards. *Keith Haddock*

Deere 344H. In 2001, John Deere announced a partnership with Liebherr-Werk of Austria. John Deere would market Liebherr-designed wheel loaders and crawler tractors in North America. Built in Austria, and with certain modifications to suit the North American market, the first wheel loaders were the 304H, 324H, and 344H of 65, 80, and 98 flywheel-horsepower. With hydrostatic transmission, these super-nimble loaders boast stereo steering. These machines not only feature frame-articulated steering, but their rear axles steer as well. This means the tightest turning circle can be achieved with less frame articulation, which results in greater machine stability. *Keith Haddock*

Dresser 4000. In 1982, Dresser Industries acquired International Harvester's Payline Division, and the trade name Dresser was adopted. New machines were introduced in the 500 Series loader line. Another change took place in 1988 when Japan's Komatsu, Ltd. and Dresser Industries, Inc. began the Komatsu Dresser Company (KDC) joint venture to market both companies' lines. The top-of-the-line Dresser 580 Payloader, upgraded to 22 yards capacity in its early life, became the 24-cubic-yard Haulpak 4000 under the KDC joint venture. The giant 1,350-horsepower loader was produced and sold under the Haulpak Division of KDC from 1992 until it was discontinued in 1996. *Keith Haddock collection*

Dressta 560C. This machine, along with other loaders in the former Dresser line, is built in Poland under Dressta. This joint venture began in 1991. The loaders are sold in North America under the Komatsu America International Company, a venture that was formed by Komatsu, Ltd. of Japan in 1996. Komatsu America International Company also markets Komatsu-designed wheel loaders. The 560C derives its heritage from the former 560 and 560B loaders that were originally introduced by International Harvester in 1970. Power increased from 370 flywheel-horsepower and a rated bucket capacity of 6.5 cubic yards in the Model 560, to 415 flywheel-horsepower and 7.5 cubic yards of capacity in the current 560C. *Keith Haddock*

Euclid L-20. General Motors' Euclid Division entered the wheel loader field in 1957 with a small rigid-frame unit known as the L-7. This 49-horsepower model with .7-cubic-yard bucket was followed in 1959 by the first version of the 2-cubic-yard L-20, shown in the picture undergoing tests. In 1962, after testing approximately 30 pre-production models in the field, Euclid released two new articulated loaders—a redesigned L-20 and the larger L-30, with buckets rated at 2.25 and 3 cubic yards. Euclid was one of the pioneering companies in the United States to build articulated loaders, and these machines attracted a lot of attention. Euclid chose to place the operator's cab on the rear half of the machine so that the operator could steer the bucket. *Keith Haddock collection*

Euclid 72-31. In the early 1960s, Euclid expanded its L Series loaders to four sizes. In 1966, the company launched an entirely new line of four models. Known as the 72 Series, the four models, 72-21, 72-31, 72-41, and 72-51, spanned sizes from 2.25 to 4 cubic yards. The mid-sized 72-31 carried a standard bucket of 2.5-cubic-yards. A 134-flywheel-horsepower GM engine provided the power. The new loader line was not affected in 1968 when anti-trust laws forced the Euclid Division of General Motors to drop the Euclid name and sell off its American haul truck business. But the new Terex name was adopted for all remaining General Motors earthmoving products. *Eric C. Orlemann*

Faun-Frisch F1400C. The F1400C was one of a long line of equipment produced by Faun AG of Germany. Powered by a 160-horsepower Deutz air-cooled diesel engine, its standard bucket held 3.25 cubic yards. This machine originated in Germany's Frisch line of graders and loaders, which were purchased by Faun in 1977, then sold under the Faun-Frisch name. These products and the Trojan line of wheel loaders, which Faun purchased in 1982, were built in Batavia, New York, and were merged with Faun's off-highway haulers. In 1986, Germany's O&K purchased this company's assets and continued to sell machines under the Trojan banner in North America, and as O&K products in Europe. *Keith Haddock collection*

Fiat-Allis 945-B. Fiat S.p.A. of Italy purchased the majority of Allis-Chalmers shares in 1974, and the Fiat-Allis joint venture was born. The former wheel loaders continued under the Fiat-Allis name with the upgraded FR Series gradually replacing the former TL models. The former Allis-Chalmers 945 loader was upgraded to the 945-B. With an operating weight of 34 tons, 450 horses under the hood, and a 6-cubic-yard standard bucket, it was the company's largest wheel loader to date. But it was still very nimble with its 45-degree articulation in each direction and twin-turbine torque converter for extra crowding power. *Keith Haddock collection*

Fiat-Allis FR20. Fiat-Allis gradually replaced the former Allis-Chalmers loader models with the upgraded FR Series, beginning in 1980. First in the series was the FR20 in the 4-cubic-yard class, which superseded the former Model 745-C. The new machine featured a Fiat diesel engine rated at 215 flywheel-horsepower, representing an increase in power over the Allis-Chalmers engine that was installed in the former model. The FR20 also boasted a new power train and increased operating weight to 42,500 pounds. In 1986, the FR20 was upgraded to the FR20B, with power increasing to 230 flywheel-horsepower and operating weight to 44,000 pounds. *Keith Haddock*

Fiatallis FR9B. The 1.5-cubic-yard FR9B was introduced in 1987 as the second model in a new generation of wheel loaders for the company. It followed the 2-cubic-yard FR10B released a year earlier. The most noticeable feature on these new models was the "Z-bar" bucket-dump linkage, which replaced the former top-mounted boom cylinders. The new design offered improved operator visibility and more efficient use of available hydraulic power. The FR9B was equipped with a 90-flywheel-horsepower Fiat diesel engine. *Keith Haddock*

Fiatallis FR160.2. In 1989, Fiatallis stopped manufacturing earthmoving equipment in North America, but new models were still being developed in Italy and exported worldwide. By 1994, Fiatallis products included a line of 10 wheel loaders ranging from the 1.3-cubic-yard FR-70 to the 5-cubic-yard FR-220. The intermediate size FR160.2, at 189 flywheel-horsepower and a standard bucket capacity of 3.6 cubic yards, was an upgrade from the former 3.3-cubic-yard FR160. In 1991, Fiat S.p.A. purchased farm equipment builder New Holland, then in 1999 merged Case Corporation into the New Holland group. After this merger, the Fiatallis name was dropped, but the machines survive under various brand names in the New Holland group. In North America, they sell under the New Holland name. *Keith Haddock*

Ford A62. In 1974, the Tractor Division of Ford Motor Company complemented its already well-established line of tractor backhoes with a range of articulated four-wheel-drive wheel loaders. The first model was the A62 sized at 1 cubic yard and powered by a Ford 89-flywheel-horsepower diesel engine. This machine was immediately accepted in the market and prompted Ford to add two larger wheel loaders over the next two years. These were the 2-cubic-yard A64 and the 2.25-cubic-yard A66. Ford acquired Sperry New Holland in 1986, and the Ford New Holland company was born. No further development took place on the wheel loaders. *Keith Haddock*

Hanomag 70E. This 230-flywheel-horsepower loader carried a standard bucket of 4.8 cubic yards. It was launched in 1986, one year after the German company celebrated its 150th year of product manufacture—albeit a checkered history in latter years. Massey-Ferguson (M-F) purchased Hanomag in 1974, and for awhile the wheel loaders were sold as M-F products. In 1980, Germany's IBH group took over the company and merged the M-F products into the Terex line when the latter became part of IBH in 1981. After the IBH empire collapsed in November 1983, Hanomag re-emerged under new ownership and continued the products under the Hanomag name. Komatsu took control of Hanomag in 1990, and the Hanomag name soon disappeared. Komatsu wheel loaders are now built in the former Hanomag plant. *Keith Haddock*

Hough O-12. One of the earliest wheel loader manufacturers was the Frank G. Hough Company, which first mounted loader attachments on farm tractors in 1920. Shown at a Historical Construction Equipment Association convention in Bowling Green, Ohio, the 1938 Model O-12 is cable-operated and dumps its bucket by gravity when a latch is released. Hough brought out its first integrated loader, the Model HS, in 1939 and called it the Payloader. With a bucket capacity of about .333 cubic yards, it was also dumped by gravity through a latch mechanism. An improved, larger model, the HL, appeared in 1941. Although some claimed that the HL was the first loader with hydraulically operated lift arms, its bucket was still gravity-dumped. *Keith Haddock*

Hough HM. In 1944, Hough unveiled its first hydraulically actuated bucket tilt. This not only allowed controlled dumping, but let the operator approach the bank in low gear and obtain a full bucket by tilting the bucket back (crowding) during loading. Of course, all loaders today incorporate this feature. Advancing further, Hough developed what can be termed the forerunner of the modern wheel loader, 1947's HM Payloader. This was the world's first four-wheel-drive, fully hydraulic loader. Its bucket was 1.5 cubic yards, and it was powered by a 76-horsepower gasoline or diesel engine. *Keith Haddock*

Hough HA. This small .5-cubic-yard Payloader was announced and put in production in 1947. The front-wheel-drive and rear-wheel-steer machine, with its tight turning radius, proved very popular in close-quarter applications such as processing plants, warehouses, farmyards, and foundries. Available with gasoline or diesel power, it could also be purchased with an extended chassis and a hydraulically dumped box of 2-cubic-yards capacity. This feature replaced the loader arms. This model was known as the HA Buggy. After International Harvester (I-H) purchased the Hough company in 1952, the Model HA with upgraded revisions remained as an I-H product until 1970. *Keith Haddock*

Hyundai HL-780-3. The Hyundai group in Korea encompasses many industrial companies and makes a wide variety of products, including ships, electronics, elevators, petrochemicals, and automobiles. In 1967, Hyundai International Inc. was founded, and in 1972, the company began to manufacture crawler tractors and wheel loaders under license from Fiat-Allis. By 1999, Hyundai's wheel loader line had expanded to six sizes from the 102-horsepower Model HL730-3 at 1.8 cubic yards to the 320-horsepower HL780-3, the company's largest with a 5.5-cubic-yard standard bucket capacity. *Keith Haddock*

International Hough H-70. In 1952, International Harvester Company (I-H) purchased the Frank G. Hough Company, giving the Hough Payloaders a marketing outlet through the already-established I-H network of dealers. I-H expanded and improved the Payloader line, bringing out new models, which gradually increased in size and sophistication. In 1958, I-H announced the 2-cubic-yard H-70 and the 3-cubic-yard H-90, powered with 110- and 125-horsepower diesel engines. These two models heralded the first of what would become the extensive range of H Series Payloaders, which formed I-H's loader line through the 1970s. The H-90 survived upgrades through to the H-90E, until it was discontinued in 1983 as the last of the H Series. *Keith Haddock collection*

International Hough H-400. International's Hough Division launched the big 10-cubic-yard H-400 loader in 1964. It was developed from the D-500 dozer, but built with a smaller engine. It was not only International's largest loader at the time, but was also the company's first loader to feature an articulated frame. Operator surveys favored the cab's location on the front section of the machine, so that location was adopted by International for all its subsequent loaders. Optional power was available from either Cummins or GM V12 diesel engines, which were capable of developing 420 flywheel-horsepower. Operating weight was 113,000 pounds. The H-400 graduated into the H-400B in 1969 with a 500-flywheel-horsepower Cummins engine. *Keith Haddock*

International H-400C. International upgraded its H-400B to the H-400C in 1973. The standard bucket was increased to 11 cubic yards and engine power reached 580 flywheel-horsepower from the V-12 Cummins engine. The example shown has its rear wheels equipped with no-tread tires to give maximum life when working on rock. The single groove in the tire provides a convenient means of measuring tire wear. The H-400C could also be supplied with Goodyear's Trak'R Tred steel-belted tires. These tires have a belt of steel shoes wrapped around special radial ply–rubber tires. *Keith Haddock*

International 580 Payloader. In 1970, International launched the 560 as the first of the 500 Series Payloaders. The following year, the giant 580 Payloader made its debut at the American Mining Congress in Las Vegas. At 18 cubic yards, it was the world's largest loader at the time, almost double the size of the previous largest Payloader, the H-400B. The 580 featured a constant-speed engine and power-modulated control, allowing the operator infinite power adjustment between the hydraulic system and drive train. By the time the 580 went into production in 1975, its capacity was boosted to 21 cubic yards. Power came from a 1,200-horsepower Detroit diesel, and operating weight tipped the scales at 134 tons. *Keith Haddock*

JCB SL3000. J.C. Bamford Excavators, Ltd. (JCB) of Rocester, England, broadened its product base with the acquisition of Chaseside Engineering of Blackburn, England, in 1968. Pioneer wheel loader builder Chaseside had a range of seven rigid-frame machines at takeover, with 15 percent of the British market. At first, JCB retained the Chaseside models and nomenclature. Then JCB introduced its articulated loaders in 1971, which were designed in-house. The SL3000, shown with a 3.25-cubic-yard bucket and Leyland 224-horsepower engine, was the largest of the Chaseside loaders and sold as a JCB product. *JCB Sales, Ltd.*

JCB 423. In 1971, JCB launched its first designed loaders, the 413 and 418 of 1.875 and 2.25 cubic yards of capacity. In keeping with the modern trend, the loaders were articulated four-wheel-drive models. JCB chose to place the operator on the front section so that he always faced the bucket. In 1974, two larger loaders, the 423 and 428 of 3- and 3.75-cubic-yards standard capacity, were designed on similar lines. The 180-horsepower Perkins-powered 423 carried a standard bucket of 3 cubic yards and tipped the scales at 31,400 pounds. *JCB Sales, Ltd.*

JCB 436B. In 1988 JCB introduced the Model 406, a new compact articulated wheel loader. Although a small machine with .75-cubic-yard bucket and weighing only 8,950 pounds, the 406 sported a significant design change. It was JCB's first loader with the operator's cab located on the rear section of the chassis. JCB gradually moved up through its loader range and replaced all its former models with this new design. By 1995, the transformation was complete when the two largest loaders in the line were replaced with the 2.3-cubic-yard 426 and 3-cubic-yard 436. The picture shows the high-lift tool-carrier version of the current 436B. It weighs 30,000 pounds and is powered by a 144-horsepower engine. *JCB, Inc.*

Kawasaki 65Z IV. Originally started as a shipbuilder in 1878, Japan's Kawasaki Heavy Industries, Ltd. expanded its product lines over the years to cover a wide array of vehicles and industrial equipment. In addition to ships, the company's current products include aircraft, railway rolling stock, industrial plants, motorcycles, and engines. In 1962, Kawasaki commenced building wheel loaders. Known as the KSS Series, the loader line had broadened to four models a decade later, ranging from the KSS6 to the KSS9 with standard buckets from 1.9 to 4.3 cubic yards. By 1985, the loaders were revamped with a two-digit model nomenclature. The 65Z shown is in the 2.5-cubic-yard size class and is powered by an Isuzu 12-flywheel-horsepower engine. *Keith Haddock*

Kawasaki 95Z IV. This Kawasaki wheel loader is one of nine current models ranging from the 1.7-cubic-yard 50Z to the 6.5-cubic-yard 115Z. The "Z" signifies the Z-type reversed link mechanism to operate the bucket. Popular on many of today's loaders, the linkage allows full hydraulic pressure to act on the bucket cylinder and maximize crowd force. Since their introduction, Kawasaki wheel loaders have gone through upgraded Series II, Series III, and to the present Series IV. The 95Z IV is the second largest in the range, carrying a standard bucket of 5 cubic yards and a Cummins engine of 315 flywheel-horsepower. *Keith Haddock*

Kawasaki/SMEC. In 1983, Kawasaki became prime contractor to the Surface Mining Equipment for Coal Technology Research Association (SMEC), an organization consisting of 11 major Japanese construction equipment manufacturers operating under the guidance of the Ministry of International Trade and Industry. This super wheel loader was developed by SMEC after over three years of research, and it easily ranked as the world's largest loader at that time. With a bucket holding 24 cubic yards and a machine operating weight of 200 tons, a pair of Cummins engines totaling 1,360 flywheel-horsepower powered the behemoth. The prototype mechanical-drive loader commenced trials in 1987. *Eric C. Orlemann collection*

Kobelco LK500. Kobelco is the product name of Kobe Steel, Ltd., which was established in 1905. As one of Japan's most diversified corporations, its construction equipment division today offers over 100 different machine models. In 1981, the parent company established Kobelco America, Inc. and began importing excavators, cranes, and wheel loaders into the United States. By 1984, the wheel loader line spanned sizes from the LK300A at 1.6 cubic yards to the large LK1500A, wielding a bucket of just under 8 cubic yards. The mid-range 2.2-cubic-yard LK500 was powered by a Nissan 105-flywheel-horsepower engine. *Keith Haddock*

Komatsu W120. Komatsu built its first wheel loader in 1956. The SW20 was a small utility machine with a boom arrangement capable of swinging 90 degrees left or right. It proved very popular in all kinds of re-handling operations and remained in the product line until the early 1970s.
In 1967, Komatsu began building International-Hough Payloaders under license. Three models were initially produced: the JH30B, JH60, and the JH65C. These carried buckets from 1.3 to 2.5 cubic yards of capacity.
In the mid-1970s, Komatsu designed a new range of loaders that gradually replaced the JH Series. A representative of this series is the 4.25-cubic-yard W120 powered by a 200-horsepower Komatsu diesel engine. *Keith Haddock*

Komatsu WA250. From its introduction of the W Series loaders with the Models W90 and W170, Komatsu expanded this series to include 10 sizes by 1982. These ranged from the Model W20 to the W260 with standard buckets from .8 cubic yards to 7.5 cubic yards of bucket capacity. In 1985, Komatsu launched nine models in a new line of loaders, the WA Series. Since the original launch, further models have joined the WA Series, including larger models at the top of the line and the WA250 shown. This machine works with a standard bucket of 2.75-cubic-yards of capacity and is powered by a 144-flywheel-horsepower engine. *Keith Haddock*

Komatsu WA800-3. Unveiled in 1986 and shown at the 1987 Conexpo equipment show in Las Vegas, the WA800-1 topped out Komatsu's loader line at that time with a bucket of 13.7 cubic yards and a big 789-flywheel-horsepower Komatsu engine. The loader was also offered in a high-lift version, boosting dumping height an extra foot to 18 feet 3 inches, but sacrificing 1 cubic yard in bucket size. The current WA800-3 was introduced in 1998 with engine power increased to 808 flywheel-horsepower and bucket size increased to 14.4 cubic yards. *Komatsu America International Company*

Komatsu WA1200-3. The current top-of-the-line Komatsu loader is the WA1200-3 introduced at the end of 1999. It boasts a standard bucket of 26 cubic yards and develops 1,560 flywheel-horsepower from its Cummins QSK60 engine. This monster loader has an operating weight of 463,400 pounds, and like the smaller WA800, is also offered in a high-lift version, sacrificing about 3 cubic yards of bucket capacity. Komatsu's biggest loader is designed for loading up to 240-ton trucks in its standard form, and up to 300-ton trucks in high-lift configuration. It tops out a long line of 19 WA Series loaders, ranging all the way down to the .5-cubic-yard WA30-5. *Komatsu America International Company*

LeTourneau SL10. LeTourneau produced some very unusual electric loaders in the early 1960s, with power transmitted to all movements by high-torque electric motors through rack-and-pinion drives. The unusual SL-10 carried a bucket of 10 cubic yards, an unheard of size when it came out in 1960. This model did not graduate past the prototype stage, but the more successful SL-40 followed in 1965. Nicknamed "The Monster," it wielded a record-beating 19-cubic-yard rock bucket and carried twin GM engines totaling 950 horsepower. Although these LeTourneau loaders were articulated, their great length negated the nifty advantage of articulation: the SL-10 and SL-40 measured over 40 feet and 52 feet! *Keith Haddock collection*

LeTourneau L-700. LeTourneau's present-day loader line is derived from the L-700 electric-drive model, which was unveiled at the 1969 Conexpo equipment show in Chicago after a two-year development period. The 15-cubic-yard L-700 was literally the shape of things to come for LeTourneau. For the first time, the loader's movements were hydraulically operated and the machine was designed on sleek modern lines, a far cry from former loaders. The L-700 graduated to the L-700A in 1973 with partial solid-state controls for the DC motors in each of the four wheels. The upgraded L-800 in 1975 added solid-state power conversion to its features, and this model eventually replaced the L-700A. *LeTourneau, Inc.*

LeTourneau L-1200. LeTourneau unveiled its largest loader to date at the American Mining Congress International Mining Show held in Las Vegas, Nevada, in 1978. The huge L-1200 LeTro-Loader was designed on similar lines to the successful L-800, but it was larger in every respect. Componentry included an AC generator, driven directly from a gearbox mounted in-line with the engine to drive the hydraulic pumps. This was an improvement from the earlier L-700 Series machines, which utilized a separate AC electric motor. The L-1200 could be purchased with Cummins or Detroit diesel engines rated at 1,200 horsepower. Operating weight was 335,000 pounds, and the standard bucket held 21 cubic yards. The worldwide recession in the 1980s caused the L-1200's production to be cut back, and only 11 had been delivered by the time the last one left the plant in 1984. *Keith Haddock*

LeTourneau L-1000. In 1982, the "smaller" L-1000 was revealed to the public at the American Mining Congress International Mining Show in Las Vegas, Nevada. This machine was rated at 17 cubic yards and offered with GM or Cummins engines rated in the 900-horsepower class. Sales were slow at first, due to the world recession at the time, but LeTourneau persevered and their order books were filled a few years later. The L-1000 is still available today as LeTourneau's smallest wheel loader! *Keith Haddock*

LeTourneau L-1800. In keeping with its long tradition of building record-breaking machines, LeTourneau expanded its line upward. It ran away with the world's largest wheel loader title in 1990 and has actually repeated that feat twice since then. In 1990, the limelight first shone on the huge L-1400 loader. It was rated at 28 cubic yards, the largest loader ever assembled. Initially, it was equipped with an engine of 1,600 horsepower, but upgrades and other engine choices provide the current machine with 1,800 horsepower. LeTourneau made an even larger loader available in 1993. Again, the largest built up to that time, the massive L-1800 weighed in at 440,000 pounds and came with a standard bucket of 33 cubic yards! *Keith Haddock*

LeTourneau L-2350. The king of all wheel loaders is this behemoth from LeTourneau. Accustomed to carrying off the world's largest titles, the company did it again in 2000 when it showed the prototype L-2350 loader at the Minexpo 2000 mining show in Las Vegas. Its 270-ton operating weight and 53-cubic-yard standard bucket measuring 22 feet, 4 inches wide, made a huge impression on show participants. A single Cummins or Detroit diesel engine rated at 2,300 horsepower provides the power via an electric generator to the traction motors in the wheels. This larger-than-life loader features state-of-the-art computer systems, and simple joystick levers to control all bucket and vehicle movements. *LeTourneau, Inc.*

Liebherr L551. Well-known for its tower cranes, excavators, and other products, Germany's Liebherr entered the earthmoving equipment business in 1974 with the PR731 crawler tractor. More tractors followed, and wheel loaders were added in the early 1980s. From the outset, all of Liebherr's mobile equipment has featured hydrostatic drive. The L551 was introduced in 1986 as Liebherr's largest loader at the time. It carried a 4.5-cubic-yard standard bucket and ran with a 244-horsepower Liebherr diesel engine. *Keith Haddock*

Lima 140. Baldwin-Lima-Hamilton Corporation (B-L-H), better known for its cranes and excavators, launched a line of wheel loaders in 1965. Four models were initially introduced, the 50, 60, 80, and 100, spanning sizes from 1.25 to 1.5 cubic yards. These models were all rigid-frame types with rear-wheel steering. The larger Model 140, with articulated-frame steering, was introduced in 1968. A 180-flywheel-horsepower GM engine powered this model and its standard bucket held 4 cubic yards. In 1970, Clark Equipment Co. purchased the B-L-H Corporation and discontinued the Lima loaders. *Keith Haddock*

Liebherr L544. In the mid-1990s, Liebherr began upgrading its loaders by placing the operator's cab on the rear half of the machine instead of the front half, and equipping them with fuel-efficient Liebherr diesel engines. The L551 was superseded by the 186-horsepower L554 in 1998. By 2001, the new line was topped out by Liebherr's largest to date, the 6.5-cubic-yard L580 powered by a Liebherr 265-horsepower engine. The mid-sized L544, with its 165-horsepower engine, carries a standard bucket of 4 cubic yards and fits into the 12-ton weight class. These loaders boast noise-reduction operator cabs with an array of digital display symbols that relay the state of all main machine functions to the operator for his assessment. *Liebherr Construction Equipment Company*

Lorain ML-153. The Thew Shovel Company, famous for its Lorain cranes and excavators, purchased the rights to a wheel loader in 1956 and added two models known as Moto-Loaders to the market the following year. These were the ML-143 and ML-157 with bucket capacities of 1.75 and 2 cubic yards. The ML-153 was available either with a 98-horsepower Continental gasoline engine or a 105-horsepower Cummins diesel engine. In 1963, Thew replaced these two models with five new Lorain loaders in sizes from the 2-cubic-yard ML-200 to the 3.25-cubic-yard ML-325. These were followed by the 3.5-cubic-yard model ML-350 a short while later. *Keith Haddock collection*

Lorain 500. In 1964, the Thew Shovel Company became the Thew-Lorain Division of Koehring Company, and the loader line was continued under the Lorain name. The company's first three articulated models appeared in 1966. These were the 300, 400, and 500, of 3, 4, and 5 cubic yards of capacity. By 1971, the model 500 had been upgraded to the L500A with a half cubic yard more in the bucket. During that same year, the three Lorain articulated loaders became the Massey-Ferguson MF66, MF77, and MF88 when Koehring sold the Lorain loader line to Massey-Ferguson. *Keith Haddock collection*

Massey-Ferguson 356. Massey-Ferguson wheel loaders originated with the Massey-Harris-Ferguson, Inc. (M-H-F) Work Bull Model 1001 wheel loader. This was a front-wheel-drive, rigid-frame loader of 1-cubic-yard capacity that became the Massey-Ferguson Model 356 after M-H-F changed its name to Massey-Ferguson, Inc. in 1957. This was the year the company formally entered the construction equipment business. The 356 remained in the Massey-Ferguson line until 1971, but its original Continental engine was exchanged for a 60-horsepower Perkins diesel soon after M-F purchased Perkins in 1959. *Keith Haddock*

Massey-Ferguson MF-11. Massey-Ferguson developed its loader line to include five sizes by 1968. The loaders included four rigid-frame models from the Model 1-cubic-yard 356 to the 2-cubic-yard MF-44. Also introduced that year was the MF-55, the company's first articulated model. This machine was sized at 2.5-cubic-yards and was equipped with a Perkins 138-flywheel-horsepower engine. The MF-11 loader replaced the former Model 356 in 1971. It retained the former model's rigid frame and rear-wheel-steer configuration, but a new Perkins engine boosted power to 76 horsepower, and its bucket size increased to 1.5 cubic yards. *Keith Haddock*

Massey-Ferguson MF-88. This was Massey-Ferguson's largest wheel loader. Formerly the Lorain L500A, it joined the Massey-Ferguson family when the Lorain line was purchased by Massey-Ferguson in 1971. At that time, three former Lorain articulated models became the MF66, MF77, and MF88 with bucket capacities of 3.5, 4.25, and 6 cubic yards. Following the Lorain tradition, Massey-Ferguson continued to situate the operator's cab on the front half of the machine. The big MF88 loader boasted a standard bucket of 6 cubic yards and a choice of Cummins or GM engines providing 285 flywheel-horsepower. Germany's IBH group purchased Massey-Ferguson in 1980 and merged the Massey-Ferguson products into the Terex line. After IBH's collapse in 1983, Hanomag emerged as an independent company and the loaders continued to be produced as Hanomag products. *Keith Haddock*

Michigan 75A. Clark Equipment Company acquired the Michigan Power Shovel Company in 1953 and established its Construction Machinery Division at Benton Harbor, Michigan. At the same time, development was under way on a new line of rugged four-wheel-drive loaders. These prototypes appeared later that same year. Using the established Michigan brand name, Clark christened the new 75A, 125A, and 175A wheel loaders at a public demonstration in 1954. Designed as earthmovers throughout, and having no relation to tractor-mounted loaders used for farming or material re-handling, the loaders handled buckets of 1, 1.625, and 2.25 cubic yards. All were powered by Waukesha diesel engines of 80, 95, and 133 horsepower. *Keith Haddock*

Michigan 275B. Clark expanded its Michigan range by announcing the Models 275A and 375A in 1957. At this same time, wheel dozer Models 280 and 380 were introduced. These machines had engines of 262 and 375 horsepower and operating weights up to 31 tons. Several more rigid-frame models were introduced until 1965, when the company announced its first articulated loaders including the 6.5-cubic-yard 275 with a 324-flywheel-horsepower engine. Although using the same model nomenclature, Clark had totally redesigned these loaders to increase weight, horsepower, and bucket size. The 275B, upgraded to 342 flywheel-horsepower, appeared in 1970 and had a production run lasting until 1980, when it was superseded by the 275C. *Keith Haddock*

Michigan 475 III. As early as 1965, Clark announced a 12-cubic-yard loader that materialized as the articulated Michigan 475A a year later. Seen here is one of the very first Michigan 475s at work near Owingsville, Kentucky, on the construction of a section of Interstate 64. Its operating weight was 60 tons and its engine developed 635 horsepower. By the mid-1960s, the Michigan range had expanded to 11 models, from the small .5-cubic-yard 12B to the large 475A. The big 475A and its upgrades through B and C versions lasted in the range until they were replaced by the similar-sized L480 in 1987. *Keith Haddock collection*

Michigan L480. After the Clark Michigan Company became a subsidiary of VME Group N.V. in 1985, Michigan loaders were gradually merged into Volvo's Swedish-designed loader line and denoted by the L Series. By 1990, the L Series consisted of 10 machines from the L30 to the L480, covering bucket sizes from 1 to 12.5 cubic yards. The L480 replaced the successful 475C loader in 1987. Its engine was the Cummins VT-28C, rated at 650 flywheel-horsepower. The L480B appeared in 1992 with the same power and bucket ratings as the L480, but it boasted an improved operator's cab that featured pilot-operated fingertip hydraulic controls. *Keith Haddock*

Michigan 675. The massive Michigan 675 carried a bucket of 24 cubic yards! It was not only twice as big as Michigan's previous largest 475 loader, at that time it was also the largest wheel loader built by any manufacturer. The first production machine was released in 1973 with a 24-cubic-yard bucket, twin Cummins engines totaling 1,270 horsepower, and an operating weight of over 190 tons. The operator sat in a cab two stories above the ground and rode on four tires over 10 feet in diameter, the largest in the industry. After only 14 production machines were built, the 675 was discontinued in 1976. The picture shows a Michigan 675 at work at a western Pennsylvania surface coal mine in 1979. *Keith Haddock*

Nelson 200. N.P. Nelson Iron Works, Inc. of Clifton, New Jersey, produced a line of wheel loaders commencing with the 150 in 1957. This model was powered by either a gasoline or diesel Hercules engine and carried a 1.75-cubic-yard bucket. In 1959, the company followed up with the 2.25-cubic-yard Model 200, again with a choice of either a 117-horsepower Continental gasoline engine or a 105-horsepower GM diesel engine. Two more Nelson loaders appeared before they faded from the scene: the 2.625-cubic-yard Model 250 in 1961, and the company's largest, the 4-cubic-yard Model 400 in 1967. All the Nelson loaders were rigid-frame models. *Keith Haddock collection*

New Holland LW130-TC. The New Holland brand name on wheel loaders resulted from the formation of CNH Global in 1999, when Case Corporation and equipment builder Ford New Holland merged under Fiat ownership. Ford had acquired New Holland in 1986, and Fiat acquired Ford New Holland in 1991. With other acquisitions, CNH brought several well-known construction equipment brands under its control. Today's New Holland loaders come in nine sizes. At the smaller end, the 1-cubic-yard LW50B and 1.5-cubic-yard LW80B were formally O&K machines, while the rest of the line, up to the 6-cubic-yard LW-270, derived from the former Fiatallis line. The 2.7-cubic-yard LW130 is shown in its TC, or tool carrier version. A tool carrier model is able to exchange its bucket for a multitude of other attachments at a moment's notice. *New Holland Construction*

O&K L6. The L6 was one of six small wheel loaders of 1.25-cubic-yards capacity or less that was produced by O&K (Orenstein & Koppel) in Germany. It was powered by a Daimler-Benz 46-horsepower diesel engine and its standard bucket held .9 cubic yards. In November 1998, New Holland announced it had acquired the O&K line of wheel loaders and excavators, then in 1999 it announced the Case–New Holland merger to form CNH Global. The result of this merger is that certain machines from the former O&K line are currently being sold in North America as New Holland products. The O&K L6, after being upgraded to the L6B in 1996, is now sold as the New Holland LW50B. *Keith Haddock*

Pettibone 125. This four-wheel-drive, rear-wheel-steer loader was produced by Pettibone-Mulliken Corporation of Chicago, Illinois. Its standard bucket held 1.75 cubic yards and it was powered by gasoline or diesel Hercules engines of 108 horsepower. The 125 was the smallest in the extensive range of loaders offered by the company. It had a production run lasting from 1955 to 1968. Pettibone wheel loaders included the Speed-Swing, with a loader attachment that could rotate 90 degrees left or right, and the 70 Carry-Shovel, which was introduced in 1962 with overhead bucket arms and a re-handling bucket capacity of 26 cubic yards. *Keith Haddock*

Samsung SL120-2. Samsung Heavy Industries began importing construction equipment into North America in 1990 through its subsidiary, Samsung Construction Equipment America Corporation. Made in Korea, the machines included hydraulic excavators, four sizes of wheel loaders, and the 270-flywheel-horsepower crawler tractor Model SD250. The loaders covered sizes from the 2.25-cubic-yard SL120-2 to the 4.75-cubic-yard SL250-2, with engines from 126 to 264 flywheel-horsepower. In 1998, Samsung became part of the Volvo organization. *Keith Haddock*

Scoopmobile LD-15A. Mixermobile Manufacturers Incorporated of Portland, Oregon, invented the Scoopmobile name in the 1930s. Its famous line of three-wheel loaders under the name Scoopmobile started in 1939 with the .75-cubic-yard Model A. Mixermobile is credited with building the first four-wheel-drive articulated wheel loader, the Scoopmobile LD-5, in 1953. Power to all four wheels was provided through an exclusive Pow-R-Flex coupling, which permits the two axles to oscillate independently, while providing articulation between the two frames. Scoopmobile rapidly added more LD Series models to its articulated loader line. The LD-15A appeared in 1959 rated at 6 cubic yards and powered by a Cummins 320-flywheel-horsepower engine. *Keith Haddock collection*

Scoopmobile 150-B. Scoopmobile further expanded its line of wheel loaders in the 1960s including the 1.75-cubic-yard 150B introduced in 1965. In 1968, the Scoopmobile line of wheel loaders merged into the Construction Equipment Division of Westinghouse Air Brake Company and the machines sold under the Wabco name. The line diminished soon after that date, and in 1974 the manufacturing rights were purchased by the Eagle Crusher Company, Inc. of Galion, Ohio. The machines continued to be built in dwindling numbers until the last Scoopmobile left Eagle's works in 1989. *Keith Haddock*

Scoopmobile 1200. Scoopmobile claimed title to the world's largest wheel loader when it announced the Model 1200 in 1965. This massive machine was offered with buckets ranging from a standard 10 cubic yards to a re-handling bucket of 20-cubic-yard capacity. Engine options were a 525-horsepower Cummins or 475-horsepower GM diesel. The 1200 debuted in an era when other manufacturers were bringing large wheel loaders on the scene. It competed against the Hough H-400, Michigan 475, and the Caterpillar 992, all in the same size class. *Eric C. Orlemann collection*

Terex 72-81. In 1968, the Euclid Division of General Motors was forced to discontinue truck manufacture in North America and divest itself of the Euclid name. In the following year, General Motors released the large 72-81 wheel loader in the 9-cubic-yard class under the new Terex name. With an operating weight of 114,800 pounds and a 438-horsepower GM 12V-71T engine, the loader was a significant achievement for General Motors, especially since it had only been seriously marketing wheel loaders for about seven years. The 72-81 turned out to be the largest loader ever to bear the Terex name. *Keith Haddock*

Terex 72-31B. The Euclid Division of General Motors began to market a new line of loaders in 1967. The machines were assigned 72 Series model numbers, a new nomenclature adopted by Euclid a year earlier. In 1968, the Terex name was announced as the product name for the Earthmoving Equipment Division of General Motors, and the 72 Series loaders continued under the Terex name. The 72-31B was released for sale in 1977 as a totally redesigned machine from the former 72-31. It featured state-of-the-art design technology and sported the Terex keystone rear-end design, now common on most Terex machines. With a standard bucket capacity of 3 cubic yards, its GM engine was rated at 146 flywheel-horsepower. The 72-31B became the Terex 60C in 1982, and was finally phased out of production in 1988. *Keith Haddock*

Terex 90C. Terex passed into the hands of the German IBH Group in 1981, and shortly afterwards the Terex loader line merged into the Hanomag loader line. Hanomag was another German company acquired by IBH. The combined line was renumbered as the C Series, and it included the 5.5-cubic-yard 80C, derived from the former 72-61, and a new top-of-the-line model, the 90C, which was rated at 7.25 cubic yards. When IBH failed in 1983, Terex returned to General Motors, but only the original GM-designed loaders were retained as Terex machines. Terex later discontinue its loaders and focused on its other products. The last loaders built, a batch of six Model 90Cs, left the Motherwell, Scotland, plant in 1994. *Francis Pierre*

Tractomotive TL-12. The Tractomotive Corporation of Findlay, Ohio, is credited with developing the world's first all-hydraulic loader mechanism. First tested in 1946 on an Allis-Chalmers HD5 crawler tractor, a second version of the loader was mounted on a farm tractor in 1948. This .5-cubic-yard machine, known as the TL-W, became the first Tractomotive wheel loader. In 1951, Tractomotive introduced the 1-cubic-yard TL-10 with torque converter drive. It was Tractomotive's first self-contained unit, designed specifically as a wheel loader. In 1954, Tractomotive unveiled its first four-wheel-drive loader, the TL-12. This machine also featured a torque converter, 63-horsepower Allis-Chalmers engine, and a standard bucket of 1.125-cubic-yards. In 1959, Allis-Chalmers Manufacturing Company purchased the Tractomotive Corporation. *Keith Haddock*

Trojan 164A. The Yale & Towne Manufacturing Company of Batavia, New York, entered the loader field in 1950 with the Yale Model LM-75 wheel loader. This was the first in a long line of machines known by the trade names "Yale" or "Trojan." During the 1950s, Yale added more models to its line of rigid-frame loaders, some with front-wheel, and others with four-wheel drive. In 1959, the four-wheel-drive 1.75-cubic-yard Model 164 was launched with a 1.75-cubic-yard standard bucket. This model was upgraded to the 164A in 1965 and continued in production until 1970. Power options included diesel or gasoline engines in the 130-horsepower range. *O&K Orenstein & Koppel, Inc.*

Trojan 8000. When the Yale company decided to produce an articulated loader, it did it in style, for the machine boasted dual-articulation with two pivots instead of one! Launched in 1966, the huge Trojan 8000 carried a standard bucket of 8 cubic yards and had an operating weight of 52 tons. Power options were GM or Cummins diesels in the 480-flywheel horsepower class. The unique machine placed the operator on the center section with the articulated sections working together in front and behind him. In a surprisingly short production life of less than three years, only 13 of the big 8000s left the factory, but it still holds the record for the largest loader Yale ever built. *Keith Haddock collection*

Trojan Yale 3000. In 1966, Yale launched two more successful articulated loaders to join the big 8000. These were the 3000 and 4000 models, sized with 3.5- and 5.5-cubic-yard buckets. The 3000 could be powered by either GM or Cummins diesel engines of 190 flywheel-horsepower. The 3000 and 4000 loaders were upgraded to B Models in 1969, and after further upgrades it stayed in production until 1974. More articulated loaders were gradually introduced, until all the rigid models were replaced. Yale loaders in the 1970s and 1980s ranged from the 1500 to the 7500, covering bucket requirements from 1.75 to 7.5 cubic yards. *O&K Orenstein & Koppel, Inc.*

Volvo LM1641. In 1950, Sweden's AB Bolinder-Munktell (B-M) was taken over by AB Volvo, and the company eventually became known as BM-Volvo. B-M was a company with a long industrial history dating back to 1832. Its products included railway locomotives, tractors, graders, engines, and all types of farm equipment. Still retaining its own identity, B-M developed Sweden's first wheel loader, the H10, in 1954. After several more extremely successful loaders bearing the BM-Volvo name throughout the 1960s, the machines gained an enviable reputation for ruggedness and reliability. In 1972, the company now known as Volvo BM introduced its largest loader yet, the articulated LM1641. Rated at 4.5 cubic yards, it was powered by a Volvo diesel engine of 240 horsepower. It stayed in production until 1980. *Keith Haddock*

Trojan 7500. In 1982, Faun AG from Germany took over the Yale & Towne Manufacturing Company and merged the machines into the Faun line of wheel loaders originally derived from the former German Frisch line it had purchased in 1977. In 1986, O&K (Orenstein & Koppel) of Germany took over the Faun company along with the wheel loaders, and continued their production at Batavia, New York. The top-of-the-line Model 7500 loader, seen here with both O&K and Trojan logos, works with a standard 7.5-cubic-yard bucket, and its Cummins engine produces 402 flywheel-horsepower. The Trojan loaders were discontinued in 1992 when the Batavia plant closed, but the former O&K heritage can still be found in the current loaders sold under the New Holland banner. *Keith Haddock*

Volvo 4500. In the late 1970s, Volvo introduced the 100 Series, which eventually replaced all of Volvo's existing models. The first was the 4300 in 1977, followed by the 4200 and 4400 in 1978, the 4500 in 1979, and the 4600 in 1980. These models spanned bucket sizes from 1 to 5 cubic yards and came equipped with Volvo engines from 59 to 252 flywheel-horsepower. The 4500 shown takes care of coal stockpiles at a generating station in Alberta, Canada, with a 4-cubic-yard bucket. *Keith Haddock*

Volvo L180D. After the VME Group N.V. was formed in 1985 with the merger of Volvo BM, Clark Michigan Company, and Euclid Inc., Michigan loaders were gradually merged into Volvo's Swedish-designed loader line, denoted by the L Series. By 1990, the L Series consisted of 10 machines from the L30 to the L480, covering bucket sizes from 1 to 12.5 cubic yards. A Volvo 275-flywheel-horsepower engine powered the 6-cubic-yard L180. It was upgraded first to the L180C, and later to the L180D, with similar size and power ratings. Volvo began its D Series with the L220D in 1998. These models boast a new load-sensing hydraulic system, increased fuel efficiency, and an improved operator's cab. *Volvo BM*

Volvo L180E. Soon after Volvo launched its modern D Series loaders in 1998, a second wave of improvements were in the works. In 2001, the 7-cubic-yard L220E was unveiled as the first new E Series loader. Four more E Series loaders were launched in 2002, including Volvo's largest, the 55-ton L330E with standard 9-cubic-yard bucket. As well as an updated appearance with rounded rear radiator and grill, the E Series are fitted with new electronically controlled Volvo engines that run at low speed for fuel economy and low emissions. The engine in the 6-cubic-yard L180E (shown) produces its maximum 303 horsepower at 1,400 rpm, and even at an idling speed of 800 rpm it still develops 98 percent of its maximum power. Volvo retained its load-sensing hydraulic system, which was pioneered on the former D Series loaders. This automatically distributes power between traction and loader movement for maximum efficiency. *Volvo Construction Equipment*

CHAPTER 6

LOADER-BACKHOES

Mount a hydraulic backhoe on the rear of a four-wheel farm tractor, then mount a hydraulic loader on the front, and you have the familiar multi-purpose excavating machine called a loader-backhoe, or backhoe-loader. However, manufacturers of these multi-purpose machines will tell you it's not quite that simple. Today's machine is designed from the ground up as an integral digging and loading machine, not a combination of a power unit carrying attachments. But that wasn't always the case. The first loader-backhoes certainly consisted of farm tractors with attachments hung on them. The concept has its roots back in the 1920s, when small agricultural-type tractors were fitted with a loader bucket. By the late 1940s, crude hydraulic backhoes were first mounted behind farm tractors, some attached to the tractor, some as a trailer unit, but the concept of using a tractor-mounted backhoe and a loader would have to wait until the early 1950s.

Whitlock Brothers of Great Yeldham, Essex, England, claim to have built the world's first backhoe-loader, the "Dinkum Digger." Whitlock first experimented with a hydraulic backhoe attachment for a Fordson Major farm tractor in 1951. The following year they added a hydraulic loader, and the first loader-backhoe was born. Next in the field was Joseph Charles Bamford, founder of the worldwide JCB organization based in Rocester, England. After building several hydraulic loaders mounted on standard farm tractors, Bamford designed and built his first backhoe attachment in 1953 following a visit to Norway. While there, he noticed an early Broyt trailer-type backhoe of crude design and immediately saw the possibilities of improving its design. He purchased one and had it shipped back to his factory, and the same year his own version appeared. Although a few of these machines were sold, it was really only a prototype version of things to come. During the stringent testing the machine undertook, it soon became apparent that its lightweight construction was a major disadvantage when used in excavation work.

In 1954 Bamford brought out a much-improved and heavier-designed backhoe, the JCB Mk.1, designed for attaching to Fordson Major or Nuffield

Allis-Chalmers 1600/160. Allis-Chalmers launched its 160 (I for Industrial) wheel tractor in 1965, available with either gasoline or diesel Allis-Chalmers engines of 56.8 or 44 horsepower. The following year, the 160 was renumbered 1600 with very little design changes. The machine in the picture is equipped with the Model 160 backhoe and loader attachment. The Henry Manufacturing Co., Inc. in Topeka, Kansas, built both. The backhoe utilized a unique hydraulic rotary joint to swing the boom, rather than the usual pair of hydraulic cylinders. This design was short-lived, and Allis-Chalmers soon replaced it with the conventional double-acting cylinder design. In 1968, Allis-Chalmers purchased the assets of Henry Manufacturing, and the 1600 was discontinued that same year.
Keith Haddock

Bucyrus-Erie 190-4. In 1971, Bucyrus-Erie Company (Now Bucyrus International, Inc.) purchased the Hy-Dynamic Company of Lake Bluff, Illinois. This company's products included a line of loader-backhoes that sold as Bucyrus-Erie products after the takeover. The tractor/backhoes, known by the name Dynahoe, were heavy-duty machines, more powerful and with greater range than the average loader-backhoe. The 190-4 (the "4" denoting a four-wheel-drive machine) was powered by a 120-horsepower engine. It boasted a digging depth of 19 feet and an operating weight of 22,750 pounds. The biggest Dynahoe was the 200-4 with 160 horsepower and a 38,490 operating weight. In 1985, Bucyrus sold the Dynahoe and its other construction machinery products to Northwest Engineering Company, which continued manufacturing the Dynahoe under its Bucyrus Construction Products division. *Bucyrus International, Inc.*

tractors. Since JCB was already selling its "Major Loader" attachment for these tractors, it didn't take long for the two to come together in a happy marriage, and JCB's first loader-backhoe was born. These early tractor-mounted backhoes could be purchased with or without the front loader. But Mr. Bamford asked, "Why would anyone want to do without the front-end loader?" and he strongly encouraged sales of machines with both attachments. As early as 1958, JCB set the standard for the loader-backhoe industry by bringing out its first completely integrated loader-backhoe built as an excavating machine.

Case was another pioneer of the loader-backhoe. Case fell into the loader-backhoe business as a result of purchasing the American Tractor Corporation (ATC) of Churubusco, Indiana, in 1957. As well as its line of crawler tractors, ATC had also developed a hydraulic backhoe and needed a suitable tractor on which to mount it. The Case takeover provided the solution, but not before a standard Model 300 tractor was beefed up to suit the application. Unlike other manufacturers at that time, the Case/ATC management did not take the easy option of mounting backhoe and loader attachments on an existing tractor. The new heavy-duty tractor Model 320 had been designed to take the rigors of excavation work.

The first tractor-mounted backhoes gained stability while digging by lowering the entire frame, with the mounted backhoe assembly, to the ground. By the end of the 1950s, manufacturers replaced this cumbersome

Case 320. Case was one of the first manufacturers to design and produce a wheeled tractor specifically to carry a hydraulic backhoe and front-end loader. Earlier attempts at mounting backhoes on farm tractors proved unsuitable in heavy industrial applications. Case introduced its first two integral tractor backhoes in 1957: the 320 early in the year, followed by the 310. The backhoe was designed by the American Tractor Corporation, which Case purchased that same year. To gain stability on these early backhoes, the entire backhoe frame was lowered to the ground, instead of using independently lowered stabilizer legs. In 1958–1959, these models were redesigned as the 310B and 320B and, that same year, the larger and smaller 410B and 210B sizes were added. *Keith Haddock*

Case 580B. Building on its experience with its early loader-backhoes, Case launched the 530 loader-backhoe in 1963. Available with Case gasoline or diesel engines rated at 52 horsepower, it was capable of digging to a depth of 14 feet. This was the first of the famous Construction King Series, and it would prove to be a milestone in the company's history by eventually propelling Case into the number-one position in sales for this type of machine. Construction Kings featured hydrostatic steering and "extendahoe," a feature permitting the boom to be hydraulically extended to give an extra 2 feet of digging depth over the standard 14 feet. The most popular of all was the Model 580, which was introduced in 1966. It was upgraded to the 580B in 1971, offering 57 horsepower from its Case diesel engine. *Keith Haddock*

Case 580K. The most popular of all the Case loader-backhoes was the 580 Series. The first model was introduced in 1966, and at the time of writing, it was still available as the much-revised and upgraded 580M. The story of the 580 metamorphosis reads like a history textbook of backhoe development in the past 35 years. Each model introduction offered the latest technology in efficient operation, improved maintenance, and operator comfort. After the 580B upgraded model appeared in 1971, the 55-horsepower 580C followed in 1975, the 580D with four-wheel drive option was introduced in 1980, and the 63-horsepower 580 Super E was first produced in 1983. Then came the 580F and 580G, available in Europe, followed by the 580K in 1986, the 580 Super L in 1995, and the 580M in 2000. All of these models were in the 14-foot digging depth class. *Keith Haddock*

design with a pair of independent hydraulically powered stabilizer legs that were either vertically telescopic or hinged. Among the early designers of this type were Massey-Ferguson in 1959 and JCB in 1961. Subsequently, all other manufacturers adopted the stabilizer leg arrangement.

Another development was the sliding kingpost. Rather than fix the boom pivot point or kingpost to the center of the rear frame, the sliding kingpost allowed the boom pivot to move to either side of the machine. This provided greater flexibility when digging alongside walls and fences. Massey-Ferguson produced an early example of this type in 1959, and JCB's Hydraslide appeared in 1961. Later, Whitlock offered its patented Swinglock device. In this design, the boom pivot was mounted on a swing-frame pivoted near the tractor's rear axle. Operated by the swing cylinders, this frame could move the backhoe boom pivot to left, right, or center positions, where it was locked in place by a hydraulically actuated pin. Because the sliding kingpost has always been more popular in Europe than in North America, the leading manufacturers continue to offer both options in their current product lines.

The various manufacturers tried many different design features during the development of the loader-backhoe; some were more successful than others. On some of Allis-Chalmers' early models, a hydraulic rotary joint was utilized to swing the boom, instead of the usual pair of hydraulic cylinders. Other swinging methods employ a chain connected to two hydraulic cylinders and wrapped around a sprocket on the king-post. Hy-Dynamic Company, later owned by Bucyrus-Erie Company, specialized in building super-sized loader-backhoes, some weighing almost 20 tons. The "Auto-Dig" feature that Ford Tractor Operations introduced on its backhoes in 1967 automatically balanced the crowd, bucket curl, and hoist forces during the digging cycle. The idea was dropped after short time.

Four-wheel drive became the fashion in loader-backhoes of the 1980s. Some manufacturers offered 2x4 and 4x4 options on the same model, while others offered separate models with four-wheel drive. At about this time, loader-backhoes became more versatile as manufacturers offered a broader choice of attachments for both ends of the machine. And then

Case 680E. For contractors wanting more power, reach, and digging depth, Case offered its 680 Series Construction King loader-backhoes with a 16.5-foot digging depth. The first version appeared in 1966, along with the 580, but it offered more engine horsepower and a torque converter that provided over 10,000 pounds of digging force on the backhoe bucket. The 680B followed in 1968, and the 680C was introduced in 1971. The latter machine sported a Case diesel engine of 80 flywheel-horsepower and outboard planetary drive to the wheels. The 680E was replaced by the 680C in 1974. It offered the same engine as the 680E, a 1.25-cubic-yard loader bucket, and the "Extendahoe" option, which provided a 20-foot digging depth. Further improved and revised models were launched—the 680G in 1978, the 680H in 1980, the 680K in 1984, and, last in the series, the 90-horsepower 680L, produced from 1988 to 1993. *Keith Haddock*

Case 780D. In 1971, Case introduced its top-of-the-line loader-backhoe, the 780 Construction King with a digging depth of 18 feet. Its Case diesel engine in standard form was rated at 89 horsepower, but a turbocharged version was also offered with power rated up to 108 horsepower. By 1979, only the turbocharged version was available, and customers could order an "Extendahoe" option, which allowed a digging depth to 20 feet. In 1981, the 780B appeared with similar power and digging capabilities. In 1984, Case installed a new 112-horsepower 6T-590 diesel engine in the replacement 780C and upgraded it to the 780D in 1988. The 780D in the picture is equipped with a hydraulically actuated tamping compactor on its rear. Case discontinued its large loader-backhoes, the 680 and 780 Series, in 1993. *Keith Haddock*

Case 580M. Case's long-running line of loader-backhoes received another upgrade in 2000 with the M Series. New features include a cast backhoe boom, improved suspension to minimize vehicle bounce, and a patented "Pro Control" system which offers automated control of the backhoe digging mode for fuel efficiency. The line consists of two-wheel- and four-wheel-drive versions of the long-running Case 580 with 14-foot backhoe digging depth, and offers different power options ranging from 73 to 90 horsepower. The North American line is headed by the 590M rated at 99 horsepower, while in Europe the four-wheel-steer 695 Super M tops the line at 106 horsepower. *Case Corporation*

Caterpillar 446. Caterpillar is a relative newcomer in the loader-backhoe market. Toward the end of the 1970s, the company recognized how large this market had become, and noted the success of pioneer builders like Case and JCB in the United Kingdom. Caterpillar decided to add loader-backhoes to its product line, and commenced an intensive development program to design and build its own machines. With production of the machines assigned to Caterpillar's plant at Leicester, England, the wraps were taken off the first model, the 416, in 1985. In the 14-foot digging-depth class, the 416 carried a 62 flywheel-horsepower engine. Special features included back-of-center carry position for the backhoe, providing superior stability when traveling, and single cylinder bucket rollback. By 1989, Caterpillar extended its backhoe-loader line to six models that ranged in size up to the 95-flywheel-horsepower 446 with a standard digging depth of 17 feet, or 21 feet with an extended arm. *Eric C. Orlemann collection*

there are the tool carriers. Like their sibling tool carrier wheel loaders, tool carrier loader-backhoes are designed to work with a multitude of different attachments such as power brooms, hydraulic hammers, plate compactors, palette forks, lifting hooks, dozer blades, and more. All can be interchanged in a matter of seconds by activating the specially designed power-operated pins that hook onto each attachment. Without ever having to leave his cab, the operator can execute all of these functions.

In 1991, JCB introduced the world's first full-sized loader-backhoe with four-wheel drive, four-wheel steer, and running on four large, equal-sized wheels. As well as providing a nimble turning radius comparable to any articulated-frame design, the makers claim that four-wheel steering based on a rigid frame results in greater stability in loading activities. The four-wheel steering concept also allows three types of steering: regular two-wheel steering, four-wheel steering for tight cornering when all wheels turn in the same direction, and crab steering when the front and rear wheels are turned in the opposite direction. The four big, equal-sized wheels provide better balance and traction during loader operations. In fact, the balance

and traction is improved to such an extent that in some trenching operations, where a wheel loader and backhoe are normally employed, the loader is not necessary. Even with the added cost of this feature, the 4x4x4 concept has caught on, and most leading manufactures offer it on certain models in their lineup.

Some of the biggest names in the earthmoving equipment business entered the loader-backhoe market relatively late—some by acquisition, and some by in-house design. Caterpillar's loader-backhoes were unveiled in 1985; Komatsu first launched two models in 1999; and Terex's version first appeared in 2001, after acquiring the Fermec machines.

For the past four decades, the loader-backhoe has been the mainstay of mechanized utility work. With the advent of the mini-excavator, the increased popularity of the skid-steer loader, and an increasing number of small companies making compact-sized machines, the loader-backhoe held its own by becoming more versatile and adapting to modern construction practices and environmental regulations. Affordable by even the smallest contractor and capable of performing a wide variety of jobs, the backhoe will be visible on almost every construction site for the foreseeable future.

Caterpillar 428. Caterpillar included two side-shift loader-backhoes in its initial line, the 428 and 438. On side-shift models, the backhoe boom assembly is carried on a sliding frame so the boom pivot can be positioned at any point from the left to the right of the machine. This simple feature, more popular in Europe than in North America, allows the operator to dig flush to walls and footings, and it offers more flexibility around obstructions. The 428's engine developed 70 flywheel-horsepower and a digging depth, with standard boom, of 15 feet, 9 inches. *Caterpillar Inc.*

Caterpillar 416C. Caterpillar redesigned its loader-backhoes to the B Series in 1992. The distinguishing feature on the B Models was the curved excavator-style backhoe boom, which first appeared on the original 446 back in 1989. This design provided more clearance when digging over obstacles, and a greater overall digging depth. The B Models were also endowed with increased engine power to 74 flywheel-horsepower for the 416B to 84 flywheel-horsepower for the 436B. Caterpillar redesigned its loader-backhoes and introduced the C Series in 1996 with slightly increased horsepower. Applicable to all models except the 446, the C models were available with four-wheel drive and four-wheel steer as an option. Caterpillar first made this option available on its 438 model in 1993. *Caterpillar, Inc.*

Caterpillar 420D. Caterpillar introduced its D Series loader-backhoes in 2001 with the launch of the 420D and 430D. These first models, rated at 85 and 94 flywheel-horsepower, are also offered in tool carrier versions known as 420D IT and 430D IT. The tool carrier replaces the standard loader bucket with a special linkage and a quick-coupler so that a wide range of attachments can be utilized. Retaining the curved excavator-type boom and the successful features of the former C models, the D Series boasts pilot-operated joystick controls for ease of operation, and increased backhoe bucket rotation to 205 degrees. Digging depth on the 420D increases from 14 feet, 5 inches, to 18 feet with the extendible arm. *Keith Haddock*

Deere 40. John Deere's loader-backhoe heritage started when it mounted loader and backhoe attachments on its farm tractors. With an abundance of tractors to choose from, loader and backhoe attachments were applied to several models of John Deere tractors by the mid-1950s. An early example is this 1957 outfit based on a John Deere Model 40 Utility tractor. Notice the bucket crowd cylinder runs parallel with the boom at all times, and the bucket arm pivot is provided by a fixed link between the arm and base of the boom. The heavier industrial tractors built from 1960 to 1965, Models 1010 of 40 horsepower and 2010 of 50 horsepower, more than fulfilled John Deere's loader-backhoe requirements for construction purposes. Backhoes with digging depths of 16.5 feet were offered for these models. *Keith Haddock*

Deere JD500-C. In 1965, John Deere got serious about its loader-backhoes and introduced three new integrated models known as the JD-300, JD-400, and JD-500. These three models formed the basis for Deere's loader-backhoes until the early 1970s. The loaders received A upgrades beginning in 1966, and then the B Series was introduced in 1969. The JD-500-B could be fitted with either diesel or gasoline engines of 80 and 77 flywheel-horsepower, and its digging depth was 16 feet. With further product improvements, Deere brought out an all-new line of loader-backhoes in 1971. The new line replaced all former models except the JD500-B, which was refined and reintroduced as the JD500-C with the same diesel engine and digging capabilities as its predecessor. *Keith Haddock*

Deere JD-410C. John Deere's revamped loader-backhoe line launched three new models in 1971 to replace similar-sized former models. The new models were the JD310, JD410, and JD510, with 52-, 66-, and 83-flywheel-horsepower ratings. Standard digging depths specified for the JD310 and JD410 were 15 feet, and 17 feet for the JD510. The models boasted state-of-the-art features including single-lever loader control and twin joystick backhoe control. John Deere has upgraded these basic loader-backhoe models over the years as technology allowed, and added models to fill specific needs demanded by the market. The B Series was presented in 1982, the C Series in 1986, the D Series in 1991, the E Series in 1996, and the G Series in 2000. *Keith Haddock*

Deere 310SG. John Deere advanced its loader-backhoes again in 2000 when it launched the G Series. The models in the 14-foot-digging-depth class consist of the 74-horsepower 310G with a naturally aspirated engine or a turbocharged option, and three models fitted with a turbocharger as standard. These are the 84-horsepower 310SG, the 85-horsepower 315SG, and the 92-horsepower 410G. All the G Series models carry the John Deere 4045 diesel engine with appropriate power ratings. They also feature larger operator's cabs with more floor space, and 30 percent more tinted glass than the former series. Options include four-wheel drive and extendible bucket arms, which push digging depth down to 19 feet. For the heaviest loader-backhoe jobs, Deere still offers the 115-horsepower 710D in 2002 with standard digging depths to 17 feet. *Keith Haddock*

109

Dynahoe Model A. The Hy-Dynamic Company of Lake Bluff, Illinois, unveiled its first loader-backhoe in 1959. Designated Model A for the gasoline version and Model AD for diesel, the machine was powered by Continental engines of 65 flywheel-horsepower. Shipping weight was 13,900 pounds. Two single-acting cylinders swung the backhoe, and it could dig down to 13 feet below grade level. The loader bucket, with power-crowding action, held 1 cubic yard. In 1966, Hy-Dynamic began building a line of rough-terrain hydraulic cranes. In 1971, Bucyrus-Erie Company (B-E) purchased the Hy-Dynamic Company and added the cranes and the Dynahoe line of loader-backhoes to its product roster. B-E expanded the product line of two-wheel- and four-wheel-drive heavy-duty loader-backhoes under its Hy-Dynamic Division established at Erie, Pennsylvania. *Keith Haddock collection*

Fermec TLK 760. Fermec of Manchester, England, was established in 1992 when Massey-Ferguson Industrial (MF) was purchased by the directors of its parent company, the Varity Corporation, and renamed Fermec International, Ltd. At that time, the former worldwide manufacturing operations of MF's Industrial Division had been consolidated at the Manchester plant, and the only products remaining were skidsteer loaders, industrial tractors, and loader-backhoes. In 1993, Fermec launched a new line of loader-backhoes, the TLK Series built in a joint venture with Japan's Kobelco. The 82-horsepower TLK 760 could dig down 14 feet, 8 inches or 19 feet, 3 inches with extendible arm. In 1996, Case acquired Fermec and certain Case-branded loader-backhoes were added to the production line at the Manchester plant. At the end of 2000, Case sold its Fermec operation, including the Manchester plant, to Terex Corporation.

Ford 655A. Ford Motor Company's involvement in loader-backhoes started in 1961 when it purchased Sherman Products, Inc., a builder of light-duty backhoe attachments. After an extensive design program, the Tractor Operations of Ford launched two loader-backhoes in 1967, the offset sliding-pivot 13-Six, and the center-pivot 16-Six with respective digging depths of 13 feet and 16 feet. Both were equipped with a 56-horsepower Ford engine, and their distinguishing feature was Ford's "Auto-Dig," a digging control system that automatically balanced the crowd, bucket curl, and hoist forces during the digging cycle. But Ford dropped this feature after a short period. The 655A of 1986 was a conventional center-pivot loader-backhoe with 15-foot-digging-depth capability, and equipped with a 72-horsepower engine. *Keith Haddock*

JCB Hydra-Digga. The founder of the worldwide JCB organization, Joseph Cyril Bamford, started fabricating trailers and farm equipment in 1945. After building several hydraulic loaders mounted on standard farm tractors, Bamford designed and built his first backhoe attachment in 1953. This was followed early in 1954 by the JCB Mk. I backhoe. When this was fitted to a Fordson Major tractor with a JCB Major Loader on the front, JCB's first loader-backhoe was born. The successful combined unit sold several hundred loader-backhoes before being replaced in 1957 by the Hydra-Digga. Larger and more powerful than its predecessor, the Hydra-Digga was designed around Fordson Major or Nuffield tractors, and could be purchased with or without the front loader. However, selling the machine without the loader was strongly discouraged by Mr. Bamford! *JCB Sales, Ltd.*

JCB Hydra-Digga Loadall 65. JCB introduced the completely integrated Hydra-Digga Loadall 65 in 1958. Designed with all the characteristics of the modern backhoe, it set the standard for the loader-backhoe industry. Based on a 52-horsepower Fordson Major tractor, this backhoe could dig to 13 feet, and its loader bucket could hold about 1 cubic yard. As with other early designs, the entire backhoe assembly was lowered to the ground for stability rather than utilizing hydraulically lowered legs. In 1960, the 52-horsepower JCB 4, a heavy-duty machine with a large, roomy cab and optional dual-joystick backhoe controls, replaced the Hydra-Digga Loadall 65. Standard digging depth was listed as 13 feet, but a fixed extension was available to push down as far as 16 feet. *Keith Haddock*

JCB 3. The JCB 3, with its subsequent derivatives, was probably the most popular loader-backhoe ever to come from JCB. Unveiled in 1961, and with many upgrades and improvements over the years through the 3C and 3D models, it continued as the backbone of JCB's product line until 1980. By this time, more than 72,000 units had been sold. Although smaller and more compact than its big brother, the JCB 4, the JCB 3 was more powerful at 57 horsepower. It had twin independent vertical stabilizers and a sliding king post that enabled the machine to dig tight against walls or other obstructions. It also boasted a swivel seat so the operator did not have to switch seats when moving from loader to backhoe operation. *JCB Sales, Ltd.*

JCB 3C. Production of the JCB 3C commenced in 1963. Instantly popular, this model caused the company's total sales to double by 1964. Built around a Ford 54-horsepower power unit, the 3C represented a breakthrough in technology: all the machine's components, including the power unit, were supported on an integrated chassis, rather than relying on bolt-ons for the backhoe and other assemblies. It wasn't long before JCB's entire line would be constructed this way. And in another move, following supply problems with the Ford power units, JCB changed to BMC Nuffield units. The first models with the Nuffield power units appeared in 1967 with the upgraded JCB 3D and 4D models. The JCB 3C Series came to an end in 1980, when the new 3CX was launched. *JCB Sales, Ltd.*

JCB 3CX Sitemaster. Soon after the introduction of the JCB 3CX in 1980, customer requests for various attachments resulted in the development of a special version, the 3CX Sitemaster, the following year. Featuring JCB's hydraulically extendible "Extradig" backhoe arm, and a six-in-one clamshell shovel bucket with flip-over forks and a crane hook, this versatile machine proved to be another huge seller for JCB. The 3CX and its Sitemaster version were powered by a 70-horsepower Perkins engine, which was capable of producing 85 horsepower with the torque converter option. Another option was four-wheel drive. *Keith Haddock*

JCB 214e Series 4. In 1991, JCB introduced the world's first full-sized loader-backhoe with four-wheel drive, four-wheel steer, and boasting four large equal-sized wheels. This concept was applied the following year to the two largest sizes, the 215S and 217S, in a new line of loader-backhoes targeted at North America. The 200 Series has since been expanded to 15 different models covering two-wheel- and four-wheel-drive, four-wheel-steer, and tool carrier versions. The power ranges from 65 to 100 horsepower, and digging depths range from 12 to 21.5 feet. The 214e Series 4 of 2002 is a two-wheel-drive model with a 14-foot, 4-inch digging depth. It focuses on ease of operation with lower noise level, sloping hood, improved seat, and low-effort levers. *JCB Sales, Ltd.*

Komatsu WB150 AWS. Komatsu introduced loader-backhoes to the North American market in 1999 with the 86-horsepower WB140-2, and the 98-horsepower WB150-2. Capable of digging down to 14 feet, 7 inches and 15 feet, 7 inches with standard arm, both models can dig 4 feet deeper when equipped with an extendible arm. Komatsu's first all-wheel-steer loader-backhoe, the WB150 AWS version, was added in 2001. This heavy-duty machine boasts four big equal-sized driving wheels for high performance in loader work. With the same engine as the standard-drive version, the WB150 AWS has a digging depth of 15 feet, 3 inches, or 18 feet, 1 inch with extendible arm. A special gear-selection feature allows the operator to select either automatic or manual transmission modes with a touch of a button. *Komatsu America International*

Massey-Harris-Ferguson Work Bull 185. In 1951, long-established Canadian company Massey-Harris acquired the tractor-building business of Harry Ferguson. The resulting company took the name of Massey-Harris-Ferguson, Inc. Under this name, the company marketed a loader-backhoe known as the M-H-F Work Bull, which was based on a Massey-Harris tractor and utilized a Davis Model 185 backhoe made by Mid-Western Industries, Inc. This hoe had a digging depth of 13 feet, and could be easily detached to allow the tractor to be used by itself as a loader. In 1957, Mid-Western was purchased by M-H-F and the company changed its name to Massey-Ferguson, Ltd. (M-F). This was the company's first production base for construction equipment. *Keith Haddock collection*

Massey-Ferguson 250/252. In 1959, M-F launched a new loader-backhoe combination based on the 37-horsepower Massey-Ferguson 702 tractor with Model 710 backhoe and 702 loader. It was one of the first to feature a sliding king post enabling flush digging alongside walls and fences. Building on this successful model, the company broadened its loader-backhoe range to seven models by the end of the 1960s. These included the loader-backhoe combination Model 250/252, based on the Massey-Ferguson 3303 tractor. This model offered digging depths down to 13 feet, 6 inches and a 60-horsepower engine. Germany's IBH group owned M-F from 1980 until the group's failure in 1983. The company re-established as MF Industrial, Ltd. but was bought by Varity Corporation in 1986. *Terex Corporation*

Massey-Ferguson MF60H. After the Varity Corporation bought MF Industrial, Ltd. in 1986, the former Massey-Ferguson loader-backhoe range was continued and upgraded. The 74-horsepower Perkins-powered MF60H with a 16-foot digging depth was typical of the machines of this era. Options on this machine included a hydraulically extended backhoe arm and four-wheel-drive transmission for increased traction in loader operations. In 1992, new management took control of MF Industrial and renamed it Fermec International, Ltd. The Fermec brand of loader-backhoes was distributed worldwide through former Massey-Ferguson outlets. From 1994, Kobelco America, Inc. sold Fermec machines under the TLK brand name in the United States. In 2001, Fermec was acquired by Terex Corporation. *Terex Corporation*

New Holland LB115.B. Ford New Holland, Inc. was established in 1986 when Ford Motor Company acquired agricultural equipment builder New Holland. Under the new Ford New Holland banner, the former Ford loader-backhoe line progressed through B, C, D, and E Series upgrades. In 1991, Ford New Holland was acquired by Italy's Fiat group, which subsequently acquired Case Corporation in 1999. The E Series loader-backhoes from the former Ford New Holland line were discontinued in 2001 in favor of New Holland's LB Series machines. The current line consists of four basic models from the 85-horsepower LB75B, to the big four-wheel-drive and four-wheel-steer LB115B rated at 106 flywheel-horsepower. Maximum digging depths range from 14.5 feet to 20 feet when using an extendible arm. *New Holland Construction*

Sherman Power Digger. In 1955, Sherman Products, Inc. of Royal Oak, Michigan, began marketing a loader-backhoe suitable for mounting on Ford industrial tractors. With a 10-foot digging depth, the hoe was equipped with hydraulically operated stabilizers, and featured an unusual hoist arrangement. As can be seen from the picture, the boom hoist cylinder and the bucket crowd cylinder work together or independently to produce the required digging action. Jointly designed and manufactured by Sherman Products, Inc. and the Wain-Roy Corporation, the machines were sold through the Ford tractor dealership network. In 1961, Ford Motor Company purchased Sherman Products, Inc. *Keith Haddock*

Terex TX760. The familiar name Terex first appeared on a loader-backhoe in 2001 after Terex Corporation purchased Fermec of Manchester, England. The deal included rights to the former Fermec and Massey-Ferguson loader-backhoes, and the Manchester plant. The Terex TX760 is a direct descendent of the former Fermec 760 loader-backhoe. It has a 77-horsepower engine, four-wheel drive capability, and torque converter. Its multi-function clamshell-type loader bucket holds 1.3 cubic yards and its maximum backhoe digging depth is 14 feet, 7 inches. With an optional extending dipper arm, its digging depth reaches 19 feet. *Keith Haddock collection*

113

Volvo BL70. After a development period lasting more than three years, Volvo unveiled its first loader-backhoes at the Conexpo 2002 equipment show in Las Vegas. Designed in-house by an international team, the new loaders are built in Poland at the same plant where Volvo makes its buses. Two models are offered, the center-pivot BL70 for the North American market, and the BL71 with sliding backhoe pivot for the European market. Both machines carry a Volvo diesel rated at 94 horsepower, and offer maximum digging depths of 14 feet. The base of the backhoe boom is a steel casting, which allows a slim boom profile to improve operator visibility. *Volvo Construction Equipment*

Whitlock Dinkum Digger. Whitlock Brothers, Ltd. of Great Yeldham, Essex, England, claim to have built the world's first tractor-mounted loader-backhoe. Whitlock designed and built hydraulic backhoe and loader attachments and mounted them on a 52-horsepower Fordson Major tractor in 1952. The Dinkum Digger was later sold as an integrated unit, and a new class of earthmovers was born. The maximum digging depth for the backhoe was 10 feet. This machine became very popular in its home country during the 1950s, and Whitlock's backhoes and loaders could be mounted on several different brands of tractors. It was also available without a loader, as the picture shows. *Keith Haddock*

Whitlock 405. During the 1960s, Whitlock broadened its loader-backhoe line to include a full range of sizes and types, most of which were built around Fordson power units. The 405, released in 1964, offered a 360-degree swing capability from its tower-mounted backhoe. But backhoe-digging depth was restricted to 9 feet, and even though the machine boasted long swing-out stabilizers, stability was a problem during travel. In 1972, hydraulic excavator builder Hy-Mac, Ltd. acquired Whitlock. The loader-backhoes continued under the Hy-Mac brand name until they were purchased by Germany's IBH group in 1979. After IBH failed in 1983, the former Whitlock loader-backhoes survived under the Hy-Mac brand, and the company underwent four more changes of ownership before the Hy-Mac products finally ceased in 1993. *Keith Haddock collection*

CHAPTER 7

SCRAPERS

Scraper is the rather nondescript name given to the spectacular digging and hauling machine that can gouge into the earth, collect a huge load in its cavernous bowl, and speed to the fill at up to 40 miles per hour. Scrapers are available in a wide range of types and sizes, and can be either self-propelled or pulled behind a wheeled or crawler tractor. The latter type, known as a towed or pull-type, is used less often today; it has been almost superseded by self-propelled types and other varieties of earthmoving equipment capable of performing similar tasks.

The history of the scraper goes far back to the time when man first used animals to undertake earthmoving tasks. Horses and mules pulled the original scrapers, and their earliest form consisted of a small scoop with handles that were maneuvered by a man walking behind it. By the 1870s, pull-type scrapers began to

Allis-Chalmers TS-300. The LaPlant-Choate Manufacturing Company, Inc. was established in 1911 as a manufacturer of stump-pulling and house-moving equipment. It also built scrapers and other tractor attachments for Caterpillar in the early 1930s, and supplied Caterpillar with a scraper to pull behind its first wheel tractor, the DW-10 in 1940. LaPlant-Choate developed its own motor scraper line beginning in 1947 with the 18-cubic-yard-heaped-capacity TS-300, powered with a 225-horsepower Buda engine. As with other motor scrapers of that era, the TS-300 was operated by cables from winches on the tractor unit. The smaller TS-200 followed in 1950. Allis-Chalmers Manufacturing Company acquired LaPlant-Choate in 1952, and for a two-year period continued producing the TS-200 and TS-300 as Allis-Chalmers products. *Keith Haddock collection*

appear with wheels. An early inventor was Abijah McCall, a blacksmith and earthmover of Fresno, California, who, with his partner F. Dusy invented an improved pull-type scraper. With a pair of wheels at the front, this device eventually became known as the Fresno, after the area where it originated. The name "Fresno" became widely used to refer to many types of drag and wheeled horse-drawn scrapers.

As power of wheeled and crawler tractors increased in the early part of the twentieth century, several varieties of pull-type scrapers were developed by many manufacturers, few of whom survive today. A popular type was known as the rotary scraper. It consisted of a cylindrical bowl that was designed to rotate into the carry position after collecting its load. An operator-controlled release mechanism caused the bowl to dump its load by rotating a full 360 degrees and returning to the carry position.

Invention of the modern scraper is credited to Robert Gilmour LeTourneau, who had established his own earthmoving business in 1920. He took the primitive contraptions of the day and developed them into efficient earthmoving machines. Shortage of equipment in 1922 led LeTourneau to start building scrapers for his own use. After experimenting with a drag scraper, he built a pull-type on wheels. Christened the "Gondola," it had a capacity of 6 cubic yards. Even at this early stage, the Gondola was built using brazed metal construction instead of rivets, and the scraper motions were powered by electric motors using rack-and-pinion drive. For LeTourneau, the rack-and-pinion drive would always be the chief method of transmitting power on his scrapers and other equipment, right up to his death in 1969.

After developing the multiple bucket principle on another self-propelled scraper called the Mountain Mover in 1923, LeTourneau invented the world's first self-propelled scraper. However, this invention turned out to be less successful. It was a long, cumbersome rig mounted on four large steel wheels. Electrically controlled from a DC generator driven by a gasoline engine, it had four telescoping buckets and a fixed bucket at the front, which incorporated the cutting edge. The fact that this scraper had a top speed of only 1 mile-per-hour probably contributed to its failure.

Allis-Chalmers TS-360. After LaPlant-Choate became part of the Allis-Chalmers organization in 1952, the parent company soon developed new models from the LaPlant-Choate designs. The three-model line introduced in the period spanning from 1954 to 1957 consisted of TS-160, TS-260, and TS-360, with respective heaped capacities of 9.5, 14, and 20 cubic yards. Still retaining its cable-operated scraper, the TS-360 had an operating weight of 49,000 pounds and was powered by an Allis-Chalmers 280-horsepower diesel engine. Hydraulic steering by two double-acting cylinders was controlled by a single valve connected with a direct linkage to the half-moon-shaped steering wheel. *Keith Haddock*

Allis-Chalmers TS-260E. This was Allis-Chalmers' contribution to the 23-cubic-yard elevating scraper market. It was introduced in 1965 as an elevating version of the existing 260, which had been on the market since 1956. The Hancock Manufacturing Company of Lubbock, Texas, made the hydrostatically driven elevating scraper, and the entire outfit tipped the scales at 58,000 pounds. In 1968, the 260E Series A replaced the original version. The new machine was restyled, its weight beefed up to 59,300 pounds, and given a new Allis-Chalmers engine of 300 flywheel-horsepower. This time the elevating scraper was designed and built by Allis-Chalmers. The 260E Series A scraper became the Allis-Chalmers 261-B in 1973, with a bigger engine at 325 flywheel-horsepower. This machine then continued as the Fiat-Allis 261-B after 1974. *Keith Haddock*

After the failure of the first self-propelled scraper, LeTourneau developed a succession of pull-type scrapers of various sizes and designs. In 1928 he pioneered the cable-control unit, where the motions of the scraper were controlled from a double-drum winch mounted on the tractor. This relatively small and inexpensive unit was actually one of the most significant breakthroughs in earthmoving equipment. R.G. LeTourneau, Inc. was incorporated in 1929 as a manufacturer and earthmoving contractor, but the company withdrew from the earthmoving business soon after 1933 in order to concentrate on manufacturing.

With the advent of larger rubber tires, LeTourneau brought out the first high-speed self-propelled scraper in 1938, the Model A Tournapull. The basic configuration of this scraper became the standard of the industry. Its single-axle prime mover and unique hitch allow the two-wheel tractor to swing more than 90 degrees in each direction. Fitted with the Caterpillar D17000 engine, developing 160 horsepower at 950 rpm, the Model A could be hitched to a choice of Carryalls up to a 42-cubic-yard heaped capacity. The scraper hit its heyday during World War II when large numbers were employed by the Allied armed forces. R.G. LeTourneau, Inc., supplied over 10,000 pull-type and over 2,000 self-propelled scrapers during the war years.

Following the success of LeTourneau's scrapers and spurred on by World War II, several other manufacturers joined the market. Along with LeTourneau, Euclid was the other company to pioneer the high-speed earthmoving capabilities of self-propelled scrapers. Euclid's prototype scraper, known as the 1SH, was in the field as early as 1938 and was the forerunner of Euclid's extensive scraper line, which developed over the next three decades. This included scrapers with two- or four-wheel prime movers and twin-powered scrapers with engines at front and rear, the first of which appeared in 1949. In 1957, Euclid launched what would become one of the most famous large scrapers of all time, the twin-powered TS-24 with a 24-cubic-yard struck capacity. It is still available today as the Terex TS-24D.

Caterpillar's first wheel tractor, the DW-10, introduced in 1941, was designed to pull a scraper of 10-cubic-yard capacity. The forerunner of the present-day Caterpillar motor scraper made its debut in 1951. The DW-21 featured Caterpillar's first two-wheel tractor unit coupled to a cable-operated scraper of 18-cubic-yard heaped capacity. In 1960, Caterpillar introduced the first of its 600 Series motor scrapers, the Model 619 of 18-cubic-yard heaped capacity. By 1962, a full line of 600 Series scrapers was available with capacities up to the 54-cubic-yard 666. This twin-engined scraper

Allis-Chalmers 562. In 1962, Allis-Chalmers began to expand its motor scraper line in a big way. It launched two of the largest scrapers it ever made, the Models TS-460 and 562 of 32 and 40 cubic yards of heaped capacity. The TS-460 topped out the Allis-Chalmers single-engine motor scraper line. The 562 was a twin-engined giant with engines in the front and rear that totaled 730 flywheel-horsepower, and weighing 51 tons. It featured a modular concept so that the scraper could be operated with or without the rear engine module. The Model 562 received an upgrade in 1965, with bowl capacity increased to 44 cubic yards heaped and weight increased to 61 tons, but the 562 was discontinued the following year. *Keith Haddock collection*

with a four-wheel tractor had a combined power rating of 980 horsepower. It was up-rated to the 666B in 1969 and lasted in Caterpillar's line until 1978. The 666 is still the largest scraper ever built by Caterpillar.

During the loading part of its cycle, a self-propelled scraper usually obtains assistance from a bulldozer pushing behind. There are, however, some true self-loading scrapers that are able to efficiently load themselves. These are the elevating and auger types. The elevating scraper, sometimes known as a "paddle wheel" scraper, utilizes a set of powered elevator flights to chop the material and hoist it into the bowl. The Hancock Manufacturing Company, founded in 1947 in Lubbock, Texas, was one of the first companies to promote and build elevating scrapers. The first models were pull-types with the elevator driven by a series of shafts from the tractor's power take-off (PTO). By the mid-1950s, Hancock elevating scrapers were operating with John Deere wheel tractors as integral units under a joint arrangement between the two companies. Hancock went on to build elevating scrapers for several other scraper manufacturers, including Wabco, Michigan, Euclid, and M-R-S. Another pioneer of the elevating scraper was Johnson Manufacturing Company from the same town as Hancock. This company introduced two elevating scraper models of 5 and 8 cubic yards in 1957, and in an agreement with Caterpillar, commenced building the elevating scraper for the J619 in 1964.

Bucyrus-Erie S112. This company, most famous for its excavators, broke into the tractor equipment business in 1936. At that time, Bucyrus-Erie had just made a deal with International Harvester to supply tractor equipment for use exclusively with International's tractors. The first scrapers were four-wheel types operated by a single cable from a winch on the tractor, but the linkage arrangement proved too complicated from a maintenance standpoint. The successful S Series soon followed in sizes ranging from the 5-cubic-yard (heaped) S-46 to the 17-cubic-yard (heaped) S-152. The S-112, at 12.5 cubic yards of heaped capacity, like all the other S Series models, was operated from a two-drum winch, but the bowl was lifted from the rear instead of the more usual front lift arrangement. In 1948, the S Series scrapers were upgraded with improved features. *Keith Haddock*

117

Bucyrus-Erie B170A. In 1948, Bucyrus-Erie released the first of its B Series pull-type scrapers, the 27.5-cubic-yard B-250, featuring the more conventional front-lifting bowl. This was subsequently joined by the 10-cubic-yard B-91, the 14-cubic-yard B-113, and the 19-cubic-yard B-170, which replaced the former S Series. In 1952, the B170 was upgraded to the larger B-170A at 21 cubic yards of heaped capacity. The B Series scrapers saw Bucyrus-Erie through to the end of its association with tractor equipment in 1953 when International announced it was about to follow Caterpillar's example, and began building its own tractor equipment. *Keith Haddock*

The other type of self-loading scraper, offering an alternative to elevating scrapers, is the auger type developed by Wotco in the mid-1970s. Caterpillar adopted the principle by 1984, and today offers auger versions of all its non-elevating scrapers above the 20-cubic-yard class, including single- and twin-powered machines. Hydraulically driven augers are mounted vertically in the center of the bowl. When the material arrives in the bowl during loading, the augers move it upwards, filling the bowl to its heaped capacity. Thus, the full tractive power of the scraper wheels is applied to cutting the material and drawing it over the cutting edge, and not wasted in raising the material in the bowl.

Still another way to cut costs in certain scraper applications is to eliminate a push dozer with use of the "Push-pull" or "Helpmate" system promoted by Caterpillar and Terex. In this system, each scraper is equipped with a large tow hook as part of its rear push-block assembly, and another push block and a power-operated bail at the front. Working in pairs during the loading part of the cycle, two scrapers are hooked together. The bail of the rear scraper is dropped over the rear hook of the leading scraper. The leading scraper is loaded first, with the rear scraper acting as a pusher. Then the leading scraper assists the rear scraper to collect its load. The scrapers then unhook and operate independently on the haul, dump, and return parts of the cycle.

No history of the scraper could be complete without mention of the monster scrapers known as Electric Diggers, built by R.G. LeTourneau, Inc. in the 1960s. Although a large number of types and sizes were built, including the largest scraper ever built, the machines

Caterpillar 70. In 1946, Caterpillar commenced building its own pull-type scrapers. The first two were the No. 70 and No. 80, with heaped capacities of 13 and 20 cubic yards. They were designed to be hauled by the D7 and D8 tractors. Other models soon followed until Caterpillar had a scraper designed specifically for each of its tractor sizes. From the hydraulically operated No. 40 at 4.5 cubic yards of heaped capacity for the D4 introduced in 1949, to the big 27-cubic-yard heaped capacity No. 90 first appearing in 1951, each tractor had a specialized scraper. *Keith Haddock*

were never a real commercial success. Beginning in 1958, five years after LeTourneau sold his earthmoving equipment business to Westinghouse Air Brake Company, LeTourneau produced an array of scrapers incorporating the familiar LeTourneau rack-and-pinion drives. Most of these machines were built in very limited numbers, and most never progressed beyond the prototype stage. The largest scraper of all time was the LT-360 Electric Digger with three bowls, making a combined capacity of 216 cubic yards. It moved on eight powered wheels driven by eight diesel engines of 635 horsepower each!

As the major tractor and scraper manufactures phased out manufacture of the pull-type scrapers, other manufacturers like Rome Industries took over the designs of the tractor manufacturers. Also joining the earthmover-scraper business were firms traditionally making light-duty scrapers, mainly used in agricultural applications. Today there are several successful pull-type scraper manufacturers, such as Reynolds and Miskin, who sell scrapers designed for the high-horsepower four-wheel-drive farm tractors, but recently Caterpillar's high-speed rubber-tracked Challenger tractors have made an ideal prime mover for hydraulically operated pull scrapers.

Caterpillar DW-10. Built in 1941, the DW-10 was the first self-propelled or motor scraper from Caterpillar. It did not follow the two-wheel LeTourneau concept. Instead, Caterpillar opted for a four-wheel tractor outfitted with a Caterpillar 100-horsepower diesel engine, which pulled a scraper of 10 cubic yards of heaped capacity and was manufactured by LaPlante-Choate. From 1947, Caterpillar offered its own No. 10 scraper of 11 cubic yards of heaped capacity to partner the DW-10 tractor. This Caterpillar combination tipped the scales at 35,200 pounds. The picture shows one of the early DW-10s with the LaPlant-Choate scraper. *Keith Haddock*

Caterpillar 463. In 1955, Caterpillar began to replace its first Series pull-type scrapers with the modernized Models 435, 463, and 491, ranging in heaped capacity from 17 to 35 cubic yards. These were designed to match the D7, D8, and D9 tractors. For the D6, the No. 60 which first came out in 1947, remained in production. Because the No. 60 proved so perfect for use in smaller applications, it persisted in the Caterpillar line until 1972. The 463, with heaped capacity of 26 cubic yards, was a common sight behind a D8 tractor. The one in the picture, pulled by a D8, is receiving a boost from an International TD-24 tractor as well. Caterpillar ceased production of all its pull-type scrapers from 1971 to 1973. *Keith Haddock*

Caterpillar DW-20. After 10 years of success with its small DW-10, Caterpillar launched two larger scrapers in 1951. These were the DW-20 with No. 20 scraper, and the DW-21 with No. 21 scraper. Both scrapers were cable-operated and rated at 20 cubic yards of heaped capacity, and both tractors came equipped with Caterpillar engines of 225 flywheel-horsepower. The DW-20 was a four-wheel tractor, and the DW-21 was Caterpillar's first two-wheel prime mover. The DW-20, as the Series E, was offered with the 1955 No. 456 scraper of 25-yard heaped capacity, and as the Series G, was offered with the 1958 No. 482 scraper of 34-yard heaped capacity. The DW Series scrapers remained in production until 1960, when Caterpillar's 600 Series motor scrapers replaced them. *Keith Haddock*

Caterpillar J619. When Caterpillar presented the first version of its 619 tractor matched with the No. 442 scraper of 18-cubic-yard heaped capacity in 1960, a completely new line of scrapers known as the 600 Series was launched. By 1961, the 619 was sold as an integral tractor/scraper unit with 250 flywheel-horsepower and an operating weight of 48,300 pounds. Caterpillar offered elevating scrapers starting in 1964 with the J619, based on 20-cubic-yard elevating scraper built by Johnson Manufacturing Company. Caterpillar expanded its elevating line to 11-, 16-, 22-, and 32-cubic-yard sizes through the 1970s. Caterpillar's largest, most powerful elevator was the 34-cubic-yard twin-powered 639D, which had a production run from 1979 to 1984. *Keith Haddock collection*

Caterpillar 631D. One of the most popular Caterpillar scrapers is the 631 Series. First appearing as the Series A in 1960, the 631 has been refined and updated through the 631B in 1962, the 631C in 1969, the 631D in 1975, the 631E in 1985, and the current 631G in 2001. With the exception of the 631A at 28-cubic-yards heaped capacity, all the other scrapers have been rated with 30- to 31-yard heaped capacities. The 631D shown in the picture, rated at 31-cubic-yards heaped capacity, is equipped with a Caterpillar 3408 diesel of 450 flywheel-horsepower, and a listed operating weight of 86,500 pounds. It could achieve a top speed of 30 miles per hour. A four-wheel version of the same scraper, the 630, was launched at the same time as the 631, but it did not survive beyond the expiration of the B Series in 1969. *Keith Haddock*

Caterpillar 666. After the introduction of Caterpillar's 600 Series scrapers in 1960, further models were introduced in larger sizes. By 1962, a full line of 600 Series scrapers was available with capacities ranging up to 54 heaped cubic yards in the Model 666. The 666 twin-engined scraper with a four-wheel tractor unit boasted 785 flywheel-horsepower from its engines mounted in the front and rear. These ratings were increased to 950 flywheel-horsepower in the revamped 666B when it came out in 1969. This unit weighed in at 142,800 pounds empty. Caterpillar decided to discontinue this size scraper in 1978, but the 666 still remains as the largest scraper ever built by the company. *David Maginnis*

Caterpillar 651E. Another big scraper from Caterpillar is the 651. First available in 1962 as a 44-cubic-yard-heaped-capacity unit, the single-engined 651, and its twin-engined brother, the 657, have undergone upgrades through the B Series in 1969 and E Series in 1983. These scraper units incorporate Caterpillar's largest single-axle prime movers. The 651E is furnished with the Caterpillar 3412E turbocharged diesel engine and offers a variable horsepower output. In first and second gears, 550 flywheel-horsepower is produced, while in gears three through eight, power is boosted to 605 flywheel-horsepower. The 651 tips the scales at 132,800 pounds empty. *Keith Haddock*

Caterpillar 611. Big is not always better. Caterpillar's smallest standard scraper, the 611, was introduced as recently as 1998. Rated at 15 cubic yards of heaped capacity, this powerful little unit puts out 265 flywheel-horsepower. The 611 joins Caterpillar's other small scraper, the elevating-type 613C, rated at 175 flywheel-horsepower and 11-heaped-cubic-yard capacity. As far back as the early 1980s, a non-elevating 13.5-cubic-yard scraper was available from Rome Industries to replace the elevating scraper on the 613, but that outfit was not officially named the 611. The Caterpillar D6-size crawler tractor makes an ideal match as a pusher for the 611 scraper. *Keith Haddock*

Clark 290M. After the U.S. Army evaluated several prototype scrapers in 1961, it invited several scraper manufacturers, including Clark Equipment Company, to bid on contracts to supply four-wheel-drive articulated rubber-tired tractors, and matching dozer blades and scrapers. With its former experience of large four-wheel-drive wheel dozers, Clark submitted its 290M tractor and won one of the orders. The four-wheel-drive articulated tractor was attached to the fully hydraulic Euclid 58SH scraper, rated at 25 cubic yards heaped. Power came from a Cummins engine rated at 350 flywheel-horsepower, and the complete outfit with dozer blade and Euclid scraper weighed 86,000 pounds. Many of these scrapers were built in the 1960s and 1970s, and many are still used today by the military. Others became government surplus and are still employed by contractors and local municipalities. *Keith Haddock*

Caterpillar 631G. The latest scraper development to boost Caterpillar's scraper fleet was the G Series, launched in 2001. The new scrapers retain all the successful Caterpillar features found in the former models, such as cushion hitch to dampen haul road bounce, a low-profile scraper design, and an electronic monitoring system. And, as with the previous models in this size of Caterpillar scrapers, the 637G offers push-pull or auger options. New features on the G Series center around the operator's cab and controls. All the scraper movements, bowl, apron, and ejector, are now controlled by a single-joystick lever. With push buttons on its handle, the same lever also controls transmission hold, cushion hitch on/off, and bail up/down for push-pull option, where fitted. A swivel seat, increased leg room, and a self-contained air compressor for the air-suspended seat tops the list of operator comfort enhancements. The 31-cubic-yard (heaped capacity) 631G has a 450-flywheel-horsepower engine up front. *Keith Haddock*

Curtiss-Wright CW-27. This name first appeared on scrapers in 1958 after Curtiss-Wright Corporation of South Bend, Indiana, acquired the Wooldridge Manufacturing Company of Sunnyvale, California. Wooldridge had developed a range of self-propelled scrapers in the mid-1940s, and at the time of the takeover, the scraper line consisted of five models with heaped capacities ranging up to 36 cubic yards. Curtiss-Wright continued to market the scrapers as the CW Series. The largest became the CW-226 with a GM engine rated at 360 horsepower. The CW27 in the picture, an update of the former Wooldridge Cobrette, could load 10 heaped cubic yards, and its GM engine developed 143 horsepower. In the early 1960s, Curtiss-Wright phased out its earthmoving equipment to focus on other products. *Thomas Berry*

121

Deere 840. John Deere's entire involvement with scrapers has been with the elevating type. It started in 1957, when a prototype John Deere 820 wheel tractor was tested with a four-wheel Hancock 8-cubic-yard elevating scraper. In 1959, John Deere introduced the 840 four-wheel tractor close-coupled to the 7E2 elevating scraper. Developed jointly by Deere and Hancock, this 7.5-cubic-yard elevating scraper was driven from the tractor power takeoff through shafts incorporating universal joints. The Deere tractors made for scraper use differed from their agricultural counterparts in that the operator's position was moved from midship to the left side. Records show that the 840 tractor was short-lived, and it was discontinued by 1961. *Keith Haddock*

Euclid 1SH. Euclid's scraper beginnings were with the rotary and pull-types of the 1920s. Long after these had been discontinued, the Euclid Road Machinery Company built a prototype self-propelled scraper designated the 1SH coupled to a 4FDT four-wheel tractor. This 12-cubic-yard hydraulically operated unit, shown under test in 1938, was the forerunner of Euclid's extensive scraper line that was developed over the next three decades. Although only one of this model was built, Euclid experimented with several self-propelled scrapers of both the overhung (two-wheel tractor) and four-wheel tractor types over the next few years. These included the 12-cubic-yard 2SH in 1939, the twin-bowl design 3SH the same year, and Euclid's first overhung tractor coupled to a 10-cubic-yard scraper in 1940. *Historical Construction Equipment Association*

Deere 762B. After a short gap in scraper production, John Deere released its 8-cubic-yard Model 5010 scraper in 1962 with 127 flywheel-horsepower. Then came the 9.25-cubic-yard Model 760 in 1965. These two models looked a lot like the former 840 except the scraper elevator was driven hydraulically. The 15-cubic-yard 860, announced at the 1969 Conexpo equipment show in Chicago was Deere's first to utilize a single-axle prime mover. By the time the 1975 Conexpo came around, John Deere announced the replacement of the 760A scraper with the model 762, which also featured a single-axle prime mover. In 1980, the 16-cubic-yard 862 replaced the Model 860 as the largest scraper in the John Deere line. Today, John Deere offers the 762B and 862B of 11- and 16-cubic-yards capacity. *Keith Haddock*

Euclid 51FDT-15SH. In the late 1940s, Euclid started work on twin-power scrapers to meet the high production requirements of the great earthmoving projects following World War II. The first unit boasting two engines was actually an 18-cubic-yard bottom-dump hauler that was introduced in 1948 using the three-axle, four-wheel tractor configuration. The first twin scraper followed in 1949, consisting of a 13SH scraper of 16 cubic yard capacity connected to a 51FDT tractor. The scraper was initially rated at 16-cubic-yards of struck capacity, but it was later up-rated to 18 yards. Both tractor and scraper utilized GM 6-71 engines, each rated at 190 horsepower, and Allison Torqmatic transmissions. This Allison drive unit, combining a torque converter and power-shift transmission, automatically adjusted for variations in load, and made the Euclid twin-power concept possible. *Keith Haddock collection*

Euclid TS-18. Euclid announced the next trio of new overhung scrapers in 1954. One of these was the TS-18, the company's first twin-powered overhung scraper. Basically an S-18 with an extra engine at the rear, this 24-yard-heaped-capacity workhorse was powered by a pair of GM 6-71 engines of 218 gross-horsepower. Euclid scrapers were now fully hydraulic, as opposed to the outmoded cable operation. The TS-18 was the forerunner of greater things to come in the way of twin and multiple-drive scrapers of the 1960s. In 1953, Euclid became a division of General Motors Corporation, and strong backing by the new parent company enabled the Euclid Division to rapidly develop each of its earthmoving machines. *Keith Haddock collection*

Euclid S-7. In 1954, Euclid announced three models of the overhung type of scraper (two-wheel tractor). These were the S-7 with 9-cubic-yard heaped capacity, and the S-18 and TS-18 of 25-cubic-yard heaped capacity. The latter model is a twin-power unit. (The Euclid model designation number indicated the scraper capacity in struck cubic yards.) These scrapers were designed with modern round-cornered engine hood and radiator, features that would endear Euclid to the market for decades. The neat hydraulic steering and scraper linkage arrangement would also become a Euclid tradition in future models. The small S-7 scraper was a great success and remained in production, with upgrades, until 1970. Its engine was the GM 4-71 rated at 143 horsepower, and the unit weighed 47,600 pounds. *Keith Haddock*

Euclid TS-24. After the TS-18 of 1954, Euclid developed larger overhung scrapers, including the 16-cubic-yard-heaped-capacity S-12 in 1955, and the TS-18's replacement, the TS-24 in 1957. The TS-24 turned out to be the most famous Euclid—and later, Terex—scraper of all time. The twin-engined, 32-cubic-yard-heaped capacity scraper was initially powered by a GM 6-110 engine of 300 gross-horsepower in front, and a GM 6-71 engine of 218 gross-horsepower in the rear. The TS-24 survived the birth of Terex in 1968, and underwent numerous upgrades and refinements. The last version was the TS-24D, which was discontinued in 2002. *Keith Haddock collection*

Euclid SS-24. Euclid is noted for its big four-wheel tractors designed to pull scrapers, bottom-dumping earth wagons, or coal trailers.
The four-wheel tractors give greater stability on long hauls and allow the scraper to achieve higher speeds than its single-axle prime mover counterpart. A typical example was the SS-24, introduced along with the TS-24 in 1957. Rated at 32-cubic-yard heaped capacity, it offered a choice of Cummins or GM engines. Like its sister, the TS-24, the SS-24 received several upgrades through its life. The last upgrade took place in 1966; production of this model ceased in 1968. *Keith Haddock collection*

Euclid TTSS-40. The huge 40-cubic-yard TSS-40, with four-wheel tractor and powered by two GM engines developing 810 gross-horsepower, came on the scene in 1963. This 52-cubic-yard-heaped-capacity monster could achieve a top speed of 37 miles per hour. It was basically a double-engined version of the Euclid SS-40 scraper of the same capacity, which was released two years earlier. The TSS-40 was a special-order model built for famous earthmoving contractor Western Contracting Corporation, that purchased four of these units. Not content with these largest scrapers available at the time, Western ordered a special fleet of five Euclid TTSS-40 scrapers in 1964. On these, three 16V-71 engines provided 1,740 gross-horsepower or 1,690 flywheel-horsepower, and the two bowls could carry a whopping 104 cubic yards when heaped. These were the largest scrapers ever built by Euclid. *Western Contracting Corporation*

Euclid S7 Hancock Elevating Scraper. Euclid entered the elevating scraper market in 1964, by teaming up the S-7 tractor with the 12-cubic-yard Model 12E-2 elevating scraper made by Hancock Manufacturing Company. This self-loading outfit was endowed with two separate power units. The front engine of 148 horsepower drove the tractor and a hydraulic system to power the scraper bowl and ejector. The rear engine powered the scraper-loading elevator through a mechanical drive. This combination machine was also known as the S-12E and continued into the Terex era until replaced by the single-engined Terex S-11E with hydraulic elevator drive. (In 1968, General Motor's earthmoving products became known by the name Terex following a Justice Department ruling that GM must discontinue manufacturing off-highway trucks in the United States for a period of four years and divest itself of the Euclid name.) *Keith Haddock collection*

Fiat-Allis 261-B. This scraper began life as the Allis-Chalmers 261-B in 1973. It was an elevating version of the conventional scraper 260-B released at the same time. Both were powered by an Allis-Chalmers engine of 325 flywheel-horsepower, and could dig and haul 21 to 23 cubic yards of heaped material. Following the purchase of Allis-Chalmers by Fiat S.p.A. of Italy in 1974, these machines took the Fiat-Allis name and retained the same model numbers. They were joined by the 262-B twin-engined conventional scraper and the 263-B twin-engined elevating scraper, all of the same capacity and utilizing the same front engines. The rear engine on the twin-powered versions provided 171 flywheel-horsepower. Another elevating scraper, the smaller 15-cubic-yard Model 161, was introduced in 1978. Fiat-Allis phased out its 200 Series scrapers after 1988, but the small 161 held on for a few more years. *Keith Haddock*

Hancock 292. As noted elsewhere in this chapter, the Hancock Manufacturing Company of Lubbock, Texas, made a name for itself in the elevating scraper field. The company provided elevating scrapers matched to several wheeled prime movers including John Deere, Wabco, M-R-S, Oliver, and Ford. Then in 1964, Hancock introduced a scraper with its own prime mover, the Model 282. This elevating scraper was available with Detroit or Oliver-Waukesha engines in the 95- to 115-flywheel-horsepower range. The scraper could heap 9 cubic yards with assistance from its mechanically driven elevator flights. The 10-cubic-yard 292 replaced the 282 with the larger Detroit 4-71N engine of 148 horsepower, and hydraulically driven elevator. Hancock Manufacturing became a division of Clark Equipment Company in 1966, but Clark continued to market scrapers under the Hancock name until about 1972. *Keith Haddock*

Heil OC-9. The Heil Company of Milwaukee, Wisconsin, was established in 1901 as the Heil Railjoint Company. A pioneer of electric welding, Heil began building truck bodies, hydraulic hoists, and later, tractor attachments such as bulldozer blades. In the early 1940s, Heil offered a line of four-wheel pull-type scrapers, the C-6, C-8, C-10, and C-15, the numbers signifying their heaped-cubic-yard capacities. In 1948, the line had been upgraded to the OC Series from the OC-6 to the OC-25 with heaped capacities ranging from 6 to 25 cubic yards. The OC-9 in the picture is being hauled by a Caterpillar D7 tractor at a meeting of the Historical Construction Equipment Association in Bowling Green, Ohio. Its empty weight is 13,500 pounds. *Keith Haddock*

Heil 2T55. Heil introduced a self-propelled scraper in 1947 featuring a two-wheeled tractor powered by a 200-horsepower Cummins engine. Known as the Model 2H700, the tractor could pull a bottom-dumping wagon of 18 cubic yards, or a 16.5-cubic-yard-heaped-capacity scraper. This machine developed into the Models 2T-55 and 2T-75 with heaped capacities of 13 and 18 cubic yards. In 1953, International Harvester purchased the patents, designs, and manufacturing rights of these two models from the Heil Company. These models formed the basis on which International developed its line of self-propelled scrapers. *Richard Yaremko*

International 2T55. International Harvester's scrapers originated in 1953 when it acquired the pull-type scraper line formerly built by Bucyrus-Erie Company, and two models of self-propelled scrapers from the Heil Company of Milwaukee, Wisconsin. Beginning in 1947, Heil introduced its two-wheeled tractor, self-propelled scrapers with the Model 2H700. When International took over the scrapers, they became known as the 2T-55 and 2T-75. The 2T-55 was a cable-operated scraper powered by a Cummins engine of 165 horsepower. It had a top speed of 23 miles-per-hour and operating weight of 37,600 pounds. *Keith Haddock*

International 295B. After success with the motor scrapers acquired from the Heil Company in 1953, International brought out its first in-house-designed scrapers in 1959. These were the 295 and 495 Payscrapers, both rated at 34-cubic-yards heaped capacity, and furnished with International diesel engines in the 375-horsepower class. As the model designations suggest, the 295 utilized a two-wheel prime mover, and the 495 utilized a four-wheel prime mover. They replaced the former 2T-55 and 2T-75 models. In 1962, the uprated 295B replaced the 295 with power upped to 396 flywheel-horsepower. In 1963, the 18-yard-heaped-capacity Model 270 joined the team, and elevating scrapers E270 and E295 were added in 1965 and 1968. *Keith Haddock*

International Dresser 433B. In 1972, International completely revamped its scraper line with the introduction of System 400, a new series of motor scrapers with different engine and elevating configurations, but with the same basic scraper of 21 cubic yards heaped. The four Model line consisted of the 431 single-engine conventional scraper; the 433 twin-powered conventional scraper; the 442 single-engine elevating scraper; and the 444 twin-engine elevating scraper. All carried the same 310-flywheel-horsepower International engine up front, and the twin-powered models carried a 185-flywheel-horsepower engine in their rear. Soon after International introduced the 400 Series, the larger scrapers were phased out. In 1978, the 400 Series models were upgraded to the B Series with power increased in the front engines to 326 flywheel-horsepower. Total weight of the 433B was 69,000 pounds. *Keith Haddock*

International Dresser 412B. This small elevating scraper had its origins in the International E-200, which was unveiled in 1966. With a 9-cubic-yard capacity bowl, a 135-flywheel-horsepower engine powered it. This model was joined by the slightly larger E-211 in 1969, with a bowl holding 11 cubic yards and an engine putting out 145 flywheel-horsepower. When International upgraded its scrapers to the 400 Series in 1972, the small 11-cubic-yard E-211 became the 412. The E-200 remained in the line for two more years before being discontinued in 1974. The 412B replaced the 412 in 1978. Weight of this scraper was 15,180 pounds. The 400 Series scrapers remained current until after Dresser Industries, Inc. purchased the Construction Machinery Division of International Harvester in 1982. They were then sold as Dresser products until the scrapers were phased out in 1984. *Keith Haddock*

Koehring WH125 Wheeler. The Koehring Company of Milwaukee, Wisconsin, famous for its shovels and cranes, first offered a motorized scraper in the 1930s. It was based on the company's Dumptor, a 5-cubic-yard hauling dumper with gasoline or diesel power of 70 horsepower. Introduced in the late 1920s, the Dumptor featured an operator's seat that could swivel 180 degrees to face the direction of travel. In the late 1930s, Koehring revitalized its Dumptor by adapting it for hauling duties. For scraper operations, an 8-cubic-yard-heaped-capacity scraper replaced the dump box, and the machine was known as the Wheeler. For hauling a bottom-dumping wagon of 12-cubic-yard capacity, the outfit was known as the Trail Dump. Neither the Wheeler nor the Trail Dump survived after World War II, but the popular Dumptor remained a Koehring product, with upgraded models, into the 1970s. *Ben Corey*

LaPlant-Choate C108. The LaPlant-Choate Manufacturing Company, Inc., established in 1911, built its first pull-type scraper, a two-wheel type, in 1924. It soon expanded its line of pull-type scrapers and, in the 1930s, offered a full line of two-wheel and four-wheel cable-operated scrapers, bulldozer blades, and other tractor attachments. In 1952, Allis-Chalmers Manufacturing Company acquired LaPlant-Choate. At the time of acquisition, LaPlant-Choate was offering its Carrimor line of pull-type scrapers: five models with heaped capacities from 2 to 20 cubic yards, including the 12-cubic-yard C108. Allis-Chalmers continued to market the pull-type scrapers as its own products until the mid-1960s. *Keith Haddock*

Komatsu WS-23. Komatsu introduced its first motor scraper in 1970, the twin-powered Model WS-16 of 21-cubic-yard heaped capacity. It had identical engines of 210 flywheel-horsepower in front and rear, and an operating weight of 74,000 pounds. The larger WS-23S scraper of 30-cubic-yard heaped capacity appeared in 1975. This single-engine conventional scraper was powered by a 425 flywheel-horsepower Cummins engine. Next came a single-engine 21-cubic-yard scraper (WS-16S), followed by a twin-engine 30-cubic-yard scraper, the WS-23. The latter machine (illustrated) had identical engines front and rear, each producing 364 flywheel-horsepower. These four scraper models fulfilled Komatsu's scraper needs through the 1980s. *Keith Haddock collection*

LeTourneau Mountain Mover. After pioneer scraper-builder R.G. LeTourneau built his first scraper, a modified drag scraper on wheels called the Gondola in 1922, he went on to develop a scraper consisting of two buckets. Each could be loaded in turn, which conserved power. He understood the principle that the last few yards of material take much more power to load into a scraper than the first few. The Mountain Mover of 1923 was the first scraper to demonstrate this concept. It incorporated electric motors and featured two bowls, one telescoping inside the other. Its capacity was 12 cubic yards and it ran on wide steel wheels to aid flotation. The Mountain Mover is now preserved, and is displayed with the Gondola scraper at the LeTourneau University of Longview, Texas. *Keith Haddock collection*

LeTourneau A. The prolific Mr. LeTourneau conceived and built a succession of pull-type scrapers, all of different designs, throughout the 1920s. A major breakthrough occurred in 1928, when LeTourneau invented the cable-control unit. On this machine, the motions of the scraper were controlled from a double-drum winch mounted on the tractor. The Highboy of 1929 was one of the first scrapers to operate from a cable-control unit. It was named for the high frame above the bowl, which supported a spring-loaded tailgate. The tailgate was pulled through an arc to sweep out the load. The Model A Carryall of 9-cubic-yards capacity was introduced in 1932 and was the first scraper to be known officially as a "Carryall." It was also the first to be equipped with pneumatic tires. *Keith Haddock collection*

LeTourneau. The Model B Carryall, built in 1933, was a significant milestone in scraper development, because it appears to be the first pull-type scraper to incorporate all the features that have since become standard. Worked from a double-drum cable-control unit on the tractor, the scraper bowl was capable of being raised clear of the ground. An apron dropped down over the load or raised slightly to aid spreading, and a separate cable-operated ejector pushed out the load through the front. The Carryall B was rated at 11-cubic-yards capacity with a weight of 16,650 pounds. *Keith Haddock*

LeTourneau YR13. LeTourneau produced a vast array of pull-type scrapers throughout the 1930s. Alphabetical letters denoted the model sizes. Models ranged from the small 3.5-cubic-yard Model Z, to the RU at 30-cubic-yards heaped capacity. A mid-sized example is this YR13 model with a rating of 16 cubic yards heaped and an empty weight of 20,340 pounds. It was produced from 1938 to 1939. The one pictured was still making money for its owner in 978. This size worked well when pulled behind one of the early Caterpillar D8 tractors of the 1930s. The larger sizes would be suitable for soft, sandy material, although they would require assistance from a push tractor in the rear. *Keith Haddock*

LeTourneau LU. The Model LU Carryall came out in 1940, and was a popular, large pull-type scraper throughout the 1940s. The largest tractors of the day, such as the various models of the Caterpillar D8 and 1947's Allis-Chalmers HD-19, would pull this 19-cubic-yard (heaped) scraper weighing 20,340 pounds empty. Notice how LeTourneau's scraper designs varied; the bowl hoist sheave-block lever on top of this scraper points to the rear, whereas it points to the front on the YR model in the previous picture. LeTourneau supplied the largest tires he could find to lower ground pressure on his scrapers. *Eric C. Orlemann collection*

LeTourneau G6. Another example of how to do it! This 6.5-cubic-yard pull scraper has its bowl lift arranged from the rear instead of the front. The G6 was produced from 1938 to 1939 with an empty weight of 7,825 pounds. These pull-type scrapers had a complicated rope-reeving system involving many sheaves, and changing ropes was a time-consuming job. The trick was to change the rope before it actually broke so that the new length of rope could be simply pulled through from the rope drum that carried the new cable, while the old length was pulled out. *Eric C. Orlemann collection*

LeTourneau A Tournapull. With the advent of larger rubber tires, LeTourneau completed manufacture of the first high-speed earthmover, the Model A Tournapull in 1938. This machine featured revolutionary concepts, several of which still appear in today's scraper designs. The major innovation was the two-wheel prime mover concept with the unique hitch, which allowed the two-wheel tractor to swing more than 90 degrees in each direction. Fitted with the Caterpillar D17000 engine, developing 160 horsepower at 950 rpm, the prototype achieved a speed of 20 miles-per-hour under tests. The Model A was hitched to a choice of Carryalls including the TU, RU, and NU of 24-, 30-, and 42-cubic-yards heaped capacity. *Keith Haddock collection*

LeTourneau Super C Tournapull. The successful Model C Tournapull earned its name as LeTourneau's best-selling motor scraper. The first version, introduced in 1940, was powered by a Caterpillar D4600 diesel rated at 90 gross-horsepower and coupled to the Model LS Carryall of 11-cubic-yard heaped capacity. A second, more powerful version called the Super C, also released in 1940, offered optional Buda, Cummins, or Hercules engines of 150 gross-horsepower. With the extra power, the Super C was paired with the LP Carryall of 15-cubic-yard heaped capacity. These two C-Pulls, as they became known, were extremely popular on the home front, as well as an important tool for the armed forces during World War II. *Keith Haddock*

LeTourneau D4 Tournapull. The unique D4 Tournapull joined many thousands of pull-type and motor scrapers used by the United States and its allies during World War II. It was made under special order for the U.S. Army Engineers. Paired with the Model Q Carryall of only 2.3-cubic-yard heaped capacity, and weighing only 3.25 tons, the D4 Tournapull was ideal to airlift into captured territory for advance airstrip construction. It was powered by a 45-gross-horsepower Continental gasoline engine. Deliveries of the D4 Tournapull started in 1943. The two scrapers on this page are owned by Bill Graham of Edmonton, Alberta. *Keith Haddock*

LeTourneau D Tournapull. In the period of 1947 to 1948, LeTourneau launched new versions of the Tournapull A, B, and C models after experimenting with several prototypes of each. In 1948, the popular 9-cubic-yard Model D Roadster Tournapull was introduced. With its successive generations, it remained in production for some 25 years and it carried the WABCO era forward. The tractor unit on these models was mechanically driven, but all other functions operated electrically. Up to this time, all Tournapulls used simple clutches and brakes applied to the drive axle, similar to a crawler tractor. A lack of rigidity made the machine prone to jackknifing. Accordingly, the new models were steered by an electric motor, pinion, and gear assembly that provided a rigid connection between the tractor and scraper. In 1953, Westinghouse Air Brake Company purchased the rights to the earthmoving products from LeTourneau, and continued the Tournapull models under the LeTourneau-Westinghouse brand name. *Keith Haddock*

LeTourneau LT-240 Electric Digger. LeTourneau scrapers built after 1958 employed DC electric motors in the wheels driven by diesel-electric power plants, and all featured power rack-and-pinion drive for their motions. Most of these machines were built in very limited numbers, or even on a "one-of-a-kind" test basis, and some bordered on the bizarre. Most famous of all were the huge tandem and triple-bowl outfits with multiple engines. The LT-240 of 1965, with a center-mounted cab, was powered by no fewer than five engines totaling 2,855 horsepower and the twin bowls combined to carry 144 cubic yards. That same year, an extra bowl and power module was added to the LT-240 to make the world's biggest scraper, the LT-360. Its three bowls could carry a staggering 216 cubic yards, and its eight diesel engines provided 4,760 horsepower. It was the largest earthmover ever mounted on rubber tires. *Eric C. Orlemann collection*

LeTourneau A4 Goliath. In 1953, R.G. LeTourneau sold his earthmoving equipment manufacturing business to the Westinghouse Air Brake Company. He then set to work designing a new line of earthmovers, which could not be marketed until 1958 because of the terms of the sale agreement with Westinghouse. The launch date eventually arrived, and LeTourneau proudly presented the first of a new earthmoving equipment line, the 50-cubic-yard-capacity four-wheel scraper known as the A4 Goliath. It featured the now-famous LeTourneau-trademark rack-and-pinion drive with high-torque motors for the scraper motions and steering. The Goliath was the largest self-propelled scraper made up to that time, and the forerunner of even bigger things to come. *Keith Haddock collection*

M-R-S 200/250-HC. M-R-S Manufacturing Company of Flora, Mississippi, was established in 1943 to build wheel tractors for pulling scrapers and wagons. Since inception, all M-R-S tractor/scraper combinations have utilized a four-wheel tractor. M-R-S scrapers incorporate an operator-controlled weight transfer system, consisting of a hydraulic ram extending from the tractor drawbar to a high point on the scraper gooseneck. When this ram extends, more weight is transferred onto the tractor driving wheels to maximize traction. Some very large scrapers were developed by M-R-S in the 1960s, ranging up to 90 cubic yards for coal hauling. The 335-horsepower M-R-S 200 tractor with 250HC scraper has a heaped capacity of 65 cubic yards. In 1986, Taylor Machine Works, Inc. purchased M-R-S, and the scrapers are still available on a manufacture-to-order basis. *Keith Haddock collection*

Michigan 410. In 1957, Michigan launched its first scrapers. Designed in-house, the scrapers were sold in three sizes, the Models 110, 210, and 310 with, respectively, 10-, 18-, and 27-cubic-yard heaped capacities. The scrapers were an outcome of the Construction Machinery Division set up by Clark Equipment Company in 1952. These three basic models were retained by Clark-Michigan for its subsequent scraper models in the 1960s and 1970s, although many variations and upgrades occurred during that period. In early 1964, Clark-Michigan introduced its largest-ever scraper. This was the Model 410, a massive single-engine scraper powered by a Cummins VT-1710-C putting out 570 flywheel-horsepower, and carrying a heaped load of 44 cubic yards. With disappointing sales, this model was discontinued in 1970. *Keith Haddock collection*

Michigan 110-15. Michigan introduced its first elevating scraper in 1965 by attaching one of its prime movers to a scraper designed and built by Hancock Manufacturing Company. The following year, Clark purchased Hancock and subsequently developed elevating options for its entire Michigan scraper line. The Michigan 110-15 was a 15-cubic-yard elevating scraper, based on the 110 tractor furnished with a 225-flywheel-horsepower GM engine. The largest elevating scraper made by Clark-Michigan was the 310-H in 1969, which boasted 32 cubic yards of capacity and a 445-flywheel-horsepower GM engine. Clark-Michigan's scraper production continued through the 1970s, with most of the models being versions of the Models 110 and 210 elevating types. In 1981, Clark-Michigan discontinued its scraper production. *Keith Haddock collection*

Terex TS-24B Loadrunner. Since its introduction in 1957 as the Euclid TS-24, and later the Terex TS-24 in 1968, this scraper has been probably the most famous of any built by the company. Over its long manufacturing run, the TS-24 has enjoyed many modifications and refinements. Carried forward from its Euclid days, the 32-cubic-yard-heaped-capacity TS-24 was joined by a new design called the TS-24B Loadrunner in 1977. This featured a nitrogen-over-oil suspended front axle, which dampened the bounce associated with scrapers traveling at speed. It also sported the new Terex "keystone-shape" front radiator. Detroit diesel engines in the front and rear put out 475 and 242 flywheel-horsepower. The last TS-24 version, the TS-24D, boasts a 34-cubic-yard heaped capacity and Detroit or Cummins power for the 480-flywheel-horsepower front engine and 260-flywheel-horsepower rear engine. In 2002, with a production life spanning almost 45 years, the TS-24D is available only by special order. *Keith Haddock collection*

Terex TS-32. The largest and most powerful regular-production scraper made by Euclid/Terex was the TS-32, of 32-cubic-yards struck (or 43-cubic-yard heaped) capacity. Equipped with two GM engines, for a total of 818 flywheel-horsepower, it was launched in 1966 as the Euclid TS-32 and carried forward into Terex's roster of scrapers after 1968. Unlike the TS-24, the TS-32 did not enjoy an everlasting production run. It did receive a significant upgrade in 1978, when the TS-32B was released with the Terex "keystone-shape" radiator, but its sheer size made it too expensive to build, so it was dropped from the line in 1980. *Keith Haddock collection*

133

Terex TS-14G. Another Terex scraper with roots way back in Euclid's early scraper development is the TS-14. Introduced in 1959 as the company's smallest twin-engined scraper, it was rated at 20-cubic-yards heaped capacity. Over the years, the TS-14 has been a huge seller for Euclid and Terex and, like its stablemate the TS-24, received several significant upgrades along the way. Initially equipped with a pair of identical GM engines totaling 269 flywheel-horsepower, its power was upped to 288 flywheel-horsepower by 1966. After further upgrades, the TS-14B debuted in 1972, followed by the TS-14C in 1990, the TS-14D in 1996, the TS-14F in 1999, and the TS-14G in 2000. All retained a 20-cubic-yard-heaped-capacity scraper bowl, but combined power rating for the current TS-14G is currently quoted as 340 flywheel-horsepower. *Terex Equipment, Ltd.*

Terex THS-15. Terex launched a radically new scraper design at the Las Vegas Minexpo 2000 equipment show. The THS-15 has a single engine, but it's rear-mounted. It drives a hydraulic pump system that provides hydrostatic drive to all four wheels. Power comes from a Detroit diesel rated at 575 horsepower, and the bowl can carry 20 cubic yards when heaped. Another unique feature is the patented Cutting Edge Crowd, which enables the scraper to collect a load in tough material without help from a push tractor. It also allows the load to be dumped without raising the apron. The climate-controlled cab provides 180 degrees of visibility, and joystick levers provide simplified scraper control. The rear-mounted engine keeps the cab away from unwanted noise and heat. *Keith Haddock*

WABCO C500. The LeTourneau-Westinghouse Company (L-W) was established in 1953 following the purchase of the earthmoving equipment business of R.G. LeTourneau, Inc. Until the early 1960s, the original LeTourneau-designed B, C, and D Tournapulls were continued by L-W with some refinements. In 1962, the products became known by the name WABCO. New models began to appear in 1959 with the introduction of the 29-cubic-yard Model B Speedpull with four-wheel-drive, and capable of reaching speeds up to 40 miles per hour. WABCO's B and C scrapers could also run with a second scraper bowl hooked on behind. The C-500, introduced in 1961, was a basic 21-cubic-yard heaped scraper with a 290-horsepower prime mover. An optional second 21-cubic-yard scraper could be added, as shown. Or, for an additional boost, a 148-horsepower engine could be added on the rear. *Keith Haddock collection*

WABCO C222F. Beginning in 1961, WABCO offered elevating versions of its scrapers. Initially, the Hancock Manufacturing Company made 10- and 21-cubic-yard scrapers for the 148-horsepower D Tournapull and the 290-horsepower C Tournapull. By 1966, the Hancock name was dropped from the scrapers and a new line of three models was offered, the 11-cubic-yard 111A, the 21-cubic-yard 222A, and the 31-cubic-yard 333A. The C222F replaced the 222A in 1967 with the same capacity, and a 300-flywheel-horsepower GM engine powered it. This model's replacement came in 1971 when the 222G appeared with an extra yard in the bowl and a modest power increase to 309 flywheel-horsepower. *Keith Haddock*

WABCO 101F. WABCO unveiled its smallest elevating scraper in 1970, the 101F. This newly designed machine boasted a gutsy Cummins engine of 162 flywheel-horsepower and carried 9 cubic yards when full. For the first time on a Wabco scraper, a hydraulic motor instead of an electric motor drove the elevator. Big-fleet Wabco scraper operators usually ran one 101F in their fleet for cleanup, precise finish grading, or work in close quarters. In 1976, Wabco replaced the 101F with the 101G. With approximately the same horsepower rating, it could carry an extra 2 cubic yards in its bowl. *Keith Haddock collection*

WABCO 333FT. WABCO aggressively promoted the elevating scraper concept throughout the 1960s. In 1966, it introduced the Model 333F, which at 32-cubic-yards capacity, was the world's largest. Next followed the twin-powered 333FT, boasting 34-cubic-yard-capacity and 900 flywheel-horsepower from its two engines. WABCO built the even larger 353FT in 1977. With a bowl heaping 36 cubic yards, and 966 flywheel-horsepower from its two engines, it was the most powerful production model elevating scraper ever built. But ironically, this record-beating 353FT signaled the end of the big elevating scrapers. They were expensive to operate, and with scraper sales generally declining, WABCO announced its exit from the scraper business in 1980. *Keith Haddock collection*

Wagner WI-14. Wagner Tractor, Inc. of Portland, Oregon, was organized in the early 1950s to build large wheeled tractors, dozers, and log skidders. Wagner was associated with Mixermobile, the famous pioneer of the Scoopmobile articulated loaders of the mid-1950s. Wagner utilized the Scoopmobile articulated steering technology in its tractors. FWD Corporation took over Wagner Tractor in 1961 to form FWD-Wagner, Inc., and the machines continued in production under that name. The big four-wheel drive, articulated wheeled tractors were useful as dozers, but could also be adapted to haul scrapers. The picture shows a Cummins-powered Wagner WI-14 tractor of 220 horsepower (maximum) coupled to a Richardson 14-cubic-yard Model G scraper. In 1971, FWD-Wagner became a subsidiary of RayGo, Inc. and operated as RayGo Wagner until 1985. *Keith Haddock*

Wooldridge OS-152. The Wooldridge Manufacturing Company of Sunnyvale, California, built scrapers in the 1930s mainly for use in the western United States. In the early 1930s, the company had contracted with the Continental Roll & Steel Foundry to have the latter build Wooldridge scrapers under license for distribution in certain areas. In the mid-1940s, Wooldridge scrapers were made especially for M-R-S tractors, and the combined scraper units were marketed by M-R-S. Wooldridge continued to build its pull-type scrapers through the 1950s, using the trade names "Terra Clipper" and "Boiling-Bowl Scrapers." The 1956 line included six sizes of pull-type scrapers, up to 41-cubic-yards heaped capacity. The OS-152 had a heaped capacity of 18 cubic yards. *Keith Haddock*

Wooldridge Terra Cobra TC-S142. Wooldridge developed a range of self-propelled scrapers in the mid-1940s. They were cable-operated scrapers known by trade names such as "Terra Cobra," which referred to a two-wheel tractor configuration, and the "Cobra Quad," which was a four-wheel tractor version. The TC-S142 could carry a heaped load of 17.5 cubic yards and was furnished with a Cummins 225-horsepower diesel engine. The Terra Cobra scrapers featured a steering system known as the "Roto-Gear," which did not use any hydraulic rams. Instead, twin hydraulic motors applied torque through a gear reduction to a bull gear attached to the scraper yoke. *Provincial Archives of Alberta*

Wooldridge Terra Cobra TH-090B. Wooldridge unveiled two new Terra Cobras in 1953, the TH-090 and TH-090B of 13.5 and 15-cubic-yard heaped capacity. Their Cummins engines provided 165 and 180 horsepower respectively. A smaller scraper, the Cobrette T-70, was introduced in 1956 with 10-cubic-yards heaped capacity. In 1958, the Curtiss-Wright Corporation of South Bend, Indiana, acquired the Wooldridge company. At the time of the takeover, the Cobra scraper line consisted of five models with heaped capacities up to 36 cubic yards. Curtiss-Wright continued to market the full scraper line as the CW Series, but in the early 1960s, Curtiss-Wright phased out its earthmoving machines as the company focused in other directions. *Richard Yaremko*

Pull-type hydraulic scraper. As a postscript to the scraper story in this chapter, many old pull-scrapers are enjoying a new lease on life. Contractors and machine shops everywhere are locating old pull-type scrapers that were thought of as obsolete and they are rebuilding them. The reborn scrapers are fitted with modern hydraulic cylinders, which operate from the hydraulic system on the towing tractor. When coupled behind today's high-powered wheel or flexible rubber-tracked tractors, they make an ideal earthmoving team. The picture shows a 300-horsepower Caterpillar Challenger 65D tractor pulling a converted Allis-Chalmers 314 pull-type scraper of 18-cubic-yard heaped capacity. *Keith Haddock*

137

CHAPTER 8

MOTOR GRADERS

Motor graders are probably the most familiar of all earthmoving machines. Seen on our highways clearing snow in winter or maintaining gravel roads in summer, the grader is often the lifeblood of our main transportation system. Today, the largest application for graders is still county and municipality road maintenance, but a close second is their use in major earthmoving projects including road construction and surface mining. This latter application is where we find the very largest graders in action. But relatively small numbers of the giant graders have been built and, as we shall see in this chapter, most had a very short production run.

Way back in the horse-drawn era, the simplest form of grader consisted of nothing more than a board pulled by a horse. Then, in 1885, entrepreneur J.D. Adams invented a new type of grader with adjustable leaning wheels. Other graders in use at that time consisted of a blade with a raising and lowering mechanism attached to the bed of a wagon. Adams observed the difficulty of working on the sloping side of the road, and to solve the problem he invented a crude grader with blade set at a fixed angle, and leaning wheels. He called it "The Little Wonder", and his machine found immediate success because the wheels could be cranked to lean against the sideways thrust of the angled blade. This leaning wheel principle has been a key feature of graders up to the present day.

It wasn't long before animal power was competing with steam power to pull graders. Initially this was risky; some of the more flimsy types designed for horsepower simply disintegrated when matched with the super power of the giant traction engines of the day.

Prior to 1919, all graders were the towed type, designed to pull behind horse teams, or behind tractors, and requiring a separate operator. The operator stood on a platform at the rear of the grader, or if he was lucky, sat on a primitive, hard seat. Blade control was by hand, usually through cranks, gear reductions, or racks operated by wheels. In 1919, the Russell Grader Manufacturing Company brought out a self-propelled machine. Although primitive, it set the stage for Russell and other manufacturers to improve on the self-propelled idea, and soon all grader makers were offering self-propelled models in their lines. Actually, the word "grader" was not applied to these machines until the late 1930s. They used to be known as road patrols, maintainers, or by various trade names.

ACCO. The largest grader ever built kicks off this selection of motor grader illustrations. This one-of-a-kind monster was built in Italy by earthmoving contractor Umberto Acco to his own designs. Constructed in 1980 for use on a major contract in Libya, the ACCO boasted a 33-foot blade. The front and rear sections articulated separately, and Caterpillar engines mounted in the front and rear produced a total of 1,700 horsepower to all six driving wheels equipped with 12 large tires.

A size comparison can be made from the man standing on the catwalk on the grader's main frame. This grader overshadows anything else built to date in the grader field. *Yvon LeCadre*

Adams 105 Pull Grader. J.D. Adams is credited with inventing leaning wheels on graders to counteract the side force produced by the angling blade. The first was 1885's Little Wonder pull grader. In 1896, the J.D. Adams Company introduced the first of its Road King Series of pull graders. Made in all sizes, the various models remained in production until they were phased out in the 1930s. The Model 105 pull grader shown was part of a new line introduced in 1935. It has a 10-foot blade and is designed for tractors with 40 to 50 drawbar-horsepower. This model has mechanical power control furnished by a single-cylinder engine. The same grader was available as the Model 104 with hand-operated controls. The 104 and 105 were sold until 1956, making them some of the last pull graders to be shipped. *Keith Haddock collection*

Adams 101. The Model 101 motor grader was launched in 1929, only one year after Adams introduced its very first self-propelled grader, the No. 10. Like the earlier model, the Model 101 was equipped with hand controls. As with most motor graders of this era, its power unit was mounted ahead of the operator's cab. This was an undesirable feature, which obstructed the operator's ability to view the blade in all its working positions. Soon after this model, graders began to appear with rear-mounted engines. This sensible position has been retained in modern grader designs. The machine shown was made at Adams' Canadian factory in Paris, Ontario. The power unit is a McCormick-Deering gasoline engine. *Keith Haddock*

Blade control by hand on the early machines was tiresome and dangerous, especially with the higher-powered tractors coming into the field in the 1920s. Consequently, powered control was introduced, starting in the mid-1920s. Some manufacturers like Galion and Huber pioneered hydraulic controls at this early date, but the blade movements on the first power-controlled graders were operated mechanically by screwed rods or cranks. It took several decades for all grader manufacturers to convert controls from mechanical to hydraulic. Some had semi-hydraulic systems operating mechanical clutches or linkages. Caterpillar did not change to hydraulic control until it introduced the G Series graders in 1973.

On the true grader, the blade, also called the mold-board, has many independently controlled operating positions, allowing a skilled operator to accomplish tasks that would otherwise require the use of hand labor. The blade is raised or lowered independently at each side, allowing a side slope or cross-fall to be shaped as the grader moves forward. The blade can rotate in the horizontal plane so that collected material can be pushed to either side. Also, the blade's pitch can be changed to cut into the material, or simply carry it on the road surface, and the blade can move sideways to reach out far beyond the wheel track. In its extreme position, the blade can be positioned in the bottom of a

Adams 512. In 1931, power-operated mechanical controls were made available on the larger Adams motor graders, and the company continued to broaden its product line. The first mono-frame grader was introduced in 1935, allowing improved blade linkage, and making it possible to swing the blade out to the side for trimming banks and shoulders. The modern-looking 512 appeared in 1944 with rear-mounted engine, mechanical controls, and full-blade functions. Powered by an International 85-flywheel-horsepower diesel engine, its operating weight when it was equipped with a scarifier was 23,680 pounds. The 512 was produced until 1953, but it was not carried forward when LeTourneau-Westinghouse took over Adams that year. *Keith Haddock*

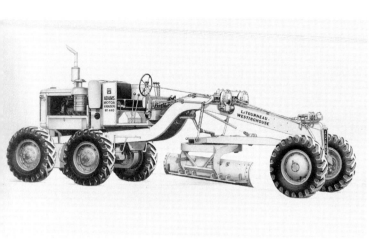

Adams 440. In 1954, LeTourneau-Westinghouse Company (L-W) purchased the J.D. Adams Company. However, the Adams name was retained as a trademark until 1962, when L-W adopted "Wabco" for its product trade name. The picture shows a Model 440, which was introduced a year before the Adams company was sold to L-W. It carries both the Adams and L-W names and was continued as an L-W product. In the 23,000-pound weight class, it remained in production until 1971. The first models were furnished with an International diesel engine of 85 flywheel-horsepower, while the later models offered a choice of Cummins or GM engines up to 125 flywheel-horsepower. *Keith Haddock collection*

Allis-Chalmers 110. Allis-Chalmers entered the grader business in 1931 by purchasing the grader line of Ryan Manufacturing Company of Chicago, Illinois. Established in 1925, the Ryan company had already made its mark in the grader industry with a broad line of products. The acquisition gave Allis-Chalmers a variety of graders, including leaning-wheel graders with power or hand controls, and a motor grader powered by the Allis-Chalmers Model U tractor. The Models 110 and 112 pull-type graders were a brand-new design for 1938 and featured round-pipe main frames. They were power-controlled leaning-wheel graders equipped with Wisconsin engines (5.4 horsepower on the 110). Allis-Chalmers phased out making pull-type graders by 1941. *Keith Haddock*

Allis-Chalmers 54 Speed Patrol. This model came to the market in 1934 and was numbered after its 54-horsepower engine. Shortly after its introduction, power was increased to 62 horsepower. Weighing 15,655 pounds when equipped with scarifier, the 54 Speed Patrol featured power-operated controls driven from the front end of the engine crankshaft. In 1936, Allis-Chalmers announced tandem-drive versions of the 54 and its smaller brother, the 42 Speed Patrol, and these soon outsold the single-drive versions. The 54 Speed Patrol illustrated is operating at the annual convention of the Historical Construction Equipment Association at Brownsville, Pennsylvania, in 1999. *Keith Haddock*

Allis-Chalmers W Speed Patrol. This handy, light-duty Model W Speed Patrol was designed to give "relief for limited budgets," as the advertisements claimed in the early 1940s. It replaced the earlier three-wheel-version known as the WC Speed Maintainer, which was launched in 1938. Built around the Allis-Chalmers Model WC farm tractor of 31 horsepower, it weighed only 6,950 pounds, but carried a 10-foot blade. Blade control was by hand; blade lift was controlled by the two large, hand wheels. The advertisements must have worked, as the W Speed Patrol proved a very popular machine for Allis-Chalmers, which sold 3,751 units between 1940 and 1950. *Keith Haddock*

Allis-Chalmers AD3. Allis-Chalmers introduced the first of its new AD grader line in 1941. This series was powered by GM diesel engines and all were tandem-drive models. A temporary gap in production occurred in 1943 and 1944 due to World War II. When production recommenced in 1944, two improved models, the AD3 and AD4 were announced. These were powered by GM engines of 78 and 104 horsepower respectively, and were in the 22,000-pound weight class. In 1952, the AD3 and AD4 were supplanted by the AD30 and AD40 heavy-duty motor graders with a new main frame design. *Keith Haddock*

highway ditch while the grader travels on the secure footing of the highway surface. In slope trimming, the blade can swing out to either side of the machine and be positioned at any angle, from horizontal to vertical.

In addition to blade movements, graders are equipped with powered front-wheel lean and are capable of mounting a dozer blade or snowplow on the front. Most graders can be equipped with a ripper or scarifier. This can be mounted ahead of the blade under the frame, or on the rear of the machine.

Graders come in all sizes. Many companies have developed a niche market for small machines, designed for grading work inside industrial plants, housing developments, and parks, as well as municipal work and other light-duty applications. With some exceptions, these small machines, weighing 5 tons or less, are built by manufacturers who don't compete with the big-grader makers.

The grader becomes a production tool when used in surface mining operations, the territory of the largest graders. Beginning in the 1960s, some huge single-purpose graders were built for mining applications such as spoil pile leveling and road maintenance for the largest off-highway trucks. Because these large graders sell in relatively small numbers, manufacturers have tended to discontinue their production after a short time. The most familiar grader manufacturers did not make some of the very largest graders. But Caterpillar, with its 16 Series and the introduction of the 24-H model in 1996, has persisted with its large graders, and now dominates this market.

Allis-Chalmers Forty-Five. In 1955, Allis-Chalmers launched the Forty-Five as its top-of-the-line grader. It replaced the former AD40 and was fitted with a modern Buda engine rated at 120 horsepower. Allis-Chalmers had purchased the Buda Company in 1953, and began switching power units in most of its construction equipment products to the company-controlled Buda models. Power to the Forty-Five was upped to 127 horsepower when the Allis-Chalmers 10000 Series engines became available in the early 1960s. Later, this grader was referred to as "Model 45" rather than "Forty-Five," and the model was replaced by the M-100 in 1962. *Keith Haddock*

Allis-Chalmers DD. The 8,500-pound Model D motor grader was introduced in 1949 to replace the former W Speed Patrol. It incorporated many features from the larger graders and was also the first from Allis-Chalmers to incorporate hydraulic blade lift. Initially powered by a 35-horsepower gasoline engine, a more powerful 50-horsepower unit was substituted in 1953. At that time, hydraulic control was extended to blade side shift, wheel lean, and blade circle. The diesel version, Model DD, of similar size and weight, was added in 1954. A diesel engine of 50 horsepower was selected from the engines built by the newly purchased Buda Company. The D and DD models were so popular that they remained an Allis-Chalmers product until 1970. *Keith Haddock*

Austin Giant Leaning Wheel Grader. This is one of many pull-type graders made by Austin Manufacturing Company of Chicago, Illinois. The operator stood on the platform at the rear and operated the grader by tugging on the various hand wheels. Originally designed, at the dawn of the twentieth century, to be pulled by a team of horses, the Giant Leaning Wheel Grader was sturdy enough to be pulled by traction engines. It was still offered in the company's 1925 catalog. Austin was purchased by the Western Wheeled Scraper Company in 1902, to form the Austin-Western Road Machinery Company. The product lines were marketed as Austin or Western machines until 1934, when all three companies merged into the Austin-Western Company.

American Coleman No. 8. Several manufacturers offered utility graders built around farm tractors. With the front wheels removed, a frame supporting the blade, circle, and leaning front wheels was added. The resulting economical light-duty machine was great for performing maintenance work on gravel roads, parking lots, and for winter snow-clearing duties. The American Coleman, built by the American Road Equipment Company of Omaha, Nebraska, was a typical type of utility grader. Based on an International tractor of 40 horsepower, the No. 8 carried a blade 10 feet wide. Blade control was hydraulic, and the manufacturer offered the No. 8 with several attachment options including scarifier and front-end loader. *Keith Haddock*

Austin-Western No. 77 Senior Dual Drive Motor Grader. Austin-Western Road Machinery Company was formed in 1902 when two long-established grader companies merged. The Western Wheeled Scraper Company of Aurora, Illinois, claimed to have built the first horse-drawn wheeled scraper in 1877. The Austin Manufacturing Company of Chicago, hard an even earlier start with its ancestry in the Chicago firm H.W. Austin & Co., formed in 1849. The Austin 77 seres of graders in the 16,500-pound weight class was an advanced design for its time when it was launched in 1934. Offered in single- or dual-drive versions with hydraulic controls, the 77 models boasted all the blade movements of today's modern grader, and contrasted with Austin-Western's horse-drawn products offered at the same time. *Keith Haddock*

Austin-Western Super 88. In 1937, the Austin-Western Company introduced the first all-wheel-drive, all-wheel-steer grader. These features were great selling points because Austin-Western could boast that there was no dead weight on an axle. In the 1940s, Austin-Western extolled the advantages of all-wheel-drive and all-whee-steer graders and brought out new four-wheel- and six-wheel-drive models. Austin-Western used the name "Super" to refer to tandem rear axle (six-wheel) machines, and "Pacer" to refer to single rear-axle (four-wheel) machines. The Super 88 was in the 20,000-pound weight class and ran with an 88-horsepower engine. It was made from 1954 to 1959. *Keith Haddock*

Austin-Western Pacer 200. In 1959, the Austin-Western grader line graduated into the 100 Series, consisting of the "Pacer" (four-wheel) and "Super" (six-wheel) versions, in sizes from the 100 to the 500 models. In typical Austin-Western tradition, every model featured all-wheel-drive and all-wheel-steer. The top-of-the-line Super 500 was powered with a GM 6V-71 diesel engine of 179 horsepower, and had an operating weight of just under 30,000 pounds. The mid-sized Pacer 200 was offered with a choice of Cummins or GM engines, ranging from 108 to 128 horsepower, and it had an operating weight around 22,000 pounds. *Keith Haddock*

Austin-Western Super 300. From the line of Austin-Western motor graders comes this Super 300, putting its four-wheel drive and four-wheel steer to full advantage. With front wheels fully locked in one direction, and rear tandem locked in the other, the blade can tackle a windrow and move it across the machine's path without interfering with its wheels. The Super 300 was offered with Cummins or GM engines of 143 horsepower and tipped the scales at around 25,000 pounds. In 1971, Austin-Western, which had become part of the Baldwin-Lima-Hamilton Corporation in 1951, became a division of Clark Equipment Company. *Berrien Springs Historical Society, Michigan*

Aveling-Barford Super 700. One of the most famous Austin-Western graders was the 99-H, introduced in 1947. This all-wheel-drive, all-wheel-steer grader was the first grader model to be adopted by Aveling-Barford, Ltd. to manufacture in the United Kingdom under license. Commencing in 1950, it sold mainly to Commonwealth countries as the Aveling-Austin 99-H, and was identical to the American machine except for its British-built Leyland engine. The 99-H remained current until the early 1970s, by which time many other Austin-Western models had been made in the U.K. The manufacturing arrangement lasted until 1973, when Aveling-Barford continued with its own line of motor graders, developed during its association with Austin-Western. The Super 700 appeared in 1974 with Leyland or GM engine options in the 204- to 228-horsepower range, and with an operating weight of 42,420 pounds. *Keith Haddock collection*

Caterpillar No. 33 Pull Grader. The acquisition of the Russell Grader Manufacturing Company of Minneapolis, Minnesota, in 1928, gave Caterpillar Tractor Company a new line of road maintenance products to join its already popular crawler tractors. For many years, Russell had produced pull-type graders, first for horse teams, and then for early farm tractors. An early example is this No. 33 double-frame blade grader with hand controls. It weighed 5,810 pounds and carried a blade that was 8 feet wide. Like most pull graders, the No. 33 was equipped with a steerable tongue, so that the grader could be steered independently from the tractor pulling it. This device allowed the grader tracking to be offset relative to the axis of the towing tractor, which permits the grader to straddle windrows or clean ditches.
Keith Haddock

Caterpillar No.10 Auto Patrol. The Russell Grader Manufacturing Company began developing a self-propelled grader as early as 1919. Known as the Motor Hi-Way Patrol, it was the first of many Russell graders designed to fit around various brands of standard farm tractors, including the Caterpillar Two-Ton crawler tractor. When Caterpillar bought the company in 1928, Russell was experimenting with hydraulic controls, but soon discarded them as unsatisfactory because of leakage and unevenness of operation when more than one control was used at the same time. Caterpillar went on to develop reliable mechanical controls, using screwed rods and worm drives, as seen on this No.10 Auto Patrol of 1931. A Caterpillar 40-horsepower gasoline engine powers the 13,460-pound machine. *Keith Haddock collection*

Caterpillar No.12. One of Caterpillar's most famous graders was the No.12 originally introduced in 1938. With its 12-foot blade, reliable mechanical controls, and Caterpillar diesel engine, it progressed through several improvements and horsepower increases to the last series in 1959. Over this period engine power went from 70 to 115, and weight increased from 21,140 to 22,410 pounds. The No.12 was replaced with the 12E, with identical horsepower, but weight increased to 24,400 pounds. The 12E became the 12F in 1965, and then the articulated 12G in 1973. Caterpillar persisted with mechanical controls on its graders, saying they were positive and not prone to creep. Finally relenting in 1973, Caterpillar launched the G Series with hydraulic control. *Keith Haddock*

Caterpillar 212. Caterpillar introduced two graders smaller than the No.12 in 1939, the No.112 and No. 212 at 52 and 35 horsepower respectively. They were of similar design, offered with either gasoline or diesel power, and offered single or tandem rear-wheel drive. The Model 212 tandem-drive grader shown is a later model powered by a Caterpillar D311 diesel engine of 50 horsepower. Caterpillar dropped this small-size grader in the 13,000-pound weight class in 1957. *Keith Haddock collection*

Caterpillar No.16. Caterpillar brought out its first No.16 grader in 1963. At 225 horsepower and an initial weight of 46,500 pounds, it represented a big jump in size for Caterpillar, and in fact was the largest grader on the market at that time. With its 14-foot blade, this grader was a larger version of Caterpillar's smaller graders of the time, the 112E, 12E, and 14D, weighing up to 30,300 pounds. Utilizing hydraulically actuated mechanical controls, the rigid-frame No.16 was powered by a Caterpillar D343 turbocharged engine. It enjoyed a production run of 10 years, and by then its weight had increased to 49,600 pounds. Caterpillar replaced the 16 with the 16G when it launched its new G Series articulated graders in 1973. *Keith Haddock*

Caterpillar 16H. Caterpillar revamped all its graders in 1973 when it introduced the G Series, a line of six models with operating weights from 25,000 to 54,000 pounds. The outmoded mechanical controls of the former models were replaced with state-of-the-art hydraulic controls and, for the first time, Caterpillar offered articulated frame design. The big 16G quickly became the standard for haul-road maintenance at surface mining and heavy construction projects. Its weight topped out at just over 60,000 pounds when equipped with ripper, and with a power increase to 250 flywheel-horsepower, the 16G could now handle a 16-foot-wide blade. The 16G stayed in Caterpillar's line for some 22 years, receiving a power increase to 275 flywheel-horsepower but with little other change. The H Series finally supplanted the G Series in 1995 with the same power and weight ratings. *Keith Haddock*

Caterpillar 24H. In 1995, Caterpillar replaced all its existing graders with the current H Series graders. The original nine model lineup encompassed the 125-horsepower 120H up to the 275-horsepower 16H. Included in the new lineup are two all-wheel-drive models, the 143H and 163H. New features include an improved operator's cab with superior forward vision, and electronically controlled transmission. The massive 24H mining grader joined the line in 1996. This truly giant grader boasts a Caterpillar 3412E engine rated at 500 horsepower and, at 131,000 pounds, it is the largest grader on the market today. Before the 24H, Caterpillar was already building the largest grader available on the market, the 16H. Thus, Caterpillar broke its own size record for graders, and remains dominant in the big-grader market. *Keith Haddock*

Champion Hydraulic Power Maintainer. The first Champion grader was the Winner, a small grader built in 1886 and designed to be pulled by two or four horses. The Champion Road Machinery Company of Goderich, Ontario, Canada, has origins in the American Road Machinery Company of Kennett Square, Pennsylvania. In 1892, Copp Brothers Company, Ltd. obtained the rights to manufacture American Road Machinery Company's products in Canada. They made the Steel Champion grader, which later inspired the company's name. Following several name changes and reorganizations, the Canadian company became known as the American Road Machinery Company of Canada, Ltd. in 1909, and operated as a subsidiary of its American parent. The company was renamed the Dominion Road Machinery Company in 1915. The Hydraulic Power Maintainer of 1936 was Champion's first grader with hydraulic controls. *Keith Haddock*

Champion D600. Champion's history is a textbook case of grader development. The Power Maintainer appeared in 1928 as Champion's first self-propelled grader. The power unit was positioned ahead of the cab, the machine featured solid rubber tires, and blade controls were hand-operated. In 1936, Champion introduced the Hydraulic Maintainer, one of the earliest successful applications of hydraulic power controls on a grader. Champion offered 90-degree blade lift on its graders in 1946, with all movements controlled from the cab. In 1958, Champion's power-plus circle turning system was introduced. This replaced the conventional circle motor with twin hydraulic cylinders. The 600 Series was Champion's mainstay of the 1960s and early 1970s. The D600 weighed 29,000 pounds and offered Cummins or GM engines of 137 and 165 flywheel-horsepower. *Keith Haddock*

Champion 507. This cumbersome-looking utility grader was actually a big seller for Champion around the early 1950s. Popular with counties and municipalities on limited budgets, the 507 boasted hydraulic controls and could use a wide range of attachments such as a scarifier, front-end loader, sweeper, weed sprayer, and fully equipped snowplow. It carried a 40-horsepower engine. In 1929 the Goderich, Ontario, plant became the sole producer of Champion graders. Champion independently prospered over the years, and gained a significant share of the grader market. In 1977, the name Champion became more than a trademark when the firm changed its corporate name to the Champion Road Machinery Company, Ltd. *Keith Haddock*

Champion D740. In 1975, Champion unveiled its redesigned 700 Series graders. The new five-model line ranged from the D720 to the D760, with operating weights ranging from 26,400 to 37,000 pounds. Also included in the line were three sizes of articulated graders, Champion's first. The articulated models were denoted by the suffix A after the model number. But the company must have initially doubted the articulated models' prospects for success, because those models were also available as rigid-frame versions. The D740 was Champion's non-articulated offering in the 30,000-pound weight class. *Keith Haddock*

Champion 740A Series IV. After the 700 models were established, Champion began to upgrade the entire line by initiating a series number to denote the upgrade. The Series III appeared in 1989, followed by the Series IV in 1995, the Series V in 1997, and the Series VI in 1999. The picture shows the articulated 740A in its Series IV guise, with an operating weight of 38,000 pounds and 210 horses under the hood. Throughout the 1990s, Champion continued to offer both articulated and rigid-frame versions for most grader sizes. In 1997, Sweden's AB Volvo purchased Champion Road Machinery, Ltd. *Keith Haddock*

Champion 780A Series V. In 1978, Champion expanded its 700 Series with the addition of the smaller 710 and 710A (articulated), and then unveiled the larger 780A at the 1981 Conexpo equipment show in Houston, Texas. Initially offered only as an articulated machine, the 780A boasted 230 horsepower and an operating weight of 46,100 pounds. It could also be purchased as an all-wheel-drive 6x6 version with hydrostatic drive to the front wheels. By the mid-1980s, a rigid-frame version became available. The 780A Series V featured a variable horsepower arrangement with its Cummins engine putting out 210 flywheel-horsepower in first and second gears, and 235 flywheel-horsepower in gears three to eight. *Keith Haddock*

Champion 100T. Champion took a bold step in 1975 when it introduced the world's largest production model grader. Originally labeled the 80T, and later the 100T, it was nicknamed the "Big Mudder." This monster of the grading world tipped the scales at 202,000 pounds. With its wide 24-foot blade, it was intended for use in surface mining operations to maintain roads for the largest haulers, or to reclaim vast areas of land. Power came from a 700-horsepower Cummins engine. Champion sold the manufacturing rights of the 100T to Dom-Ex Corporation of Hibbing, Minnesota, in 1989. *Keith Haddock collection*

Clark 501S. In 1971, the Austin-Western Company became a division of Clark Equipment Company, and the former Austin-Western Pacer and Super graders from the 100 to the 500 models were continued for a couple of years. In 1973, the entire line was consolidated into two basic ranges, the 301 and 501 Series machines with horsepower ratings from 146 to 187 flywheel-horsepower. Like the former Austin-Western graders, the Clark models boasted all-wheel drive and all-wheel steer. The Pacer 301 and 501 were four-wheel models, and the Super 301 and 501 were six-wheel models. Clark discontinued grader manufacture in 1981. *Keith Haddock*

CMI Autograde AG-55. In addition to the double-ended Autoblade, CMI also produced more conventional-looking graders. The AG-55 and AG-65 graders had respective operating weights of 55,000 and 60,000 pounds, and hydrostatic drive provided infinite travel speeds up to 18 miles per hour. A Caterpillar D336 engine capable of developing 300 horsepower powers the AG-55 shown. It could also work in fine grading applications when it was equipped with an automatic stringline-guiding mechanism. CMI graders were phased out in the early 1980s. *Keith Haddock*

CMI Autoblade. CMI Corporation, famous for its automated profiling and paving equipment, came out with a giant grader in 1969. Dubbed the Autoblade, the 40-foot-long double-articulated unit had a power module at each end that consisted of a 225-horsepower diesel engine driving four wheels through hydrostatic drive. The eight-wheel-drive machine featured a centrally mounted cab that could swing 180 degrees to face in either direction. In addition to heavy-duty grading, CMI also promoted the Autoblade as a precision grader, suitable for fine grading in paving operations. The 65,000-pound machine could be guided in both alignment and grade from a single stringline reference. *CMI Corporation*

Deere JD-570B. John Deere entered the grader market in 1967 with the 83-flywheel-horsepower JD-570. This advanced machine carried a 12-foot blade, and boasted an articulated frame as well as front-wheel steering that created excellent maneuverability. At that time, no other manufacturer offered articulated graders, but today, with the exception of some small light-duty machines, all grader manufacturers offer articulated-frame machines. In 1972, the popular JD-570 became the JD-570A, which carried on the tradition until 1986 when the improved 90-flywheel-horsepower JD-570B took over. *Keith Haddock*

Deere JD-670B. Deere introduced this model in 1986, replacing the former JD-670A, which had been in production since 1978. The JD-670B offered direct-drive or power-shift transmission, and was powered by a John Deere diesel of 135 flywheel-horsepower. Employing frame articulation, a characteristic of all John Deere graders, the JD-670B is in the 30,000-pound weight class. The JD-672B is a six-wheel-drive version of the same grader, with hydrostatic drive to the front wheels. These B Series models were superseded by the JD-670C and JD-672C in 1997, with power ratings increased to 140 flywheel-horsepower, and weight boosted to 32,000 pounds. *Keith Haddock*

Deere JD-770. John Deere unveiled the innovative 770 at the 1975 Conexpo in Chicago. At 33,000 pounds, the new grader was not only John Deere's largest to date, it also replaced hand levers with push-button hydraulic controls for all motions except the blade lift. Although this system was not the most reliable, it continued in the JD-770A that was introduced in 1978 and survived until 1986, when the JD-770B reverted to lever control. The 770-size model was the only grader equipped with push-button controls. The John Deere grader line has progressed through the B Series, introduced in 1986, and the present C Series that began in 1997. The six-model lineup consists of tandem-drive and six-wheel-drive models from 140 to 210 horsepower. All models carry a 12-foot standard blade. *Keith Haddock*

Fiat-Allis M65. The former Allis-Chalmers D and DD grader models were replaced in 1971 with the similar-sized M65. Improvements over the former model included hydrostatic steering, power circle turn, new sheet metal, and increased power to 59 flywheel-horsepower. In January 1974, Allis-Chalmers and Fiat S.p.A. of Italy formed a joint venture, and the Fiat-Allis trademark was born. For the next 15 years, construction equipment was manufactured in existing plants of both companies, and bore the Fiat-Allis name. The M65 continued the success of its predecessor as a Fiat-Allis product. In 1979, as the 65-B, it received an 80-flywheel-horsepower Fiat engine. The 65-B was made at the Vermeer plant in Pella, Iowa, until 2001. *Keith Haddock*

Fiat-Allis FG85. The former Allis-Chalmers M Series graders were continued as Fiat-Allis products until the early 1980s, when FG Series gradually replaced them. For the first time, Fiat-Allis now offered articulated graders, but the line still included rigid-frame models. In 1982, Fiat-Allis became Fiatallis, and the FG Series graders eventually consisted of six sizes from 80 to 196 horsepower. In 1989, Fiatallis announced it would cease manufacture of earthmoving products in North America. In 1991, Fiat S.p.A. purchased farm equipment builder New Holland, then in 1999 it merged Case Corporation into the New Holland group. After this merger, the Fiatallis name was dropped, but the graders survive under the New Holland name in North America as imports from Brazil. *Keith Haddock*

Galion No. 14. David Charles Boyd founded the Galion Iron Works Company of Galion, Ohio, in 1907. In its early years, the Galion name appeared on a wide range of road and other construction equipment. By 1911, Galion had begun production of its own road grader, a light-duty, horse-drawn appliance. The company changed its name to the Galion Iron Works and Manufacturing Company in 1913. Galion was famous for building some of the heaviest pull-type graders in the industry such as this 15,000-pound No. 14, which carried a 14-foot blade. Popular throughout the 1920s and 1930s, they were capable of being pulled by the largest traction engines and crawler tractors available. Galion continued selling its pull-type graders until 1945. *Historical Construction Equipment Association*

Galion C Patrol. In 1922, Galion developed one of the first self-propelled motor graders with the engine at the rear and the operator positioned in the center of the frame. Also in the 1920s, Galion began development work on another milestone achievement, the Galion hydraulic control. Used on both pull-type and self-propelled graders, this hydraulic system was among the first to be applied to grader controls. Shown on the Model C Patrol in the picture, the hydraulic pump is driven by belt from the front of the engine crankshaft, and the extended lever linkages into the cab operate the hydraulic valves. This machine has a 50-horsepower engine and weighs in at 15,000 pounds. *Barbara Haddock*

Galion T-700. Galion introduced the "king" of graders when the company unveiled the T-700 in 1955. Larger than anything else in the grader industry at that time, it boasted 190 horsepower, a 14-foot blade, and an operating weight of over 40,000 pounds with scarifier. In typical Galion tradition, the T-700 was fully hydraulic and equipped with the patented Grade-O-Matic power-shift transmission, producing a top speed of 20 miles per hour. By 1960, the T-700 had its power upped to 220 horsepower and its weight increased to 42,000 pounds. Before production ceased in 1965, Galion's largest grader had reached 250 horsepower. *Galion Historical Society*

Galion 118. In 1950, Galion introduced the mid-sized 118 grader, boasting full hydraulic control of all grader operations. Working weight was listed at just under 25,000 pounds, and a 12-foot blade was standard. The 118 proved so popular with townships and contractors alike that it enjoyed a production run of some 21 years. Before production ended, the machine was upgraded to the 118B, with optional engines now rated at 135 and 145 horsepower. Galion celebrated in 1955 when it announced the first power-shift transmission installed on a grader. Called the Galion Grade-O-Matic drive, it utilized a torque converter, output shaft governor, and power-shift transmission to provide simple two-lever control of speed and direction. *Keith Haddock*

Galion 160L. The 160 Series was another successful grader model for Galion. With a choice of Cummins or GM engines of 160 horsepower, the 160 was a tandem-drive, fully hydraulic grader. Operating weight was around 30,000 pounds when equipped with a scarifier. Introduced in 1958 and not discontinued until 1971, the popular 160 finished its production days as the 160L with its specifications listing Cummins 160-horsepower or Detroit 190-horsepower engine options. After exactly 60 years with the same name, the Galion Iron Works & Manufacturing Company was renamed the Galion Manufacturing Company in 1973. In the following year, an industrial transaction resulted in Galion becoming a division of Dresser Industries, Inc. *Keith Haddock*

Galion A550. Galion launched its first articulated graders in 1979, quite late for such a well-established name in the grader industry. But the machines were very modern looking with a distinctively sloping rear hood. Identified as the A Series for "Articulated," the first three were the A-500, A-550, and A-600 with weights up to 30,000 pounds. The mid-sized A550 in the 29,000-pound weight class was powered by a Detroit diesel of 163 flywheel-horsepower. Beginning in 1986, Galion products took on the name of the parent company, Dresser, and the Galion name was temporarily dropped. In 1988, Dresser consolidated the grader line into three articulated models: the 830, 850, and 870. That same year, the graders became part of the Komatsu Dresser Company (KDC) joint venture. KDC reinstated the Galion name for a few years after 1992. Today the Galion name has disappeared, but its heritage can be traced into the current Komatsu grader line. *Keith Haddock*

Huber-Warco 5D-190. When the Huber Manufacturing Company acquired the W.A. Riddell Corporation (Warco) in 1957, the Huber-Warco name was born. Huber had been established since 1875 at Marion, Ohio, and the W.A. Riddell Corporation of Bucyrus, Ohio, was established in 1854. Huber built its first graders in the 1920s, and introduced hydraulic control as early as 1926. W.A. Riddell claimed the distinction of designing one of the very earliest motor graders in 1921. Warco graders included some of the most powerful built at that time. The big 5D-190, built between 1955 and 1959, was billed as the world's most powerful motor grader at 195 horsepower and 30,000 pounds of operating weight. *Keith Haddock*

Huber 10-D. When Huber acquired Warco in 1957, the range of graders consisted of the big 5D-190, the 4-D Series of five standard-transmission models from 75 to 123 horsepower, the 6-D and 7-D Series of torque converter models ranging from 102 to 150 horsepower, and the small M-52 Maintainer. In 1960, three new graders appeared, the 9-D, 10-D, and 11-D, with respective horsepower ratings of 100, 134, and 162, and weights ranging from 22,100 to 27,100 pounds. In the early 1960s, the Warco name was dropped and the single Huber name was adopted. The Huber 9-D and 11-D were discontinued in 1966, but the 10-D (illustrated) survived for two more years until the last of the D Series were replaced by the new 1000 Series. *Keith Haddock collection*

Huber F-1900. Huber revamped its grader line in 1966 and brought out the D-1000 Series graders with constant mesh transmission. The five sizes covered weight classes from the 23,000-pound D-1100 to the 29,000-pound D-1700, and horsepower ratings from 107 to 195 horsepower. These graders had a distinctive rear-sloping engine hood. The F-1000 Series soon followed, boasting a torque converter and power-shift transmissions. These were the F-1500 and F-1900 graders with engines of 156 horsepower and 195 horsepower, respectively. By 1968, the D Series and F Series had replaced all the earlier models in the Huber grader line, with the exception of the small Maintainer, which continued as the M650. *Keith Haddock collection*

Huber M-500. When Huber launched the first model of its small Maintainer utility grader in 1943, it was never imagined that this would become the company's longest-lived machine. Looking like a farm tractor with a blade slung below its frame, the light-duty 66-horsepower Maintainer has survived through its various guises to the present day. The M-500 appeared in 1963, taking over from the former M-52. This popular little grader progressed to the M-600 in 1967, with only slight changes to specification and horsepower. After 1970, the Huber company went through several changes of ownership. In 2002, the Huber M-850-C hydrostatically driven Maintainer is made in Galion, Ohio, by Enterprise Fabrications, Inc., and since 1994 has been the only product surviving from the former Huber line. *Keith Haddock collection*

Komatsu GD670A. Japan's Komatsu began building motor graders for the home market in 1952. Three years later, large numbers of graders were exported to Argentina, marking the first export of Komatsu products. By the late 1960s, four models were offered, the GD30-5M, GD31-3H, GD37-5H, and GD37-6H. These came in sizes ranging from 17,330 pounds to 26,680 pounds of operating weight, and spanned from 68 to 125 flywheel-horsepower. In 1979, Komatsu launched the first seven models in a new line of graders with a three-digit nomenclature. These ranged from the 125-flywheel-horsepower GD500R to the 165-flywheel-horsepower GD655A. In 1988, the Komatsu Dresser Company (KDC) joint venture was established and the former Galion graders (also part of Dresser) merged into Komatsu's grader line with modified specifications. The Komatsu GD670A shown was formerly the Galion 670 in the 32,400-pound weight class. *Keith Haddock*

Komatsu GD825A-2. Komatsu launched its flagship grader, the GD825A, at the 1987 Conexpo equipment show in Las Vegas, Nevada. With its 16-foot blade, 280-horsepower engine, and 58,250 pounds of operating weight, it remains Komatsu's largest grader at the time of writing. It features an articulated frame and a load-sensing system, which automatically adjusts the amount of oil to the hydraulic cylinders according to the work at hand. Since 1997, the GD825A has been sold as a surface mining product with the largest of Komatsu's other earthmoving machines. *Komatsu America International Company*

Komatsu GD750A-1. This modern-design Komatsu grader was announced at the Conexpo 1999 equipment show in Las Vegas, Nevada. In the heavyweight class, the GD750A is powered by a Cummins engine developing 225 flywheel-horsepower, and weighing 43,000 pounds in operating condition. Its standard blade is 14 feet wide. Highlights of this model include load-sensing hydraulics, full power-shift transmission, and a torque converter with a lock-up feature that allows the machine to operate in direct-drive mode. *Komatsu America International Company*

Meili-Blumberg Power Grader. The Meili-Blumberg Corporation, established in 1922, produced several grader models designed for attaching to heavy-duty farm tractors. With the front wheels removed, a frame supporting the blade, circle and leaning front wheels were added. Typical of similar units built around farm tractors by several other manufacturers, these outfits were an economical way to obtain a grader for light-duty utility work. The Meili-Blumberg operated hydraulically. The one shown is mounted on a Minneapolis-Moline Model R tractor. Another version was available for a 40-horsepower International tractor and could apply approximately 7,000 pounds of pressure on the blade. Attachments for the M-B grader included scarifier, power broom, snowplow, and front-mounted blade. *Keith Haddock*

New Holland RG200. The name New Holland first appeared on a grader in 1999. The company had acquired the construction equipment division of Orenstein & Koppel (O&K) from Germany's Hoesch-Krupp group a year earlier, then in 1999 Case Corporation was merged into its empire. In 1991, New Holland had been purchased by Fiat S.p.A. of Italy, which also included the Fiatallis range of motor graders. From 1999, the various graders were consolidated into New Holland's North American product line as imports from Brazil. Currently, the line consists of three models: the 140-horsepower RG140, the 170-horsepower RG170, and the 205-horsepower RG200. The smallest machine carries a 12-foot blade while the other two handle 14-foot blades. *Keith Haddock*

O&K G350. In 1980, Orenstein & Koppel (O&K) added a huge mining grader known as the G-350 to its established grader line. The machine had an operating weight of over 90,000 pounds and was the largest grader in production during the time it was built. It was a true grader, with all of the blade movements of its smaller brothers, and it was used in large mining applications where haul trucks were rapidly increasing in size. O&K sold 34 of the G-350 graders to many different countries, but in 1986, the model was phased out. The current O&K grader line consists of three sizes from 23,800 to 35,000 pounds of operating weight. *Keith Haddock collection*

Pettibone-Mulliken 402. This company announced a four-wheel motorized grader in 1930. Like other motor graders of the day, the operator's station was mounted behind the engine at the rear, and blade controls were hand-operated through bevel gears and screwed rods. The power unit was based on farm tractors such as the McCormick-Deering I-30 and the Massey-Harris 25. After introducing its first grader, Pettibone-Mulliken continued to include graders in its wide product line. The 1960 grader lineup consisted of five sizes from the 69-horsepower 401 to the 125-horsepower 404, spanning weights from 21,000 to 26,800 pounds. The mid-sized 402 weighed 23,000 pounds, and could be equipped with Hercules or GM diesel engine in the 107- to 125-horsepower range. Today, Pettibone, LLC no longer makes earthmoving equipment, but is the parent of a diverse range of industrial companies. *Keith Haddock*

Puckett 510. Looking rather untidy, but a veritable workhorse, this little grader is made by Puckett Brothers Manufacturing Company, Inc. of Lithonia, Georgia. It is one of many small utility graders built by specialist manufacturers who don't make the big graders. The niche market for these graders is found in landscaping, housing developments, parks, and work in confined spaces that would otherwise have to be performed by hand. The Puckett 510 not only functions as a grader, but as seen in the picture, it can work with several different attachments including a front-end loader, ripper, power broom, and vibratory plate compactor. A 76-horsepower engine powers this hydrostatic machine. Puckett sold its grader rights to Gehl Corporation in 1989. A descendent of this machine is now sold by PSI, Inc. *Keith Haddock*

Raygo Giant. This grader certainly lived up to its name. The double-articulated Giant had a GM 318-horsepower diesel engine driving a single-axle module at each end. With a weight of 106,000 pounds, it was one of the largest grader-type machines ever built. Although suitable for heavy-duty leveling and reclamation of surface mines, its blade was fixed to the central frame instead of the usual circle mounting, so it did not possess all the blade functions of a regular grader. Established in 1964, RayGo began manufacturing the Giant in 1969. Raygo went out of existence in 1985, when CMI Corporation purchased the company. Rights to the Raygo products passed to Caterpillar, Inc. in 1987. *Keith Haddock*

Russell No. 3 Motor Patrol. After Caterpillar Tractor Company was established in 1925, its first venture into products other than tractors was to purchase the Russell Grader Manufacturing Company in 1928. This company had already been developing self-propelled graders since 1919, and at the takeover date Russell was producing a line of graders known as Motor Patrols. The Motor Patrol No. 3 carried a McCormick-Deering power unit, and was made from 1926 to 1929. This tandem-drive outfit with hand controls formed the basis of Caterpillar's grader development in the 1930s. *Keith Haddock*

Volvo G780 VHP. AB Volvo of Sweden purchased Champion Road Machinery, Ltd. in 1997. At first, the existing Series VI Champion graders remained unchanged and continued to be marketed as Champion products. In January 2001, the Champion name was officially dropped, and for the first time the Volvo name appeared on a motor grader. The line was rationalized and identified with a "G" prefix. The current range is sold in five sizes: the G710, G720, G730, G740, and G780, with weights spanning from 30,600 to 42,700 pounds. Volvo offers a VHP (variable horsepower) version for each of its graders, where increased horsepower is available in the higher gear ratios. The top-of-the-line Cummins-powered G780 VHP provides 210 flywheel-horsepower in gears one and two, and 235 flywheel-horsepower in gears three through eight. Volvo also offers four sizes of compact graders from 85 to 110 horsepower. *Keith Haddock*

WABCO 660. In 1954 LeTourneau-Westinghouse Company (L-W) purchased the J.D. Adams Company, but the Adams name was retained as a trademark until 1962 when L-W adopted "WABCO" as its product trade name. The picture shows a WABCO 660, which was originally introduced as an Adams product in 1953 when it replaced the former Adams 610 model. The 660 was then carried forward into the new L-W company product line. In the 27,000-pound weight class, it was produced until 1962. The Cummins-powered machine was initially rated at 140 horsepower, but subsequent revisions brought this up to 190 horsepower by the time production ended. *Keith Haddock collection*

WABCO 888. The biggest grader produced by WABCO was the Model 888. Unveiled in 1967, it was in the heavyweight class at 41,000 pounds. It pushed a 14-foot-wide blade and was powered by a 230 flywheel-horsepower GM diesel. By 1970, the refined 888B model was in production, but the big grader was dropped from the product line in 1974. WABCO utilized hydraulically actuated mechanical blade controls on its graders, providing all the usual blade functions including side shift, angle, tilt, and bank-sloping capability up to 90 degrees from the horizontal. The 1980s saw a decline in the grader market, and by 1983 WABCO had ceased producing graders. *Eric C. Orlemann collection*

Wehr Power Grader. The Wehr Company of Milwaukee, Wisconsin, patented the One-Man Power Grader in 1921. It was based on a standard Fordson tractor and sold as a unit through all Fordson tractor dealers. With hand-operated controls, the operator was positioned ahead of the engine, near the center of the frame, where he had a bird's-eye view of the blade. The outfit weighed 8,300 pounds and carried a standard blade that was 8 feet wide. Soon after its introduction, the Power Grader was offered with a steel-cleated tire option. This unique system consisted of a series of cleats attached to spring-loaded, radially positioned rods around the wheel. When not required, the cleats could be turned 90 degrees and snapped into a recessed groove between the twin solid-rubber tires on each driving wheel. *Keith Haddock*

Wehr U26. After the Wehr Company introduced its first power grader in 1921, it expanded its line to the U Series, which included a range of models designed for power units other than Fordson. The U26 model shown is based on a Case tractor. The hand-operated blade lift is actuated through screwed rods, which are helped by the long tension springs. The tension springs carry the dead weight of the blade assembly. Most grader manufacturers progressed from pull-type graders to self-propelled units, but Wehr took the opposite strategy. Ten years after its Power Grader had been in the field, the company announced what would be a short-lived line of six pull-type graders ranging up to the 10,500-pound P-12. *Historical Construction Equipment Association*

CHAPTER 9

ARTICULATED DUMP TRUCKS

The articulated dump truck is a unitized tractor trailer vehicle with an articulated frame and rear-dumping body. Manufacturers offer four-wheel and six-wheel versions in 4x4, 6x4, or 6x6 drive configurations. This nimble hauling vehicle, known today as the ADT, is one of the newest categories of equipment to enter the earthmoving field.

Articulated hauling units actually date back to the 1940s, when prime movers designed for pulling scrapers were coupled to rear-dumping or bottom-dumping trailers. Following Letourneau's Tournarocker, leading manufacturers such as Allis-Chalmers, Caterpillar, International Harvester, Wooldridge, Euclid and others, offered earth-hauling trailer options for their scraper prime movers. All these units were articulated haulers by definition, but were not designed on the same lines as the modern-day ADT that has gained worldwide popularity over the past two decades. In fact, the modern ADT has developed into a new class of earth-moving vehicle that is a far cry from the scraper-type prime mover. It is faster on the road, built to a lighter specification, and designed for one purpose in mind: to haul excavated material.

The ADT owes its recent popularity to several design features, such as its articulated frame, providing superb maneuverability, and its oscillating hitch that separates the front and back frames. This keeps all wheels on the ground, lessens stresses in the truck's frame, and provides a longer working life.

In highway construction, industrial development, and where haul distances are medium-length, fleets of ADTs loaded by excavators have replaced conventional scrapers. The ADT is cheaper to operate than a comparably sized scraper because it is designed specifically to haul material, and not to excavate like a scraper. The digging capability of a scraper is only used for a small portion of its operating cycle, and that portion decreases as hauls grow longer. Thus, the ADT's lighter construction, smaller engine, and higher speed contribute to lower-cost operation. The ADT also doesn't carry the complicated scraper mechanisms to operate and maintain. But contractors have to compare the merits of each equipment type for a certain project, and must figure in the total cost of a dirt-moving spread. ADTs need an excavator to fill them, and

Allis-Chalmers TR-200. This is an example of an articulated hauling unit utilizing a scraper-type prime mover. The rear-dumping trailer has replaced the usual scraper for which this machine was originally designed. The Allis-Chalmers TR-200 Motor Wagon was designed for a load of 18 tons or 15 heaped cubic yards. It was powered by a Buda 176-horsepower diesel engine and could achieve a top speed of 21 miles per hour. Beginning in the 1940s, other manufacturers such as LeTourneau, Caterpillar, International Harvester, Wooldridge, and Euclid offered earth-hauling trailer options for their scraper prime movers. All these units were articulated haulers by definition, but were a different class of machine compared to the modern-day articulated dump truck (ADT), which is a single-purpose high-speed hauler built to a lighter specification. *Keith Haddock collection*

scrapers need a push tractor to load efficiently. There is a place for all types of equipment, and the experienced contractor knows which machines to use for maximum efficiency in each application.

With its roots going back to the United Kingdom in the 1950s, the present-day articulated dump truck has been popular with European earthmoving and construction contractors since the mid-1960s, but has only risen in popularity in North America over the past two decades. After the advantages of this medium-sized, high-speed earth hauler were recognized in the United States, unit population rapidly increased 40 percent since 1995 and 65 percent since 1991. Total population now exceeds 6,000 units.

In the 1950s, several manufacturers began to offer earth wagons coupled with reinforced agricultural

Bell B30B. South African manufacturer Bell Equipment launched its first articulated dump truck in 1985. The 25-ton B25 made an immediate impact that resulted in a broadened line of sizes extending to 40-tons capacity. Bell states that most of the main components in its trucks are mass-produced by other manufacturers, so there are no obscure parts to find, and the company can choose the best manufacturer for the product. During the early 1990s, Bell phased in upgraded B Series versions of its trucks, represented here by the B30B rated at 30-tons capacity and fitted with a Mercedes-Benz engine of 261 flywheel-horsepower. In 1998, Bell revised its trucks to the C Series with improvements focusing on the operator's cab and machine access. *Keith Haddock*

tractors. These early tractor-trailer combinations were the forerunners of today's ADT. English manufacturers such as Shawnee-Poole, Horley, and Hudson, as well as Lihnell of Sweden built early examples of this type. The first two-axle integrated hauler designed as an integral unit was built by Northfield of England in 1957. This forerunner of the modern-day ADT could carry 12.5 tons, and boasted most features found in today's ADTs, including 180-degree articulation actuated by two pairs of hydraulic rams. Camill and Whitlock, also of England, each produced similar trucks in the early 1960s. Whitlock made a brave attempt in 1963 to launch a very modern-looking 12-ton ADT featuring hydrostatic drive on all four wheels. But the market was not ready for this advanced design, and Whitlock soon discontinued the project.

During the 1960s, these articulated dump truck pioneers fell by the wayside except Sweden's Lihnell. Founded in 1946, this company built a tractor-trailer unit in 1959 consisting of a Bolinder-Munktell farm tractor pulling a trailer with a powered axle. Persevering with the powered trailer concept, the company marketed several 8x4 and 6x4 outfits designed around four-wheel farm tractors. The big breakthrough came in 1965 when Lihnell launched the DR630, a dump

Bell B40D. Bell launched its latest D Series ADTs in late 2001. The new machines boast Mercedes-Benz fuel-economy engines utilizing four-valve technology with electronically managed high-pressure injectors. Further economy is gained by the slower-running engines rated at 1,800 rpm. The sloping front hood affords the operator maximum visibility. He sits in a quiet cab where all-important operating conditions, such as cycle data, fuel usage, and machine malfunctions, are monitored on a display unit. The top-of-the-line B40D carries a payload of 40.5 tons, and its engine puts out 413 flywheel-horsepower. In 1999, Bell Equipment formed a strategic alliance with Deere & Company to distribute Bell trucks in North and South America under the Deere name. *Bell Equipment*

CAMILL 6/10

Camill 6/10. Another early pioneer of the ADT was this Camill dumper of 1963. Contractors Campbell & McGill of Devon, England, initiated a design based on a six-cylinder Fordson tractor power unit of 105 horsepower. The machine was adopted and marketed by E. Boydell & Company, makers of the Muir-Hill line of dump trucks and front-end loaders. The Camill ADT did not gain much popularity, but was used extensively by its design contractors on their own projects.

truck with a 4x4 configuration and a single-axle tractor. That same year, Volvo established a marketing agreement with Lihnell, whose design spawned the very successful Volvo range of ADTs. The Volvo name soon became the world market leader, and the company's efforts to promote this type of vehicle on a worldwide basis are a big reason for the ADT's popularity today.

Toward the end of the 1960s and in the early 1970s, several other companies began to experiment with ADT designs, and most of these are still around today under various guises. In 1971, Moxy Industries

of Norway introduced its first ADT, a robust 6x6 design that had a slow start due to financial difficulties. But under different management and with perseverance, Moxy trucks are one of the market leaders today. From 1986 to 2000, Moxy made ADTs for Komatsu sold under Komatsu's name.

Another milestone date in ADT history was 1973. That's the year David John Brown formed DJB Engineering in Peterlee, England, after a successful career in the heavy equipment industry, including a stint in West Africa as a logging contractor. DJB launched its

Case 325. Case is a recent name to appear on ADTs. The truck originated as a product of DDT Engineering, Ltd., established in Yorkshire, England, in 1994. This company became part of CNH Global, following the merger of Case and New Holland in 1999. Subsequently, the DDT articulated truck has been marketed and sold under several brand names within the group including Fiat-Hitachi, Link-Belt, O&K, New Holland, and Case, all companies within the CNH empire. The Case 325 is one of two offered by the company in 2002. It has a 25-ton payload capacity and is powered by a Case 260-horsepower diesel engine. *Case Corporation*

Caterpillar D400D. Caterpillar entered the ADT market in 1986 when it acquired the design rights to the line of ADTs designed and built by DJB Engineering, Ltd. of Peterlee, England. The DJB units had already featured Caterpillar engines and drivetrain componentry since their inception in 1973. So, coupled with the outstanding success these trucks had achieved in the field, Caterpillar's acquisition came as no surprise. At the time of takeover, the truck line consisted of 4x4 and 6x6 models, filling out capacities from 20 to 55 tons. Under Caterpillar's control, upgraded models soon appeared. This D400D was upgraded from the former 40-ton DJB D400 in 1989. The cutaway drawing shows the separate drives for all three axles on this 6x6 model powered by a Caterpillar 385-flywheel-horsepower engine. *Caterpillar, Inc.*

Caterpillar D40D. Caterpillar continually revised and upgraded its ADT line after acquiring the DJB products. The 55-ton D550B, largest in the industry, was dropped in 1987, but the line was broadened with new models up to the 40-ton size. Revised C and D Series began to appear in the late 1980s. The two-axle 4x4 ADTs were given a two-digit model number following a nomenclature established by the former DJB company. Here is the D40D, which was introduced in 1989. It has the same 40-ton capacity and 385-horsepower engine as the three-axle D400D. *Caterpillar, Inc.*

first ADT, the D250, at the London Public Works Exhibition in 1974. It created immediate interest both in the U.K. and overseas, and production commenced at a rate of one per month. The DJB units featured Caterpillar engines and drivetrain components and proved very successful in the field—so successful that Caterpillar acquired the DJB design rights and entered the ADT market in 1986.

In South Africa, Bell Equipment launched its first articulated dump truck in 1985, the 25-ton B25. This was the first of a very successful line of ADTs that rapidly penetrated the world market. In 1999, Bell Equipment formed a strategic alliance with Deere & Company to distribute Bell trucks in North and South America under the John Deere name.

Another company to gain worldwide notoriety is DDT Engineering, Ltd. Established in Yorkshire, England, as recently as 1994, the company rapidly made a name for itself through its successful line of ADTs. To its advantage, the DDT company was caught up in the huge merger of Case and New Holland in 1999, and the DDT articulated truck marketing and distribution was

Caterpillar D400E Ejector. As with most leading ADT manufacturers in the late 1990s, Caterpillar took part in the resurrection of the ejector-type truck, which had been around in small numbers since the late 1940s. Caterpillar chose its upgraded D400E, originally launched in 1996, for its first ejector model. This machine has a capacity of 40 tons and is fitted with a 405-flywheel-horsepower engine. The ejector advantages include safe dumping without raising the center of gravity, uniform spreading on the move, and safety under overhead obstructions because the body isn't raised during dumping. *Caterpillar, Inc.*

Caterpillar 730. In 2000, Caterpillar launched the first two models, the 725 and 730, in a redesigned line of ADTs. These 25- and 30-ton models were joined by the 40-ton 740 in 2001. New features include a high horsepower-to-weight ratio, and an electronically controlled transmission that completely integrates engine and ground speeds for smooth gear shifting. An engine compression brake enhances downhill braking, and four modes of operation allow retarding power to be matched with operating conditions. The radiator is mounted behind the cab to improve forward visibility. The 730 is equipped with a 305-flywheel horsepower engine. *Caterpillar, Inc.*

taken over by the new company known as CNH Global. Since then, the DDT dump trucks have not only been sold under their own name, but have been incorporated into the product lines of Case, Fiat-Hitachi, Link-Belt, and O&K, all companies within the CNH empire.

Terex developed its own ADT design at its plant in Scotland, and began marketing it in early 1983. Terex soon developed a full range of ADTs up to 40-tons capacity that have since become probably the most successful of all Terex product lines since the company's formation in 1968.

The ADT basic design permitted the mounting of several other types of equipment on its chassis in place of the rear-dumping body. Water tanks, log and pipe carriers, fuel trucks, hydraulic booms, drill rigs, and special trailers for just about anything that needed to be carried were designed onto the basic tractor-trailer unit. This strategy expanded the ADT's sales areas and gave the user of this equipment mobility and off-road capability never before experienced. Special dump bodies adapted for hauling coal and wood chips further penetrated new markets. There are even low-profile versions for working underground in tunnels and mines.

Recent improvements in the ADT's basic design include electronic controls and diagnostics, higher horsepower engines, more robust components and frame design, and smoother gear selection. Tilt and telescoping steering wheels are now standard equipment, as are well-situated controls and easy-to-read

Deere JD760. Another example of an early type of articulated hauler derived from a scraper-type prime mover. This is the John Deere JD760 that normally pulled a 9.5-cubic-yard elevating scraper. It is shown with an Athey model PR760 rear-dumping trailer of 15 tons capacity, although the trailer in the picture has received welded sideboards to add a few more cubic yards. The Model 760 carried a 143-flywheel-horsepower John Deere engine. It first appeared in 1965, and with the upgraded JD760A, it lasted in the product line until replaced by the 762 in 1975. *Keith Haddock*

gauges. Today's operators expect air conditioning and sound suppression to reduce noise. Operator comfort has come a long way since the first machines moved dirt, as each manufacturer has made improvements to increase operator comfort, visibility, and safety.

161

Deere 250C. In 1999, Deere announced it had formed a strategic alliance with Bell Equipment of South Africa to market the latter's ADTs badged as Deere products in North and South America. The line consists of four models from 25- to 40-tons capacity. They feature a centrally mounted cab with air-suspension seat to smooth the operator's ride. Power is automatically distributed equally to all three axles by limited-slip differentials, providing constant traction in slippery conditions. The 250C is powered by a DaimlerChrysler diesel of 237 flywheel-horsepower. In unison with Bell, Deere upgraded its four models to the D Series in late 2001. *Keith Haddock*

DJB D25B. In 1973, DJB Engineering was established in Peterlee, England, to build articulated dump trucks. The company launched its first model, the 25-ton 6x6 D250, at the London Public Works Exhibition in 1974. An extended line of sizes were designed and built with both 6x4 and 6x6 drive options. The picture shows an original DJB D25B, a 25-ton two-axle design with 4x4 drive configuration. DJB trucks featured Caterpillar engines and drivetrain componentry, and benefited from being sold through the worldwide Caterpillar dealer network. Caterpillar acquired the DJB design rights and entered the ADT market in 1986. *Keith Haddock*

Euclid S-12. Another example of an early articulated hauler is this 1950s Euclid S-12 tractor unit coupled to a rear-dumping trailer built by the Easton Car & Construction Company of Easton, Pennsylvania. The outfit weighed 22 tons empty and could carry a load of 22 tons. When loaded, each of the four wheels shared the load almost equally. The Euclid S-12, which normally pulled a 12-cubic-yard (struck) capacity scraper, was equipped with a GM 6-71 diesel developing 218 flywheel-horsepower. Euclid also offered similar rear-dump options for its S-7 and S-18 tractor units. *Keith Haddock collection*

Euclid A-464. This ADT made its debut at the Conexpo 1981 equipment show as the H-35-T by Haulmasters, Inc. of Olathe, Kansas, founded in 1969. The machine became a Euclid product in 1983, after Euclid's parent company Daimler-Benz purchased Haulmasters, and incorporated the truck into the Euclid line as the A-464. The 35-ton-capacity unit carried a Cummins NT-855-C engine of 311 flywheel-horsepower driving through an eight-speed power-shift transmission. The front and center axles were driven through limited-slip differentials, and the rear tandem-axle suspension was designed on the oscillating beam principle, providing a low center of gravity and equal weight distribution on all four wheels. *Eric C. Orlemann collection*

Hitachi AH400. In 2000, Hitachi Construction Products announced an alliance with Bell Equipment of South Africa to market the latter's ADTs badged as Hitachi products. The line consists of four models, the AH250, AH300, AH350, and AH400 with capacities denoted by the first two digits of the model number. They feature a sophisticated automatic transmission that selects the optimum shift points based on the load and driving conditions. Power is automatically distributed equally to all three axles by limited-slip differentials that provide constant traction in slippery conditions. The 40-ton-capacity AH400 is powered by a Daimler/Chrysler diesel of 413 flywheel-horsepower. *Hitachi Construction Products*

ISCO IC-A22R. Cline Truck Manufacturing Company, established in 1952, made a variety of off-highway trucks. The company was a division of ISCO Manufacturing Company, Inc. from 1972 to 1978. During that era, the off-highway trucks bore the name ISCO, and the range included rigid-frame dump trucks as well as this articulated model. Initially introduced in 1973 as the 20-ton IC-A20R, the vehicle was revised with two additional tons to the IC-A22R. The engine installed was a Cummins NHD-230 stated as 220 gross-horsepower. The front wheels were driven via a torque converter and four-speed power-shift transmission. *Keith Haddock collection*

JCB 716. JCB presented a prototype ADT known as the 6D as far back as 1959, but it never went into production. Almost three decades later, the company re-entered the ADT market when it launched the two-axle 13-ton 712 in 1988. The 17-ton Model 716 followed this two years later. Fitted with a 139-flywheel-horsepower engine, the 716 drove through a six-speed transmission with power to all four wheels. In the mid-1990s, JCB temporarily withdrew from the dump truck market. *JCB Sales, Ltd.*

JCB 718. JCB launched a new ADT in 2000. This is the Model 714 with a design capacity of 14 tons. It boasts a modern, curvy appearance and state-of-the-art operator's cab featuring a high-suspended seat giving good visibility fore and aft. JCB followed this up with the similarly designed Model 718 in 2001. The larger-capacity machine carries a payload of 18 tons and comes with a 167-horsepower engine. Transmission is a six-speed electrically operated automatic type incorporating a torque converter. On JCB dump trucks, the operator can select two- or four-wheel drive at the throw of a switch. *JCB Sales, Ltd.*

Link-Belt D300. LBX Company LLC entered the ADT market with its Link-Belt branded models in 2000. The trucks resulted from a supply agreement between LBX and ASTRA, the heavy-duty truck division of Italy's Fiat. The trucks originated from the former British DDT line which ASTRA purchased just before it became part of CNH Global with the merger of Case and New Holland in 1999. The LBX Link-Belt truck line initially consisted of four models from 16- to 30-tons capacity including the 30-ton E30 with ejector discharge. In 2002, the company announced its second-generation ADTs consisting of four models, the 25-ton D250, the 30-ton D300, the 35-ton D350, and 40-ton D400. A Cummins 300-horsepower engine powers the D300 shown. *Keith Haddock*

Komatsu HM400-1. Komatsu entered the ADT market following a joint venture set up with Norway's Moxy in 1986. The first models, the 27.5-ton HA250 and the 30-ton HA270 appeared in 1987, each fitted with a Komatsu diesel of 240 flywheel-horsepower. A year after the joint venture ended in 2000, Komatsu released in North America the first of a new line of ADTs, designed in-house by the company. The HM400-1 can achieve a top speed of 35 miles-per-hour with its rated load of 40 tons. A 430-horsepower Komatsu diesel is up front, driving a six-speed fully automatic transmission utilizing electronic control that senses speed and load for precise shifting. In 2002, Komatsu launched 30- and 35-ton similarly designed ATDs on the market. *Komatsu America International Company*

MackPack MP404X. Mack Trucks introduced this unusual articulated dump truck in 1973. The bottom-dumping vehicle carried 35 tons and measured over 46 feet from front to rear. All four wheels were driven from a Detroit 12V71N 475-horsepower engine mounted in the rear, and the vehicle could achieve a top speed of 50 miles-per-hour according to the specification sheet. The front wheels were driven via a propeller shaft over 20 feet long, running through a trough in the body! The MackPack turned out to be Mack's last fling at the off-highway market, as the company announced its withdrawal from off-highway trucks in 1979. *Tom Berry*

Moxy D16B. In 1971, Moxy Industries of Norway introduced its first ADT, the 18-ton-capacity D16. It was soon followed by the upgraded D16B, one of which is shown working on highway construction in southern England. The robustly designed D16B was equipped with a Scania 210-horsepower engine and Clark transmission. In 1982, Brown Engineering of Yorkshire, England, took over manufacturing and distribution of Moxy trucks. Under the Brown management, the line was expanded until, by 1987, the range included seven models ranging from 13- tons to 38.5-tons capacity.

Moxy 6225B. Moxy introduced a new series of ADTs beginning in 1982 with the Model 6200S. It boasted an advanced-design independent suspension system and a capacity of 27.5 tons. More trucks were announced during the next five years including this 6225B with an extended-capacity body for hauling coal. The 6225B is rated at 27.5 tons capacity, and is powered by a Scania engine of 254 horsepower affording a top speed of almost 30 miles per hour. The smallest Moxy model, the 13-ton-capacity 3212 introduced in 1984, was actually manufactured by MT Agricultural Engineers of Essex, England, a company founded in 1975 to manufacture agricultural products.

Moxy MT30. In 1986, Moxy established an arrangement to make trucks for Japan's Komatsu to be sold under that company's brand name. In 1990, financial problems hit the company when its parent owner Brown Group went into receivership. But Komatsu desired to keep the Moxy factory in production and enlisted the help of theNorwegian mining group Olivin. From 1991, Moxy was owned jointly by Moxy and Olivin, and the Moxy trucks continued with the introduction of the MT Series of ADTs. The example shown is the MT30 of 30-tons capacity with a 262-horsepower engine. From the outset, all Moxy trucks have been designed on the all-wheel-drive principle, either in 4x4 or 6x6 configuration.

165

Moxy MT36 II. In 2001, Moxy began to introduce a new line of trucks designed on what the company calls its "Plus 1" concept. This concept blends a number of important elements into the truck's design: power, traction, stability, reliability, productivity, operator comfort, and environment. The latest MT36 Series II, revised from the former MT36 introduced in 1999, is designed with these elements in mind. The 36-ton-capacity ADT carries a Scania 388-horsepower engine, claimed by Moxy to be the highest engine power rating of any other ADT in the 35-ton weight class. The MT36 Series II is one of Moxy's lineup for 2002 covering sizes from 26 to 40 tons. *Moxy Trucks*

New Holland AD300. New Holland became heavily involved with construction equipment when it merged with Case Corporation in 1999. It had already purchased manufacturing and distribution rights from several other well-known equipment manufacturers, and the resulting conglomeration became known as CNH Global. Each of the manufacturers' products under this organization were subsequently marketed in different parts of the world under different brand names within the CNH empire. The two New Holland ADTs, 25-ton AD250 and 30-ton AD300, have their heritage in the British DDT trucks. They feature automatic six-speed transmission with manual override, and rear-view closed-circuit TV for safe operation. A Cummins 300-horsepower engine is under the AD300 hood. *Keith Haddock*

Northfield F7. Recognized as the forerunner of the modern-day articulated dump truck (ADT) is this Model F7 built in 1957 by Northfield Industrial of Yorkshire, England. It was the first two-axle tractor-trailer hauler designed as a single-purpose integrated unit. It could carry 12 tons, and boasted most features found in today's ADTs, including 180-degree articulation actuated by two pairs of hydraulic rams. Northfield faded from the scene in the mid-1960s but not before two larger ADTs had been introduced, the 14-ton F9 and 20-ton F12. The earthmoving industry was just not ready for this type of hauler—a classic case of a machine ahead of its time.

Shawnee-Poole FD 750. The Shawnee-Poole "system of mobility and economy" was designed in the mid-1950s by H.G. Poole & Partners, Rhodesia, Africa, and manufactured by Steel Fabricators (Cardiff), Ltd., Cardiff, Wales. It represents one of the earliest forms of articulated hauling units applied to a standard farm-type tractor. The designers recognized the advantages of hauling a load behind the tractor as long as the right type of hitch was used. In this case, a full gooseneck was employed resulting in an extremely tight turning circle and superior stability because of its low-mounted hitch point. The FD 750 utilized a 55-horsepower Fordson Major as prime mover and a 10-ton-capacity trailer. Shawnee-Poole trailers up to 20-tons capacity were marketed until at least the 1980s. *Keith Haddock*

Terex TA30. Terex took advantage of the latest technology in electronic engine management, emission control, and operator comfort when it replaced its former ADT line with the new TA Series in 1998. In 2002, this line consists of the TA25, TA30, TA35, and TA40 with capacities from 25 to 40 tons. They feature automatic-slip differentials with three axles in permanent six-wheel drive. Each can achieve a top speed of 34 miles-per-hour. Large numbers of these trucks have left the factory since their introduction, including a record 800 in 1999 alone. The 2002 version of the 30-ton TA30 shown is powered by a 287-flywheel-horsepower Cummins engine. *Terex Equipment, Ltd.*

Terex 4066C. Terex designed and developed its own ADT at its plant in Scotland, and released the first model early in 1983. Known as the Model 32-04, the 25-ton, three-axle 6x4-drive ADT was the forerunner of probably the most successful of all Terex product lines since the company's formation in 1968. In 1985, Terex changed its models to a new four-digit nomenclature. The first two digits indicated the truck's capacity, while the last two digits indicated 6x4 or 6x6 drive configuration. Thus the 32-04 became the 2364 (23-metric-tons capacity). With frequent revisions and updates, Terex phased its ADTs through B and C models, and broadened its range up to 40-tons capacity. The 40-ton 4066C 6x6 model was powered by a 375- flywheel-horsepower Detroit diesel. *Terex Equipment, Ltd.*

Volvo DR631. This was the first ADT to carry the Volvo name. Volvo acquired the design from Sweden's Lihnell company in 1965. Lihnell developed its first tractor-trailer unit in 1959 consisting of a Bolinder-Munktell farm tractor pulling a trailer with a powered axle. The DR631 was a four-wheel-drive updated version of the former DR630 released a year earlier. It was based on a Bolinder-Munktell BM350 tractor. This machine spawned the very successful Volvo range of ADTs.

Volvo DR860. With Volvo's successful DR631 under its wing, the company introduced the much larger DR860 in 1968. With a capacity of 20 tons, and a 150-horsepower Volvo turbocharged engine, the machine had virtually no competition for its ability to move on rough terrain with a full load. The front axle, as well as the front tandem axle, was powered in this 6x4 design. The Volvo ADT was the first to use long hydraulic rams mounted outside the chassis, a design later copied by others. Volvo released the updated DR860A in 1970, and then nine years later replaced it with the DR861 in 1979. The DR861 was Volvo's first truck offered with an all-wheel-drive (6x6) option, a configuration that would later become standard in the entire Volvo range. *Keith Haddock*

Volvo A25. A new line of ADTs appeared from the Volvo stable in 1979, spearheaded by the 22-ton 5350. This 6x4 truck sported a modern look with the latest technology in engine efficiency, transmission and operator comfort. It was powered by a 190-horsepower diesel engine with its radiator positioned at the side. The tractor axle and the front trailer axle were powered. In 1984, the 5350 became the 25-ton 5350B, a full 6x6 model. This machine evolved into the A25, one of Volvo's new A Series ADTs launched in 1987. The A25 in the picture has a 25-ton-capacity high-volume body for hauling coal, and a Volvo 240-flywheel-horsepower engine. *Keith Haddock*

Volvo A40. Forty tons, 6x6 drive, 395 flywheel-horsepower—that's the specification in a nutshell for the top-of-the-line Volvo A40, one of the company's A Series ADTs. The others were the A20, A25, A30, A35, and included both 4x4 and 6x6 wheel configurations covering payload capacities from 20 to 40 tons. These forerunners of Volvo's present ADT line utilized Volvo engines and were equipped with Volvo's own planetary transmission specially designed for dump trucks, as well as a fully floating bogie with high ground clearance. *Keith Haddock*

Wagner Fullback 645. Starting in 1958, Wagner Mining & Construction Equipment Company of Portland, Oregon, and its predecessor companies, built a well-respected business producing front-end loaders and haul trucks for underground mining. In 1989, the company was acquired by Sweden's Atlas Copco AB, and, in 1993, unveiled its first ADT designed for general construction. Initially marketed as the 45-ton Fullback 645, it was uprated to the 50-ton Fullback 650 the following year, making it the largest-capacity ADT in production at that time. The 6x6 vehicle featured totally enclosed, liquid-cooled brakes, a centrally mounted climate-controlled operator's cab, and a 450-horsepower Detroit diesel engine with torque converter. These machines were produced up to 1996 when the company decided to concentrate on its other products. *Atlas Copco Wagner, Inc.*

Volvo A30D. With the latest rounded look, Volvo's new D Series line of ADTs is represented here by the 31-ton A30D. This model, and the A25D, were released in 2002 rounding out Volvo's four Model D Series line initiated in 2000 with the launch of the A35D and A40D up to 40 tons capacity. Apart from their appearance, these latest from the ADT world market leader, in terms of sales, boast a unique "load and dump" brake. This safety feature allows the operator to apply all brakes and neutralize the transmission by pressing a single button during loading and dumping. The brakes are automatically released when the transmission lever is moved from neutral to drive. The A30D comes with a 324-flywheel-horsepower electronically controlled Volvo engine. *Volvo Construction Equipment*

Whitlock DD95. Whitlock of Essex, England, was one of the pioneers of the single-axle tractor concept for ADTs. This 95-horsepower Model DD95 had a hauling capacity of 11 tons and a standard mechanical transmission with six forward and two reverse speeds. The company also offered the DD75 with the same capacity but equipped with a smaller engine of 67 horsepower. These dump trucks were only marketed for few years in the early 1960s. Whitlock was better known for its tractor backhoes and claimed to have built the world's first in 1952. Whitlock machines were based on Fordson agricultural tractor power units.

Whitlock DD105. Whitlock made a brave attempt in 1963 to launch a very modern-looking 12-ton articulated dump truck, the DD105. Its advanced design featured hydrostatic drive on all four wheels. Its engine developed 105 horsepower, and its top speed in four-wheel drive was 7 miles-per-hour. However, the rear drive could be disconnected, allowing a top speed of 20 miles per hour in front-wheel-drive. The market was not ready for this advanced design, and the project was soon discontinued. In the early 1970s, British excavator manufacturer Hy-Mac took over the Whitlock company, but the haul trucks had long been discontinued by that time.

CHAPTER 10

OFF-HIGHWAY HAULERS

Off-highway haulers developed from a need to haul vast amounts of material on unpaved roads. From their early beginnings, when attempts were made to adapt highway-type trucks to off-road use, these vehicles have gradually increased in strength and capacity. Now the largest behemoths can carry loads of over 400 tons with a gross vehicle weight of over 1,300,000 pounds. These are truly the monster trucks of today.

As one might expect, off-highway trucks don't operate on public highways. Their width usually places them in the "wide load" category, even when running empty, and their weight and wheel arrangements don't comply with highway regulations. The largest trucks today measure over 30 feet wide. That's almost the width of a three-lane highway! So the big trucks must be broken down into transferable components to enable them to move from job to job. And although the term "off-highway" implies that these trucks might be at home on rough, uneven roads, the opposite is in fact true: hard and stable roads are essential to run these huge vehicles efficiently. Frames can twist over uneven ground, resulting in premature cracking.

Bumps in the road can ruin suspensions, so most open-pit mines spend a lot of time and money constructing roads, and maintaining them in top condition so the trucks run trouble-free with minimal maintenance.

Vehicles designed for off-highway use cover a wide range of types. They include small site dumpers used on building sites, articulated types covered in the previous chapter, and off-highway rigid-frame haulers ranging in size from about 10-tons capacity to the giant haulers found in surface mines. Most of these latter types have a rigid-frame with single- or tandem-drive axles, but some are the tractor-trailer type, usually consisting of a four-wheel tractor unit pulling a semi-trailer.

While articulated in the true sense of the word, these tractor-trailer outfits differ from the articulated dump truck (ADT) described in the previous chapter because they are not integrally designed vehicles. The tractor unit consists of a modified rear-dump hauler with a fifth wheel coupling in place of its regular dump box. A specialized trailer manufacturer usually builds the trailer to a specification that matches the hauling unit. What really sets these vehicles apart, when compared to an ADT, is their sheer size. Very few of the

Autocar AP40. This rugged-looking off-road hauler was the largest of a range of quarry and mine trucks built by Autocar in the 1950s. With a capacity of 40 tons, and powered by a Cummins VT-12 engine developing 600 horsepower, it boasted planetary gear drive to the rear axles. The Autocar Company, founded in 1908, became a division of the White Motor Company in 1954. Based at Exton, Pennsylvania, it was one of several well-known highway truck companies that temporarily ventured into the off-highway truck business. Subsequently most companies withdrew from the market because these vehicles continued to grow in size and their manufacturing concept became entirely different from that required for highway trucks. *American Truck Historical Society*

Aveling-Barford RD150. A builder of road rollers since 1865, the English firm Aveling-Barford launched its first site dumper in 1939 based on a Fordson tractor. Expanding its hauler line, the company released its very successful SN Series haulers of 30- and 35-tons capacity in 1958. These Rolls-Royce-powered haulers were shipped to all five continents, and continued in production to 1970, when the entire line of Aveling-Barford trucks was replaced by the Centaur range in sizes up to 50 tons. The Centaurs were gradually developed into the current RD Series, consisting of six rigid-frame haulers from 30 to 65 tons, including the 50-ton RD150 (shown) with a Cummins engine of 560 flywheel-horsepower. *Keith Haddock*

Belaz 256B. This military-style 15-ton Russian truck was initially made for use in the former Soviet Union. Since the 1970s, this model has been exported around the world. The 256B is powered by a 165-horsepower V-8 diesel engine, utilizes a five-speed manual transmission, and can attain a top speed of 42 miles-per-hour. Belaz claims to be the world's largest maker of off-highway trucks, building some 4,000 to 4,500 trucks per year. It introduced a 200-ton truck in 1981, and currently supplies trucks from 33 to 310 tons. The largest model, still in prototype stage, is of articulated-frame design, powered by a Russian-made, low-speed locomotive engine, and propelled by DC electric motors in all four wheels. *Keith Haddock*

tractor-trailer types operating today carry less than 100 tons, and the largest carries over 300 tons. These haulers are confined to the large surface mines where coal is hauled several miles on relatively flat roads.

Yet another type of coal hauler is the rigid-frame bottom-dumping type known as a unitized truck. Introduced by Kress in 1970, this vehicle is carried on four-wheel assemblies, one at each corner, and is driven by a rear-mounted engine through a mechanical transmission. Other manufacturers such as UnitRig, Goodbary, and Wabco, brought out unitized bottom-dumping haulers during the 1970s, each one different in its configuration or drive type. Of these, only Kress survives today; that company recently put 300-ton-capacity unitized trucks to work in North Dakota.

When dirt-moving jobs called for steam shovels in the 1920s, they needed trucks to load. The only ones available were the highway type, built with light-duty frames, wooden bodies, and narrow wheels. The comparatively advanced shovels pounded the flimsy truck bodies with rocks, and the trucks frequently became stuck in muddy conditions. Highway trucks proved totally unsuitable to work off-road, and a robust off-highway hauler was desperately needed.

Some early attempts had been made to beef-up highway truck designs for on-site use, but it took a project the magnitude of the Boulder Dam (now the Hoover Dam) for true off-highway trucks to come into their own. Truck builder Mack completely redesigned some of its trucks in 1931 for Boulder Dam use, then expanded the line to include special off-road models in the 1930s.

The first company to specialize in haulers designed and built for off-highway duty was Euclid Road Machinery Company of Euclid, Ohio, beginning in 1934. The off-highway truck filled a much-needed role in the earthmoving contractor's spread of equipment, and its success prompted many other manufacturers to enter the field. Some were established truck makers, such as Dart and Mack, while others were specialist off-road vehicle builders. Experience proved that a highway-type truck could not be beefed-up enough for regular off-highway service. It wasn't enough just to strengthen the frame and axles. Every component of the unit, including wheel rims, springs, door hinges, even down to the last nut and bolt had to be designed to withstand the most rugged site use.

By the end of the 1930s, an array of off-highway truck types was available, including some very large, high-capacity units such as those built by the Hug and Trojan companies. By 1940, some of these were carrying loads up to 70 tons. Another type of hauler developed

Caterpillar 769. Caterpillar introduced its first rigid-frame off-highway truck in 1962. The 35-ton Model 769 was styled ahead of its time, as its curved appearance gave it a 1990s look! It featured oil-cooled disc brakes and a new power-shift transmission built for this truck. Its Caterpillar diesel engine was initially rated at 375 flywheel-horsepower, but was later increased to 400 flywheel-horsepower. Upgraded truck specifications resulted in the 769B in 1967 (415 flywheel-horsepower), the 769C in 1978 (450 flywheel-horsepower), and the 769D in 1995 (485 flywheel-horsepower). By 1990, the 769's capacity was also boosted to 40 tons. *Keith Haddock collection*

Caterpillar 772B. The Model 769/769B was Caterpillar's only rigid-frame truck for some eight years until the 50-ton 773 appeared in 1970. Of similar design and appearance to its smaller brother, the 773 was simply a larger version of a very successful hauler. The 600-flywheel-horsepower truck remained current until 1978, when the 773B was unveiled with power boosted to 650 flywheel-horsepower. The picture shows the fifth-wheel tractor version known as the 772B hauling coal in a surface mine in Alberta, Canada. In this configuration, the tractor unit can haul a trailer of 100-tons capacity, double the capacity of the same hauler in its rear-dump version. *Keith Haddock*

Caterpillar 783. After the company launched its first off-highway truck in 1962, Caterpillar went straight into designing and testing a range of large diesel-electric trucks. Three sizes were eventually built between 1965 and 1969 before Caterpillar decided to concentrate solely on mechanical-drive trucks. The picture shows the three-axle Model 783 side-dumping truck rated at 100-tons capacity. Its center axle drove, while the front and rear axles steered. This model was never developed beyond the prototype stage, but Caterpillar's other electric trucks did achieve a fair degree of success. These were the 75-ton Model 779 in production from 1965 to 1969, and the 786, a 240-ton bottom-dumping coal hauler with a cab and power module at each end for shuttle service. *Caterpillar, Inc.*

around this time was the trailer type, pulled by a tractor unit as described above. This type, consisting of a two-wheel or four-wheel tractor, was developed from the earliest form of wagons first pulled by horses, and later by steam traction engines. Manufacturers such as Caterpillar, LeTourneau, M-R-S, Dart, and Euclid, started to make this type at an early date. Today, tractor units of this type include those made by Caterpillar, Euclid, and Komatsu. The wagons or trailers are built by specialist manufacturers, such as Maxter Industries, Ltd. of Montreal, Quebec, that build rear- and bottom-dumping trailers up to 290-tons capacity.

After World War II, hauler sizes continued to increase, and many well-known highway truck manufacturers, including Autocar, Mack, Walter, International, Kenworth, and Oshkosh, continued off-highway vehicles in their production programs, alongside the specialist manufacturers. However, the development of larger trucks was limited by the available size of engines, transmissions, and tires. This situation prompted Euclid to adopt twin power in the late 1940s, which involved doubling up engines, drive trains, and drive axles so heavier loads could be carried.

In the 1960s, as stronger, more powerful components became available, truck design reverted to single-drive axle and single-engine designs. This cycle was repeated in the early 1970s, when the demand for increased capacity once again overtook technology

Caterpillar 797. In 1998, Caterpillar officially rolled out its flagship mining truck, the Model 797, from the Decatur, Illinois, plant. Although some 50 percent bigger than Caterpillar's previous largest, the 240-ton 793C, the 360-ton 797 retained proven Caterpillar features such as mechanical drive, sealed and oil-cooled disc brakes, and electronically-controlled power-shift transmission. This monster truck measured over 30 feet wide and 23 feet, 9 inches high. Its 24-cylinder engine developed 3,211 flywheel-horsepower. In 2002, Caterpillar launched the successor to its flagship truck, the 797B, with larger tires, power increased to 3,370 flywheel-horsepower, and payload capacity boosted to 380 tons, making this one of the largest trucks ever built. *Keith Haddock*

available to produce large enough components. Tandem-drive trucks reappeared in the largest sizes. Today, tires and engines have advanced to the point where the largest trucks in production are once again of the single-drive axle, single-engine design.

A major breakthrough came with the perfection of electric-wheel-drive, consisting of a diesel engine driving a generator to provide DC electric current for a motor in each driving wheel. R.G. LeTourneau developed one of the first electric haulers in conjunction with Anaconda Company of Butte, Montana. This was the trolley-assisted TR-60, a 75-ton articulated hauler shipped to the Montana site in 1959. That same year, Unit Rig brought out its prototype diesel-electric Lectrahaul. Today, there is much debate between manufacturers as to whether mechanical- or electric-drive trucks produce the lowest cost per ton hauled. Both types have their advantages and disadvantages, and both can make money for their owners in the right conditions.

By the 1970s, the only companies making both highway and off-highway trucks were International and Mack. Other highway truck builders had ended off-highway truck building at some time in the previous two decades. It appears that truck builders had to specialize to survive. Those specializing in highway trucks found the market lucrative and shied away from the relatively small market for off-highway haul trucks. The new generation of large off-highway vehicles demanded heavy steel castings, and technology quite different from what was required to build road vehicles. Accordingly, Mack dropped its off-highway hauler line in 1979, and International sold its off-highway Payhauler Division to a new company, Payhauler Corporation, in 1982. International's departure from the off-highway truck scene marked the end of an era. From that time on, highway truck and off-highway truck manufacture moved on as entirely separate industries, with no manufacturer producing both types.

Caterpillar 771D. In 1992, Caterpillar launched special beefed-up versions of its two smallest trucks following a demand for a tough hauler to work in rock quarries. The quarry versions of the 40-ton 769C and 60-ton 773B were upgraded to the 44-ton 771C and 65-ton 775B, respectively. The new trucks were additions to Caterpillar's truck line as the 769 and 773 models continued in production. The quarry trucks received a flat-floor body made of high-strength steel (Brinell hardness 400) and other upgrades consistent with their increased capacity. In 1995, Caterpillar upgraded the quarry trucks to the 771D and 775D with new operator controls and improved hydraulics and steering systems. *Caterpillar, Inc.*

Caterpillar 777. Caterpillar pushed upward in size when the 777 was released for service in 1975. The 85-ton rear dump took the surface mining industry by storm, selling several thousand over next decade. Its 870-flywheel-horsepower Caterpillar engine drove through a seven-speed automatic transmission, and its box-section frame with heavy steel plates and steel castings in critical stress areas ensured trouble-free operation. The 777 was upgraded by 10 more tons to the 777B in 1984, and to the 777C in 1992. The 777D, introduced in 1996, is currently running as a 100-ton truck, boasting improved operator comfort and 938 flywheel-horsepower from its engine. *Caterpillar, Inc.*

Caterpillar 785. Caterpillar boosted the top end of its truck line in 1985 when it introduced the 150-ton 785, and again the following year with the 195-ton 789. These mechanical-drive trucks were equipped with Caterpillar diesel engines of 1,290 and 1,705 flywheel-horsepower. Another boost came in 1990 with the launch of the 793 at 240-tons capacity with a 2,057-flywheel-horsepower Caterpillar D3516 diesel. These models placed Caterpillar firmly in the worldwide large-truck market, and since their introduction, all have received upgrades. The current 785C, with improved operator's station, comes with a 1,348-flywheel-horsepower engine and has a payload range of 130 to 150 tons. *Keith Haddock*

Cline SD456. In 1952, Max Cline started Cline Truck Manufacturing Company in Kansas City, Kansas, after being top salesman at Dart. A variety of heavy trucks followed, including crane carriers and underground trucks. This 25-ton-capacity quarry truck, Model SD456, was one of a line of rear dump trucks from 12- to 50-tons capacity that Cline offered in the 1960s. These included a 35-ton 6x4 coal hauler that became very popular in the Appalachian coalfields. Cline built its largest truck in 1970, a 72-ton tandem-drive coal hauler with a 635-horsepower Cummins diesel. *Keith Haddock*

Cline 50-ton Coal Hauler. Helping to promote Cline's rugged trucks in the early 1970s was this 50-ton tandem-drive coal hauler. Offered with Detroit or Cummins power in the 420-horsepower range, it came with a six-speed power-shift transmission with torque converter. This truck became the Isco IC-250C when Cline became a division of Isco Manufacturing Company, Inc., in 1972 (see under Isco). In 1979, the Cline name re-emerged under new owner T & J Industries, Inc., who kept the company until 1985. Since then, Cline Truck Manufacturing, Inc., has operated as a division of C.B.T. Corporation. C.B.T. discontinued building the trucks in the mid-1990s, but still rebuilds older Cline trucks. *Keith Haddock collection*

Dart 75TA. Established in 1903 as a highway truck builder, the Dart Truck Company built its first heavy-duty off-highway truck in 1937. In the early 1950s, Dart discontinued its highway truck line in favor of off-highway trucks, which it built in ever increasing sizes. The company claimed title to the world's largest truck in 1951 with the official launch of the tandem-drive 75-ton Model 75-TA, designed by Ralph Kress. This monster truck of its day sported two Buda diesel engines under the hood, each developing 300 horsepower. Only one of these trucks was built. It is shown at its launch at the Bagdad Copper Mine in Arizona, with Ione Dickey, wife of the mine's general managers. *Keith Haddock collection*

Dart 6050T. This Dart Model 6050T bottom-dump tractor-trailer outfit is hauling 60 tons of coal at a West Virginia surface mine operation. The tractor unit was equipped with a Cummins NDH V-12 diesel engine, and Allison 5840 transmission with oil retarders. This was one of many types of off-highway haulers developed by the company during the decade leading up to the 95-ton-capacity, rear-dumping tractor-trailer unit known as the 95EDT launched in 1960. Dart later sold substantial numbers of these units as 100-ton-capacity haulers, some of the largest trucks available at that time. *Keith Haddock collection*

Dart 50S-BDT. Dart's tractor-trailer outfits became a standard hauling unit in Midwestern U.S. surface coal mines. Here, one of Green Coal Company's haulers receives a load from a Northwest 80-D shovel at a Kentucky mine in the mid-1950s. The tractor unit is a Dart Model 50S-BDT equipped with a 300-horsepower Cummins engine, power steering, and three-speed power-shift transmission with torque converter. The unit could run 50-ton loads at speeds up to 24 miles-per-hour on the level. *Keith Haddock collection*

Dart D-2771. Dart claimed it was the first to build a mechanical-drive, two-axle hauler to break the 100-ton barrier. The Dart Model D-2771 debuted in 1965 at 110-tons rated capacity. A GM 12V149 engine of 740 flywheel-horsepower powered it, but an optional turbocharged version put out 920 flywheel-horsepower. The truck featured Dart's own design of front and rear axles and suspension system combining steel springs with compressed air. Dart also offered an electric version, the DE2771, of the same tonnage, featuring a diesel-electric module comprising a Cummins engine, radiator, General Electric DC generator and exciter mounted on one frame to form a single exchangeable unit. *Keith Haddock collection*

Dart D4651. Dart's tractor-trailer coal haulers kept pace with its rear-dump developments during the 1960s. Dart offered mechanical and diesel-electric drive in its truck line. In 1970, the line consisted of three sizes of two-axle mechanical-drive trucks up to 110-tons capacity, and 120-ton and 150-ton two-axle electric-drive trucks. The mechanical drive models could also be equipped with trailers, providing capacities up to 120 tons. A 120-ton-capacity trailer is shown being hauled by the mechanical-drive D4651 that could be equipped with a GM or Cummins engine of 650 flywheel-horsepower and six-speed power-shift transmission. Overall length of the unit measured 66 feet, 5 inches. *Keith Haddock collection*

Dart 3100. In 1976, Dart updated its haulers and adopted a new numbering system for its models. The last three digits of the four-digit model number signified the tonnage capacity while the first digit indicated the type of vehicle (4 for tractor-trailer, 3 for single rear-axle, and 2 for tandem drive). By this time, Dart produced only mechanical-drive trucks, citing several advantages over electric drive: increased efficiency, less dead weight in the power train, lower repair costs, and only one maintenance skill required for servicing. The 100-ton 3100 could be provided with a Detroit or Cummins diesel in the 1,050-horsepower class driving a power-shift transmission with torque converter. *Keith Haddock collection*

Dart 2085. This Dart-designed hauler was claimed to be the largest tandem-drive mechanical truck ever built. The 2085 measured over 40 feet long, 15 feet, 4 inches wide and could carry 85 tons. Optional Cummins or Detroit engines provided 800 horsepower to this oversize highway-type brute. In 1984, Dart was acquired by Unit Rig & Equipment Company of Tulsa, Oklahoma. The Dart mechanical-drive products made a perfect marriage with Unit Rig's electric-drive truck line, giving customers a choice of their favorite drive type. In 1988, however, Unit Rig became a division of Terex Corporation, and Dart mechanical-drive truck production diminished soon afterward. *Keith Haddock collection*

Dresser Haulpak 210M. The Dresser name first appeared on haul trucks in 1984 when the Wabco line became a division of Dresser Industries, Inc. (see under Wabco). Under the new company, the entire Wabco truck line was revamped and the Wabco name was dropped. The new Dresser model designations reflected the gross vehicle weight (GVW) of the vehicle, and by 1987 the Dresser line ranged from the 35-ton mechanical-drive 140M with 140,000-pounds GVW, to the 240-ton electric-drive 830E at 830,000-pounds GVW. The 210M mechanical-drive truck could carry 55 tons, and its Cummins diesel was rated at 641 flywheel-horsepower. *Keith Haddock*

Dresser Haulpak 830E. The biggest truck to bear the Dresser Haulpak name was this 240-ton-capacity 830E. The electric-drive truck was powered by two General Electric DC motors, one in each rear wheel hub driven by a 2,054-flywheel-horsepower, 16-cylinder Detroit diesel-electric generator. The truck boasted latest-technology electronic engine control and an advanced monitoring system to protect 54 critical functions. In 1988, Japan's Komatsu, Ltd. and Dresser Industries, Inc. began a joint venture known as Komatsu Dresser Company to manufacture and market construction and mining equipment (see under Komatsu). Subsequently the haul trucks were sold under the name Komatsu Haulpak. *Keith Haddock*

Euclid Trac-Truk. The Euclid Road Machinery Company of Euclid, Ohio, was established from predecessor companies in 1931, and two years later the company experimented with a 5-cubic-yard bottom-dumping semi-trailer intended for off-highway use. Euclid built its first off-road truck in 1934, the rear-dump type shown here, christened the "Trac-Truk." It boasted a modern single-cylinder hydraulic dumping system and 7-cubic-yards carrying capacity. The success of this truck established Euclid as the first company to specialize solely in off-highway haulers. Euclid's experience with these early trucks enabled it to develop a vast range of types and sizes including the world's largest by 1951. *Eric C. Orlemann collection*

Euclid R-15/FD Series. Euclid's reputation for tough off-road vehicles was exemplified by the R-15 rear dump truck, or FD Series, to use its engineering nomenclature. The 15-ton-capacity rear dump truck was a welcome addition for many a quarry owner and surface mine operator. This very successful truck, small by today's standards, had a very long production run. From 1936 to 1963, Euclid produced 63 different FD models, each with a sequential prefix number. They had slight variations in engines, transmissions, axles, and other components, but all were of 15-tons capacity. Euclid Road Machinery became a division of General Motors Corporation in 1953. *Keith Haddock collection*

Euclid FDT Bottom Dump. Euclid produced tractor versions of its FD Series trucks, broadening the application of this reliable vehicle. The "FDT" nomenclature was Euclid's engineering reference for this model, a system used for all its models to denote size, power type, and vehicle configuration. (In this case 15 to 20 tons, diesel power, and trailer type.) Euclid bottom-dumping trailers utilized a patented wheel wind door-closing mechanism. After releasing the doors by gravity, the doors were closed by a cable system. A spring-loaded wheel was pressed into contact with one rear trailer wheel to drive a drum that wound in the cable. When the doors were fully closed, an automatic clutch disengaged the drum wheel from the trailer wheel. *Keith Haddock collection*

Euclid 1LLD. This was the real monster truck of the early 1950s–the largest production truck of the day. With two Cummins NHRS engines under the hood for a total of 600 horsepower, each driving one rear axle, this giant rear dump could carry 50 tons. It measured 13 feet, 9 inches wide, and 12 feet high. Euclid pioneered the twin-drive concept to overcome the limitations of available engine and transmission capability. The key to this technology was the Allison Torqmatic Drive, a system that enabled two transmissions to be shifted simultaneously by a single gear lever. Beginning in 1948 with an 18-cubic-yard twin-powered bottom-dump hauler, Euclid followed with the 34-ton 1FFD rear dump a year later, and then the record-breaking 1LLD in 1951. *Keith Haddock collection*

Euclid 1LLD/Western 80. The initial demand for the 50-ton 1LLD rear dump trucks just described came from famous earthmoving contractor Western Contracting Corporation for use on their large dam projects in South Dakota. By 1952, the contractor was running a fleet of 30 of these behemoths. Not content with running a fleet of the largest trucks available, Western rebuilt one of the LLDs in 1958 to receive two 375-horsepower engines, a fifth-wheel assembly, and semi-trailer capable of hauling 150 tons. More power was added in 1960, when the same truck was fitted with twin 425-horsepower GM 12V-71 engines. *Western Contracting Corporation*

Euclid 36LDT Coal Hauler. Euclid's tractor-trailer units enjoyed a major portion of the company's off-road hauler business from the 1940s thru the 1960s. As well as the initial FDT models with capacities of 15 to 25 tons, sizes included the TDT models (22 to 40 tons) and the LDT models (30 to 70 tons). The 36LDT, in production from 1958 to 1964, was coupled to a 51-ton-capacity-trailer (Model 138W) designed for coal hauling. The tractor unit carried a Cummins NVH12 engine rated at 450 horsepower, and the drive train included an Allison six-speed transmission and torque converter. *Keith Haddock collection*

Euclid R-X. In 1965, Euclid unveiled the R-X, a rear-dump hauler with a unique four-wheel-drive, articulated frame concept. A pair of tires on each of the four wheels carried an equal share of the loaded truck. Steering was activated through hydraulic cylinders between the front and rear frames. The Euclid R-X truck was offered with capacities from 85 to 105 tons, and with a choice of Detroit 16V-71T or 12V-149T diesel engines of 650 and 912 flywheel-horsepower. From 1969, the R-X was known as the Euclid R-105. *Keith Haddock collection*

Euclid R-85. Euclid remained a division of General Motors (GM) from 1953 to 1968, when it became a subsidiary of White Motor Corporation. This followed a Justice Department ruling that GM had to discontinue the manufacture and sale of off-highway trucks in the United States for a period of four years, and divest itself of the Euclid name. Thus, the White Motor Corporation took hold of the famous Euclid name, and the GM plant in Scotland was allowed to continue building trucks, but under the new name of Terex. Under the White era, Euclid continued to develop new models including the 85-ton R-85 powered by Detroit or Cummins engines in the 800-flywheel-horsepower class. *Keith Haddock collection*

Euclid R-210. In 1971, after three years of development, Euclid took the wraps off a 210-ton-capacity prototype haul truck. This unique vehicle ran on gas turbine power and electric-wheel drive. Power came from an Avco-Lycoming 1,850-horsepower gas turbine power unit. It ran on eight of the largest tires available, each 10.5 feet high. The tires were mounted in pairs on each of the hauler's four wheels, and the truck's design resulted in equal weight distribution on all four wheels when loaded. The only R-210 built was shipped to the island of Bougainville to haul copper overburden. It was subsequently wrecked and scrapped at that site. *Eric C. Orlemann collection*

Euclid CH-120 Twin-Power. Another power concept developed by Euclid during the White Motor Corporation era was the CH-120 coal hauler with an extra engine in the rear. This throwback to the early Euclid twin-power days was intended to boost the tractor-trailer units, normally designed for level hauls up steep, short ramps often found in surface coal mines. Euclid offered this 120-ton tractor-trailer combination in the 1970s utilizing its R-85 tractor unit. Doubling up on the engines also meant that on level hauls, a second 120-ton trailer could be pulled behind the first. *Keith Haddock collection*

Euclid R-170. From 1977 to 1984, Euclid was a subsidiary of Daimler-Benz AG of Germany. During this time the worldwide surface mining industry standardized on 170 tons as a proven and reliable truck size. Euclid's contender in this class was the diesel-electric R-170. Actually developed during the White Motor ownership and announced in 1975, the R-170 would be Euclid's flagship hauler for more than a decade. It could be fitted with Detroit or Cummins 16-cylinder engines of 1,492 and 1,519 flywheel-horsepower respectively and, from 1982, the MTU 12-cylinder 1,492-flywheel-horsepower engine was available. The picture shows a Euclid R-170 with a high-volume coal body. *Keith Haddock*

Euclid R-32. In 1984, Daimler-Benz sold Euclid to Clark-Michigan Company. The following year, Clark entered into a joint venture with Volvo AB from Sweden, and VME Americas, Inc. was established to market products from Volvo, Michigan, and Euclid. The former Swedish Kokum line of haulers, already part of the Volvo organization, was merged into VME, and certain models were sold with the Euclid brand name. One of these was the 35-ton R-32, shown as a Euclid product. It carried a Volvo engine of 276 flywheel-horsepower and five-speed automatic planetary transmission with torque converter.
Volvo Construction Equipment

Euclid CH-160. A popular coal hauler from Euclid in the 1990s was the CH-160 bottom-dumping unit of 160-tons capacity. The tractor unit was based on the Euclid R-90 truck with turbocharged 982 horsepower, but a fifth-wheel trailer hitch substituted for its 90-ton rear-dump body. The trailer was not built by Euclid but was chosen by the customer from a number of specialized trailer builders such as Mega Corporation of Albuquerque, New Mexico, and Maxter Industries, Ltd. of Montreal, Quebec. *Keith Haddock*

Euclid-Hitachi EH-4500 AOS. In 1992, VME teamed up with Japan's Hitachi to form Euclid-Hitachi Heavy Equipment, Inc., which manufactures and markets the current line of Euclid haulers. Euclid unveiled its largest hauler to date at the 1996 Minexpo equipment show in Las Vegas, Nevada. This was the electric-drive R-260 of 262-tons capacity. A year later, Euclid topped this with the 280-ton R-280 with 2,646 flywheel-horsepower and AC electric-wheel motors. In 2000, Euclid-Hitachi renumbered its haulers to the EH Series. The R-260 became the EH4000 and the R-280 became the EH4500. Shown here is the EH4500 AOS (Alberta Oil Sands) version with 300-tons capacity. For 2003, Euclid-Hitachi presents the EH5000 with 330-tons capacity and 3,000 gross-horsepower. *Keith Haddock*

Goodbary CP2400. Goodbary trucks were built from 1976 to 1980, taking their name from the company founder, E.R. Goodbary, formerly with the Unit Rig company. They were sold in capacities from 100 to 170 tons, and offered with engine choices of Caterpillar, Detroit, or Cummins in the 1,000- to 1,200-horsepower range. Goodbary trucks were diesel-electric drive (rear-wheel-drive only), and were the unitized (rigid-frame) bottom-dumping type designed for coal hauling. The rights to manufacture and market the Goodbary haulers were acquired by Dart Truck Company in 1980, but no further units were built. *Keith Haddock*

Holland 180. The Holland Loader Company began building its own haulers in the early 1980s. It offers the Model 180 bottom-dump hauler capable of carrying loads up to 200 tons. The 180 is the tractor-trailer type built of unique design—the trailer dumps its load like a clamshell with the gates opening 16 feet wide. These outfits are offered in two power configurations: a single Cummins or Detroit upfront engine of 1,050 horsepower, or with an engine mounted on the rear of the trailer. In the latter case, both front and rear engines are Cummins KTA1150C diesels of 600 gross-horsepower. *Holland Loader Company*

International PH95. International Harvester Company entered the off-highway truck business in 1957 with the introduction of the Models 65 and 95 Payhaulers of 18- and 24-tons capacity. They were powered with International engines of 250 and 335 horsepower. With upgrades, the 65 lasted in the line until 1973, by which time the 65C was rated at 22 tons. The 95 remained until 1965 when it was supplanted by the Payhauler 100, released a couple of years earlier as a 30-ton truck. The 100, in its final B Series version, was in production from 1967 to 1971. *Keith Haddock*

International 350. International's greatest achievement in off-road trucks was the launch of the Payhauler 180 in 1963. This four-wheel-drive, rigid-frame 45-ton rear-dump hauler, with dual tires and equal weight distribution on all four wheels, had no competition in the field. It was perfect for construction sites and surface mines when soft ground was encountered. In 1973, the Payhauler models were revamped and renumbered as the 330, 340, and 350, covering sizes from 36 to 50 tons. When International sold its construction equipment lines in 1982, the Payhaulers were sold to a new company, Payhauler Corporation of Batavia, Illinois. Only the 50-ton Model 350 was marketed, but it progressed through the 350B and 350C models with added improvements. Terex Corporation purchased Payhauler in 1998 and continued to sell the trucks as Terex products. *Keith Haddock*

ISCO IC-23R. The ISCO name on off-highway trucks was the result of the Cline Truck Manufacturing Company, established in 1952, becoming a division of ISCO Manufacturing Company in 1972. The former Cline trucks bore the name ISCO until 1978, when the company was sold to T & J Industries, Inc. (see under Cline). During the ISCO era, the off-highway trucks included rigid-frame dump trucks from 13- to 50- tons capacity, a 22-ton articulated dump truck, and a tandem-drive tractor unit capable of pulling 90-ton wagons. The IC-23R was a 23-ton rear-dump truck powered by Cummins or Detroit engines in the 245-gross-horsepower class. It drove through an Allison six-speed power-shift transmission. *CBT Corporation*

Kenworth 802. Famed highway truck builder Kenworth Truck Company of Seattle, Washington, built off-highway trucks in the early 1950s. Models included the 32-ton Model 803 with a 400-horsepower (gross) engine, and this 24-ton-capacity Model 802. The 802 employed a three-speed Allison transmission with torque converter, while the similar Model 802A was also offered with a manual-shift 10-speed Fuller transmission. Power to both versions was provided by a Cummins 300-horsepower (gross) diesel engine. Maximum visibility was afforded by the offset cab design with minimum frontal obstructions. *Keith Haddock collection*

Koehring Dumptor. The Dumptor was a Koehring product originating in the 1920s and lasting in production for more than 45 years. The nifty four-wheel dumper, with swivel seat and dual controls so the operator could drive in either direction, became popular on construction sites, quarries, and surface mines alike. In the 1940s, Koehring utilized the basic Dumptor chassis and power units as prime movers for Koehring's "Trail-Dump" bottom-dumping wagons in 8-, 10-, and 12-cubic-yard sizes, and also for the 10-cubic-yard Koehring "Wheeler" scraper. In the early 1960s, models produced were the 8-ton 60, the 15-ton 100, and 18-ton 140, powered by GM engines of 109, 168, and 227 flywheel-horsepower respectively. In the late 1960s, the 140 became the 1860, and the new larger 2460 of 24-tons capacity appeared. Koehring shipped its last Dumptor in 1970. *Keith Haddock collection*

Komatsu HD785-3. In 1969, Komatsu introduced the HD180 with a capacity of 20 tons and powered by a 230-flywheel-horsepower Cummins engine. Developed from the former HD150, it was Komatsu's only off-road truck at that time. The 1970s were a period of rapid expansion for Komatsu's truck line as new models appeared almost every year, gradually increasing in size. By 1980, the line consisted of 10 models from the HD180 to the 132-ton HD1200. All were mechanically driven, but the HD1200 was offered with optional diesel-electric drive. The HD785-3 shown is rated at 96-tons capacity and runs with a Komatsu diesel of 1,010 flywheel-horsepower. It was upgraded from the original 85-ton HD785 available in 1980. *Keith Haddock*

Komatsu 730E. In 1988, Japan's Komatsu, Ltd. and Dresser Industries, Inc. started a joint venture, Komatsu Dresser Company (KDC), to manufacture and market construction and mining equipment in the Western Hemisphere. Dresser had previously taken over the former Wabco Haulpak truck line in 1984, and these large electric trucks complimented Komatsu's existing mechanical models. Today the trucks sport the Komatsu Haulpak name since Komatsu acquired 100 percent interest in KDC. The Komatsu 730E is a 200-ton truck with a Cummins 1,860-flywheel-horsepower engine. This example, at the Barrick Goldstrike Mine in Nevada, is equipped with "trolley-assist" so that its wheel motors can receive a boost from overhead power during the uphill climb out of the pit, saving fuel for its on-board diesel engine. *Eric C. Orlemann collection*

Komatsu 930E. The top-of-the-line truck from Komatsu is the 930E with a payload rating to 320 tons. Apart from its size, the real breakthrough on this vehicle is its electric-wheel drive using AC motors, the first in the industry to do so. Launched at Minexpo Las Vegas in 1996, the 930E truck is 27 feet wide, and 24 feet high. The 930E initially came with an MTU engine of 2,500 flywheel-horsepower, but a "2SE" version was announced in 2000 with a Komatsu 2,550-flywheel-horsepower engine developed jointly by Komatsu and Cummins. *Komatsu America International*

Kress CH-160. The Kress Corporation of Brimfield, Illinois, was formed in 1965 to design special-purpose vehicles such as slag pot carriers primarily for steel mills. The company is now the world leader in this market. The coal haulers were initiated in 1971 when the first of six started work at the Captain Mine in Illinois. Kress haulers are of the rigid-frame, bottom-dumping type designed specifically as coal carriers. Sizes range from 110- to 300-tons capacity. This CH-160, owned by Luscar, Ltd., hauls coal to the Boundary Dam Generating Station at Estevan, Saskatchewan. It is fitted with a Detroit 1,200-horsepower engine and features oleo-pneumatic suspension. *Keith Haddock*

Kress CH-300. The CH-300 haulers operating at a mine in North Dakota are the largest Kress trucks built to date. Carrying over 300 tons, these huge units are powered by a rear-mounted Caterpillar 3516 engine producing 1,800 gross-horsepower. All Kress trucks are mechanically driven and designed to haul loads at high speeds up to 60 miles-per-hour. when the road is smooth. The four front wheels, straddle-mounted in pairs, are capable of turning up to 90 degrees to the truck frame, allowing extremely tight turns in a narrow coal cut. *Eric C. Orlemann*

LeTourneau Cradle Dump. R.G. LeTourneau designed an early vehicle for off-road hauling called the Cradle Dump buggy. It was a side-dumping carrier built for use with a Caterpillar RD8 tractor. It could also be used without the front axle as a semi-trailer behind heavy-duty trucks such as those produced by the Hug Company. Introduced in 1935, it carried 35 heaped cubic yards and was dumped by a cable and sheave arrangement operated from the tractor's power control unit. The curved bottom was fixed to the trailer frame while the three-sided body was pivoted at the top. It dumped when the cable pulled the body through a short arc to the side, allowing the load to fall out by gravity. *Eric C. Orlemann collection*

LeTourneau TR-60. R.G. LeTourneau, Inc. has made many different types of haulers over the years since its incorporation in 1929. Most were trailer types, rear- and bottom-dumping, hauled behind Tournapull prime movers. In 1960, the first of LeTourneau's TR Series electric-drive trucks went to work for Anaconda Company's Berkeley Pit in Montana. This vehicle was a trolley-assisted rear dump carrying 75 tons. The picture shows the truck at the dump, away from the overhead power system. It drove under the overhead power line to save fuel on the long uphill haul from the pit. After a useful life, this truck is now preserved at the Butte Mining Museum in Butte, Montana. *Keith Haddock collection*

LeTourneau T-2240. LeTourneau's large electric mining trucks are descendants of the former Terex Titan haulers designed by General Motors' Diesel Division of London, Ontario (later GM Titan Division). In 1985, Marathon-LeTourneau Company of Longview, Texas, purchased rights to these trucks. At that time LeTourneau was owned by Marathon Manufacturing Company. The trucks included the former 170-ton Terex 33-15B and the world record–beating 350-ton 33-19, but only the former was continued by LeTourneau. Upgrades and revisions followed and LeTourneau's T Series appeared in 1987 with capacities ranging from 170 to 200 tons. In 1990 the 240-ton Model T-2240 was added with MTU or Detroit engines rated at 2,467 and 2,250 horsepower. *Eric C. Orlemann collection*

Liebherr TI272. This is the latest truck development from Liebherr. Resulting from a Technology Licensing Agreement between Liebherr and BHP Coal Proprietary, Ltd. of Australia, a truck of radical new design has reached beyond the prototype stage. The TI272, in the 320-ton class, was designed from a "clean slate" with the objective of decreasing structural weight, thereby increasing payload-to-weight ratio. The design features four in-line rear wheels, straddle-mounted in pairs, and a rear frame with no lateral support. Necessary strength is provided by a beefed-up truck box, which transmits the necessary stresses when the vehicle is on the road. Power comes from Cummins or Detroit/MTU engines of 2,700 horsepower. *Liebherr Mining Equipment*

Liebherr T282. In 1995, Liebherr-America, Inc. acquired Wiseda, Ltd. of Baxter Springs, Kansas, builder of the 240-ton KL-2450 electric mining truck. Liebherr continued to manufacture the KL-2450 and, a year later, added a new, smaller model, the KL-2420 in the 200-ton size class. In 1998, Liebherr established a new division, Liebherr Mining Equipment Company, to market its haul trucks and the largest of its hydraulic excavators. That same year, Liebherr adopted a new model nomenclature, the T Series, for all its haulers. The top-of-the-line 340-ton truck became the T282 featuring an AC electric-wheel-motor-drive system developed jointly by Siemens and Liebherr. In 2000, this truck was upgraded to 400-tons capacity and offered with engines to 3,500 horsepower. *Keith Haddock*

Linn Half-Track. The Linn Manufacturing Corporation of Morris, New York, established in 1916, made this hybrid crawler tractor and truck. The half-track vehicle represents an evolutionary step between trailer haulage by crawler tractor, and the first off-highway trucks. It offered superb traction on jobs where haul roads were nonexistent. Linn advertised a top speed of 7.5-miles-per-hour achieved for its six-cylinder model, double the speed of current crawler tractors. Bill Rudicill of Petersburg, Kentucky, owns this immaculately restored Linn. It was built in 1952 from spare parts after the Linn company closed in 1950. *Keith Haddock*

Mack LV. Mack's reputation for heavy-duty trucks was in no small part due to the success of its Model AC Bulldog that remained in the line until 1938, by which time over 40,000 had been built. The reliability of the Mack Bulldog and the need for a robust off-highway vehicle intensified Mack's interest in the off-highway hauler market. Mack's F Series chain-drive trucks, with gross vehicle weights to 50,000 pounds, took over from the A Series in the quarry market. Then, from 1940 to 1960, Mack catered to the off-highway industry with its L Series of four-wheel and six-wheel tandem trucks. The LV shown here had a capacity of 22.5 tons and could be equipped with either a 300- or 335-horsepower Cummins engine with eight-speed manual transmission. *Keith Haddock collection*

Mack AP Bulldog. Highway truck builder Mack Trucks, Inc. of Allentown, Pennsylvania, established in 1902, brought out its famous Model AC chain-driven truck in 1915. In the late 1920s this truck was upgraded to produce the Model AP. Beginning in 1931, both ACs and APs played a major role in the construction of the Boulder Dam on the Colorado River. The trucks were fitted with specially designed, welded steel bodies built by the Heil Company, and the trucks themselves underwent many design changes to meet the tough conditions of this project. These included a new type of underslung rear axle and spring assembly to increase the truck's capacity without raising its loading height. These trucks were the first on record to be built specifically for off-highway use. *Eric C. Orlemann collection*

Mack LRVSW. Mack broadened its L Series off-highway rear-dump haulers up to its largest, the LYSW of 40-tons capacity, fitted with a 450-horsepower Cummins NVH12V1 engine. More popular was this LRVSW of 34-tons capacity introduced in 1951. Operated extensively on the Iron Range of Minnesota, the LRVSW carried the same engine as its larger brother, but was rated at 400 horsepower. Overall width was 11 feet, 3 inches, and overall height 11 feet, 8 inches. Mack's own eight-speed manual transmission provided the LRVSW with a top speed of 28 miles-per-hour on the level. *Keith Haddock*

Mack M35AX. After two decades of successful off-highway hauling, Mack's L Series was replaced with the M Series in 1960. With modern styling, the line consisted of both single- and tandem-drive axle types, denoted by the suffixes AX and SX. The M35AX of 35-tons capacity boasted a high power-to-weight ratio with a 420-horsepower Cummins engine and 26-ton unladen weight achieved by the use of high-strength alloy steel. Standard transmission was a six-speed power-shift unit with integral torque converter. *Keith Haddock*

Mack 75SX. Mack's largest off-highway haulers were the big M Series tandem-drive units of the 1960s. These were the 70-ton M70SX, the 75-ton M75SX, and the 100-ton M-100SX. Only three of the largest type were made, but the smaller M-70SX unveiled in 1965, and its successor the M-75SX in 1970, were much more popular. These were fitted with 700-horsepower Cummins engines and drove through a six-speed Allison transmission with integral torque converter. In 1979, Mack announced it was withdrawing from the off-highway truck market, and the last truck left the factory in 1981. *Ray Bentley*

Michigan T-65. Well-known for its wheel loaders and scrapers, Clark Equipment Company added an off-road rear-dump haul truck to its Michigan-branded earthmoving line in 1965. It was the modern-looking T-65 of 65-tons capacity, equipped with air-over-oil suspension, and offered with Cummins or GM diesels of 700 horsepower. Intended to be the first of a line of haulers, the T-65 had a short life, with only about eight being built. These all operated in the United Kingdom in various open-pit coal mines. *Keith Haddock collection*

M-R-S Mississippi Wagon. The M-R-S Manufacturing Company (Mississippi Road Services) was established in 1942. The company produced the Mississippi Wagon, which bore a unique, patented load transfer system. Under the control of the operator, a hydraulic cylinder mounted between the tractor drawbar and the yoke of the trailer could raise the front trailer axle, transferring weight to the rear tractor wheels and thereby increasing traction. M-R-S developed a line of haulers from 13- to 20-tons capacity based on International prime movers. By the 1950s, M-R-S was producing a range of their tractors in sizes up to the Model 250 with 500-horsepower Cummins diesel power. They could pull wagons up to 50-tons capacity. The Taylor Machine Works purchased the rights to M-R-S products in 1986. *Taylor Machine Works*

Oshkosh 25-Ton W Series. Oshkosh Motor Truck, Inc. of Oshkosh, Wisconsin, played a small but significant part in off-highway truck design over the years. In 1933 it built the Model TR, a four-wheel-drive, four-wheel-steer prime mover used with a bottom-dump semi-trailer or scraper. This made it the first rubber-tired earthmover. After World War II, Oshkosh's W Series trucks were expanded into off-road applications with 4x4 and 6x4 models culminating in 1960 with the W-3000, a 60-ton tractor-trailer rear-dump truck. The Cummins-powered 25-ton W Series truck is shown receiving a load from a Bucyrus-Erie 88-B shovel. *Keith Haddock collection*

Rimpull R3051. Rimpull Corporation of Olathe, Kansas, was established in 1971 and began developing a line of mechanical-drive haul trucks. "Back to Basics" was the company's slogan at a time when most manufacturers were promoting electric trucks with elaborate drive and suspension systems. The first two Rimpulls were 100-ton bottom-dumping types delivered in 1973. By 1979, Rimpull offered five rear-dump haulers from 65- to 120-tons capacity, and five tractor-trailer bottom-dump haulers from 100- to 170-tons capacity. Representing the line of Rimpull rear-dump haulers is this current 110-ton Model R3051, which can be powered by either Cummins or Detroit diesels in the 1,200-horsepower class. *Rimpull Corporation*

Rimpull CW-300. In 1980, Rimpull introduced the CW-200, a 200-ton-capacity bottom-dump unit equipped with a 1,200-horsepower Detroit diesel engine. This was followed by Rimpull's largest, the CW-300, designed to carry 300-ton loads in its cavernous bottom-dumping trailer. Detroit or Cummins engines of 1,600 horsepower power it. Today, Rimpull continues to build mechanically driven trucks and offers rear-dump and tractor-trailer units in the range from 85- to 300-tons capacity. It also builds trailers and water tankers for other manufacturers. *Rimpull Corporation*

Terex R-65. The Terex name was born in 1968 when a Justice Department ruling forced General Motors' (GM) Euclid Division to end the manufacture of off-highway trucks in the United States for four years and discontinue using the Euclid name. White Motor Corporation purchased Euclid, and Terex was chosen for GM's remaining earthmoving equipment lines and the trucks still being made in GM's plants in Scotland and Canada. One of these was the Terex R-65 rear-dump hauler introduced in 1968. One is shown here in a deep open-pit coal mine in South Wales. Its power came from a GM 16V-71T engine developing 654 flywheel-horsepower. *Keith Haddock*

Terex 33-15. When GM's forced hiatus on truck manufacture in the United States expired in 1972, GM was once again free to manufacture and sell off-highway haulers on a worldwide basis. It immediately announced its new line of 33 Series haulers. The first was the 33-15, a 150-ton diesel-electric rear-dump hauler, designed and built by the GM Diesel Division in London, Ontario, Canada, at the same plant where GM builds its diesel-electric railroad locomotives. It was powered by a GM 16V-149T engine of 1,445 flywheel-horsepower driving a GM DC generator to power two GM DC traction motors in the rear axle. In 1975, GM upgraded the 33-15 hauler to the 33-15B, keeping the same engine but adding 20 tons to its payload. *Ron Nelson Photography*

Terex 33-03B. In 1972, when Terex recommenced off-highway hauler manufacture in the United States, it applied the 33 Series designation to its entire line of haulers, eventually replacing the former R Series, which enjoyed continuous production at its Scottish plant established by Euclid in 1950. GM also renumbered the trucks built in its Canadian plant from the R Series to the 33 Series. The former 22-ton, 226-flywheel-horsepower R-22 became the 33-03. This was upgraded to the 33-03B in 1977 with new-style cab and distinctive Terex keystone-shaped radiator. *Keith Haddock*

Terex 33-19. When launched in 1974, the 350-ton Terex Titan Model 33-19 was by far the world's largest truck. It held on to this title for 22 years until Caterpillar unveiled its Model 797 truck at 360-tons capacity in 1996. The Titan 33-19 was designed and built at the GM Diesel Division in London, Ontario, Canada, using the same diesel-electric drive technology as GM's railroad locomotives. Powered by a 16-cylinder GM 16-645E4 engine rated at 3,000 flywheel-horsepower, it ran at a low 900 rpm flat out, and 315 rpm at idle speed. This drove a GM generator to power four GM traction motors, two in each rear axle. *Keith Haddock collection*

Terex 33-19. The world's largest truck, the Terex Titan 33-19, was first shown at the American Mining Congress Exhibition, Las Vegas, in October 1974. Grabbing all the attention with its raised body containing five GM automobiles, the behemoth measured almost 67 feet long by 26 feet wide, weighed 509,500 pounds empty, and boasted a gross vehicle weight of 1,209,500 pounds. It ran on 10 40x57 tires, which were over 11 feet in diameter. A unique feature of the 33-19 was its rear bogie, which steered automatically with the front wheels to reduce tire scuffing. The only Titan 33-19 built spent a long and productive life at the Balmer Mine of Westar Mining, Ltd. in British Columbia. Today, the Titan is restored and is a tourist attraction at Sparwood, British Columbia. *Keith Haddock collection*

Terex 33-14. The largest Terex mechanical-drive truck was this 33-14, unveiled at the American Mining Congress Show in Las Vegas in 1978. In the 120-ton class, it was powered by a 1,092-flywheel-horsepower Detroit 12V-149T1 diesel driving through a six-speed Allison automatic transmission with integral torque converter. In 1981, German conglomerate IBH purchased the Terex division from GM, but GM retained the diesel-electric portion of the product line made at its Diesel Division at London, Ontario. When IBH failed in 1983, GM purchased Terex back, then sold it to Northwest Engineering Company in 1986. The following year, Terex Corporation succeeded Northwest as the parent company name. *Keith Haddock collection*

Terex 34-11. Some of Terex's large mechanical-drive trucks were sold as tractor units for hauling bottom-dumping earth wagons and coal trailers. The 34-09, with 624-flywheel-horsepower Detroit 16V-71T engine, was initially announced with a 100-ton-capacity trailer, but was later up-rated to 120 tons. The 34-11C (shown) debuted in 1978 as a 150-ton tractor-trailer outfit. Its Detroit 16V-92TA diesel developed 840 flywheel-horsepower, and drove a six-speed Allison automatic transmission with integral torque converter. *Keith Haddock*

Terex 33.08E. Throughout the ownership changes from GM to IBH to Terex Corporation, Terex's Scottish plant continued unabated to roll out the 33 Series mechanical-drive haulers, introducing new models and updating others throughout the 1980s and 1990s. In 1992 the line consisted of five sizes of rear-dump haulers from the 34-ton 33-05B to the 94-ton 33-11E, plus five sizes of articulated dump trucks from 25- to 40-tons capacity. The 33-08E carried 55 tons and was powered by a 570-flywheel-horsepower Cummins KTA 19-C engine in its standard version, but was also offered in a 33-08E "Plus" version with an additional 75 flywheel-horsepower obtained from a two-stage torque converter. *Keith Haddock*

Terex TR100. In 1995, Terex revised its hauler designs and began a new nomenclature for its rear-dump haulers with the last two digits denoting the capacity in tons. For example, the 45-ton 33-07 became the 3345, and the 33-11E became the 100-ton 33100. In 1998, Terex adopted another new nomenclature for its haulers. This time it was the TR Series (Terex rear dump) and TA Series (Terex articulated) prefix followed by the payload capacity. The top-of-the-line TR100 is sold with a Cummins KTA38-C engine developing 975 flywheel-horsepower and Allison six-speed transmission with integral torque converter. *Terex Equipment, Ltd.*

Trojan 70-Ton. The Trojan Truck Manufacturing Company built the world's largest trucks from 1938 to 1940. With an enormous payload of 70 tons, these outsize vehicles were equipped with a pair of Caterpillar D17000 diesel engines. Notice how the load was ejected over the rear without raising the body. To discharge the load, the front of the body was pulled to the rear by the hoist mechanism. There were triple tires on each of the four rear wheels. A 1938 Fageol truck heads the trailer outfit hauling the Trojan to the job site. *Leigh Knudson collection*

Trojan 35.5. This Trojan bears no relation to the Trojan just described. The 35-ton truck with 384-horsepower engine, derives its heritage from the former Faun line of off-road dump trucks built by Faun A.G. of Germany. In 1982, Faun took over the Trojan wheel loader line of Yale & Towne and its plant at Batavia, New York. It then merged the two lines, but retained the Trojan name for its trucks and graders sold in North America. In 1986, Orenstein & Koppel (O&K) from Germany took over the Faun products, and marketed them through its North American dealer network. These models were gradually phased out until 1992 when the Batavia plant closed. *Keith Haddock*

Electric-Wheel Motor. This cutaway view shows all the components of the General Electric wheel motor mounted in the wheel hubs of diesel-electric haulers such as the Unit Rig. The motor armature can be seen in the center; it drives the sun gear at the right meshing with the three planetary gears. The pinions on the planetary gear shafts mesh with an internal ring gear, which drives the wheel mounted on roller bearings. The brake shoes are on the left. The entire wheel assembly is bolted to the truck main frame. The success of these electric wheels paved the way for general acceptance of the electrically driven truck in the world's surface mines. *Keith Haddock collection*

Unit Rig M-85. Established in 1935 to build oil well servicing equipment, Unit Rig & Equipment Company first entered the off-highway truck field in 1963 with the M-85 diesel-electric truck. The company had previously tested a prototype articulated diesel-electric truck, the 64-ton M-64 in 1960. The electric-drive principle found immediate acceptance with the world's surface mines and, using the trade-name Lectrahaul, the line expanded in the 1960s to include nine models with payloads from 85- to 200-tons capacity. The M-85 was rated at 85-tons capacity, but, in most applications it carried loads up to 100 tons. Engine choices of 700 to 1,000 horsepower were offered. *Keith Haddock*

Unit Rig M-200. In 1968, Unit Rig created a stir throughout the truck industry when it unveiled the world's largest truck, the M-200 rated at 200-tons capacity. It was not only the world's largest, but also remarkable because it could carry that outsize load on only four wheels. The diesel-electric drive provided smooth variable speed from zero to maximum without the usual gear changes. It also eliminated conventional gearboxes and drive shafts. The M-200 was supplied with a 1,650-horsepower engine, and it measured 24 feet wide by 20 feet, 7 inches high—truly the monster truck of its day. *Keith Haddock*

Unit Rig Mk. 36. By the 1970s, the standard size of haul trucks in the world's surface mines reached 170 tons. Unit Rig's contender in this category was the Lectrahaul Mk. 36 with a choice of Detroit or Cummins engines with 1,450 flywheel-horsepower. Electrically driven haul trucks have a fuel-saving advantage not possible in mechanically driven trucks. On downgrades, the wheel motors act as generators providing a powerful retarding action. The kinetic energy so generated is dissipated through an air-cooled resistor bank. By 1979, Unit Rig had delivered its 2,500th Lectrahaul and the company boasted it had produced more diesel-electric trucks than all other makes combined. *Eric C. Orlemann*

Unit Rig BD-30. Unit Rig produced a rigid-frame, bottom-dump hauler of 160-tons capacity known as the BD-30. This was an upgrade from the former 145-ton Model BD-145 prototype hauler, which first appeared in 1977. The 1,200-horsepower engine in the BD-30 was mounted in the rear, and electric-wheel motors were provided in the rear wheel hubs. When loaded, the overall weight was distributed evenly on all four-wheel assemblies for increased stability and better control on grades. The eight-tire wheel configuration included straddle-mounted dual tires on the front-steering wheels. The retired BD-30 shown is preserved at the Jacobs Ranch Mine in Wyoming. *Keith Haddock*

Unit Rig MT-5500. In 1988, Unit Rig became a division of Terex Corporation. The line remained unchanged, as the electric-drive trucks complemented the mechanical-drive trucks in the existing Terex stable. Unit Rig pushed the size envelope higher in 1995 when it announced the MT-4400 which, at 260 tons, was the largest production truck available at that time. Then in 1998, Unit Rig debuted a new top-of-the-line hauler, the MT-5500 with 320-tons capacity. It boasted a new electric-drive system featuring AC electric-wheel motors driven by a General Atomics brushless alternator. *Garry Middlebrook*

V-Con 3006. The Vehicle Constructors Division (V-Con) of Peerless Manufacturing Company, Dallas, Texas, was formed in 1969 with a vision to build the world's largest mining truck. This they did when the Model 3006 started a testing program in 1971. Rated at 260 tons and fitted with an Alco 3,000-horsepower locomotive engine, the diesel-electric truck moved on eight wheels, straddle-mounted in pairs. The 3006 truck, and the V-Con large wheel dozers described in chapter 3, attracted the attention of Marion Power Shovel Company, who acquired the V-Con Division in 1973. Much promotion was done, and several truck sizes were offered, but nothing more was achieved in sales. *Eric Orlemann collection*

WABCO 75A. By 1961, WABCO's truck line had expanded to include 22-, 27-, 32-, 42-, and 60-ton mechanical-drive trucks. In 1965, the 75-ton 75A rear-dump hauler was introduced with either Cummins or GM engines of 665 flywheel-horsepower. Wabco trucks employed the patented "Hydrair" suspension using a combination of air and hydraulic oil. The wheel assemblies were attached to a piston that compressed the air inside a heavy-duty cylinder bolted vertically to the main truck frame. The 75A was upgraded to the 75B in 1967 with minor upgrades and an increase in unladen weight. The 75 A and B models were also available as tractor units which could pull 120-ton bottom-dumping coal trailers. *Keith Haddock*

WABCO 80 Bottom Dump. WABCO was formed in 1953 when Westinghouse Air Brake Company (WABCO) purchased R.G. LeTourneau's earthmoving business, including the Peoria, Illinois, plant. In 1955, Ralph Kress, famous off-highway truck designer, was hired to design a new line of off-highway trucks. The trucks were of innovative design with offset cab, sloping windshield, and V-shaped dump body, a style that has remained basically unchanged for almost five decades. The first two trucks were a 30-ton rear-dump and an 80-ton tractor-trailer bottom-dumping coal hauler with a 450-horsepower Cummins engine. The first WABCO truck to leave the plant led the 1957 Thanksgiving Day Parade on its way to Midland Coal Company's mine, 25 miles west of Peoria. *Keith Haddock collection*

WABCO 170C. To haul over 100 tons, WABCO adopted electric drive by General Electric for its rear-dump trucks. The 105-ton 120A appeared in 1965 with a 930-horsepower V12 Fairbanks Morse engine. Two years later this was up-rated to 120-tons capacity and GM power. For the 1970s, WABCO's 170-ton contender was the 170C electric truck with a choice of Detroit or Cummins engines with 1,450 flywheel-horsepower. One of Northern Strip Mining's fleet is shown at a coal mining operation in central England. In 1980, WABCO upgraded the 170C to the 170D. Revisions included an improved operator's cab and new General Electric "Statex" drive system with solid-state componentry and diagnostic capabilities. *Keith Haddock*

WABCO 200B. In the 1960s, when operators were demanding haul trucks in sizes approaching 200 tons, WABCO offered the 200B tractor-trailer rear-dump hauler for use where grades were not too steep. Upgraded from a former 160-ton model based on a 120A rear dump, the 200B achieved its 200-ton load capability by utilizing a WABCO 150B rear dump truck and replacing its body by a fifth-wheel assembly and a huge rear-dumping trailer. Electric traction motors were installed in the trailer wheels as well as the rear tractor wheels. A GM 16V-149T engine with 1,440 flywheel-horsepower was under the hood. *Eric C. Orlemann collection*

WABCO 3200. WABCO unveiled the giant Model 3200 tandem-drive diesel-electric truck in 1971. WABCO chose the GM 645-E4 locomotive engine to power this brute. This engine was rated 2,475 gross-horsepower, but for the 3200 it was downgraded to 1,800 flywheel-horsepower running at only 900 rpm. The 3200 was initially designated a 200-ton truck, but the 3200B announced in 1974 with the same engine was boosted to 235-tons capacity. It measured 24 feet wide and over 54 feet long. By 1976 this model achieved a 250-ton capacity rating with its engine up-rated to 2,250 flywheel-horsepower. It had a single 1,125-horsepower traction motor in each rear axle. The 3200 Series was phased out in the early 1980s after some 48 units were produced. *Keith Haddock collection*

WABCO 170 Coalpak. In 1977, WABCO sought increased presence in the coal hauling business when it announced the Coalpak, a rigid-frame (unitized) bottom-dumping coal hauler. With a capacity of 170 tons, it featured diesel-electric drive and a top speed of 32 miles-per-hour. The power rating for the Coalpak was 1,470 flywheel-horsepower from a Detroit or Cummins engine. Because the rear-positioned engine resulted in the placement of about two-thirds of the loaded vehicle weight on the rear axle, the hauler demonstrated superior gradeability over its tractor-trailer counterparts. In 1984, WABCO became a division of Dresser Industries, Inc. *Komatsu America International*

Wiseda KL-2450. Wiseda, Ltd. of Baxter Springs, Kansas, started at the top when it launched its first truck, a 220-ton monster, at the Las Vegas mining show in 1982. The company concentrated on this one large model, and after tests at several coal mining operations, the truck was boosted to 240-tons capacity. Known as the Model KL-2450, it was the first in that size range to run on two axles. It was an electric-drive truck with General Electric DC motors in the rear wheel hubs. Power came from a 2,000-horsepower diesel provided by Detroit, Cummins, or MTU. In 1995, Liebherr-America, Inc. acquired Wiseda and continued to develop the truck and add new models. *Liebherr Mining Equipment*

CHAPTER 11

CABLE EXCAVATORS

Cable excavator is the name given to the type of excavating machine that utilizes wire ropes (cables) to apply its digging forces to a single bucket (dipper). It usually consists of a revolving machinery house (upper works) connected via a turntable to a self-propelled crawler or wheeled base (lower works). The cable winding drums and the excavator's other functions, such as rotation (swing) and propelling are driven from the power unit (engine) through clutches, gears, and chains.

The English language is inadequate when it comes to describing earthmoving machines and the work they do, and the cable excavator is no exception. Almost every descriptive word applied to an excavating machine has a different meaning when used in another context. For example: crane, scraper, drum, crawler, boom, dozer, blade, bucket, etc., all have familiar meanings in other areas. Even the machines themselves are referred to by different names in different parts of the world, or even different localities in the same country. In modern-day terminology, the use of the word "excavator" has tended to imply that the machine being described is a backhoe. But this is incorrect. "Excavator" refers to a class of machine available in many forms, including stripping shovels, walking draglines, and bucket-wheel excavators. Hydraulic excavators (described in chapter 12) may operate as backhoes, but with different attachments they may also operate as shovels, clamshells, hammers, and a host of other machines. A cable excavator is even more adaptable. As well as shovel, backhoe, and skimmer (now obsolete), the cable excavator has long-boom capabilities, enabling it to work as a dragline, clamshell, crane, or pile driver. These attachments are called front ends, and an adaptable cable excavator with these attachments is referred to as universal or fully convertible. Front ends of a universal excavator are shown in the first photo.

The cable-operated excavator was the earliest documented self-powered machine ever used to move earth. Its earliest form, the steam shovel, has roots going back to the very first mechanical excavator, the Otis Steam Shovel of 1835. From this machine, the half-swinging railroad shovel was developed, its name derived from the fact that the early shovels were mounted on standard-gauge rail tracks, and most of the early shovel work was in railroad construction. These machines are described in chapter 1.

Whitaker & Sons of Leeds, England, built the world's first fully revolving in 1884. But it was not until well into the twentieth century that the revolving shovel became popular. The 1920s was a revolutionary decade for the cable excavator. The railroad shovel, the usefulness of which was restricted by its rail mounting and half-swinging boom, was gradually being replaced by highly mobile wheel and crawler outfits that could swing a full circle. The last railroad shovel was shipped in 1931, almost 100 years after the advent of the Otis shovel. Manufacturers in the business either adapted to

American 750. The American Hoist & Derrick Company was founded in 1882 at St. Paul, Minnesota. Its initial products were steam railroad cranes, but the company soon broadened its output to include all types of lifting equipment. Its first excavating machine was the "American Railroad Ditcher" of 1905, a fully revolving, rail-mounted steam shovel used for the purpose its name implies. In 1928, the company commenced building the Gopher Series, a line of crawler-mounted universal excavators. They were built in seven sizes ranging in .25-cubic-yard increments from .5- to 2-cubic-yards capacity. Built in relatively small numbers, the Gopher Series was discontinued during World War II. In the 1950s, American Hoist regained its interest in building crawler excavators and produced a new line of crawler cranes and excavators beginning with the .75-cubic-yard 375 in 1951. The 750 crawler excavator appeared in 1953 and remained in production until 1979. The machine shown was working in 1991, equipped as a 2-cubic-yard shovel. *Keith Haddock*

American 175. In 1955, American Hoist & Derrick Company purchased the American Steel Dredge Company of Fort Wayne, Indiana. The purchase included rights to a line of small cranes and excavators. These were added to American's line and became the 100 Series and 200 Series American machines of .5-cubic-yard and .75-cubic-yard capacity. The smallest American was the .5-cubic-yard 175 which could also be rigged as a 9-ton crane. A GM 3-53 engine rated at 57 horsepower powered it. The machine in the picture is in backhoe configuration, capable of digging to 16 feet. The 100 Series was discontinued in 1969. *Keith Haddock*

American 1221O. More widely known for its giant lift cranes, American Hoist was also a strong contender in the excavator business throughout the 1960s and 1970s. The largest American crawler excavators were the Model 12210 dragline introduced in 1978, and its successor, the 12220, in 1980. These machines, available as draglines only, could handle a 10-cubic-yard bucket on a 140-foot boom. This big diesel crawler was mechanically operated through clutches and brakes, and utilized "interlock" by which the hoist and drag drums could be locked together under the control of the operator. When locked, the gravitational pull of the loaded bucket on the drag rope as the bucket was hoisted reduced power needed to hoist the bucket. A Cummins KT-2300 engine rated at 900 horsepower powered the 1200 Series machines. *Keith Haddock*

diesel- or gasoline-powered machines or failed completely. The 1920s also saw dozens of new excavator manufacturers emerge. They had skipped the steam era, and offered sophisticated mechanical features with diesel or gasoline power on their machines. Many of these companies did not survive the Great Depression of the early 1930s, but those that did became the backbone of the excavator industry for the next three decades.

The 1920s also witnessed the development of another class of excavator known as the quarry and mine shovel. In this decade, excavation with shovels that loaded trucks or rail cars became prevalent and organized. There were still many railroad shovels at work—heavy and robust for digging hard rock. But these could not swing 360 degrees, so their use was severely restricted. The fully revolving shovels of the day were long-boomed, gangly outfits, not robust enough for hard digging. Thus, the market demand led the Bucyrus Company to design a shovel that combined the robust qualities of the railroad shovel with the 360-degree capability of the stripping shovel. The result was the 120-B, the world's first mine and quarry shovel. First built in 1925, this 5-cubic-yard machine revolutionized the shovel industry, and over 300 had been built by the time it was discontinued in 1951. (A 120-B appears on page 14 in chapter 1.)

Many of the two-crawler, cable-operated shovels could be fitted with a boom of extended length. Thus, the two-crawler shovel could then do the work of a stripping shovel, although on a smaller scale than the giant multi-crawler machines described in chapter 13. The long boom, and correspondingly long stick or handle, allowed the shovel to dump the material far enough away without the need to load trucks. These types of stripping shovels, sometimes called highlifts, were most popular in the 1940s and 1950s in the shallow overburden coal regions of Ohio, West Virginia, and western Pennsylvania. This shovel option allowed many excavator manufacturers to sell machines to the surface mining industry, a market they would not normally serve. Manufacturers in this category include Koehring, Lorain, Northwest, and Osgood.

Bay City R. Initially founded as the Bay City Dredge Works in 1913, the company became known as Bay City Shovels, Inc. in 1929. Its first products included the Bay City Land Dredge, a long-range rail-mounted shovel used in land drainage. This was followed in 1920 by the One Man Excavator of similar design. Bay City's first crawler excavator, the 16-B, appeared in 1923. This was a half-swinging shovel or dragline of .5-cubic-yard capacity. (The boom swung about 180 degrees only.) The Model R (the R stands for revolving) was Bay City's first fully revolving excavator. Introduced in 1930, this fully convertible machine was rated at .75-cubic-yards capacity. As a backhoe it could dig down 20 feet, and as a crane it could lift 9 tons. Original power was a 76-horsepower Climax gasoline, or Atlas 69-horsepower diesel engine, but the machine in the picture has been re-powered with a Caterpillar diesel. *Keith Haddock*

Bay City 65. This was a 1.25-cubic-yard fully convertible (universal) crawler-mounted excavator produced by Bay City from 1936 to 1951. A Hercules 114-horsepower diesel or gasoline engine provided power. As a backhoe, digging depth was specified as 21 feet, and as a crane, the 65 was rated at 20 tons. The Bay City 65 in the picture has been exported to Russia and is shown being commissioned in 1947. In 1960, Unit Crane & Shovel Corporation purchased Bay City Shovels, Inc., and the Bay City excavators and cranes continued to be sold under the Bay City name. In 1966, Bay City became a subsidiary of the Manitowoc Company, Inc. Under the new company Bay City-Manitowoc Corporation, Bay City products were continued until 1969. *Keith Haddock collection*

Hundreds of manufacturers have designed and built cable-operated crawler excavators over the years, but relatively few have ventured into sizes much above the 6-cubic-yard class. These have included Weserhütte and Menck & Hambrock from Germany; Ruston & Hornsby from England; Clark/Lima, Manitowoc, P&H, Bucyrus-Erie (now Bucyrus International), Marion, and American Hoist from the United States; as well as some makers in the former Soviet Union.

By the 1980s, cable excavators were all but eclipsed by other types of equipment, such as hydraulic excavators, wheel loaders, and tractor-mounted attachments. The demise of the cable excavator was a gradual process beginning in the 1950s with the advent of the hydraulic excavator. Traditional cable excavator manufacturers added hydraulic excavators to their rosters, and then gradually phased out their cable machines. Some formed alliances with foreign hydraulic excavator manufacturers, especially those from Japan, while others were taken over and their cable product was dropped.

Bucyrus 50-B. Known today as Bucyrus International, Inc. and founded as the Bucyrus Foundry and Manufacturing Company in 1880, this company built its first steam shovel, a railroad type, in 1882 (see chapter 1). These half-swing railroad shovels were the company's main products well into the twentieth century. Bucyrus built its first fully revolving shovels in 1912. The company rapidly introduced a full range of revolving shovels, and in 1922 brought out one of its most famous models, the 50-B. Up-rated from 1.75- to 2-cubic-yards capacity, the 50-B proved itself as a heavy-duty excavator that thrived on the toughest excavation assignments. Convertible to shovel, dragline, or crane, its power options were diesel, gasoline, steam, or electricity. The diesel version utilized a four-cylinder Bucyrus-Atlas engine with 9x12-inch bore and stroke, running at a low 300 rpm. The 50-B was produced up to 1934. *Bucyrus International, Inc.*

Bucyrus Class 24. The Class Series from the Bucyrus Company signified draglines of the non-walking type. They were mounted on rails, crawler tracks, or skids and rollers. The steam-powered Class 24 in the picture is mounted on skids and rollers, the standard form of mounting for this machine. Heavy timbers were laid out in front of the machine for the rollers to run on, then the machine simply pulled itself along with its bucket. A sizeable ground crew was needed to construct the timber path and place the hardwood rollers ahead of the machine. The standard configuration for the Class 24 was a 3.5-cubic-yard bucket on a 100-foot boom. Operating weight was 145 tons. Class 24 machines were produced from 1911 to 1930. One is preserved at the Reynolds Alberta Museum, Wetaskiwin, Alberta, Canada. *Bucyrus International, Inc.*

Bucyrus Class 375. Before the advent of the walking type, draglines moved on crawler tracks or rails. The Bucyrus Company did not make walking draglines until it purchased the Monighan Manufacturing Corporation in 1932. Prior to that time, the company built some very large crawler and rail-mounted draglines. The largest of these was the Class 375 introduced in 1929, which could handle buckets up to 10 cubic yards and booms up to 160 feet in length. Operating weights were up to 438 tons for the crawler version. The example shown was electrically powered and rail mounted. *Keith Haddock collection*

Bucyrus-Erie 37-B. In 1927, the Bucyrus-Erie Company (B-E) was formed by the consolidation of Bucyrus Company and the Erie Steam Shovel Company of Erie, Pennsylvania. The Bucyrus Company had achieved great success with its large shovels and dredges, but it needed a line of small machines to compete in the rapidly growing construction market. One of the earliest machines to come from the merger was the 37-B. This ruggedly designed shovel was unveiled in 1931 as a fully convertible 1.5-cubic-yard machine available with gasoline, diesel, or electric power. The 37-B belonged to the B-E family of machines with a chain-driven rack-and-pinion crowd motion and twin dipper sticks. Production of the 37-B continued until 1943, but the British 37-RB version continued until 1949. *Keith Haddock collection*

Today, the cable backhoe has become obsolete, and the cable shovel is only found on the very largest of electric models used in surface mining operations. Hydraulic excavators (chapter 12) are today favored over cable machines because they are cheaper to buy, easier to operate, and faster traveling. Also, they have positive action in all movements instead of relying on gravity to provide some of the digging forces. Only two North American manufacturers supply cable shovels today: P&H and Bucyrus, both of Milwaukee, Wisconsin. These two companies compete in the large electric mining shovel market in sizes above 20 cubic yards, and also produce draglines. Of all the other manufacturers covered in this chapter, only American Hoist, Link-Belt, Little Giant, and Manitowoc still produce cable excavators, and these are only in dragline form.

The boom in surface mining in the 1970s brought larger two-crawler shovels to load the bigger trucks then available. This trend has continued into the 1990s, with trucks available to carry up to 400 tons. Since customers demand three-pass loading of these large trucks, shovel manufacturers respond. Consequently, unlike the giant stripping shovels and walking draglines that reached their peak size over three decades ago, the two-crawler electric shovel has continued its upward trend in size.

Bucyrus-Erie 10-B. The smallest of Bucyrus-Erie's long line of excavators was the 10-B. This popular shovel with a dipper capacity of .375 cubic yards sold by the thousands to contractors around the world. Weighing a mere 10 tons and initially powered by a Buda HP260 gasoline engine of 38 horsepower, the 10-B was easily transported on a light trailer. Equipped with any one of a full slate of front-end attachments (shovel, dragline, backhoe, clamshell, crane, pile driver, and skimmer), the 10-B was the mainstay of small-scale excavation and trenching duties in city and industrial development before the advent of the crawler loader and hydraulic backhoe. The 10-B was produced from 1934 to 1959, and the British 10-RB version continued until 1969. *Bucyrus International, Inc.*

Bucyrus-Erie 30-B. A popular mid-sized excavator was Bucyrus-Erie's 30-B introduced in 1956. From the outset, the 30-B boasted air control for its clutch operations, a feature that would eventually be adopted on all the company's cable excavators. Initially rated at 1 cubic yard, the 30-B progressed through several series upgrades to the Series V machine, produced from 1981 to 1984. This machine was also made in Lincoln, England, as the 30-RB by Ruston-Bucyrus, Ltd., who continued with the Series VI machine until 1995. The 30-B in the picture is equipped with a cable backhoe and tractor-type "Hi-Walker" undercarriage ready for pipelining duties. *Bucyrus International, Inc.*

Bucyrus-Erie 88-B. The largest of the "construction-sized" cable excavators from Bucyrus-Erie was the 88-B. Introduced as a 4-cubic-yard shovel in 1946, it grew through several series upgrades to 5.5-cubic-yards capacity in the Series IV machine, produced from 1968 to 1985. The design of the 88-B belonged to the family of Bucyrus-Erie cable shovels produced in the 1960s and 1970s that sported an independent rope crowd motion with single internal dipper stick. The 88-B Series IV machine weighed 140 tons as a shovel, and offered Cummins or GM power units in the 360-horsepower range. A heavy-duty version was also offered for crane and dragline duties with buckets available up to 6 cubic yards. *Keith Haddock collection*

Bucyrus-Erie 395-B. Probably the best-known name in the excavator industry is Bucyrus-Erie. The extensive line of excavating and drilling machines produced by this company since its inception is unmatched by any other organization. Products ranged from the largest machines to move on land—the giant shovels and walking draglines—to rough-terrain cranes and backhoe loaders. Today, the company specializes in electric mining shovels, walking draglines, and drills for the surface mining industry. Bucyrus built the first quarry and mining shovel, the 5-cubic-yard 120-B in 1925 (see chapter 1). The modern 395-B electric mining shovel, shown here loading a 320-ton truck with its 34-cubic-yard dipper, was launched in 1979. The current upgraded 395-B Series III version is rated at 44 cubic yards and has an operating weight of 1,144 tons. *Keith Haddock*

Bucyrus 595-B. In 1996, Bucyrus-Erie Company changed its name to Bucyrus International, Inc. The following year, it took over archrival excavator builder, Marion Power Shovel Company of Marion, Ohio. The 595-B was formerly the Marion-designed 351-M, but upgraded with state-of-the-art technology. With its standard 57-cubic-yard dipper, the 595-B is able to load a 400-ton truck in four passes. Several of these machines have been sold into the oil sands operations in Alberta, Canada, where soft ground conditions dictate a special undercarriage design to support the 1,300-ton weight of the machine. The oil sands shovel shown boasts crawler shoes 140 inches wide. *Keith Haddock*

Byers Bearcat 27. The John F. Byers Machine Company was established in 1886 at Ravenna, Ohio. The town also was the original home of the Quaker Oats Company, and around 1890 John F. Byers invented a machine for slicing the grain. Byers' first excavator was the "Auto-Crane" in 1914, a flimsy-looking clamshell/crane mounted on four steel wheels. The famous "Bearcat" excavator appeared in 1923 with a .5-cubic-yard bucket capacity. This half-swing excavator could operate with all front-end attachments including skimmer. A 48-horsepower Hercules four-cylinder gasoline engine powered it. Byers brought out a new model of Bearcat each year from 1923 to 1927. The fully restored 1927 version in the picture was demonstrated at a convention of the Historical Construction Equipment Association in 1993. *Keith Haddock*

Byers 63. In 1926, the John F. Byers Machine Company became the Byers Machine Company under new ownership. In the 1930's Byers offered a broad line of crawler-mounted conventional universal excavators up to 1.25-cubic-yards capacity. By 1943 the line had been consolidated to four models: the .375-cubic-yard, half-swing Bearcat Junior; the .5-cubic-yard Model 65, the .625-cubic-yard Model 75, and the .75-cubic-yard Model 83. The Model 63, which replaced the Model 65, was Byers' contender in the .5-cubic-yard class in the early 1950s. With an operating weight of 15 tons, it offered diesel or gasoline engines of 44 horsepower. In 1953, Byers Machine Company was purchased by the Thew Shovel Company, who discontinued the Byers products in 1958. *Keith Haddock*

Erie B. The Ball Engine Company of Erie, Pennsylvania, began building a .75-cubic-yard fully revolving steam shovel in 1914. Known as the Erie B, its wheel-mounted mobility and relatively low cost proved to be just what the average contractor was looking for. Advertisements boasted that "a four-man crew can do the work of fifty men." Another advantage touted at the time was that "all machine parts are machined to jigs and gauges so as to be absolutely interchangeable when replacement becomes necessary." A crawler version soon followed and an upgrade, the B2, appeared in 1925. The Model B wheel version weighed 22 tons, while the crawler-track option added another 4 tons to its operating weight. The B2 was carried forward under the Bucyrus-Erie banner from 1927. It was revised to the B3 model in 1929 and was available up to 1936. *Keith Haddock*

Erie A. With its business committed to steam shovels, the Ball Engine Company changed its name to the Erie Steam Shovel Company in 1922. Following the success of the Erie B, the company introduced the smaller .5-cubic-yard steam shovel known as the Erie A in 1918. Weighing 13.5 tons on wheels or 18 tons on crawlers, the Erie A was advertised as "light enough to cross ordinary county bridges, but powerful enough to dig stiff clays and lighter shales without blasting." Never as popular as its sister machine the Erie B, the Erie A did chalk up respectable sales, and was valued enough to be carried forward as a Bucyrus-Erie product from 1927 to 1931. The Bucyrus Company of South Milwaukee, Wisconsin, took over the Erie Steam Shovel Company in 1927, and the Bucyrus-Erie Company was born. *Keith Haddock collection*

Erie GA-2. In the mid-1920s, gasoline-powered shovels were becoming popular. Not to be outdone, the Erie Steam Shovel Company developed a unique gasoline-powered excavator that utilized compressed air for crowding and swinging. The directly driven hoist drum was connected to the engine through an air-operated clutch, but the crowd and compressed air motors designed like steam engines drove swing motions. This hybrid machine reflected Erie's deep steam heritage and lack of confidence in marketing a fully mechanical machine at that time. The GA-2 (for gas plus air) was advertised as being "just as fast, smooth and flexible as a steam machine." After Bucyrus took over Erie in 1927, the Bucyrus-Erie Company pursued the "gas-plus-air" concept on a small scale. Diesel versions and a GA-3 upgrade were released, but the concept finally died in 1935. *Keith Haddock collection*

General Invincible. The General Excavator Company was established in 1926 at Marion, Ohio, by the owners of shovel-builder the Osgood Company in the same town. Starting with a single .5-cubic-yard excavator known as the Series I, the company did not introduce further models until 1935, when the .625-cubic-yard Series II and the .75-cubic-yard Invincible were unveiled. The latter machine, an example of which is shown, was powered by a six-cylinder Cummins engine of 87 horsepower or a six-cylinder Buda gasoline engine of 84 horsepower. As a shovel, the Invincible weighed 24 tons. General concentrated only on gasoline- and diesel-powered fully revolving excavators that were fully convertible to all front ends. *Keith Haddock*

General 310 and 320. In 1948, the General Excavator Company introduced the Model 310, a .75-cubic-yard excavator with air-controlled clutches, an advanced feature for its day. Weighing 22 tons as a shovel, the 310 could be powered by Buda gasoline or diesel engines in the range of 74 to 84 horsepower. General also offered the Model 320, an excavator of similar capacity and range as the 310, but with mechanical controls instead of air. Both models appear in the picture; a 1953 Model 320 is on the left, and a 1950 Model 310 is on the right. In 1954 the Marion Power Shovel Company took over the General Excavator Company as well as its parent, the Osgood Company. The former General 320 became the Marion 32-M before it was discontinued in 1958. *Keith Haddock*

Hanson 28. The Hanson Clutch and Machinery Company was incorporated in 1918 at Tiffin, Ohio, to manufacture friction clutches. In 1924, the company built its first excavator, the .375-cubic-yard Model 28, claimed by its makers to be the first fully revolving gasoline excavator in the United States. The machine utilized a McCormick-Deering engine mounted longitudinally instead of across the back of the revolving frame. Power to the drums was transmitted through a right-angle drive. The fully restored Hanson 28 shown here moves dirt at a meeting of the Historical Construction Equipment Association in 2001. Hanson expanded its product line to include truck cranes, but none of the company's excavators exceeded .75-cubic-yards capacity. Pettibone-Mulliken Corporation purchased the Hanson company in 1966, but only the former Hanson truck cranes were continued as Pettibone products. *Keith Haddock*

Insley K-12. Founded in 1905 as the Insley Iron Works at Indianapolis, Indiana, the company initially built concrete mixing and handling equipment. Changing its name to the Insley Manufacturing Company in 1911, the company built a prototype excavator in 1924, a .375-cubic-yard half-swinging machine based on a Fordson tractor. The first production machine was the half-swinging, fully convertible excavator Model C in 1925. This Buda-powered, heavily built machine had an operating weight of almost 23 tons as a .5-cubic-yard shovel. Insley presented its fully revolving excavator, the Model R, in 1928. Then in 1936, the highly successful Model K appeared. Starting out as the .375-cubic-yard K-10 and evolving into the .5-cubic-yard K-12, this model sold more than twice the number of all Insley's other cable excavators combined, by the time production ceased in 1971. The machine shown is the "Swamp Cat" version with 48-inch crawler shoes proving a ground pressure of 3.1 psi. *Keith Haddock*

Insley M. From 1958 to 1971, Insley produced the Model M, a .875-cubic-yard fully convertible excavator. Available with diesel or gasoline power and optional engines made by Minneapolis-Moline, GM, or Caterpillar, the Model M had an operating weight of 26 tons as a shovel. At the time the M was in production, Insley's line consisted of the .375-cubic-yard K, the .75-cubic-yard L, the 1.25-cubic-yard WT, and the 1.5-cubic-yard WB. The WB was the largest cable excavator made by the company. In 1971 the company made the bold decision to discontinue its cable excavators and concentrate on its hydraulic excavators. Badger Construction Equipment Company of Winona, Minnesota, took over Insley in 1986 and continued the Insley hydraulic excavators until 1996. *Keith Haddock*

Koehring 303. Founded as the Koehring Machine Company in 1907 to build concrete mixers, the company changed its name to Koehring Company in 1920. The first Koehring excavator appeared in 1921 as a prototype fully revolving crawler-mounted gasoline excavator. Over the next three years, Koehring released three sizes of its universal excavators known as the No. 1, No. 2, and No. 3. With the launch of the .75-cubic-yard Model 301 in 1927, the company adopted a new numbering system whose first digit signified the machine's capacity in quarter cubic yards. The modern-looking, and upgraded 303 replaced the 301 in 1937 with similar capacity. The machine shown in the picture was purchased by Vern Schield of Waverly, Iowa, and was the machine that motivated Mr. Schield to produce his own machines, and establish the Schield-Bantam Company. *Keith Haddock*

Koehring 205. Koehring expanded its excavator line throughout the 1930s to include machines up to the 2-cubic-yard capacity 803 which appeared in 1939. The successful 205, introduced in 1944, tipped the scales at 14 tons. This .5-cubic-yard, fully convertible machine was a big seller throughout the 1950s, and, in 1957 Koehring developed the 2-cubic-yard Skooper hybrid hydraulic/cable shovel attachment for this model (see chapter 12). The 205 was also one of the models built in England by Newton Chambers & Company, Ltd. under a manufacturing agreement started in 1947. Sold under the NCK brand, the Newton Chambers excavators eventually included most of the Koehring models produced after that date. *Keith Haddock collection*

Koehring 1205. Koehring released its largest shovel to date in 1956, the heavy-duty 1205. Initially rated at 3 cubic yards, it was later up-rated to 3.5-cubic-yards capacity. Convertible to shovel, dragline, or crane, it was also available as a long-boom stripping shovel for use in coal mining operations (illustrated). This shovel boasted a 50-foot-long boom providing a 53-foot dumping radius, but its dipper was correspondingly reduced to 2.5-cubic-yards capacity. Power options were Buda 230-horsepower or Cummins 300-horsepower diesel engines, or a single AC electric motor. In 1961, Koehring introduced a wider-undercarriage version known as the 1295, designed for lifting crane and dragline duties only. In 1986, Koehring was purchased by Northwest Engineering Company and two years later, was merged into the Terex organization. *Keith Haddock collection*

Lima 601. Famous for its big steam railroad locomotives, the Lima Locomotive Works of Lima, Ohio, entered into excavator manufacturing when it purchased the Ohio Power Shovel Company in 1928. The first fruits of the acquisition resulted in the Model 101, a convertible crawler-mounted excavator of 1.25-cubic-yards capacity. The success of the 101 prompted Lima to rapidly expand its line of cable excavators during the 1930s to include a full range of sizes from .75 to 2.5-cubic-yards capacity in quarter-yard increments. The Model 601 shown is equipped with a 1.5-cubic-yard heavy-duty shovel and independent chain crowd. The 601 was produced from 1933 to 1935, when it was superseded by the 302 of similar capacity. *Keith Haddock*

Lima 802. In 1933, Lima lunched the 1.75-cubic-yard Model 701 and added the larger 2-cubic-yard 801 the following year. These machines featured heavy-duty chain crowd shovels with twin dipper sticks. The 801 was also available as a 3-cubic-yard dragline. Both were offered with gasoline, diesel or electric power options. In 1939, Lima brought out the 2-cubic-yard Model 802 derived from combining a Model 701 upper works with a Model 801 lower works (undercarriage). The 802 could be converted for shovel, dragline, backhoe, and crane duties. A common power unit for this model was the Caterpillar D17000 diesel engine. The 802 was superseded by the 2.5-cubic-yard 803 in 1954, which remained in production until 1963. *Keith Haddock*

Lima 2400. Lima's flagship excavator was the Model 2400, which was unveiled in 1948. This legendary machine would become the mainstay of Lima's excavator line until the company's demise in 1981. With hundreds sold around the world, the 2400 built a solid reputation as a tough mining-sized, diesel-powered shovel or dragline in the 6- to 8-cubic-yard class. The picture shows a mid-1960s-vintage Lima 2400 working in a limestone quarry in 2001. Diesel power for this machine was the Caterpillar D397 of 473 flywheel-horsepower. After several mergers and name changes, the Baldwin-Lima-Hamilton Corporation emerged in 1950. This group was eventually sold to Clark Equipment Company in 1970. The upgraded 2400B appeared in 1969, and this lasted until the Lima plant closed in 1981. *Keith Haddock*

Link-Belt K-2. The long-established Link-Belt Company of Chicago, Illinois, began making rail-mounted and locomotive cranes as far back as 1894. In 1922, Link-Belt shipped the first of a new line of crawler-mounted, fully convertible excavators, the .75-cubic-yard K-1. This was followed in 1923 by the larger K-2 rated at 1-cubic-yard bucket capacity or 15-tons lifting capacity as a crane . The fully restored K-2 in the picture, owned by the Historical Construction Equipment Association, is shown at work in 1994. It is equipped with a clamshell and powered by a Waukesha engine. In 1939, Link-Belt purchased the Speeder Machinery Company of Cedar Rapids, Iowa, builder of a line of small excavators up to .75-cubic-yards capacity since 1919. This merger broadened the line of Link-Belt machines, which became known by the brand-name Link-Belt-Speeder. *Keith Haddock*

Link-Belt-Speeder LS-85. During the 1930s, Link-Belt developed a full line of crawler-mounted cable excavators comprising models derived from the former Speeder designs up to .75 cubic yards, and its own Chicago-built K Series covering all popular sizes up to 2 cubic yards. In 1940, Link-Belt's extensive line consisted of eight models up to the .75-cubic-yard size, the 1-cubic-yard LS-100, and the 1.25-cubic-yard LS-120, as well as the K-300, K-400 and K-500 Series machines covering sizes up to 2.5-cubic yards. The LS-85, a fully convertible crawler machine, was in production from 1940 to 1954. The LS-85 in the picture is working in a gravel pit in 2001. *Keith Haddock*

Link-Belt K-580. Link-Belt's K-500 Series of seven different models of shovels, cranes, and draglines was introduced in 1940. Shovel models in this series were the two-yard K-560, the 2.25-cubic-yard K-570, and 2.5-cubic-yard K-580, with diesel power of 160, 175, 200 horsepower respectively. The dragline and crane models were derived by increasing the length and shoe widths to allow greater ranges. The K-580 in the picture, built in 1943, has a twin-stick chain crowd. Later models were supplied with a single-stick rope crowd. The 500 Series machines were built up to 1956. *Keith Haddock*

Link-Belt LS-98. Probably the most popular of all Link-Belt's cable excavators was the LS-98 introduced in 1954, shown here as a 1-cubic-yard chain-crowd shovel. Fully convertible, it featured Link-Belt's Full-Function Design, which provided a separate set of spur gears on each side of the four main shafts in the upper works. Running in opposite directions, these gears provided reverse power to each of the main motions. When equipped with a tractor-type undercarriage and shoe grousers, the LS-98 was a favorite among pipeline contractors. The LS-98 also featured Speed-o-Matic control used on Link-Belt excavators since 1936. In this system, the clutches are activated by oil under pressure, controlled by light-load levers in the operator's cab. The LS-98 legacy continued into the 1990s, with the LS-98C and LS-98D offering crane and dragline capability up to 1.5 cubic yards. *Keith Haddock*

Link-Belt LS-108H II. In 2002, Link-Belt offers a line of Japanese-designed crawler cranes available for dragline duties, and is one of few companies still building these machines in North America. The LS Series of hydraulic cranes, up to the LS-308H Series II, can swing buckets up to 6 cubic yards. They are powered by hydraulic motors for all motions, including an independent propel drive in each crawler assembly. The LS-108H in the picture shows its free-spooling capabilities as the operator casts the 2-yard bucket way beyond the boom point. The machine is powered by an Isuzu engine of 157 horsepower and can handle boom lengths up to 160 feet as a 50-ton crane. *Link-Belt Construction Equipment*

Thew Model O. Captain Thew designed a fully revolving shovel with a telescopic crowd motion in 1895. Built by the Variety Iron Works, Cleveland, Ohio, it was the first fully revolving shovel in the United States. Following its success, Thew decided to build his own machines, and established the Thew Automatic Shovel Company at Lorain, Ohio, in 1899. By 1911 the company was offering six sizes of shovels mounted on rails or steel wheels in sizes from .625 to 1.75-cubic-yards capacity. The illustration shows a rail-mounted .625-yard type O with Thew's patented telescopic crowd. This model was made until 1929, but later versions appeared with crawler tracks and a conventional shipper-shaft boom. *Harry E. Young II collection*

Little Giant C48. Lewis Grundon built his first excavator in 1946 intended for his own use. It was a truck-mounted excavator with a .5-cubic-yard bucket capacity. Its inventor claimed that it was the world's first excavator mounted on a ball-bearing turntable. This machine was so successful that Grundon sold it and began making more. He founded Little Giant Crane & Shovel, Inc. in 1947 at Des Moines, Iowa. Over the years the company has manufactured a wide range of excavators sized at 1 cubic yard or less, as well as truck and rough terrain cranes. Little Giant found its biggest market with the railroad companies; thus, most of its models could be fitted with hi-railer kits so the machines could run on standard-gauge rails. The C48 shown handles a .75-cubic-yard clamshell. In 1996, Avis Industrial Corporation purchased Little Giant, and in 2002, Avis still offered Little Giant products. *Keith Haddock*

Lorain 75. In 1920, the Thew Automatic Shovel Company passed to new owners, who re-established it as the Thew Shovel Company. In 1925, Thew brought out one of its most famous models, the 75. This 1.25-yard shovel or dragline set the standard for the company's future excavators, and was the first to be known as a "Lorain." More models followed, and by 1927, Thew was the sixth-largest excavator company in terms of sales in the United States. The 75 featured Thew's patent "center-drive" whereby the crawlers were driven by the two center tumblers instead of an end tumbler. The 75 and its upgrades stayed in production until 1939. By that time it had become the 1.5-cubic-yard Lorain 75D. The prolific Thew company brought out an extensive line of Lorain excavators up to 2.5-cubic-yards throughout the 1930s and 1940s. *Keith Haddock*

Manitowoc 2000. Formerly established in 1902, the Manitowoc Shipbuilding Company of Manitowoc, Wisconsin, built its first crane in 1925 under license from its designers, the Moore Brothers. Known as a Speedcrane, the steam-powered, wheel-mounted machine could operate as a 15-ton crane or carry a .75-cubic-yard bucket. Manitowoc promptly took over the Moore patents and designed a gasoline-powered universal excavator on a crawler base known as the Model 125 (later renumbered the 1500) with 1.25-cubic-yards capacity. In 1932, Manitowoc introduced the completely-redesigned 1.5-cubic-yard Model 150 (later renumbered the 3000). In 1936, the former 1500 was upgraded to the 2000, a fully-convertible excavator powered by a 115-horsepower engine and weighing just over 42 tons as a shovel. Manitowoc retained the Speedcrane logo until the mid-1950s. *Keith Haddock collection*

Lorain 50. The 1-cubic-yard Model 50, built from 1949 to 1963, was powered by a Caterpillar D318 diesel of 77 flywheel-horsepower. The 50 was a strange blend of old and new technology. It was offered with twin joystick levers to control all digging functions through air-operated clutches, but its crawler steering, as on older Lorains, was activated by a mechanical dog that dropped down from the turntable to engage a lever operating the steering clutches. Steering was thus accomplished by swinging the turntable. The Lorain 50 illustrated is working as a crane on a Brazilian pipeline job in 1976. The Thew Shovel Company merged with Koehring in 1964 to become the Thew-Lorain Division of Koehring Company. After this time, the Lorain products were gradually phased out until by 1976 the only crawler crane still in production was the L-790. After further ownership changes, the remnants of the company have been controlled by Terex Corporation since 1988. *Keith Haddock*

Manitowoc 3500. Manitowoc produced this 2.5-cubic-yard excavator from 1938 to 1958. As a heavy-duty shovel or dragline it was a favorite with surface mine and quarry operators. The machine in the picture is operating at a meeting of the Historical Construction Equipment Association in Brownsville, Pennsylvania, in 1999. This particular machine is equipped with a special high-lift stripping shovel front, a style synonymous with Manitowoc. The boom is 45 feet long and the dipper arm or sticks measure 34 feet. In this configuration, the machine weighs 84 tons, but because of its extended reach, dipper capacity is reduced to 2 cubic yards. *Keith Haddock*

Manitowoc 4600. In 2002, Manitowoc Cranes, Inc. is better known for its heavy lifting cranes than for excavators. It builds some of the world's largest cranes with capacities exceeding 1,000 tons. However, Manitowoc also made an enviable name for itself in the surface mining industry during the 1960s and 1970s with its large diesel-powered shovels and draglines. Foremost amongst these was the Model 4600 in the 6- to 8-cubic-yard class. Derived from the former 4500 introduced in 1947, the first version of the 4600 appeared in 1961. The 200-ton machine was powered by two GM engines, one of 387 horsepower for the main drums and another of 186 horsepower for the swing and travel functions. Manitowoc shipped the last 4600 in 1994, but like the one in this picture taken in 2001, many still enjoy an active life. *Keith Haddock*

Marion 37. Famous for its giant stripping machines (see chapters 13 and 14), the Marion Power Shovel Company of Marion, Ohio, got its start in 1884 when Henry M. Barnhart and two other partners established the Marion Steam Shovel Company to build a shovel designed by Barnhart (see chapter 1). The company went from strength to strength and, by the turn of the twentieth century the company was one of the leading steam shovel manufacturers. Marion built its first fully revolving shovel in 1908 and its first gasoline-powered shovel in 1915. The Model 37 was typical of the heavy-duty shovels of the 1920s. Produced from 1922 to 1929, it was rated at 2 cubic yards and available with steam, gasoline, or electric power, and wheel or crawler mounting. The 37 steam shovel shown is preserved in the Crawford County Historical Museum, Pittsburg, Kansas. *Tom Pierce*

Manitowoc 6400. Manitowoc's largest excavator was the 6400 dragline built from 1977 to 1988. Weighing in at 554 tons and available only as a dragline, it carried a standard 15-cubic-yard bucket on a 160-foot boom. A V16 Cummins engine of 1,600 horsepower powered the upper works (hoist, drag, and swing), while a separate 450-horsepower engine in the lower works powered the crawler tracks. Manitowoc's big draglines utilized its patented Vicon control system, first applied in 1958. This system (an acronym for Variable Independent Control) allowed the operator to individually control the speed and output of each engine. When the operator moved a clutch lever, the clutch engaged with the engine running at idle speed; then, further movement of the lever accelerated the engine. *Keith Haddock*

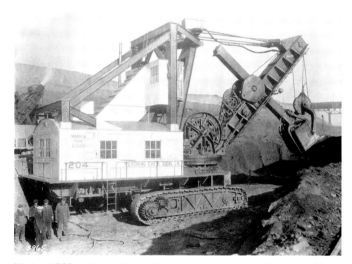

Marion 6200. In the twilight of the railroad shovel era (Marion built its last in 1931), the company produced two of these Model 6200 electric shovels in 1929. Looking like a throwback to the railroading pioneering days, the giant 5.5-cubic-yard shovel was built on the obsolete half-swinging principle but incorporated the latest technology for its day. Notice the elevated cab and exposed hoist drum mounted on the boom turntable. We can only speculate that owner Mahoning Ore & Steel Company was so accustomed to operating half-swing railroad shovels that its pit layout could not accommodate a revolving shovel. *Keith Haddock collection*

Marion 4121. Marion produced dozens of shovel and dragline models over the years and became a leader in the industry. Although its steam-powered machines were obsolete by the early 1930s, the company did not change its name to the Marion Power Shovel Company until April 1946. Marion introduced an electric mining shovel in 1934 known as the 4121. After 1940, this model was equipped with a special "knee-action" shovel front, a design borrowed from the big Marion stripping shovels (see description in chapter 13). This type of shovel lent itself to loading coal in surface mining operations as it provided a much greater clean-up radius and, with the lighter-density coal, the dipper capacity was boosted to 7.5 cubic yards. The 4121 coal shovel weighed 177 tons. *Keith Haddock*

Marion 93-M. Although Marion offered a full line of excavators from the smallest to the world's largest, the mid-sized range, represented by the 93-M, 101-M, and 111-M, proved to be the most popular in terms of numbers sold. The 2.5-cubic-yard 93-M and the 4.5-cubic-yard 111-M were introduced in 1946, with the 3-cubic-yard 101-M first shipped in 1953. These stalwart machines, equipped as cranes, shovels, or draglines, and powered by diesel or electric motors, found homes in quarries, surface mines, and construction projects. The 93-M in the picture loads blasted rock in a quarry. It was furnished with a Cummins diesel engine rated at 268 horsepower, and tipped the scales at 83 tons. The last of this series of machines was shipped in 1975. *Keith Haddock collection*

Marion 151-M. Marion took the wraps off the first 151-M in 1945. Originally designed as an electric mining shovel of 6-cubic-yards capacity, the 151-M was soon adapted for dragline work with buckets up to 8 cubic yards, and as a 12-cubic-yard shovel for coal-loading duties. In 1970, Marion offered a diesel-electric version employing two Cummins engines providing 700 horsepower to independent electric motors for the hoist, swing, and crowd motions. In the 1960s, Marion gradually pulled away from the small "construction-sized" machine market, preferring to concentrate on the large mining machines such as stripping shovels, walking draglines, blast hole drills, and large two-crawler excavators. By the mid-1970s, the 151-M was the smallest excavator in Marion's product line. It continued until 1982 offering dippers up to 12 cubic yards. *Keith Haddock collection*

Marion 191-M. When Marion designed and built the first 191-M in 1951, at 10-cubic-yards capacity it was the world's largest shovel on two crawlers. Although nearly all subsequent 191-Ms were electrically powered, this first machine, sold to Western Contracting Corporation, was diesel powered with three engines totaling 1,700 horsepower. It was employed on dam construction in South Dakota, along with several more 191-Ms, and then used on many other jobs by Western Contracting. One of the most successful mining shovels of all time, the 191-M continued in production until 1989, by which time it had been upgraded to carry a standard dipper of 15 cubic yards. The 1967-vintage machine in the picture is loading a Caterpillar electric truck in an Arizona copper mine. *Keith Haddock collection*

Marion Superfront. Marion's Superfront shovel was designed to increase dipper capacity of a given shovel size. Prior to its announcement in 1974, Marion performed an extensive testing program starting in 1967 when a Marion 101-M was retrofitted with the first Superfront of 5-cubic-yards capacity (illustrated). This represented an increase of 66 percent over its standard dipper size. The Superfront's increased capacity came from its geometry and its weight-saving front end utilizing a moveable stiff leg replacing the boom. The production model Superfront was known as the 204-M and carried a standard dipper of 30 cubic yards. Ten of these were shipped to the former Soviet Union and further orders were received from Australia, New Guinea, and coal mining companies in the western United States. *Keith Haddock collection*

Marion 351-M. Keeping pace with the increasing size of off-highway trucks, Marion designed the 301-M, a 57-cubic-yard mining shovel designed to load 240-ton trucks in three passes. The first of these 1,150-ton shovels was sold in 1985. In 1995, the 301-M was upgraded to the 351-M, Marion's largest-ever two-crawler shovel, with similar dipper range to its predecessor, but weight upped to 1,300 tons. In 1997 Bucyrus International, Inc., purchased the Marion Shovel Company and all production was transferred to the South Milwaukee plant of Bucyrus. The 351-M was upgraded, and is sold in 2002 as the Bucyrus 595-B. *Keith Haddock*

Marion 195-M. Some customers preferred crawler draglines to walking draglines. Although more expensive to build, crawler machines offer greater mobility and flexibility when working in close quarters. Marion had offered crawler versions of its electric mining shovels for many years when it announced its largest to date in 1969. Designed only for dragline duties, the 195-M all-electric machine could handle a 17-cubic-yard bucket on a 130-foot boom. Its operating weight was 527 tons. The machine illustrated uncovered coal at a surface mine being worked by British contractor G. Wimpey & Company. Marion's largest two-crawler dragline was a single Model 305-M shipped to Australia in 1991. It weighs 1,225 tons in operation, and in 2002, was carrying buckets up to 24-cubic-yards capacity. *David Wootton*

NCK 605. Originally derived from the Koehring line of excavators, the NCK brand was manufactured at Sheffield, England, by Newton Chambers & Company, Ltd. under a manufacturing agreement started in 1947. In 1959, Newton Chambers amalgamated with excavator builder Ransomes & Rapier, Ltd. to form NCK-Rapier, Ltd. Under this company the Newton Chambers/Koehring partnership continued to build most of Koehring's excavator models until 1974. The NCK 605 was a 1.5-cubic-yard convertible excavator introduced in 1952. The picture shows an electrically powered version (note the trailing power cable), removing overburden at a surface coal mine in the United Kingdom. Since 1974, British-designed NCK machines have been continued as the company endured several changes of ownership. In the 1990s, fully hydraulic crawler cranes were introduced. *Keith Haddock collection*

Northwest 80-D. Northwest prospered in the 1940s, and in the 1950s it reached its peak as one of the leaders in the excavator industry. Backbone of the company's products was the 2.5-cubic-yard Model 80-D that made a name for itself as a tough rock shovel in quarries all over the United States. Introduced in 1937 as an upgrade to the former Model 80 originally released in 1933, the 80-D was convertible from shovel to dragline, crane or pullshovel (Northwest's name for a backhoe). The pullshovel in the picture had a digging depth of 32 feet. *Keith Haddock collection*

Northwest 105. Northwest Engineering Company of Green Bay, Wisconsin, built its first prototype excavator in 1920. It was a fully revolving crawler machine of advanced design, and was said to be the first excavator steered through the center pin by the operator in his cab. The following year production commenced, and the 1.25-cubic-yard machine known as the Model 104 became an instant success with over 500 machines sold in the first four years. The slightly smaller 1-cubic-yard Model 105 was added in 1922. The 105 and 104 were convertible to the usual front ends, and their operating weights were 31 tons and 36 tons, respectively. Northwest discontinued both models in 1929, and replaced them with the Model 4 and Model 5 of similar capacities. *Keith Haddock*

Northwest 190-DA. Northwest unveiled its largest machine to date at the 1963 Chicago Road Show. Available in two models, the 180-D was designed primarily as a 4.5-cubic-yard shovel, or dragline, and the 190-D, with longer and wider crawler base, for crane, dragline or pullshovel work. This 190-DA pullshovel is able to dig to 37 feet deep on this sewer job with its 6.5-cubic-yard bucket. In the late 1970s and 1980s, sales of Northwest machines dwindled, and after several financial transactions involving different owners, the company arrived under the Terex umbrella in 1988. Terex Corporation closed the Green Bay plant in 1990 and transferred Northwest manufacturing to the former Schield Bantam plant in Waverly, Iowa. In 1993, M.D. Moody Corporation purchased the manufacturing rights of Northwest machines from Terex Corporation. Moody built several machines until the last Northwest was shipped in 2002. *Keith Haddock collection*

Osgood 18. The Osgood Company's roots can be traced back to the very first steam shovel. Jason C. Osgood and Daniel Carmichael took out a patent for a dredge in 1846. Carmichael an was uncle of steam shovel inventor William S. Otis (see chapter 1). The Osgood name was associated with a number of shovel builders prior to forming the Osgood Dredge Company at Troy, New York, in 1875. This company supplied several large steam shovels for the French attempt to build the Panama Canal. The company also built a fully revolving shovel in 1890 and the world's first electric excavator in 1899. Of .75-cubic-yard capacity, the Osgood 18 was produced from 1914 to 1922 and was designed to take the limelight away from the popular Erie B shovel. The Model 18 crawler version as shown had an operating weight of 27 tons. *Keith Haddock collection*

Osgood Victor V. In the 1920s Osgood built a line of heavy-duty crawler shovels. In fact, Osgood's trade name became Heavy Duty. Ranging in sizes from .75 to 2 cubic yards in quarter-yard increments, the models were identified only by size in cubic yards, prefixed by the letters HDS or HDG to signify Heavy Duty Steam or Heavy Duty Gasoline. In the 1930s, Osgood adopted names for its excavators: the .5-cubic-yard Invader, .75-cubic-yard Commander, 1-cubic-yard Challenger, 1.25-cubic-yard Conqueror, 1.5-cubic-yard Victor, and 1.75-cubic-yard Chief. All these machines were available with gasoline, diesel, or electric power. The 1.75-cubic-yard Victor V shown was introduced in 1936 as an upgrade of the earlier 1.5-cubic-yard Victor that first appeared in 1929. Its operating weight was 50 tons. *Keith Haddock collection*

Osgood 200. The .5-cubic-yard Osgood 200 was launched in 1930 and enjoyed a very long production run. Many were sold to the U.S. armed forces in World War II. Its handy size and reliable performance endeared it to many loyal contractors. Power options were Buda or Chrysler gasoline engines of 57 and 60 horsepower, or Buda or Hercules diesel engines of 55 and 51 horsepower. Operating weight was 14 tons as a shovel. In 1953, this model was upgraded to the Osgood 250 now rated at .75 cubic yards, and with some extra horses provided by Continental diesel or gasoline engines of 88 and 79 horsepower, respectively. The 250 was manufactured up to 1957, the latter three years as a Marion machine following Marion Power Shovel Company's acquisition of Osgood in 1954. *Keith Haddock*

Page 222. Page Engineering Company of Chicago, Illinois, was a specialist dragline builder. In fact, company founder John W. Page invented the first dragline machine in 1904, and established Page Engineering Company in 1912. Before Page became known for its walking draglines in the 1920s, most of its machines were rail-mounted. The Model 222 ran on four rail trucks traveling on parallel pairs of rails. It carried a 2.5-cubic-yard bucket on a 100-foot boom, and power came from a 150-horsepower Page two-cylinder, 13x20-inch bore and stroke diesel engine running at 250 rpm. Its swing system comprised a cable wrapped around its circular base and fed to a drum in the house. This provided about 400 degrees of rotation. The Page 222 shown is preserved by Big Brutus, Inc., at their Weir, Kansas, site. Harnischfeger Corporation purchased Page Engineering in 1988 (see chapter 14). *Mark Bridle*

P&H 210. The present range of large crawler shovels and draglines from Harnischfeger Corporation (P&H) has a long pedigree going back to the company's founding by Alonzo Pawling and Henry Harnischfeger in 1884. Looking to expand its markets, the company decided on mobile digging machines, and its first excavator, the gasoline-powered Model 210 appeared in 1914. Initially mounted on steel traction wheels, it was later available on crawler tracks and carried a standard 1.25-cubic-yard dragline bucket on a 40-foot boom. It remained in production until 1925. The success of this model spurred the company to develop an extensive line of excavators up to the early 1930s. In 1935, an entire new excavator line was launched, incorporating welded construction. *P&H Mining Equipment*

P&H 1250WL. Harnischfeger built its first electric shovel, the P&H 1200WL, in 1933. With a 2-yard capacity, it was the forerunner of the present-day P&H mining shovel line. The larger 1250WL appeared in 1937 with a dipper of 2.5 cubic yards on a standard 30-foot boom, and an operating weight of 95 tons. These early shovels exhibited the basic features of the modern P&H electric mining shovel that would eventually dominate the market. The boom-mounted crowd motor, twin arms (handles) to support the dipper, and welded structures are apparent on this early machine. The 1250WL also featured crawler steering accomplished from the operator's cab, and all high-speed gearing operating in an enclosed oil bath. *Keith Haddock*

P&H 315. Over the years, Harnischfeger Corporation produced excavators and cranes from the smallest .375-cubic-yard capacity models to the largest two-crawler mining shovels available. When cable excavators were popular in smaller sizes for construction applications, Harnischfeger played a significant part with a full line of crawler excavators up to 3.5-cubic-yards capacity, as well as a broad line of rubber-tired and truck-mounted cranes. The modern-looking P&H 315, in production from 1961 to 1976, incorporated an isolated cab and tractor-type undercarriage. Like other P&H excavators of this era, the P&H 315 utilized P&H's power box drive. The power box contained all the shafts and gears necessary to transmit power to every machine motion. All gearing was completely encased and splash lubricated. As a shovel, the 315 tipped the scales at just over 25 tons. *Walter Bennett*

P&H 955A. A popular mid-sized crawler excavator in the 1960s was the 2.5-cubic-yard P&H 955A. Beginning life in 1940 as the P&H 955, the model was revised over the years. The 955A utilized the P&H-patented Magnetorque to replace the normal swing clutches. This frictionless system consisted of two electromagnetic couplings, each with a "driving" and "driven" member, and utilizing controlled magnetic force to transmit power to the swing motion. As more current was introduced in the driving member, the faster the driven member turned. This system was also utilized in the P&H large electric mining shovels to power the dipper hoist. The 955A weighed 88 tons as a shovel and could be furnished with Cummins or Waukesha diesel engines in the 210-horsepower range. *Claes Nilsson*

P&H 2100B. After Harnischfeger introduced its first electric shovel in 1936, it promoted and developed this type of excavator intensively over the next two decades. This early experience positioned the company to build electric excavators in sizes larger than the economic limit of diesel machines, and paid off handsomely when sales of the small "construction-size" cable excavators dwindled in the 1960s. This mining machine expertise contributed largely to Harnischfeger becoming the dominant force in the mining shovel industry by the 1980s. In 1963, Harnischfeger shipped its first 15-cubic-yard electric shovel, the 390-ton Model 2100, a machine that would soon became the standard for large open-pit mines around the world. The upgraded 2100B of the same dipper range appeared in 1969, but weighed some 65 tons heavier. *P&H Mining Equipment*

P&H 4100. Harnischfeger kept pace with the increasing size of haul trucks, and industry demands for larger equipment to take advantage of economies of scale. It introduced larger shovels and improved the performance of its existing shovel models. A big jump in size occurred in 1969 when the first P&H 2800 shovels were shipped with dippers of 25 cubic yards. The 2300 followed in 1972 in the 20-cubic-yard class, and the same year P&H unveiled the world's largest shovel on two crawlers, the 5700, with dippers up to 44 cubic yards. The first 4100 was shipped in 1991 with a 56-cubic-yard dipper designed to load a 240-ton truck in three passes. This shovel incorporated state-of-the-art electronic control and integrated diagnostics, a means of alerting operator or maintenance personnel of any pending malfunction. *Keith Haddock*

P&H 2355. Harnischfeger developed some large two-crawler draglines based on its electric shovels. The first was the 8-cubic-yard P&H 1855, introduced in 1954 as a diesel-electric dragline. It was P&H's largest excavator at the time. The 1855 was superseded in 1962 by the P&H 10-cubic-yard diesel-electric 2155 dragline, of which only two were built. In 1981 the company introduced its largest crawler dragline yet, the P&H 2355. This state-of-the-art, two-crawler dragline was supplied with either diesel or electric power. The diesel version came with a choice of two big Cummins, Caterpillar, or GM engines, totaling approximately 2,000 horsepower. The electric version shown had an operating weight of 765 tons and swung an 18-cubic-yard bucket on a 160-foot boom. *Keith Haddock*

P&H 4100 BOSS. Since the first Series P&H 4100 was launched its 1991, it has become the most popular large mining shovel with over 100 sold by the end of 2001. The original 4100 was upgraded to the 4100A in 1994, and then to the 4100XPB in 1999. Operating weights increased from 1,200 tons in the original model to 1,500 tons in the latest 4100XPB. Dipper size was also upped to 67 cubic yards, enabling it to load 320-ton trucks in three passes. Since 1998, P&H Mining Equipment has been shipping the special 4100TS and 4100 BOSS shovels designed to work in the Alberta, Canada, oil sands operations, where underfoot conditions are extremely soft. Consequently, these shovels are fitted with extra-wide crawler shoes—138 inches compared with 87 inches on the XPB model. The 4100 BOSS in the picture has a 62-cubic-yard dipper and obeys the latest electronic control. *Keith Haddock*

Rapier 423. After the Rapier-Marion agreement terminated, Rapier continued to develop new models of excavators. One of the first all-British machines was the Rapier 423 introduced in 1936. Convertible to all front ends, the 423 was rated at .625-cubic-yards capacity and powered by a 57-horsepower diesel engine. As a shovel it weighed 21 tons. As a backhoe it could dig down to 19 feet, 6 inches. Toy collectors will recognize this machine as the 1:25 scale Model Triang Shovel of the 1950s. The 423 remained in production until 1953, when it was upgraded to the .75-cubic-yard Rapier 424. *Keith Haddock*

Quick-Way E. In 1922, Luke E. Smith built America's first truck-mounted shovel, a war-surplus crane mounted on a second-hand truck. After much testing and development, Smith put the machine into full production in 1929, and established the Quick-Way Truck Shovel Company at Denver, Colorado. The company prospered, and during World War II, supplied 2,225 Quick-Ways to the armed forces. Up to 1953, four sizes of truck shovel/cranes were produced in sizes up to .333-cubic-yards, or 10-tons lifting capacity. The .5-cubic-yard Model E shown was built in 1945 and mounted on a Coleman E55 four-wheel-drive truck. Quick-Way expanded rapidly in the 1950s, adding new models up to 1-cubic-yard capacity, and crawler excavators from 1957. In 1961, Quick-Way was purchased by the Marion Power Shovel Company. *Keith Haddock collection*

Ransomes-Rapier-Marion Type 7. Ransomes & Rapier, Ltd. was established in 1869 at Ipswich, England, and built a wide variety of heavy industrial equipment. In 1924 the company entered into an agreement with the Marion Steam Shovel Company of Marion, Ohio, to build Marion excavators under license. The first excavator produced under this arrangement was a Type 7 of 1-cubic-yard capacity. Power optionswere steam, full-electric, or a gasoline-electric version in which the engine drove a generator supplying current to separate DC motors for each machine function. Rapier built further Marion-based excavators, including shovels up to 11 cubic yards. These machines were sold as "Ransomes-Rapier-Marion" excavators until the Rapier-Marion agreement terminated in 1936. Rapier then continued producing excavators to its own designs. *Keith Haddock*

Ruston-Bucyrus 22-RB. In 1930 the excavator interests of Ruston & Hornsby, Ltd. of Lincoln, England, were merged with Bucyrus-Erie Company, and a new, jointly owned company, Ruston-Bucyrus, Ltd., was established at Lincoln. The new company was able to fuse designs from both partners and develop new excavator models that were built on both sides of the Atlantic. Probably the all-time most popular .75-cubic-yard excavator in terms of numbers sold was the 22-RB and its American sister, the 22-B. The British 22-RB was launched in 1950, and by the time this legendary machine had run its course, more than 10,200 units had been shipped, including special crane and dragline versions. The last was shipped in 1994. The American 22-B sold another 8,828 between its introduction in 1938 and 1976, when it was discontinued. *RB International*

Rapier 4142. Built from 1943 to 1955, the Rapier 4142 electric quarry and mine shovel was an upgrade from the former 4140 shovel introduced in 1934. Designed as a heavy-duty rock shovel of 3.5-cubic-yards capacity, the machine weighed just less than 140 tons in working condition. The dipper connection to the crowd arms (handle) featured an unusual swivel bearing designed to eliminate twisting forces on the dipper handle. This shovel employed the "Ward-Leonard" type of electric drive, common on electric shovels of all makes up to the 1980s. In this system, an AC induction motor drives a DC generator to power separate DC motors for hoist, crowd, and swing through a variable-voltage control. Ransomes & Rapier, Ltd. merged with Newton-Chambers, Ltd. in 1959, and the Rapier products were absorbed into the NCK-Rapier line of excavators. *Keith Haddock*

Ruston-Bucyrus 195-B. Ruston-Bucyrus released the 110-RB in 1955 and the larger 150-RB, rated at 6 cubic yards, two years later. Like the 110-RB, the 150-RB was sold mainly as an electric shovel, but a few dragline versions with buckets up to 7 cubic yards were also sold. In 1974, Ruston-Bucyrus commenced building the 195-B electric mining shovel, which had been built by Bucyrus-Erie since 1968. With dippers from 12 to 16 cubic yards and an operating weight of 377 tons, the Ward-Leonard-controlled machine utilized a 600-horsepower main hoist motor, two 130-horsepower swing motors, and a 130-horsepower crowd motor. After adequately serving surface mining operations running trucks up to 100 tons, the last 195-B was shipped in 1985. *RB International, Ltd.*

Ruston-Bucyrus 110-RB. The American-designed 110-RB was built by Ruston-Bucyrus from 1955 to 1978. This 4.5-cubic-yard quarry and mine excavator, sister to the 110-B built by Bucyrus-Erie, was mainly sold as a Ward-Leonard electric shovel, but a few diesel-electric and dragline versions up to 5.5 cubic yards were also shipped. The shovel working weight was 170 tons, and the diesel-electric version utilized a Ruston-Paxman V-12 engine of 520 horsepower. With some 152 British-built units and another 92 made by Bucyrus-Erie, the 110-RB/110B proved to be the mainstay of surface mining operations and quarries running haul trucks of 50-tons capacity and under. *Keith Haddock*

Schield Bantam M-47. In 1941, inventor Vern Schield built a homemade dragline and mounted it on a surplus International truck. It performed its intended duties so well that Schield started to built similar machines for sale to his neighbors. By the time the Schield Bantam Company was incorporated in 1946, more than 35 truck-mounted draglines had been sold, and construction of a new plant had commenced at Waverly, Iowa. The first model produced in the new plant was the M-47, capable of swinging a dragline bucket of .375 cubic yards, or working as a crane. In 1949 the M-47 was upgraded to the M-49 of the same capacity but embodying improvements for greater reliability. *Keith Haddock*

Schield Bantam C-35. The Schield Bantam Company unveiled a new excavator in 1952, the T-35, designed to replace the M-49. The following year Bantam's own carriers were utilized for the first time. In 1954, Models C-35 and CR-35 crawler- and wagon-mounted versions were offered. All the 35 Series machines were rated at .375-cubic-yards capacity and were convertible to shovel, dragline, backhoe, clamshell, and crane. The C-35 backhoe in the picture has a digging depth of 14 feet, 6 inches. In 1959 the 35 Series machines were renumbered the 350 Series machines with the same capacity. Schield Bantam became a division of Koehring Company in 1963, but the excavators were continued as Schield Bantam products at the Waverly plant. The last cable machine was shipped in 1973. *Keith Haddock*

Wayne 66. The prototype Wayne Crane was completed in 1943 by the American Steel Dredge Company and put into production in 1946. Founded in 1906, the company initially manufactured dipper dredges, and later progressed into hydraulic dredges. The first machine, known as the Model 22, was a wheeled mobile crane mounted on four pairs of rubber tires. It was also convertible to shovel, backhoe, clamshell, and dragline of .5-cubic-yards capacity. The crawler-mounted .5-cubic-yard Wayne Crane Model 66 appeared in 1950. A 62-horsepower gasoline engine powered the Model 66, and its operating weight was listed at 15 tons. In 1955, American Hoist & Derrick Company purchased American Steel Dredge, and the Wayne Crane models of .5- and .75-cubic-yard capacity became the American 100 and 200 Series excavators. *Keith Haddock*

Unit 1020. Known as the Unit Crane & Shovel Corporation from 1945, this company traces its origins to the Universal Power Shovel Company established in 1926 in Detroit, Michigan, by William Ford, brother of automaker Henry. The company began by making the Wilford shovel, a .375-yard, crawler-mounted .75-swing outfit based on a Fordson power unit. In 1928 manufacturing was moved to Milwaukee, Wisconsin. The following year, fully revolving crawler and truck-mounted excavators were being produced. Many more cable excavator models, crawler- and truck-mounted, were introduced up to the 1950s, all under .75-cubic-yards capacity. Most popular was the .75-cubic-yard 1020, offering digging depths as a hoe to 19 feet. Its 75-horsepower GM 3-71 engine was mounted longitudinally, its 90-degree power take-off utilizing a worm gear. *Keith Haddock*

CHAPTER 12

HYDRAULIC EXCAVATORS

With the possible exception of the bulldozer, the hydraulic excavator is probably the most familiar of all earthmoving machines. Hydraulic excavators can be seen working on every kind of construction job from road maintenance, trenching, and foundation work to mass excavation on major industrial sites, as well as in quarries and surface mining operations. Their sizes range from the smallest "toys," weighing less than 2 tons, to some of the largest excavators being produced today. They are made by hundreds of manufacturers in every industrialized country around the world. Thousands of new machines are produced each month.

Hydraulic excavators have largely replaced the cable-operated types, except in the very largest sizes. Compared to cable excavators, they are cheaper to buy, easier to operate, travel faster, and have positive action in all movements instead of relying on gravity

American 45-A. American Hoist & Derrick Company, founded in 1882 and well known for its heavy lifting cranes, began manufacturing a series of hydraulic excavators in the early 1970s. First came the .25-cubic-yard Model 25 Pow'r Hoe in 1971. The following year saw the 2-cubic-yard Model 35 Pow'r Hoe, and in 1973 American Hoist launched its Model 45 Pow'r Hoe, biggest from the company to date. The three machines featured heavy-duty crawler crane undercarriages with tumblers, but a hydraulic motor in each crawler side frame provided independent drive and counter-rotation of the crawlers. The three models were upgraded to A Models in 1977. The 45-A illustrated carried a standard bucket of 3.5-cubic-yards, tipped the scales at 82 tons, and could reach down to 34 feet, 6 inches with standard arm or 38 feet with extended arm. *Keith Haddock*

to provide some of the digging forces. Although backhoe and shovel fronts are the most common for hydraulic excavators, manufacturers have developed a vast array of attachments so the machines not only do an excellent job of digging a hole, but also rip, knock, hammer, lift, drill, scrape, saw, cut, and compact as well. These attachments have greatly enhanced the excavator's usefulness and contributed to its rapidly increasing popularity.

Hydraulic excavators were first used in the nineteenth century, but those early attempts used water instead of oil to transmit the power, and were not a success. Unrelated Armstrongs built two early railroad-type water hydraulic shovels. The earliest was in 1882 by the British firm Sir W.G. Armstrong & Company, and was used to construct the Hull docks in England. Frank H. Armstrong, mechanical engineer for the Penn Iron Mining Company in the United States, tested the other machine in 1914. On both machines, a hydraulic cylinder operating a set of multiplying sheaves provided the hoisting power. The Kilgore Machine Company of Minneapolis, Minnesota, designed another hydraulic shovel, patented in 1897. This machine used direct-acting cylinders, dispensing with all ropes and chains. Reportedly, only five of these machines were built, including one shipped to Mexico.

Today's hydraulic excavator has a relatively recent history, developing almost simultaneously in Italy, France, and the United States in the late 1940s. Carlo and Mario Bruneri produced a prototype wheeled hydraulic excavator at Turin, Italy, in 1948. Several further prototypes followed, and the machine was named the Yumbo around 1950. In 1954, the Bruneri brothers ceded manufacturing and patent rights to a French company, SICAM. That same year, SICAM produced its first Yumbo, the S25 truck-mounted excavator. Interest in the new machine increased, and further wheeled and crawler models were developed. In the early 1960s, SICAM extended manufacturing agreements for Yumbo machines to be produced by Drott in the United States, TUSA in Spain, Mitsubishi in Japan, and Priestman in the United Kingdom.

In France, Poclain produced a truck-mounted loader in 1948 and built its first hydraulic excavator, the TU, in 1951. The tractor-drawn machine did not

American 780. In the early 1980s, American Hoist replaced its three-model line of hydraulic excavators with four new upgraded models that were more productive and operated at higher hydraulic pressures. The models were the 185, 480, 680, and 780, ranging in size from 1 to 4 cubic yards. The former largest model, the 45-A, was replaced by the 3.5-cubic-yard 680, keeping the same Detroit 12V-71N diesel engine but receiving a power increase from 420 to 456 horsepower. The same engine was also fitted in the new, larger model, the 780 (illustrated), weighing in at 86 tons. This model achieved similar digging ranges to the 680 but wielded a larger 4-cubic-yard standard bucket, or a 6-cubic-yard coal bucket. American Hoist shipped its last hydraulic excavator in 1985. *American Crane Company*

Badger 450. The Badger Machine Company of Winona, Minnesota, was established in 1946. It developed a hydraulic backhoe called a "Hopto" (Hydraulically-Operated Power Take-Off). From 1958 to 1977, the Warner & Swasey Company owned the company. Badger developed the Hopto line of crawler- and truck-mounted hydraulic excavators (see under Warner & Swasey). In 1977, Badger was sold to Burro Crane, who established Badger Equipment Company and continued the Hopto product until 1991. Badger's excavators included the wheeled Model 450 shown here, powered by a 171-horsepower engine and weighing 18 tons. In 1994 Badger purchased the manufacturing rights to the former Case 1085 Cruz-Air wheeled excavator. In 2002 this was sold as the 1085D powered by a 133-horsepower Cummins diesel mounted in the carrier, and boasting a road speed of 29 miles per hour. *Badger Equipment Company*

Bucyrus-Erie H-5. The Milwaukee Hydraulics Corporation was one of the pioneer companies in the United States to apply hydraulic power to cranes and excavators. The first machine, the H-2 Hydrocrane, was launched in 1946. Bucyrus-Erie Company (now Bucyrus International, Inc.) purchased this company in 1948, and further developed the Hydrocrane into the H-3 and H-5 models, which could be converted into hydraulic excavators known as Hydrohoes. When operating as a crane, the hoist motion was derived from hydraulic rams working between two multiple-part sheave blocks to extend and retract the cables. The H-3 and H-5 were very successful products for Bucyrus-Erie Company, and upgraded models continued in the company's product line until 1981. *Bucyrus International, Inc.*

possess full swing capability, and hydraulic power was obtained from a pump driven by the tractor. Poclain grew steadily, launching the TY45, its first fully revolving machine, in 1960. Poclain's rapid development in the 1960s resulted in the unveiling of the monster EC1000 in 1970, which awed the industry with its record-beating 10-cubic-yard capacity.

In the United States, contractor Ray Ferwerda of Cleveland, Ohio, invented a telescoping-boom excavator and mounted it on a truck. This machine became known as the famous Gradall excavator, and the Warner & Swasey Company purchased the rights to its manufacture in 1946. The new owners developed the machine utilizing advanced hydraulics, ideal to provide the various actions of the bucket, which could simulate the movement of the human hand. Since 1950, Gradalls have been built in New Philadelphia, Ohio. The Milwaukee Hydraulics Corporation was another U.S. company which made an early entry into the hydraulic field when it launched the H-2 Hydrocrane in 1946. Bucyrus-Erie purchased this company in 1948 and further developed the Hydrocrane into the H-3 and H-5 Hydrohoes. These machines and their derivatives remained in the B-E line until 1981.

Bucyrus-Erie 20-H. With the Hydrohoe hydraulic machines already well established, Bucyrus-Erie expanded its product line by introducing a completely new design of fully hydraulic excavator beginning in 1965. The first model was the .75-cubic-yard 20-H powered by Cummins or GM diesel engines of 106 horsepower and weighing 17 tons in operating condition. The 20-H featured a heavy-duty crawler-crane undercarriage with tumblers, and the hydraulic propel motor was mounted in the upper works. Drive to the tracks was through the center pintle transmitted by gears and shafts, and steering was accomplished through jaw clutches, just like a cable excavator. *Bucyrus International, Inc.*

Bucyrus-Erie 40-H. Bucyrus-Erie broadened its hydraulic excavator line by introducing the .5-cubic-yard 15-H in 1966, the 1.75-cubic-yard 30-H in 1967, and the 3-yard 40-H in 1970. The three smaller models initially propelled from the upper works like the 20-H, but by the time the 40-H appeared in 1970, this outmoded form of propel was already replaced by independent hydraulic motors in each crawler side frame, providing independent drive to each crawler as well as counter-rotation capability. The smaller 15-H and 20-H also received independent crawler drive in their Series II and Series II upgrades respectively. In 1975 the 40-H was also stretched to the IPA (Improved Production Attachment) version, a backhoe with special short stick and 5-cubic-yard bucket for coal loading. *Bucyrus International, Inc.*

Bucyrus-Erie 350-H. In 1975, Bucyrus-Erie unveiled the forerunner of a new line of advanced excavators with a high-pressure hydraulic system. The machine was the 350-H, a 46-ton backhoe of 2.5-cubic-yards capacity, powered by Cummins or GM engines in the 250-horsepower range. By the end of the decade, this new line had superseded all previous models and was topped by the 5-cubic-yard 500-H and a 10-cubic-yard shovel version, the 550-HS, which came out in 1982. Two years later, Bucyrus-Erie announced it had sold its entire construction equipment business to Northwest Engineering Company, and the hydraulic excavators were discontinued. *Keith Haddock collection*

Case 40. The Case name first appeared on an excavator in 1968 after the Drott Manufacturing Company was purchased by Tenneco Corporation and became a division of J.I. Case Company. Drott had acquired the manufacturing rights of the French Yumbo excavators in 1962 and marketed them as Drott machines in the United States. Under Tenneco, Case expanded the line from the former Drott 30 Series and 40 Series to include the 1.25-cubic-yard 50 Series and 1.75-cubic-yard wheel-mounted Model 80 by 1970. The Model 40 shown is one of the first adopted by Case from the former Drott line. It had a 180-horsepower GM engine and 40,600-pound operating weight. *Keith Haddock*

Case 880. In 1971, Case introduced the first of a new line of excavators with a new nomenclature. The Model 880 boasted a digging depth of 19 feet, 5 inches and was powered by a 120-horsepower Case diesel engine. An interesting optional feature on this .625-cubic-yard machine was the turntable leveler. This provided a sideways tilt of about 8 degrees in either direction so the machine could be leveled when working across a slope. This feature also provided an additional 2 feet of digging depth when working over the side of the crawlers. The revised 880B appeared in 1978, followed by the 880C in 1980 and the 880D in 1984. When this model was discontinued in 1987, its appearance had benefited from improved cab cosmetics. *Keith Haddock collection*

Case 1080B. Case added the 1080 excavator to its 80 Series in 1983 and upgraded it to the 1080B three years later. The 1080B weighed 22 tons and carried a standard bucket of .75-cubic-yard capacity. Power came from a Case diesel engine developing 153 horsepower. Like the 880 described above, the 1080B also could be provided with optional turntable leveler. In 1976, Tenneco, Case's parent company, became a major shareholder in Poclain, and over the next few years, Poclain excavators and Tenneco's existing Case/Drott excavators were merged into a single line. Poclain machines covered the larger machine applications, while the Case/Drott machines covered the small machine market. *Keith Haddock*

The advent of the early hydraulic excavators in Italy, France, and the United States laid the foundation for a complete revolution of the excavator industry. The 1950s were the pioneering years when many manufacturers ventured into making this new type of machine. Compared with the previous cable-operated machines, manufacture was relatively simple, needing only a power unit, hydraulic pumps and valves, and hydraulic rams to power the excavator's movements. However, unreliable hydraulic systems, unable to withstand the rigors of the excavation site, slowed development, and the hydraulic machines were thought by many to be just a passing phase. Fortunately, the perseverance of the manufacturers gradually alleviated the problems.

The 1960s were the developing years when hydraulic excavators rapidly increased in size and still more manufacturers entered the field. Excavator popularity increased with the evolution of reliable hydraulic systems utilizing higher hydraulic pressures first proved on the early Poclain and other European machines. Many of the staunch cable excavator manufacturers entered the new field in the 1960s, but their engineering was steeped in cable shovel design, and most found it extremely difficult to compete with their "hydraulics-only" counterparts. It took some manufacturers many years to forsake features like jaw-clutch steering and tumbler-type excavator track shoes, and change to hydraulic motors in each crawler frame and tractor-type crawlers. Some manufacturers made a brief entry, then abandoned hydraulics altogether. North American manufacturers tended to employ low-pressure hydraulic gear pumps working at around 3,000 psi or less, whereas most European manufacturers utilized piston pumps operating as high as 5,000 psi. As excavators increased in size, the low-pressure systems became less efficient and introduced severe limitations.

By the end of the 1960s, hydraulic excavators had graduated into a major force in the excavating industry. Cable excavator manufacturers observed Poclain's EC-1000 record-beating 10-yard machine with some apprehension. Here was a machine encroaching well into territory believed to be the sole domain of cable machines. The concerns of the competition were justified, as by the end of the next decade, much larger hydraulic mining shovels and backhoes were fully established and selling in large numbers by just a few dominant manufacturers. By 1980, the O&K RH-300, an excavator with a bucket capacity of 30 cubic yards, three times the size of the Poclain EC-1000, was already at work.

The dominance of Japanese technology in the hydraulic excavator industry took hold in the 1970s, and by the end of the millennium had all but taken

Case 988 Super Railer. The Case excavator line weathered some radical changes beginning in the mid-1980s. The large Poclain machines were dropped and a new Case 88 Series was introduced at the 1987 Conexpo equipment show in Las Vegas. The Models 688 and 888 excavators, with respective operating weights of 15 and 18 tons, were introduced at that time. By 1998 the 88 Series had expanded to a six-machine lineup. Made in France at a former Poclain factory and targeted mainly for the European market, the line spanned from the 13.5-ton 588 to the 39-ton 1488. The line included the 988, shown here with a special adaptation calledthe Super Railer made by Rexquote of England. The modified undercarriage allows the machine to run on rails or road.
Keith Haddock

over the construction-size and mini-excavator markets. Japanese excavator technology has infiltrated into nearly all excavators available in the Western world to the extent that familiar brand names formerly associated with American manufacture are actually Japanese machines, or made under license from a Japanese company.

This rise to dominance by Japanese manufacturers developed in three distinct phases. In the 1960s, the Japanese initiated their hydraulic excavator industry by manufacturing machines under license that were designed by established firms in the United States and Europe. This resulted in such combinations as Sumitomo-Link-Belt, Komatsu-Bucyrus, Kobelco-P&H, and Mitsubishi-Yumbo. After learning how to build and market a successful machine, the Japanese then entered the second phase of their development by designing their own machines and ending ties with Western manufacturers. Further development took place, with Japanese-exported machines gaining a reliable reputation and selling at very competitive prices.

The third phase was largely brought on by politics and economics. Shipping costs, foreign currency exchange rates, and import tariffs imposed by governments made it increasingly difficult for the Japanese to export their machines. Thus, they established their own factories in foreign countries, making machines for local markets. In a number of cases, the Japanese took over or became the major shareholder in, established American companies. Today, nearly all the major excavator manufacturers in the Western world are building excavators of Japanese design.

Another major influence on the excavator industry during the 1990s was South Korea. That country's four major manufacturers, Daewoo, Hyundai, Samsung, and Halla, all obtained substantial technology through manufacturing agreements or technical affiliations with Japanese firms or the French Poclain company. By 2002, the Korean excavator export industry was represented by only two companies, Daewoo and Hyundai. Sweden's Volvo took over Samsung's excavator business and factory in 1998, and Hyundai took over the management of Halla in 1999, subsequently phasing out excavator production.

While Japanese excavators dominate the construction size market (50 tons and lower), the giant mining class excavators originate in Germany from three manufacturers: Liebherr, Demag (taken over by Komatsu Mining Systems, Inc. in 1997 and sold as Komatsu products from 1999), and Orenstein & Koppel (O&K) (taken over by Terex Mining in 1997 and sold as Terex products). Although challenged by Caterpillar's 360-ton Model 5230B and Hitachi's 570-ton Model EX5500, the largest hydraulic excavators available in 2002 remain of German origin. These are the Liebherr R996 (720 tons, 44-cubic-yards capacity), Komatsu PC8000 (755 tons, 46-cubic-yards capacity), and Terex/O&K RH-400 (1,000 tons, 57-cubic-yards capacity). The size of these machines is gradually allowing them to penetrate the large surface mines of the world, where they work alongside similar-sized electric cable-operated shovels to load the world's largest off-road haul trucks.

Case CX800. In 1999, New Holland took over Case, and the new company CNH Global (Case New Holland) was formed. With a large group of companies now under the CNH umbrella, including New Holland, O&K, FiatAllis, and Link-Belt, the doors were opened for cross-pollination among excavator brands. Case initiated the CX Series excavators in 2000 with the Models CX130 and CX210 in the 14- and 23-ton weight classes. The top-of-the-line Case CX800 was unveiled at the 2000 Intermat equipment show in Paris, France. At 88-tons operating weight, the CX800 carries a 4.3-cubic-yard standard bucket. In 2002, the CX line, all designed by Sumitomo in Japan, consists of six models ranging from 14 to 88 tons. They feature an Auto Power Boost, which instantly increases power by 10 percent when the auto-control system detects increased resistance. *Case Corporation*

Case 9050. While it marketed the 88 Series excavators mainly in Europe, Case adopted another new line, the 90 Series introduced in 1992 for the North American market. These machines, which graduated to the B Series in 1994, were based on designs by Sumitomo of Japan, and initially comprised a range of six models from 14- to 50-ton operating weights. These machines featured a "work mode select" function allowing the operator to select one of three pump output settings. These could be set to match the work at hand: high speed for maximum productivity, and standard or low speed for precision work and increased fuel economy. From 1999, the Sumitomo-designed 90 Series were amalgamated with the European-built 88 Series machines, and the combined lines marketed as the Case excavator line in Europe. The mid-sized 9050 had a standard bucket of 1.75 cubic yards and weighed 69,000 pounds. *Keith Haddock*

Caterpillar 225. Caterpillar's launch of its first hydraulic excavator in 1972 followed an extensive market research and development program begun in the mid-1960s. This included building a series of prototype excavators starting with the X-1 in 1968. In the two years leading up to the machine's launch, 20 pre-production machines were subject to controlled testing and contractor evaluation at job sites. The first production machine, the 225, powered by a Caterpillar 125-flywheel-horsepower engine, weighed 52,000 pounds, and its standard bucket held one cubic yard. It incorporated state-of the-art hydraulics, independent crawler-drive motors, and joystick controls. The upgraded 225B appeared in 1986, followed by the 225D in 1989. By the time this model was superseded in 1991, power had been boosted to 165 horsepower and operating weight to 56,860 pounds. *Keith Haddock collection*

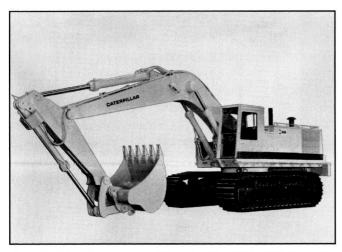

Caterpillar 245. After the successful launch of the 225 in 1972, Caterpillar broadened its excavator range by adding the Model 235 in the 40-ton class in 1973, followed by the 70-ton Model 245 in 1974. Caterpillar's first line of hydraulic excavators was completed in 1975 when the smallest in the line, the 19-ton 215, was unveiled at that year's Conexpo equipment show in Chicago, Illinois. These four 200 Series excavator models were the foundation of Caterpillar's hydraulic excavator line and, with upgrades, were marketed until the early 1990s. The 245, available in both front shovel and backhoe configurations, was powered by a Caterpillar 325-flywheel-horsepower engine and carried a standard bucket of 2.5 cubic yards. *Caterpillar, Inc.*

Caterpillar 213. In the early 1980s, Caterpillar commenced a program to rapidly expand its excavator products. It entered into a number of marketing agreements with foreign excavator manufacturers to augment its existing models and reach out to a wider variety of markets. Many of the models, such as wheel-mounted excavators, were more popular abroad than in the United States. In 1984, Caterpillar began marketing a line of excavators designed and built in Germany by Eder. These consisted of the 205, 211, and 213 crawler models, and the 206, 212, 214, and 224 wheeled models. All these were powered by Deutz or Perkins engines, and covered weight categories from 13 to 21 tons. The Eder-designed machines were phased out in the early 1990s when Caterpillar's 300 Series machines started to arrive on the scene. *Keith Haddock collection*

Caterpillar E140. In 1987, Caterpillar and Mitsubishi of Japan reorganized an earlier joint-venture operation to form Shin Caterpillar Mitsubishi, Ltd. Under this new company, existing Mitsubishi excavators were updated, fitted with Caterpillar engines, and sold as Caterpillar products. This line was designated the E Series, and consisted of nine basic models: E70, E110, E120, E140, E200B, E240, E300, E450, and E650, plus long-track versions. Engines ranged from 52 to 375 flywheel-horsepower, and operating weights ran from 7 to 70 tons. Some of the models, such as the 89-flywheel-horsepower E140 shown, retained their Mitsubishi engines. Most of these excavators received B Model upgrades, and the E240 reached a C Model, briefly marketed from 1992. The entire E Series machines were superseded in the early 1990s by Caterpillar's 300 Series excavators. *Keith Haddock*

Caterpillar 345B. By 1991, Caterpillar's range of hydraulic excavator models had expanded to almost overwhelming proportions with no less than 24 basic models. In addition to Caterpillar's own machines designed in the United States, the vast range comprised machines designed by Eder and Mitsubishi, plus long-track, shovel front, clamshell, and logging versions and a host of special application machines. In 1992, Caterpillar began introducing its 300 Series hydraulic excavators, which eventually replaced all previous models. The machines were a result of a joint engineering team set up under the Shin Caterpillar Mitsubishi joint venture in Japan. The first to appear were the 320 and 325 with weights of 21 and 28 tons. New models were rapidly added, including the 49-ton 345B, shown here with a hydraulic hammer. *Keith Haddock*

Caterpillar M320. During the 1990s, Caterpillar expanded its excavator line until once again it comprised 24 basic models—but this time all in the 300 Series. They spanned from the smallest mini excavator weighing less than 2 tons to the giant 5230 with a weight of over 350 tons. Caterpillar offers a wide variety of boom, stick, and bucket configurations suited to different material densities, deep excavation for pipe work, or mass excavators for earthmoving production. Undercarriage options provide for different underfoot conditions from rock to soft material. The line also includes four sizes of wheeled excavators designed and built in Germany. The M320, fitted with dozer blade and stabilizers as shown, weighs 21 tons and is powered by a Caterpillar 140-flywheel-horsepower engine. *Caterpillar, Inc.*

Caterpillar 320C. This model is the first of Caterpillar's C Series excavators introduced in 2000 to replace the former 320B. The 320C retains most of the popular features of the former machine but includes a new automatic work and power mode priority system, eliminating the manual mode selection found on other machines. The best mode for the task at hand is automatically selected, based on the amount of joystick movement by the operator. Machine weight is 46,300 pounds and standard bucket capacity is 1.5 cubic yards. Power is boosted to 138 horsepower, up from 128 on the former model. Since the 320C release, Caterpillar has been busy replacing its smaller B Series excavators with C Series designs. *Keith Haddock*

Caterpillar 5230B. In 1992, Caterpillar unveiled its first "mining" shovel at the Minexpo show in Las Vegas. The 5130 weighed 193 tons and its bucket range was from 11 to 14 cubic yards. Power came from a 755-flywheel-horsepower Caterpillar engine. In 1994 the larger 5230 was announced, powered by a single Caterpillar diesel engine of 1,470 horsepower and buckets ranging from 16 to 22 cubic yards. With a weight of just over 350 tons, the 5230 is the largest machine of any type ever built by Caterpillar. The 5130 and 5230 firmly established Caterpillar as a supplier of excavators to the surface mining industry. In 2001 the 5230 was upgraded to the 5230B, with power increased to 1,550 flywheel-horsepower and weight increased to 360 tons. Backhoe and shovel buckets are offered in the 22-cubic-yard range. *Eric C. Orlemann*

Caterpillar 385B. Caterpillar showed this machine for the first time at the Conexpo 2002 equipment show in Las Vegas. The 385B is the largest 300 Series excavator and tips the scales at 94 tons. It replaces the former 375 which had been in production since 1993. The 385B is equipped with an advanced electronic control system that does away with the operator having to select work modes. This is the same system as installed in Caterpillar's C Series excavators as described above. Optional excavator attachments include a special long-boom version that enables the 385B to dig down to 38 feet, 7 inches, and a short mass-excavation boom that allows the machine to dig with a 7.25-cubic-yard bucket. *Caterpillar, Inc.*

Daewoo 280LC-III. Daewoo Heavy Industries, Ltd. was established in South Korea in 1976 following the merger of Choson Machine Works with Korea Machinery Industries, Ltd. Hydraulic excavator manufacture commenced the following year under a joint venture with Japan's Hitachi. The first models were the 11.9-ton DH04-2 and the 20.4-ton DH07-3. The line expanded upwards to the 57-ton DH20 by 1981. In 1984, Daewoo commenced designing its own excavators, the Solar Series, which were imported into North America soon afterward. The picture shows one of the Solar Series III excavators launched in 1994. The 280LC-III shown is equipped with a demolition clam replacing its standard bucket. This machine has a 190-horsepower Daewoo diesel engine and an operating weight of 62,000 pounds. *Keith Haddock*

Daewoo 470LC-V. Following the establishment of Daewoo Heavy Industries America Corporation, the company expanded its excavator line throughout the 1980s and 1990s to include mini excavators as well as wheeled machines. It also added crawler tractors and wheel loaders to its product line. The Solar Series III machines introduced in 1994 were superseded by the Solar Series V in 1997. The top-of-the-line Solar 470LC-V was introduced at the Conexpo 2002 equipment show in Las Vegas. Operating weight is 104,900 pounds, and it carries a standard bucket of 2.8 cubic yards. The operator's joystick controls operate through pilot pressure, which reduces operator fatigue. Power comes from a 312-horsepower Daewoo diesel engine. *Daewoo Heavy Industries*

Deere 690B. Deere & Company's Industrial Division entered the crawler hydraulic excavator market in 1969. The first machine was the 690, a model number that would become a legend in Deere's excavator world. The first upgrade was released two years after the initial launch in the form of the 690A. In 1973 the machine was revised again to the 690B, powered with a John Deere diesel of 131 horsepower; in the 20-ton weight class, it dug with a standard bucket of .75-cubic-yard capacity. The 690 excavators were Deere's only excavator until the larger 890 went into production in 1978. The 890, a 45-ton-class machine, was actually announced at the 1975 Conexpo equipment show in Chicago. The popular 690B remained in production until 1985, when it was replaced by the 690C. *Keith Haddock*

Deere 690E LC. Again at the forefront of technology, Deere upgraded the 690C to the 690D in 1987. Then, in 1988 a joint venture company, Deere-Hitachi Construction Machinery Corporation, was set up to serve the North and South American markets, with access to machines designed by Hitachi in Japan. By 1984, certain models of Hitachi excavators were already selling under the John Deere name in North America. In 1991 the first of the Hitachi-designed E Series excavators was launched. This was the 690E LC, which kept the same 690 designation, by now a tradition with John Deere. In addition to state-of-the-art electronic controls, the new model gained a modest increase in power and weight over the 690D. *Keith Haddock*

Deere 892E LC. After the 690E LC was introduced in 1991, Deere released more models in it E Series. The 14-ton 490E and the 25-ton 790E LC appeared in 1992, and the following year the 34-ton 892E LC was added. In 1994, Deere upgraded the former top-of-the-line 992D LC, which had been in production since 1989, to the 49-ton 992E LC. The 892E LC sported a digging depth of almost 27 feet, and its engine developed 220 horsepower. All Deere's E Series excavators featured electronic controls with four operator-controlled work modes. Each mode was a pre-programmed engine speed and hydraulic flow combination set to match different work tasks. *Keith Haddock*

Deere 750. In 1996, Deere launched a new breed of excavators beginning with the 200LC. Over the subsequent four years, all former models were replaced with the new designs. The emphasis was on fuel economy, operator comfort, lower noise levels, and emission-compliant engines. In addition, the computerized automatic hydraulic management system was simplified to just two work modes: Full-Power and Economy. In 2001, Deere's line of hydraulic excavators included 16 different sizes from the 3.8-ton 17ZTS mini excavator to the big 750, Deere's largest-ever excavator weighing 84 tons and equipped with a 434-horsepower engine. Beginning in 2002, Deere began the process of further upgrading its excavator models to the C Series. *Keith Haddock*

Demag B504. This famous machine holds the distinction of being the world's first fully revolving crawler-mounted hydraulic excavator. It represented Demag's entry into the hydraulic excavator field in 1954. The long-established German firm had been building cable excavators since 1925, when it took over the excavator line from Carlshutte, established in 1820. The .5-cubic-yard B504 boasted characteristics well ahead of its time, such as continuous 360-degree swing, and independent hydraulic crawler drive in the lower works. Not such a good idea was the use of steel piping and rotary joints to transmit the hydraulic oil to the cylinders; hoses are not used! Check out the hole in the back of the bucket to let the air out. *Demag Komatsu GmbH*

Demag H65. After its initial attempt at building a hydraulic excavator in 1954, Demag continued full production of its cable excavators. It was not until 1965 that continuous hydraulic excavator production commenced. At that time, Demag introduced the .875-cubic-yard Model HB-1, and also sold the French-made Richier machines under the Demag name. The introduction of the 51-ton H-41 in 1968 put Demag's excavators on a firm footing, and although the company still offered two cable excavators up to 1982, the hydraulic excavators became the primary product.

Until the early 1970s, Demag filled out its H Series excavators with more models designed in-house and produced at its factory at Benrath, Germany. The H-65, shown here with 5.6-cubic-yard front shovel, weighed 75 tons in operation. *Urs Peyer*

Demag H-111. The foundation of Demag's giant hydraulic excavators was laid in 1972 when the company launched the H101, breaking into the 100-ton-plus class. It carried a 6.5-cubic-yard shovel bucket, and was powered by a pair of Caterpillar diesels totaling 560 horsepower. This machine was upgraded to the H-111 in 1976. Now with a standard 10-cubic-yard face shovel bucket, the H-111 retained the same engines from the former model, but weight increased to 120 tons. Most of these large Demag shovels were sold with the "bull-clam" type of bucket, which discharged the material through the bottom like a clamshell. *Keith Haddock*

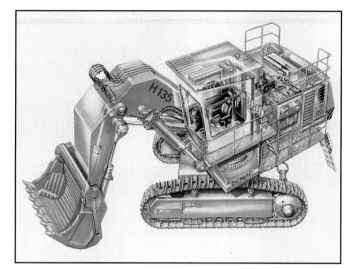

Demag H-135. For Demag, the 150-ton H-135 is only a mid-sized machine! Introduced in 1989, the machine could be equipped with a backhoe or a bullclam-type shovel of 12.4 cubic yards for general excavation. Buckets up to 19 cubic yards were offered for coal. Power came from a single Cummins or Caterpillar engine developing 730 horsepower. The H-135 featured pilot-operated controls through joystick levers for digging functions. Another single joystick lever controlled all travel functions, including counter-rotation of the tracks. The artist's impression shows the engine and hydraulic pump arrangement. *Demag Komatsu GmbH*

Demag H-241. In 1978, Demag claimed the world size record for a hydraulic excavator when it launched the huge H-241 with an 18-cubic-yard capacity. At 262-tons operating weight, this machine was only the first of a long line of supersized hydraulic excavators to come from the house of Demag. The H-241 was powered by a single Cummins or GM diesel with over 1,300 horsepower. About 80 H241s were sold worldwide by the time it was upgraded to the 21-cubic-yard H285 in 1986. The H-241 in the picture is loading a 170-ton Terex truck at the oil sands operations near Fort McMurray, Alberta, Canada. *Keith Haddock collection*

Demag H-485. In 1986, Demag again took title to the world's largest hydraulic excavator when it sold the first H485 shovel to Coal Contractors, Ltd. for coal stripping in Scotland. This machine was powered by a single MTU diesel engine rated at 2,106 horsepower; it weighed 620 tons and carried a 34-cubic-yard bucket. The H-485 electric-powered shovel is shown working in Alberta's oil sands. The upgraded and larger H485S version came out in 1993, with shovel capacity boosted to 44 cubic yards and operating weight to 689 tons. Power on this machine is provided by dual Cummins diesels totaling 3,000 horsepower. *Keith Haddock*

Demag H-685 SP. The oil sands operations of Alberta, Canada, are home to the world's largest hydraulic shovels. One of the major contractors on location is Klemke Mining Corporation. After placing a Demag H-485 to work in 1989, Klemke added an even larger machine, the Demag H-685 SP, in 1995, retaining the distinction of operating the world's largest hydraulic excavator. The H-685 SP wields a 46-cubic-yard bucket and weighs in at 755 tons. This massive shovel is powered by two Caterpillar 3516 diesels totaling 3,732 horsepower. Two joystick levers electrically activate the hydraulic controls for all digging functions. *Keith Haddock*

Drott 30YM. This machine has its heritage in the French Yumbo excavators. SICAM commenced production of those excavators in the early 1950s, having obtained manufacturing rights from Italy's Bruneri Brothers, who had built one of the world's first hydraulic excavators in 1947. In 1962, Drott Manufacturing Company purchased the rights to make Yumbo excavators in the United States, and produced the Drott 30 Series and 40 Series up to 1-cubic-yard capacity. They were mounted on crawlers (YC designation), rubber tires (Cruz-air), or a truck (YM). The standard engine for the 30YM illustrated is an International UC-263. Even at this early date, the crawler version featured hydrostatic propel in the lower works, and a turntable leveler for working on side slopes. In 1968, Drott became a division of J.I. Case Company. *Keith Haddock*

Demag H-740 OS. In 1998, Demag built another record breaker, the H-740 OS. This machine, built specially for the oil sands operations, was put to work by Klemke Mining Corporation at the same location as the Demag H-685 described above. The H-740 OS (oil sands) carries a bucket of 54 cubic yards. It retains the same Caterpillar engines as the H-685 (maximum horsepower 4,400), but operating weight is increased to 772 tons. The operator's eye level is almost 28 feet above ground elevation, enabling him to see into 400-ton trucks, which the machine can load in five passes. In 1997, Demag excavators came under Komatsu Mining Systems, Inc., which subsequently took full control of the Demag product. The former Demag mining excavators were renumbered as Komatsu machines. *Keith Haddock*

Fiat-Allis S-15. Fiat of Italy purchased the Simit line of hydraulic excavators in 1972. Mario Bruneri, one of two brothers who originated the hydraulic excavator, and his two sons-in-law, founded the new company, Simit, in 1965. The purchase of Allis-Chalmers by Fiat in 1974 gave birth to Fiat-Allis, and the new company continued the former excavator line. The S-15 headed the original five-model lineup of S Series excavators up to 27.5 tons and 139 horsepower. Notice the extra boom joint controlled by a hydraulic cylinder on this S-15 backhoe. The S Series was superseded by the FE Series in 1981, which eventually included nine basic crawler models from the 12.7-ton FE12 to the 46.8-ton FE45. *Keith Haddock*

Fiatallis FX250 LC. In 1986, the Fiat-Hitachi joint venture was formed, with access to the Hitachi-designed excavators from Japan. Subsequently, Fiat-Hitachi FH Series models were introduced, and the FE Series models were phased out until the last was shipped in 1989. A new line of Hitachi-designed excavators was launched in North America from 1993 to 1994 and badged as the Fiatallis FX Series. Six models were introduced with Cummins engines, including the 27-ton FX250 LC. The example shown is equipped with a hydraulically operated bucket tilt for precise bank sloping. In 1998, a further group of FX Series excavator models were marketed by Fiatallis. These were based on Germany's O&K designs, a company acquired by New Holland that year, and in which Fiat has controlling interest. *Keith Haddock*

Fiat-Hitachi EX455. The Fiat-Hitachi joint venture, started in 1986, initially produced the FH Series excavators under the Fiatallis name for North America, and under the Fiat-Hitachi name for Europe. Beginning in 1993, these were replaced by the Fiatallis FX Series excavators. Then in 1998, Fiat announced a new line of Fiat-Hitachi EX Series excavators that would replace the former Fiatallis FX Series over the next three years. The picture shows the largest Fiat-Hitachi excavator so far built. Released in 2000, the EX455 is in the 53-ton weight class and is powered by an Isuzu diesel of 305 horsepower. In 2002 Fiat announced that the Fiat-Hitachi joint venture was terminated and that future excavators would be sold under the Fiat-Kobelco name. *Keith Haddock*

Gradall (early machine). Contractor Ray Ferwerda of Cleveland, Ohio, invented a telescoping-boom excavator and mounted it on a truck. This machine became known as the famous "Gradall" excavator, and the Warner & Swasey Company purchased the rights to its manufacture in 1946. The following year, the first hydraulic machine was produced. The Gradall boom not only telescopes to provide the digging action, but also rotates about its longitudinal axis. This, coupled with the bucket wrist movement, allows the Gradall to "simulate the movements of the human hand." The machine in the picture was the third Gradall to be produced by Warner & Swasey. It is mounted on a Linn half-track truck. *Keith Haddock*

Gradall G-1000. Under Warner & Swasey control, Gradall developed new models including crawler- and wagon-mounted versions by 1955. Optional remote control was available so the operator could drive the truck carrier from his cab in the excavator. Gradall strongly promoted the adaptability of the machine, and a host of attachments was designed for a variety of jobs. The machines became favorites with counties, townships, and municipalities, where one Gradall could do the work of several other machines. The big G1000 Gradall appeared in 1965. It carried two GM diesel engines each of 108 horsepower and was available as a crawler machine or mounted on an 8x4 carrier designed and built by Warner & Swasey. The carrier had its own engine, a 256-horsepower International diesel. Digging depth was quoted as 18 feet, with 34 feet, 6 inches ground-level reach. *Keith Haddock*

Gradall XL2200. In 1992, Gradall launched a new line of excavators, the XL Series with load-sensing high-pressure hydraulics. The first machines were the crawler-mounted XL5200, and the truck-mounted XL5100. These excavators were powered with a Cummins 162-flywheel-horsepower engine, and a Cummins 225-flywheel-horsepower engine powered the XL5100 carrier. Gradall added more XL models: the XL4200 and XL4100 crawler and truck models in 1993, and the small XL2200 crawler and XL2300 wheeled excavators in 1998. The XL2200 weighed 26,600 pounds and carried a Cummins 80-horsepower engine. In 1999, Gradall announced its 3100XL Series available on crawlers or wheels, or truck-mounted. These models rounded out Gradall's modern excavator line and supplanted the last of its former G Series machines. In 2000, JLG Industries acquired Gradall. The machines are still made at the New Philadelphia, Ohio, plant where they have been built since 1950. *Keith Haddock*

Halla HE220LC. Halla Engineering & Heavy Industries, Ltd. was established in Korea in 1990. Its predecessor companies had made excavators for the domestic market under license from Poclain (1974 to 1983) and Hitachi (1983 to 1992). Halla started manufacturing models of its own design in 1993, and that same year commenced exports. The first machines were sold into North America in 1996 under the newly established company Halla America, Inc. By 1999 the Halla line consisted of six crawler excavators, from the 6-ton HE50A to the 50-ton HE450LC, and three wheeled excavators. Bucket sizes ranged from 0.2 to 2.4 cubic yards. The 23-ton HE220LC carried a 1.1-cubic-yard bucket and was powered by a Cummins 153-flywheel-horsepower engine. In 1999, Hyundai took over the Halla management and announced excavator production would be phased out. *Keith Haddock*

Hein-Werner C-32. The Hein-Werner Corporation, established in 1919, began manufacturing hydraulic excavators in 1961 under license from the Hydraulic Machinery Company of Butler, Wisconsin, who later produced the Hy-Hoe line of excavators. Hein-Werner began with the crawler C-10 and truck-mounted T-10 models, and continued these until 1971. In addition, Hein-Werner commenced making models of its own design in 1962 and developed a full line of crawler and truck models. The 1.5-cubic-yard C-32 was released in 1970, and the one in the picture was made in 1971. In 1981, Ackermans of Sweden acquired Hein-Werner, and at that time the line consisted of four crawler models with weights from 20 to 54 tons. Akermann models were built in the former Hein-Werner plant at Waukesha from 1982 until 1992, but the last Hein-Werner excavator was shipped in 1983. *Keith Haddock*

Hitachi UH03. Established in 1910, the parent company of Hitachi Construction Machinery Company, Ltd. built it first excavator, an electric cable-operated mining shovel, in 1939. It was not until 1965 that Hitachi unveiled its first hydraulic excavator, the .375-cubic-yard UH03, the first to be developed using Japan's own excavator technology. This machine weighed just less than 10 tons, and power came from a 50-horsepower Isuzu diesel engine. Its hydraulic-propelled motors were mounted in the car body, and the tracks were driven by chains to drive tumblers in each side frame. From this small beginning, Hitachi rapidly expanded its UH Series excavator models and penetrated world markets. By 1973, Hitachi had achieved 20,000 excavator sales. *Hitachi Construction Machinery*

Hitachi UH30. By 1975, Hitachi's original UH Series excavator line extended up to the UH30. This heavy-duty machine boasted two Isuzu diesel engines totaling 400 flywheel-horsepower and an operating weight of 80 tons. Its standard backhoe bucket, with 30-foot digging depth, held 4.5 cubic yards, and its standard shovel bucket held 6 cubic yards. The UH30 continued in production until 1984. In 1978, Hitachi began replacing the original UH Series machines with upgraded models and a new three-digit nomenclature. The first machine in this series was the 13-ton UH045. The new models eventually replaced all former UH Series excavators, and sales went from strength to strength. By the early 1980s, Hitachi was building excavators at a rate of 7,000 units per year, reaching total sales of 70,000 by 1983. *Keith Haddock collection*

Hitachi UH801. Hitachi has been one of the few Japanese manufacturers to challenge the "mining" excavator market, and it certainly has made its mark. Hitachi's first mining hydraulic excavator was the UH801 introduced in 1979. Originally designed as the UH80, it was renumbered to fit in with Hitachi's new three-digit numbering system that was introduced in 1978. The UH801 was rated at 800 horsepower derived from dual Cummins diesels, and weighed 173 tons in operating condition. The one in the picture dug with a 15-cubic-yard bucket uncovering coal in West Virginia. This machine was also available as a 10-cubic-yard backhoe. *Keith Haddock*

Hitachi EX200LC. In 1986, Hitachi introduced the revised and upgraded EX Series hydraulic excavators with state-of-the-art electronic control and a choice of three or four operator-selected work modes, depending on the model. The first machines in this series were the 12-ton EX100 replacing the UH053, the 13-ton EX120 replacing the UH063, and the 20-ton EX200 replacing the UH083. The LC versions have extended undercarriages for increased lifting capacity and for working on soft ground. The EX200LC shown has a 132-horsepower Isuzu engine and weighs 22.5 tons. *Keith Haddock*

Hitachi EX1100. The top end of Hitachi's excavator line, the mining machines, received the benefit of the EX Series in 1987. The 100-ton EX1000 replaced the former UH501, the 193-ton EX1800 replaced the UH801, and a new top-of-the-line, the EX3500, was introduced. These three mining excavators carried standard shovels of 7, 15, and 30 cubic yards respectively. The EX3500 was upgraded in 1991 to the 364-ton Super EX3500-2, and carried a pair of Cummins diesels rated at 1,684 horsepower. The EX1100 appeared in 1991 as an upgraded replacement for the EX1000. It was powered by a single Cummins diesel rated at 550 horsepower. Operating weight was just under 120 tons. The backhoe version in the picture wielded a 6.5-cubic-yard bucket and could dig down to 30 feet. *Keith Haddock*

Hitachi EX5500. Firmly placed in the large hydraulic mining excavator market, Hitachi has brought out larger machines and boosted its existing models since 1996. The intermediate EX2500 model appeared in 1996 fitting into the 18-cubic-yard class, with an operating weight of 263 tons. Hitachi's largest excavator at the time of writing is the EX5500. The first of these was delivered in 1998 to North American Construction, an overburden removal contractor at the oil sands operations near Fort McMurray, Alberta, Canada. The machine in the picture loads a 320-ton Wabco 930E truck with a 35-cubic-yard bullclam-type bucket. The huge excavator weighs 570 tons and is powered by two Cummins KTA50-C diesels developing a total of 2,500 flywheel-horsepower. *Keith Haddock*

Hitachi ZX450. Progressing further with its hydraulic excavator development, Hitachi introduced the first of its new Zaxis excavators, the ZX450, in 2001. Replacing the EX Series, these machines have received a reshaped box-design undercarriage, and boast a computerized on-board information carrier to track operational data that can be downloaded to analyze machine performance and maintenance needs. Power for the 51-ton ZX450 is a 314-horsepower Isuzu engine. In 2002, Hitachi released seven more models up to the 84-ton ZX800. They replaced their similar-sized counterparts in the former EX Series. *Hitachi Construction Products*

Hyundai 360LC-3. Hyundai Heavy Industries Company, Ltd. was established in 1973 from a former Hyundai company. That same year, the company began building excavators under license from Poclain. In 1989 Hitachi opened an office in Chicago, Illinois, to import machinery for sale in North America. In 1991, Hyundai Construction Equipment U.S.A., Inc. was established to market the Robex excavator line that had been introduced in 1990. By 2002, this line had expanded to include 12 crawler models from the 6-ton R55-3 to the 83-ton R755-3, and five wheeled models from the 6-ton R55W-3 to the 22-ton R200W-3. Bucket sizes span from .2 to 4.5 cubic yards. The 360LC-3 is in the 41-ton weight class. In 2002, Hyundai began to introduce its upgraded LC-7 Series machines. *Keith Haddock*

Insley H-2250. Insley Manufacturing Corporation of Indianapolis, Indiana, was an early American entrant into the hydraulic excavator field. It had built cable excavators since 1922, and unveiled its first hydraulic machine, the H-100, in 1963. The following year, this machine was replaced by the H-560, a .625-cubic-yard backhoe. In 1965, only two years after producing its first hydraulic excavator, Insley shone the spotlight on its H-2250, the largest fully hydraulic backhoe ever built up to that time. The giant H-2250 could be equipped with a hoe bucket of 2.25-cubic-yards or, in shovel form known as the HL-5000, it could dig with a 5-cubic-yard bucket. With an operating weight of 46 tons, it remained in production until 1972. *Keith Haddock collection*

Insley H-875. Insley's success with hydraulic excavators led the company to fill out its line between its smallest and largest machines. The 1-cubic-yard H-875 appeared in 1967, and the H560 was upgraded to the 560B in 1969. These excavators featured fully hydraulic propel, but their crawlers were chain driven from hydraulic propel motors mounted inside their car bodies. Steering was achieved through jaw clutches and band brakes on each propel shaft. Insley had such confidence in its hydraulic products that in 1971, it decided to break its long tradition of cable excavator manufacture and turn production entirely to hydraulic machines. *Keith Haddock collection*

Insley H-1500C. Insley's last cable excavator was shipped in 1971, the same year it launched the first of a new line of excavators, the 1.5-cubic-yard H-1500 weighing in at 70,500 pounds. The new machines featured independent hydraulic propel motors in each crawler frame. More models were added until 1975, when seven sizes were offered. That year, the H-1500 was upgraded to the H-1500B, and then the H-1500C appeared in 1978 with weight increased to 78,300 pounds. In 1986, Badger Construction Equipment Company purchased Insley, and production moved to Winona, Minnesota. The last excavator produced by the company was the 69-ton H-3500D. One of these was the last Insley machine built when Badger decided to discontinue the Insley product line in 1996. *Keith Haddock*

International 3964B. International's name first appeared on excavators after the company purchased the rights to the French Yumbo company in 1970. Yumbo's predecessor, SICAM, was one of the companies that obtained manufacturing rights from Italy's Bruneri Brothers, who built one of the world's first hydraulic excavators in 1947. The first International machines were the crawler-mounted 12-ton 3944 and 15-ton 3964, and wheeled versions 3945 and 3965. They carried International diesel engines rated at 62 and 104 horsepower respectively. These machines superseded the former Yumbo crawler Y Series and wheeled H Series models of similar size. The upgraded 3964B gained an extra 2 tons in weight and was offered with International or Deutz engines. *Keith Haddock*

JCB 7. After establishing its very successful line of backhoe loaders, the British company JCB, with its founder Joseph Charles Bamford, took a new direction in 1964 with the launch of its first fully revolving crawler excavator. The machine was manufactured under license from Warner & Swasey's American Hopto design. It carried a standard bucket of .75 cubic yards and was powered by a Ford 96-horsepower engine. JCB rapidly expanded its crawler line with the introduction of the JCB 6 and JCB 7B in 1966, the JCB 5C in 1969, and the JCB 8D in 1971. The latter model was JCB's largest to date at 25 tons. *JCB Excavators, Ltd.*

International 3980. International added this 18.5-ton model in 1972. It utilized the same 104-horsepower International engine as the smaller 3964, but deployed a high-pressure variable displacement piston hydraulic system in contrast to the low-pressure gear pumps on the smaller machine. In 1982, Dresser Industries purchased the Construction Machinery Division of International Harvester, and from 1986 reintroduced the Yumbo-designed excavators, which had been upgraded to the 600 Series beginning in 1979. This line included the 630, 635, 640, 645, and 650B from 15- to 35- tons weight. These models were discontinued in 1989 when Dresser began marketing Komatsu-designed excavators under the joint-venture Komatsu Dresser Company. In the United States these machines were marketed as the Dresser 6000 Series, with the "6" replacing the "PC" prefix on the same Komatsu model (e.g., Dresser 6220 was a Komatsu PC220). This arrangement only lasted until 1992. *Keith Haddock collection*

JCB 808. In 1973, JCB presented its 800 Series, which replaced all former excavator models. The new machines boasted quieter operation, variable-flow hydraulic pumps, and tilt-away cab for servicing. First came the 17-ton Perkins-powered JCB 806. Then JCB announced the 807 and the 808 in 1974. The JCB 808 was in the 24-ton weight class and worked with a 1-cubic-yard standard bucket. It was produced from 1975 to 1982. Rounding out its four-model basic 800 Series, JCB introduced the smaller 805 in 1976. Three years later, this model was upgraded to the 805B after an extensive testing program. The upper portion of the booms on these machines could be pinned in one of two positions so the operator could choose between maximum capacity and maximum working range. *Keith Haddock*

JCB JS200LC. In 1991, JCB and Sumitomo Construction Machinery (SCM) established the joint venture JCB-SCM. JCB immediately began producing the Sumitomo-designed crawler hydraulic excavators known as the JS Series, which supplanted the former in-house-designed JCB models. The new line consisted of eight Isuzu-powered crawler models from the 7.8-ton JS-70 to the 48-ton JS450LC covering standard bucket sizes from .3 to 2.7 cubic yards. The JS200LC shown is reducing rock size in a quarry with a hydraulic hammer. Its Isuzu engine puts out 122 flywheel-horsepower, and the machine weighs 24 tons. *Keith Haddock*

JCB JS330L. The JCB-SCM joint venture came to an end in 1998, but JCB continued to produce excavators utilizing Sumitomo technology to develop a new line of JS excavators. In 2002 this line consisted of 11 sizes of crawler machines with weights from 7.7 to 51 tons, and three wheeled excavators from 14- to 24-tons operating weights. The JS330L, in the 35-ton class, is powered by an Isuzu engine developing 219 flywheel-horsepower. The machine in the picture is equipped with a short arm and maximum bucket size of 1.8 cubic yards for mass excavation. With optional long arm, the hoe can reach down almost 27 feet. *JCB Sales, Ltd.*

JSW BH70. The Japan Steel Works (JSW) was established in 1907 by Hokkaido Colliery and Steamship Company, Ltd. and two English companies, Sir W.G. Armstrong Whitworth & Company, Ltd. and Vickers Sons & Maxim, Ltd. The company produced a variety of industrial products including steel castings and forgings. In 1964 hydraulic excavators were added to the range of products. These were built under license from Germany's O&K, starting with the RH5. The license agreement ended in 1979, at which point JSW launched its own excavators. Initially they were based on O&K designs such as the BH70 shown here, which is a modified version of the O&K RH6. *Keith Haddoc*

Kobelco K907C. The giant industrial concern Kobe Steel was founded in Kobe, Japan, in 1907. The company has the distinction of building Japan's first electric mining shovel in 1930. Since then, Kobe has built electric mining shovels and a wide range of smaller cable-operated excavators. From 1956, these were built under license from Harnischfeger Corporation as the P&H brand, a licensing agreement still in force at the time of writing. Kobe's first hydraulic excavator appeared in 1967 based on P&H hydraulic designs; other models followed. In 1972, Kobe commenced production of its own in-house-designed excavators starting with the R Series and progressing to the revised and upgraded K Series launched in 1980. The Kobelco K907C, itself an upgrade from the earlier K907B and K907A, was in the 21-ton weight class and utilized a 118-horsepower Mitsubishi engine for its power. *Keith Haddock*

JSW BH110-2. After JSW separated from the O&K manufacturing agreement in 1979, it began its own line initially based on O&K designs, but soon developed completely new designs starting with the NC Series for the Japanese domestic market only. These were expanded to include a new line of BH Series machines from the 6.8-ton BH30 to the 30-ton BH110-2, which were exported worldwide. From 1979 to 1983, JSW excavators were sold as Pettibone machines for the U.S. market. *Keith Haddock*

Kobelco K916LC II. In 1980, the same year it launched the K Series excavators, Kobe commenced using the brand name Kobelco to identify its products. It rapidly expanded its K Series excavators and, by 1984, the line included nine basic sizes from the .4-yard K903B to the 2.5-cubic-yard K935. Most of these were upgraded to the Mark II Series in 1989. They featured a heavy-lift mode by which, at the touch of a switch, 14 percent more power was available for hoisting heavy loads. Another advanced hydraulic feature enabled the boom and bucket circuits to be linked together so that the weight of the boom assisted bucket movement. Retaining its Mitsubishi power, the K916LC II had a 286-horsepower engine. Its operating weight in standard trim with a 2.4-cubic-yard bucket was 96,600 pounds. *Keith Haddock*

Kobelco SK210 LC. Kobe purchased Japan's Yutani in 1983, and initiated the first SK Series excavators jointly designed by Kobe and Yutani. After several upgrades, this series graduated into the advanced SK Dynamic Acera machines. Here, for the first time, the computerized control does not require the operator to choose from a confusing set of up to 10 work modes. Instead, he has just three choices: assist mode, where the machine recognizes the various tasks and automatically adjusts the machine's response to job conditions; manual mode, where the operator takes full control; or breaker mode, used when increased pump flow is required for attachments like hydraulic breakers or demolition nibblers. The 47,000-pound SK210 LC is one of 11 SK Dynamic Acera excavators, weighing up to 53 tons, offered by Kobe in 2002. Its Mitsubishi engine puts out 143 horsepower. *Keith Haddock*

Koehring 205 Skooper. Koehring Machine Company started building concrete mixers in 1907, then broadened its line to include other construction machinery. Changing its name to Koehring Company in 1920, it built its first excavator, a fully revolving cable-operated excavator, in 1921. The picture shows Koehring's first attempt at introducing hydraulic power into an excavator. Introduced in 1957, the hybrid 205 Skooper utilized a Koehring 205 base machine on which was mounted a 2-cubic-yard shovel attachment. The shovel crowd was activated hydraulically, and the linkage provided an automatic 7-foot level crowding action. Everything else on the machine, including the hoist, was mechanically operated as in the standard Koehring 205 cable machine. This machine did enjoy a fair degree of success, which prompted Koehring to develop the concept further. *Keith Haddock collection*

Koehring 505 Skooper. With the success of the 205 Skooper just described, Koehring developed the larger 505 Skooper in 1960 designed on similar lines. Although the first machines were hybrid mechanical/hydraulic like the 205, Koehring brought out a full-hydraulic version in 1962, as shown in the picture. The 505 could handle buckets from 3.5 to 5 cubic yards depending on the material, and power options were GM, Allis-Chalmers, or Caterpillar diesel engines rated at 162 horsepower. Machine weight was 78,315 pounds. The 2-cubic-yard Koehring 505 hoe version, which appeared in 1964, was claimed to be the world's largest at that time. It remained in production until 1972. *Keith Haddock collection*

Koehring 1466 Shovel. The first of Koehring's new 66 Series appeared in 1967 as the 1-cubic-yard Model 466. This was joined by the .75-cubic-yard Model 366 the following year, and the big 1066 in 1969. The latter machine boasted a 3-cubic-yard-heaped-capacity hoe bucket and a ground reach of almost 52-feet, the largest in the industry at the time. By 1983, Koehring's 66 Series consisted of 10 sizes up to the company's largest, the 10-cubic-yard Model 1466 available as a hoe or shovel, and tipping the scales at 150 tons. Power on this machine came from two GM engines totaling 898 horsepower. The 1466 illustrated was loading coal at an Ohio surface mine. *Peter N. Grimshaw collection*

Koehring 6625. Over the years, Koehring established several international partnerships with other excavator manufacturers, and exchanged their technology. One of these partnerships was with Japan's IHI, and it spawned a new 66 Series of excavators, this time with the "66" placed in front of the model number. This series, marketed from 1984, eventually grew to 10 machine sizes, from the 6-ton 6608 to the 49-ton 6644, and spanned bucket sizes from .2 to 2 cubic yards. In 1993, Koehring withdrew from the excavator market, but three models remained in production as scrap handlers only. *Keith Haddock*

Komatsu PC300LC-3. Komatsu started production of excavators in 1963 using America's Bucyrus-Erie (B-E) technology through an agreement between B-E, Komatsu, and Mitsui Engineering. Both cable and hydraulic excavators were produced, most notably the 15-H and 20-H hydraulic machines from B-E's line. This agreement lasted until 1981, a year after Komatsu launched its own-design PC Series excavators. By 1986, the PC line included nine basic sizes from the 7-ton PC60-5 to the 72-ton PC650-1, which was launched in 1982, as well as three sizes of wheeled, and five sizes of mini excavators. All were powered by Komatsu diesel engines. The 197-flywheel-horsepower PC300LC-3 shown is the long-track version weighing 67,900 pounds and carrying a 1.75-cubic-yard bucket. *Keith Haddock*

Komatsu PC240LC-6. In 1988, Komatsu began introducing the PC-5 (also known as the Dash 5) excavators incorporating computerized control systems to give the operator a choice of four working modes: heavy duty, general operation, finishing operation, and lifting. Komatsu moved to the PC-6 (Dash 6) in 1994 when it introduced the Avance Series of excavators that utilized a system known as "Hydraumind," which automatically adjusted the hydraulic power to the application at hand. Initially, five sizes were offered from the 13-ton PC120-6 to the 30-ton PC300-6. By 1997 the line had expanded upward to include the 82-ton PC750-6 and the PC240LC-6, shown in the picture with a special coal-loading shovel bucket. Its standard bucket capacity is 1.5 cubic yards and operating weight is 53,500 pounds. *Keith Haddock*

Komatsu PC1100-6. Komatsu's top-of-the-line construction-sized excavator in 2002 was the PC1100-6. Introduced in 1998, this Avance Series excavator replaced the former PC1000-1, which had been produced since 1986. It is available in shovel or backhoe form. The backhoe has optional boom and arm lengths to provide either maximum digging depths to 31 feet with a 4.5-cubic-yard bucket, or a short boom swinging an 8.5-cubic-yard bucket for mass excavation. As a shovel, the PC1100-6 carries a 9-yard bullclam-type bucket. It boasts all the computerized refinements of its smaller brothers, and fits into the 120-ton weight class. *Keith Haddock*

Komatsu PC1800-6. Komatsu entered the world of giant mining excavators in 1981 when it unveiled the PC1500 hydraulic shovel at the 1981 Conexpo equipment show in Houston, Texas. The 175-ton machine was one of the first to feature a microcomputer for fuel economy and increased efficiency. With two Cummins KT1150 diesels putting out a total of 820 flywheel-horsepower, the machine worked with 13-cubic-yard shovel or backhoe front ends. In 1987, Komatsu upgraded the PC1500-1 to the PC1600-1 with similar power and weight but fitted with dual Komatsu diesel engines. This machine was replaced by the PC1800-6 in 1999 incorporating Avance computer technology. Its standard shovel or backhoe buckets hold 15 cubic yards, and machine weight is approximately 200 tons. Power comes from dual Komatsu engines totaling 908 flywheel-horsepower. *Keith Haddock*

Komatsu PC4000. In 1997, Demag excavators came under Komatsu Mining Systems, Inc., which eventually took full control of the Demag product. Beginning in 1999, the former Demag mining excavators were renumbered as Komatsu machines. The PC1400 replaced the former Demag H135S, the Demag H255S became the PC3000, the PC4000 replaced the Demag H285S, The H455S became the PC5500, and the PC8000 was updated from the Demag H655S. The latter machine is one of the giants of the industry with an operating weight of 755 tons and standard shovel capacity of 46 cubic yards. The smaller PC4000 has an operating weight of 400 tons and loads with a 28-cubic-yard shovel bucket. A single Cummins QSK 60 engine of 1,875 horsepower powers this machine. *Francis Pierre collection*

Liebherr L300. Liebherr entered the hydraulic excavator market in 1955 with this wheeled model. The company was already well known for its tower cranes introduced in 1949. Founded by Hans Liebherr, who took over the family construction business in 1938, Liebherr prospered and expanded rapidly in the 1950s and 1960s. Many subsidiary companies were set up in foreign countries, including the Colmar factory in France in 1961, which would become the world center for hydraulic excavator manufacture. A year after the L300 was released, crawler- and truck-mounted versions became available. In 1957, the revised .5-cubic-yard L350 appeared, and further upgrades brought the wheeled A353 and crawler R353 machines of the same capacity. *Liebherr-France, Colmar*

Liebherr 961. Liebherr expanded its excavator line in the early 1960s to include the 1-cubic-yard wheeled A750 in 1960, the company's first with a hydraulically driven undercarriage, and the 1.25-cubic-yard crawler RT1000 in 1966, the company's largest at that time. In 1968, Liebherr presented its 900 Series excavators, which laid the foundation on which all subsequent models have been based. The line initially comprised models renumbered from former machines plus new additions. It ranged from the 10-ton R901 through the 33-ton R961, Liebherr's largest in 1968. The models were identified by prefix letters "A" for wheeled or "R" for crawler-mounted versions. Liebherr excavators gained in popularity around the world, and in 1970 the company opened its Newport News, Virginia, factory to manufacture machines for the North American market. *Keith Haddock*

Liebherr R994. Since Liebherr launched its 900 Series in 1968, the top end of the line has progressively pushed upward in size through the 50-ton R971, the 70-ton R981, and then a big jump in size to the 180-ton R991 released in 1977. This machine, with its standard rock bucket of 10 cubic yards as a shovel, firmly positioned Liebherr in the large hydraulic excavator market for the mining industry. The R991, with dual Cummins engines totaling 720 horsepower, was upgraded to the R994 in 1984, with a weight increase to 227 tons. A single Cummins diesel of 1,050 horsepower powered the first R994. Weight and power subsequently increased to 250 tons and 1,142 horsepower for the machine shown in the picture. *Liebherr-France, Colmar*

Liebherr R996. Liebherr's drive for the world's mining excavator market is currently spearheaded by the R996. Introduced in 1995 with an operating weight of 584 tons and standard shovel bucket of 36 cubic yards, by 2002 this monster machine weighed 720 tons and had standard shovel buckets up to 44 cubic yards. The R996 is also offered as one of the world's largest backhoes, carrying a bucket of 43 cubic yards. Power is supplied by two Cummins engines with a combined output of 3,000 horsepower. *Liebherr-France, Colmar*

Liebherr A904. As well as the large quarry and mine machines just described, Liebherr has always catered to the small contractor with a full range of wheeled and crawler excavators in sizes under 1 cubic yard. The A904 is one of nine wheeled excavators offered in 2002. Powered by a 135-horsepower engine, it has an operating weight ranging from 18 to 21 tons, depending on the attachment. The A904 in the picture sports a hydraulic tilt arrangement on its backhoe bucket, and its undercarriage has the standard dozer blade on one end and stabilizers on the other. All current Liebherr excavators incorporate the patented Litronic hydraulic system, which monitors, controls, regulates, and coordinates all key systems of the excavator. *Keith Haddock*

Lima 4505. Lima's first excavator was the cable-operated Model 101 manufactured in 1928. More models were introduced, and their success spurred Lima to rapidly expand its line of cable excavators, including the 8-cubic-yard type 2400 in 1948. Lima's first hydraulic excavator appeared in 1970 with the release of the Model 945 advertised as a 2.25-cubic-yard backhoe. In 1973, Lima announced three new models, the 1.5-cubic-yard 205, the two-yard 3505, and the 2.5-cubic-yard 4505. The latter machine weighed just over 50 tons and was powered by a GM diesel rated at 300 horsepower. These excavators had a relatively short production life and had disappeared by the end of the 1970s. The Lima plant at Lima, Ohio, closed in 1981. *Keith Haddock*

Link-Belt LS-3500. Link-Belt got serious about hydraulic excavators in 1967 when it launched four machines, the .75-cubic-yard LS-3500, the 1-cubic-yard LS-4000, the 1.25-cubic-yard LS-4500, and the 1.5-cubic-yard LS-5000. These machines incorporated mechanical drive for swing and travel functions through friction clutches, just like a cable-operated machine. Drive to the crawlers was via shafts and gears through the center pintle, and then via chains to the crawler drive tumblers. Jaw clutches in the lower works actuated the steering. Working weight for the LS-3500 was just over 27 tons, and power came from GM or Caterpillar engines in the 140- to 150-horsepower range. *Keith Haddock*

Link-Belt HC-2000. The long-established Link-Belt Company of Chicago, Illinois, shipped its first crawler-mounted excavator in 1922. Link-Belt purchased the Speeder Machinery Company of Cedar Rapids, Iowa, in 1939, and combined the excavator lines of both companies. Link-Belt's entry into the hydraulic excavator market occurred in 1963 after it purchased the manufacturing rights to a machine called the Hydraxcavator. This machine (Model 100HT truck-mounted or 100HS wheel-mounted) boasted a telescopic boom that could also rotate 160 degrees longitudinally. This patented device was known as a Rotascope. In 1966 this model became the Link-Belt HC2000, with a bucket capacity of .333 cubic yards. The picture emphasizes the great lengths the designers went to accommodate the hydraulic hoses for the bucket wrist action. *Keith Haddock*

Link-Belt LS-5400. Independent hydraulic propel motors in the crawler side frames, permitting counter-rotation steering, appeared on Link-Belt excavators in 1975 when the company launched three new machines. These were the 1.25-cubic-yard LS-4800, the 1.75-cubic-yard LS-5800, and the 3-yard LS-7400, to replace the earlier mechanically driven models. Link-Belt rounded out its excavator line in the 1970s with the addition of the .75-yard LS-2800 in 1976, the 1.5-cubic-yard LS-5400 in 1977, and 1.25-cubic-yard LS-3400 in 1978. The 40-ton LS-5400 hoe carried a GM engine rated at 208 horsepower, and could dig down 25 feet. *Keith Haddock*

Link-Belt 3900. In 1986, FMC Corporation, parent company of Link-Belt since 1967, entered into a joint venture with Sumitomo to form Link-Belt Construction Equipment Company. The following year, Link-Belt brought out four models of its C Series excavators with computer-aided control and operator-selected work modes utilizing Sumitomo technology. These models, all powered by Isuzu engines, were updated in 1994 to initiate the Quantum Series excavators. These boasted state-of-the-art computer controls that automatically matched machine output to the work at hand, and provided the operator with four work modes. The initial Quantum models ranged from the 14-ton 2650 to the 50-ton 5800. By 1996, Cummins diesels were utilized on the larger Quantum models, and additional models joined the line including the 32-ton 3900 in 1998. This was powered by a 178-horsepower Cummins engine. *Keith Haddock*

Link-Belt 8000. In 1998, Sumitomo Construction Machinery Company and Case Corporation announced a global alliance to manufacture and market hydraulic excavators. As part of this alliance, a joint-venture company, LBX Company, LLC, with 50 percent ownership by each company, was formed to market Link-Belt-branded excavators in North America. One of the first fruits of this alliance was the top-of-the-line Link-Belt Quantum excavator 8000 announced at the 1999 Conexpo equipment show in Las Vegas. Weighing in at 176,400 pounds, the 800 had a Cummins engine developing 445 horsepower, and the machine could be fitted with hoe buckets from 3 to 6 cubic yards depending on the material. *LBX Company*

Link-Belt 210LX. Moving ahead still further, Link-Belt announced a new upgraded line of excavators in 2000, the LX Series, based on Sumitomo designs. In 2002, this line consists of six sizes from the 130LX weighing 27,100 pounds to the 330LX weighing 78,000 pounds, all powered by Isuzu engines. Two of the models are offered as a long-front option with extended reach to 60 feet. Hoe bucket sizes span from .5 to 2.5 cubic yards. The new line is represented here by the 210LX, which has an operating weight of 44,800 pounds and a 138-horsepower engine. This model is also offered with long-front attachment extending its reach to 51 feet. *Keith Haddock*

Little Giant 34TX. Lewis Grundon in Des Moines, Iowa founded Little Giant Crane & Shovel Company in 1946. Over the years the company manufactured a wide range of crawler- and truck-mounted cable excavators up to one-yard capacity. In 1963, the company built its first hydraulic excavator, the Combo 12, with mechanical swing and propel. Two years later, Little Giant unveiled the .75-cubic-yard Combo-J, claimed to be the world's first hydraulic excavator fully convertible for dragline duties. The 34TX truck-mounted telescoping excavator appeared in 1972. The one in the picture demonstrates its long reach and its capability to dig straight down. In 1996, Avis Industrial Corporation purchased Little Giant and changed its name to Little Giant Corporation. In 2000, manufacture was moved to Winona, Minnesota, where production continued as a division of Badger Equipment Company. *Keith Haddock collection*

Lorain L-48H. Following the success of Captain Thew's fully revolving shovel in 1895, the Thew Automatic Shovel Company was established at Lorain, Ohio, in 1899. The company produced and marketed an extensive line of cable excavators and, by 1927, became the sixth-largest excavator manufacturer in the United States. The Thew Shovel Company merged with Koehring in 1964 to become the Thew-Lorain Division of Koehring Company. Its only hydraulic excavator, this Lorain L-48H, was introduced in 1967. Standard bucket capacity was 1.25 cubic yards, machine weight topped 40 tons, and power came from a 240-flywheel-horsepower Cummins diesel. Its hoe could dig down 28 feet. *Keith Haddock collection*

Marion 3560. The Marion Power Shovel Company's only contribution to the hydraulic excavator industry was the giant 3560. It holds the distinction of being the largest first Model hydraulic excavator made by any manufacturer, and is still one of the largest hydraulic excavators ever designed and built in North America. Weighing over 300 tons, the Model 3560 was offered as a standard 20-cubic-yard shovel or 16-cubic-yard backhoe, and with diesel or electric power. The diesel version carried two Caterpillar 3412 engines totaling 1,400 horsepower. In 1988, Marion revised the machine to the 3560B, with weight increased to 328 tons in backhoe configuration, and 1,410 horsepower from dual Cummins engines. A total of eight 3560s were built between 1981 and 1989. *Keith Haddock collection*

Massey-Ferguson MF 350. Agricultural group Massey-Ferguson (M-F) commenced hydraulic excavator manufacture in 1968 at a new factory at Aprilia, Italy. The machine designs came from the former Beltrami company, which M-F had previously purchased. The first models were the .5-cubic-yard MF 350, and the .75-cubic-yard MF 450 available in crawler, wheeled, or truck-mounted options. The picture shows an MF 350 receiving final inspection at the plant. M-F upgraded its two excavator models in the 1960s to the 15-ton MF 350S and the 17-ton MF 450S, powered by Perkins engines of 69 and 88 flywheel-horsepower respectively. Notice the three-position pinned boom arrangement on the M-F machines. This allowed the operator to choose between maximum digging depth (19 feet, 6 inches), or increased lifting capacity. *Keith Haddock collection*

Massey-Ferguson MF W450D. In 1974, Massey-Ferguson purchased the German Hanomag company, which at that time was marketing excavators designed by Eder Hydraulikbagger. These designs were infused into the existing Massey-Ferguson excavators, and the resulting models commenced production at the German and Italian plants. These included the MF W450D mounted on a four-wheel-drive undercarriage with planetary gears in each wheel hub. It handled a standard bucket of .875 cubic yards and weighed 16 tons in roadable condition. Due to adverse business conditions, M-F sold its Italian plant in 1978, but continued excavator production at its Hanomag plant. Germany's IBH group purchased the company in 1980. After IBH failed in 1983, the excavators were reborn under the Hanomag name produced by an independent company. *Keith Haddock collection*

New Holland EW200. The New Holland brand name on excavators resulted from the merger of Case Corporation and equipment builder Ford New Holland to form CNH Global in 1999. Fiat had acquired Ford New Holland in 1991, and in 1998 acquired excavator builder O&K in Germany as well as several other companies. As part of its global plan, CNH chose O&K excavators to represent the New Holland name in North America. The initial line consisted of 11 sizes of crawler excavators from the 19,200-pound EC90-LC to the 139,400-pound EC600-LC, as well as three wheeled excavators: the EW160, EW200, and EW220. The EW200, shown equipped with dozer blade and stabilizers, has a Deutz engine of 111 horsepower, and an operating weight of 40,800 pounds. *New Holland Construction*

Northwest 100-DH. Northwest Engineering Company of Green Bay, Wisconsin, builder of cable excavators since 1920, unveiled its first hydraulic excavator in 1969. This was the 1 cubic-yard 30-DH backhoe, which was fully convertible to dragline or crane service. The Northwest management initially believed this feature was mandatory when it came to hydraulic excavators, so subsequent models over the next few years were designed with this capability. The 1.5-cubic-yard 35-DH was added in 1971. The top-of-the-line 100-DH was displayed for the first time at the 1975 Conexpo equipment show in Chicago. Able to handle an 8-cubic-yard standard hoe bucket, its operating weight was 237,000 pounds. As a crane, it was known as the Model 1200-C, and rated at 150-tons capacity. In the late 1970s and 1980s, Northwest faced dwindling sales, and discontinued its hydraulic machines in 1983.

O&K RH6. The German firm, Orenstein & Koppel (O&K), established in 1876, built its first steam shovel in 1908, and soon established itself as one of the leading German excavator manufacturers. This company was one of the few old-established cable excavator manufacturers that successfully made the transition from cable to hydraulic excavators—and in a very short space of time. O&K released its first hydraulic excavator in 1961, the RH-5, a small .5-cubic-yard machine, of which over 20,000 were eventually sold. The similar-looking .75-cubic-yard RH-6 followed, and a rapidly expanding line of hydraulic excavators found immediate acceptance. *Keith Haddock*

O&K RH-60. In only 10 short years after its first hydraulic excavator, O&K launched the world's largest series-produced hydraulic excavator, the RH-60. This 124-ton machine was equipped with two Deutz diesel engines totaling 760 horsepower, and an 8.5-cubic-yard shovel bucket. The time was ideal to launch such a large, diesel-powered hydraulic excavator. Contractors found the nimble machine perfect for use in the expanding surface coal mine industry, especially in the United Kingdom. In operation, it wasn't dependent on the trailing power cable of an electric machine, and, when it came time to move jobs, the big shovel could be dismantled easily and moved in modular units. In 1976 the RH-60 was superseded by the larger RH-75, with bucket size increased to 10 cubic yards, and weight to 150 tons. *O&K*

O&K RH-300. As early as 1979, O&K took a huge step in hydraulic excavator technology when it unwrapped the world's largest hydraulic excavator. With an operating weight of 535 tons and a 34-cubic-yard bucket, the RH-300 easily surpassed anything built up to that time. Purchased by contractors Northern Strip Mining, Ltd. (NSM), who were already operating large fleets of RH-60s and RH-75s in British surface coalmines, the first RH-300 was powered by two Cummins KTA2300C diesel engines, each of 1,210 horsepower. Unfortunately, the industry was not quite ready for such a revolutionary machine and only three were built. O&K gained experience to build even larger machines with improved technology. *Keith Haddock*

O&K RH-City. While O&K were making noises in the large mining excavator field, the company did not neglect the small-machine construction market. Innovative machines adapted for special applications were forthcoming from the company. The Model RH-City released in the early 1990s was such a beast. As its name suggests, it was designed for use on city streets. Based on an RH-4, its large undercarriage resulted in low ground pressure, preserving pavement surfaces and protecting underground services. Its small rear-end swing radius allowed the machine to carry on working while occupying only one traffic lane. Its engine was a Deutz 70-horsepower unit, and operating weight was approximately 17 tons, depending on the crawler width selected. *Keith Haddock*

O&K RH-120C. In the 1980s, O&K's mining excavators continued to gain ground. Important additions during the decade were the 245-ton RH-120C in 1983, the 176-ton RH-90C in 1986 and, launched at the Bauma equipment show in Germany in 1989, the 512-ton RH-200 carrying a 34-cubic-yard shovel bucket. A distinguishing feature of O&K's mining shovels is their TriPower system. This mechanical linkage provides automatic bucket leveling through a trunnion system, which also amplifies the crowding force during hoisting. The RH-120C in the picture is working with a 17-cubic-yard bullclam-type bucket, and is powered by dual Cummins KTTA 19C engines, each rated at 1,180 flywheel-horsepower. *David Wootton*

O&K MH-6. Wheeled excavators have always been a big part of O&K's product line and, over the years, it has offered the smaller models under the 1.5-cubic-yard size class both in crawler and wheeled versions. In 2000, O&K offered no less than 10 different models and variations of wheeled excavators ranging from the 9.4-ton MH-2.8 to the 26-ton MH-6 HD. The MH-6 shown in the picture is of 1991 vintage. Mounted in the undercarriage, its single hydraulic propel motor transmits power through a two-speed gearbox to all four wheels. The four stabilizers are lowered when the machine is digging. *Keith Haddock*

P&H H-312. The Harnischfeger Corporation, founded by Alonzo Pawling and Henry Harnischfeger in 1884, built its first excavator, a gasoline-powered cable-operated machine, in 1914. The company developed an extensive line of excavators with brand name P&H, and gained an enviable reputation with its construction-sized cable machines as well as its large electric mining shovels. The company's first entry into the hydraulic excavator market was in 1964 when it acquired rights to a small excavator designed by Cabot Corporation. From this model, P&H developed the popular .75-cubic-yard H312 and 1-cubic-yard H418, which remained in production until 1976. The H-312 weighed 18 tons and boasted five vane-type hydraulic pumps to work its various motions. *Keith Haddock*

O&K RH-400. O&K's crowning excavator achievement is the RH-400, which went to work in 1997 at the Syncrude oil sands operation in Alberta, Canada, where it is matched to 380-ton trucks. Developed jointly by Syncrude and O&K, the machine once again puts O&K's name on the world's largest hydraulic excavator. This 1,000-ton hydraulic behemoth wields a 57-cubic-yard bucket, and takes its power from dual Cummins K2000E engines totaling 3,350 horsepower. Several RH-400s are now at work at the massive Syncrude site, where they toil alongside cable shovels of the same capacity. In 1997, Terex Corporation purchased the rights to O&K's mining excavators from the 100-ton RH-30E up. They are now sold under Terex Mining, one of the Terex Companies. *Keith Haddock*

P&H H-1250. Harnischfeger's hydraulic excavators received a boost when the company entered into a technical collaboration with Germany's O&K from 1970 to 1974. During this time, Harnischfeger manufactured O&K excavators under license and sold them as P&H machines. The 3.25-cubic-yard O&K RH-25B was sold as the P&H RH-25 shovel and, after 1974, this machine became the P&H H-2500. P&H also revised its earlier models in 1976. The H-312 became the H-750, and the H-418 became the H-1250. The H-1250 (illustrated) is in the 30-ton weight class, and able to dig down 22 feet, 9 inches with its .875-cubic-yard hoe bucket. *Keith Haddock*

Poclain TU. In France, Georges Bataille, founder of Poclain, produced a truck-mounted loader in 1948. After further experimenting with hydraulic pumps and valves, he built one of the world's first fully hydraulic excavators, the model TU, in 1951. The tractor-drawn machine did not swing full circle, and the operator had to climb off the excavator and onto the tractor to move to a new digging location. Hydraulic power was obtained from a pump driven by the tractor. The Model TU in the picture was the second one made. The large bucket was presumably intended for re-handling stockpiled material. The bucket door was opened on release of a rope-operated latch. *Keith Haddock collection*

P&H 2250. Harnischfeger went to Germany again when it decided to enter the hydraulic mining shovel market. This time the excavators were designed and built in the company's own German facility, and the first to appear was the Model 1200 in 1979. Weighing 190 tons and carrying standard shovel or backhoe buckets of 13 cubic yards, the P&H 1200 stood firmly in the hydraulic heavyweight class. In 1988, Harnischfeger pushed upward to the 226-ton Model 1550, and followed up two years later with the 372-ton 2250. The standard buckets on these machines were 17 and 23 cubic yards respectively. They could be equipped to operate from a trailing power cable or with a single diesel engine. The diesel version of the 2250 ran with a Caterpillar 1,800-horsepower engine. Harnischfeger shipped its last hydraulic excavator in 1996. *Harnischfeger Corporation*

Poclain TL. With experience gleaned from its first machines, Poclain introduced several types and variations throughout the 1950s. It was usual practice to mount these early Poclains on the customer's own truck or, in the case of the Model TL in the picture, on an ex-army vehicle. And most of these models had the unusual feature of the hoist cylinder attached to the bucket arm instead of the boom. The TL of 1957 had a gravity-dumped bucket operated by a latch system, and auto-leveling capability from the pantograph linkage. The machine in the picture has two additional safety struts temporarily positioned to support the boom when roading from job to job. *Keith Haddock collection*

Poclain FC30. Poclain started the 1960s with a most successful machine, the full-swing TY-45, of which over 30,000 were eventually sold. Mounted on its own wheeled carrier, this machine earned Poclain worldwide attention and enabled the company to develop many new models of both crawler and wheeled excavators introduced throughout the 1960s, including the FC30, Poclain's smallest. This machine had a capacity of .5 cubic yards, weighed 9 tons, and ran a Deutz 33-horsepower engine. The hydraulic system in Poclain excavators utilized piston pumps and operated with oneof the highest pressures in the industry: up to 4,500 psi compared with an average of 2,500 psi on most other machines utilizing gear pumps. *Keith Haddock collection*

Poclain EC1000. Headlines were made in 1970 when the Poclain EC-1000 was displayed at the Paris Intermat equipment show. With an operating weight of approximately 160 tons, the EC-1000 could operate as a 10-cubic-yard front shovel or 6.5-cubic-yard backhoe. Power came from no fewer than three GM 8V71 diesel engines developing 840 horsepower. The independent crawler drive and tractor-type crawlers and sprockets endowed this monster machine with remarkable agility. There was absolutely no doubt that Poclain had built the world's largest hydraulic excavator up to that time. *Keith Haddock*

Poclain 1000CK. In 1975, the 1000CK replaced the EC1000, and subsequent upgrades increased its weight to 210 tons and standard shovel bucket to 13 cubic yards. In fact, the only thing smaller on this machine than on its predecessor was the number of engines. Poclain managed to obtain the required 900 horsepower from just two Cummins diesel engines. In 1976, Tenneco became a major shareholder in Poclain and, over the next few years, Poclain excavators and Tenneco's existing Case/Drott excavators were merged into a single line. Due to the recession in the early 1980s, the Case/Drott excavator line underwent some changes, and large mining excavators were discontinued. The last 1000CK left the factory in 1984 after 59 had been produced. *Gary Middlebrook*

Poclain 220. After Tenneco became a major shareholder in Poclain in 1976, the former Poclain excavators and Tenneco's existing Case/Drott excavators were merged into a single line. The Case/Drott machines covered the small machine market, while the Poclain machines took care of the larger end. The 50-ton Case Poclain 220, formerly the Poclain 220, operated with a 4.25-cubic-yard standard shovel bucket. This machine was later upgraded to the 220B in 1986. During the 1980s, Poclain excavators were made at the former Drott factory at Wausau, Wisconsin. Poclain's hydraulic technology survives today in the Case 88 Series excavators still manufactured at the former Poclain plant established at Crepy-en-Valois, France, in 1948. *Keith Haddock collection*

Samsung SE210 LC-2. Samsung Heavy Industries was established in South Korea in 1974 from predecessor Samsung companies. From 1983 to 1987, it manufactured Poclain excavators under license, and in 1993 a technical affiliation was initiated with Hitachi. In 1988, Samsung launched its in-house-designed SE Series excavators. These were upgraded to the Dash 1 models in 1991, the Dash 2 models in 1995, and the Dash 3 models in 1997. The following year, Sweden's Volvo acquired Samsung's excavator line, and continued producing the machines badged as Volvo products. At the time of the takeover, Samsung's line consisted of seven sizes of crawler machines from the 5.4-ton SE50-3 to the 48-ton SE450LC-2, and three wheeled models from 14.5 to 21 tons.

The SE210LC-2 in the picture dates from 1996. It carries a 1-cubic-yard standard bucket and tips the scales at 23 tons. *Keith Haddock*

Priestman VC-15. The VC (variable counterweight) excavators invented by Priestman are touted as the the hydraulic dragline. These machines can achieve an extremely long reach without increasing machine weight. As the arm extends outward, a moveable counterweight attached to the boom assembly moves backward. It not only balances the bucket and arm, but also counterbalances the weight of the boom, which is pivoted midship. Instead of a hydraulic cylinder, the machine utilizes a hydraulic winch to pull the bucket inward, offering superior control. Announced in 1982, the range included the 21-ton VC-15 and the 32-ton VC-20, with reaches of 50 feet and 65 feet, 6 inches respectively. Many of these machines were used to fight oil well fires in Kuwait during Operation Desert Storm. They are still available today from RB Cranes, Ltd. at Retford, England. *Keith Haddock*

Schield-Bantam C-450. Vern Schield incorporated the Schield-Bantam Company in 1946 at Waverly, Iowa, to build the truck-mounted excavators he had been building since 1941. Expanding into a successful line of crawler and truck-mounted cable excavators, the company released its first hydraulic excavator in 1964 after testing a pilot machine for a year. The C-450 crawler and T-450 truck-mounted excavators were powered by a Chrysler 105-horsepower engine, and could dig 18 feet deep with a standard .625-cubic-yard backhoe bucket. The crawler machine weighed 27,000 pounds. The C-450 became the C-450A in 1967, then was upgraded to the C-451 in 1972. In 1974, the Bantam .625-cubic-yard tradition was carried forward to the renumbered Model C166, which became the Koehring 166 in 1982. *Keith Haddock collection*

Schield-Bantam T-744. Joining several others in the field with a telescoping-type boom excavator, Schield-Bantam launched its Telescoop C-744 crawler and T-744 truck-mounted version in 1976. The excavators were powered by Detroit or Allis-Chalmers diesels of 107 flywheel-horsepower, and offered standard buckets of .75-cubic-yards capacity. Schield Bantam became a division of Koehring Company in 1963, but the excavators continued as Schield Bantam products at the Waverly plant until 1982, when the remaining Bantam products were sold under the Koehring name. Updated Telescoops (Koehring Models 4470 and 4475) appeared in the mid-1980s. In 1988, Koehring became a division of Terex Corporation after being purchased by Northwest Engineering two years earlier. *Keith Haddock*

Unit H-201-C. Started in 1926 as the Universal Power Shovel Company in Detroit, Michigan, by William Ford, brother of automaker Henry, the firm changed its name to the Unit Crane & Shovel Corporation in 1945. The company began making hydraulic excavators when it introduced the Model H-201-C Hydra-Unit in 1964. This .75-cubic-yard machine boasted independent hydrostatic travel motors in each crawler frame. In addition, each crawler frame could be hydraulically extended or retracted. The machine weighed just under 20 tons and power came from a GM 120-horsepower engine. The unit expanded its hydraulic excavators to a full lineup with the 50-ton H-471 by 1975, but sales dropped drastically and the last Unit excavator was shipped in 1982. In 1988, Offshore Crane Company purchased the company. *Keith Haddock*

Volvo EC360. This 40-ton EC360 is one of a line of excavators offered by Sweden's Volvo Construction Equipment. It carries a standard 2-cubic-yard bucket and is also available with a quick-hitch attachment, allowing a multitude of different buckets and tools to be interchanged quickly. After dropping its Akerman-derived excavator line acquired in 1991, Volvo acquired Samsung's excavator line in 1998 and continued their manufacture in Korea. In 2002, Volvo upgraded its excavator line to the B Series, distinguished by less-rounded new-style cabs, and the former Cummins engines replaced by Volvo's own turbocharged engines meeting the latest emission standards in Europe. Volvo's excavator line consists of six basic B Series models, from the 15-ton EC140B to the 50-ton EC460B, plus five wheeled models and a line of mini excavators. *Volvo Construction Equipment*

Warner & Swasey Hopto 1900. The huge Hopto 1900 was America's largest hydraulic excavator when introduced in 1972. This 100-ton, 4-cubic-yard backhoe came equipped with two GM 8V-71 diesels totaling 616 horsepower. Each engine was coupled to two gear-type pumps in the low-pressure hydraulic system, which operated at 2,750 psi. The 1900 boasted a digging depth of 35 feet, 7 inches and reach at ground level of 48 feet, 10 inches. The most amazing thing about this outsized machine was its eight-motor tractor-type undercarriage utilizing two hydraulic motors at both ends of each crawler assembly. The four driving sprockets were driven by spur gears and planetary reductions consisting of no fewer than 48 gears! The 1900 enjoyed a lengthy production run, latterly as the Badger Hopto 1900. The last one was shipped in 1990. *Keith Haddock*

Warner & Swasey Hopto 200TM. The Badger Machine Company, incorporated in 1946, developed a tractor-mounted hydraulic backhoe called a Hopto (Hydraulically Operated Power Take-Off). From 1958 to 1977, Badger was owned by the Warner & Swasey Company, who developed the Hopto idea into a line of crawler-, wheel-, and truck-mounted hydraulic excavators. The .375-yard Model 200TM shown here, dating from the early 1960s, could be mounted on any truck of minimum 18,200-pounds GVW, or on a purpose-built carrier by the Duplex Division of Warner & Swasey Company. From 1977, the Hopto machines were made by Badger Construction Equipment Company at their factory in Winona, Minnesota; the last one, a Model 900B, was shipped in 1991. *Keith Haddock*

Warner & Swasey Hopto 311. The introduction of the Hopto 311 backhoe by Warner & Swasey in 1974 heralded a new line of excavators from the company. Along with the 27-ton 211 and 57-ton 411, the 311 sported a new cab design, tractor-type undercarriage, and a Power-Demand hydraulic system that automatically adjusted force and speed to the job requirements. The 311 hoe could dig down 24 feet, 7 inches with its standard arm, and could reach over 34 feet at ground elevation. It weighed 37 tons, and power came from a 235-horsepower GM diesel engine. From 1977, the Hopto machines were made by Badger Construction Equipment Company at their factory in Winona, Minnesota. The last 311 was shipped in 1991, when the Hopto line was discontinued. In 2002, Badger Equipment Company manufactures and markets its own line of Hydroscopic excavators. *Keith Haddock*

CHAPTER 13

STRIPPING SHOVELS

Stripping shovels are the kings of the mobile machine world, and include the 15,000-ton Captain shovel, the heaviest piece of equipment ever to move under its own power on land. Stripping shovels work in surface mines or large quarries, and, as their name implies, they strip away earth and rock (overburden) to uncover valuable minerals like coal, ironstone, or limestone. They work in the same way as regular cable shovels, but unlike their smaller counterparts, they don't need to load another vehicle to carry away the material. Stripping shovels are of necessity built in huge proportions, giving them a much greater range. This allows them to dig from a high face, swing around, and dump the material clear of the working area.

In operation, the stripping shovel sits on top of the mineral it is uncovering, and moves forward as the digging face advances. The shovel digs long strips or cuts, and casts the overburden into the adjacent cut from which the mineral has already been removed.

Bucyrus 175-B. The Bucyrus Company built the first full-circle long-boom stripping shovel in the United States soon after it purchased the Vulcan Steam Shovel Company in 1910. Known as the Class 5 and built to Vulcan designs, the fully revolving shovel carried a 1.5-cubic-yard dipper on a 55-foot boom. The following year, Bucyrus engineers designed two sizes of stripping shovels with pioneering features: the 2.5-cubic-yard 150-B and the 3.5-cubic-yard 175-B. They were rail-mounted, steam-powered machines, and the first with a three-point suspension system utilizing an equalizer beam and screw jacks for leveling the machine. By the end of 1912, one each of these two shovels was already at work, stripping coal in the southeast Kansas coal fields. *Keith Haddock collection*

Because of the huge costs and the engineering and manufacturing challenges involved, only a very small number of companies have ventured into designing and building these giant specialized machines. In the United States, two companies have dominated manufacture: Marion Power Shovel Company and Bucyrus-Erie Company. The latter, now known as Bucyrus International, Inc., purchased Marion Power Shovel in 1997. Before the merger, these two companies were archrivals for decades, vying time and time again for the latest innovation or the largest machine.

With a few exceptions, the Marion and Bucyrus companies have supplied the entire world market with large stripping shovels. Several other manufacturers did produce this type of machine in the early part of the twentieth century. They included Whitaker, Grossmith, and Taylor & Hubbard in England, and Browning in the United States. In addition, Ransomes & Rapier, Ltd. built stripping shovels in England from 1934 to 1943. The German firm Menck built some in the 1920s, and a few have been built in the former Soviet Union for use in that country. But there was never any serious competition for Marion and Bucyrus, whose names will forever be synonymous with stripping shovels.

The very first stripping shovels were actually steam railroad shovels fitted with a long boom. Vulcan built the earliest documented in 1899. But even when fitted with a long boom, a railroad shovel was severely limited as a stripping shovel because of its limited-swinging boom. When the big, fully revolving shovels became popular after 1910, they were also mounted on rails, and required two sets of parallel railroad tracks to support their weight.

Stripping shovels first traveled on crawler tracks in the early 1920s. Crawlers were slow to be accepted at first because of their much higher cost, about 40 percent more than the traditional rail mountings. But one or two pioneering owners found the extra cost was soon offset by the shovel's superior mobility when not limited by rails. Also, since the ground crew could be reduced from about eight men to one, crawler mountings soon became very popular, and orders for rail-mounted shovels diminished.

Bucyrus 320-B. Following Marion's introduction of the world's largest shovel, the Model 350, in 1923, Bucyrus offered a similar-sized machine in 1924: the Bucyrus 320-B in the 8-cubic-yard class, weighing some 430 tons. Initially steam driven and rail mounted, crawler tracks and electric power were offered on later models. The 320-B proved to be a great success, as 29 shovels plus eight dragline versions were sold before the last one was shipped in 1930. During this era, Bucyrus opted for twin dipper handles (sticks) driven by rack and pinions mounted outside the boom, while Marion preferred a single dipper stick running through the upper portion of the boom. In later years, both companies would build both types. *Keith Haddock collection*

Bucyrus 200-B. Carrying dippers from 5 to 7 cubic yards, the 200-B was designed on similar lines to the larger 320-B. Introduced in 1927, this stripper weighed 372 tons in operation. It produced well where the cover was not too deep, such as at this U.S. Gypsum Company's quarry near Alabaster, Michigan. The electrically powered 200-B shown is actually the first of 13 shipped. The same year the 200-B was introduced, its manufacturer, the Bucyrus Company, merged with the Erie Steam Shovel Company to form Bucyrus-Erie Company. Consequently, later 200-Bs were sold as Bucyrus-Erie products. The last remaining 200-B is preserved at the Reynolds Alberta Museum at Wetaskiwin, Alberta, Canada. *Keith Haddock collection*

Although some stripping shovels were mounted on two large crawler tracks, by far the majority has been mounted on an eight-crawler undercarriage with the crawler assemblies mounted in pairs at each corner of the machine. The first application of crawler tracks on a stripping shovel was in 1925, when Bucyrus replaced the rail mountings on its large model 7.5-cubic-yard 320-B stripping shovel with crawler tracks. Marion quickly responded by fitting crawler tracks on its record-size Model 350, which had an 8-cubic-yard dipper.

Bucyrus and Marion adopted entirely different engineering solutions to support these mammoth machines when traveling over uneven ground. In order to minimize stress in the lower frame, Bucyrus utilized a power-driven screw system on two of the legs supporting the crawler assemblies, while the other two were mounted under an equalizing beam, which compensated for uneven terrain during traveling. Marion pioneered a hydraulic system where each two-crawler assembly was attached to a large vertical hydraulic cylinder. By directing hydraulic fluid to and from the four cylinders, the machine stayed on an even keel. On the early machines, the ground man controlled this leveling device, but later machines employed a pendulum system to automatically level

Bucyrus-Erie 1050-B. The innovative 950-B stripping shovel, launched in 1935, was uprated to the 1050-B in 1941. Design features on both these machines included a single tubular dipper handle operated by wire ropes instead of racks, a two-part boom pinned at its center to eliminate bending stresses, an automatic hydraulic leveling system dispensing with the earlier screw-types, and a counterbalanced hoist system. That elevator-like structure at the back of the machine houses a moveable weight that is hoisted up and down in unison with the bucket. It saves electrical energy by compensating for the weight of the empty bucket. Twelve 1050-Bs were made between 1941 and 1960 having dipper capacities ranging from 33 to 45 cubic yards. Machine weight was approximately 1,500 tons. *Urs Peyer*

Bucyrus-Erie 1650-B. Designed with all the successful features on B-E's earlier stripping shovels, the first of the super strippers from Bucyrus-Erie was shipped from the factory in 1955. Designated the 1650-B and named the "River Queen," the first machine went to work with a 55-cubic-yard dipper for Peabody Coal Company at the River Queen Mine, Kentucky. The other four 1650-B's subsequently shipped up to 1964, ranged up to 70-cubic-yards capacity. The picture shows the second 1650-B just starting work at Sunny Hill Coal Company's mine at New Lexington, Ohio, in 1958. This machine wields a dipper of 65 cubic yards, and total machine weight tops out at 2,450 tons. *Keith Haddock collection*

Bucyrus-Erie 3850-B. The picture shows the largest shovel ever built by Bucyrus-Erie Company. It was the second of two Model 3850-B stripping shovels purchased by Peabody Coal Company, and was erected at the River King Mine in Illinois in 1964. The cavernous dipper held 140 cubic yards, the boom was 200 feet long, and this second largest of all stripping shovels weighed approximately 9,350 tons. The first 3850-B shovel was announced in 1960 with a slightly longer boom at 210 feet and a dipper holding 115 cubic yards. It went to work at the Sinclair Mine in Kentucky in 1962, with a 115-yard dipper. The first 3850-B finished work in 1985, and the second finished work in 1992. *Bucyrus International, Inc.*

the machine. By the mid-1930s, all manufacturers had adopted the hydraulic leveling system. These eight-crawler mountings, pioneered in the 1920s, became the standard configuration for all giant stripping shovels in later decades.

Up to the late 1920s, rail-mounted and crawler-mounted stripping shovels were propelled by power from one of the motors in the revolving frame. Power was transmitted through the center pintle via a series of bevel and spur gears to the driving wheels or tracks. Since then, stripping shovels have been provided with independent propel motors for each crawler assembly. On the larger machines, eight powerful motors are installed, one to drive each crawler track. Despite all this power, the top speed of a stripping shovel is only about a quarter-mile-per-hour. That doesn't seem like much, but a shovel's worth is measured by how much material it can move in an hour, not how fast it can travel. In fact, when a shovel is moving, it's not making any money for its owners.

The first stripping shovels were powered by steam, but electric-powered machines soon followed, and since the mid-1920s almost all have been powered by electricity. In 1919, both Marion and Bucyrus applied an improved control system to their electric machines known as Ward Leonard control. This produces precise variable speed, similar to steam power, and proved well-suited to excavators. Ward Leonard uses AC-powered motor generator sets to power DC motors for the machine's motions. With Ward Leonard control, maximum pull is available at motor stall speed, and a motor will not burn out when overloaded. Bucyrus first applied Ward Leonard control on a 225-B stripping shovel, while Marion put it on the Model 300-E. Since then, Ward Leonard control has been standard on all stripping shovels.

The idea of stripping coal with large shovels caught on very quickly, spurred on by the demands of World War I. By the time World War II arrived, the coal stripping industry was very well established with modern stripping equipment wielding buckets of up to 40-cubic-yards capacity. During the 1950s, the boom in coal-fired power created a demand for even

Bucyrus-Erie 1950-B. This shovel was christened the Silver Spade, and was the first of two built by Bucyrus-Erie Company for the Hanna Coal Company, a division of Consolidation Coal Company. The Silver Spade began uncovering coal in 1965 near Georgetown, Ohio. Equipped with a 105-cubic-yard dipper on a 200-foot boom, the machine weighs approximately 7,200 tons. The 1950-B's most distinguishing feature is its knee-action front end, Bucyrus-Erie's only model to be so equipped. In this arrangement, the dipper arm is pivoted to a moveable stiff leg instead of being mounted on the boom. Its numerous advantages include increased bank penetration force and elimination of bending stresses on the boom. The Silver Spade still works for the same company, not far from where it was built. The other 1950-B, named the Gem, started work in 1967 and was scrapped in 1992. *Keith Haddock*

larger, more efficient stripping machines. The Hanna Coal Company (now Consolidation Coal Company) ordered a shovel of record size for its operations in eastern Ohio. The Marion-built monster, the Model 5760, wielded a 60-cubic-yard dipper and could tackle a face over 100 feet high. Christened the Mountaineer, this giant shovel took its first bite in January 1956, and the era of the "super strippers" was born.

After the Mountaineer, the size of stripping shovels increased astronomically. Almost immediately, Bucyrus-Erie Company (B-E) responded with a shovel of similar size, the 55-cubic-yard 1650-B River Queen ordered by Peabody Coal Company for its River Queen Mine in Kentucky. Shovel size records were continuously broken in the 1960s. The decade kicked off with what would turn out to be B-E's largest shovel model, the 3850-B. Two were ordered by Peabody Coal Company and shipped in 1962 and 1964 with buckets of 115 and 140 cubic yards, respectively. In between these, B-E shipped the 90-cubic-yard 1850-B in 1963. Rounding out B-E's contribution to the super stripper era were two Model 1950-Bs shipped in 1965 and 1967. These, known as the Silver Spade and the Gem, swung buckets of 105 and 130 cubic yards, respectively.

Over at the Marion stable, two giant 5860 shovels with 80-cubic-yard buckets were shipped in 1965 and 1966. And in 1965, Marion broke the shovel size record for the last time when it shipped the incredible Marion 6360, named The Captain, ending the race for the largest stripping shovel ever built. Purchased by the Southwestern Illinois Coal Corporation to work at their Captain Mine near Percy, Illinois, the behemoth weighed an estimated 15,000 tons and carried a bucket of 180 cubic yards. Marion built three more monster shovels after the 6360 went to work: a Model 5960 in 1969 swinging a 125-cubic-yard bucket, and two Model 5900 shovels in 1968 and 1971 with 105-cubic-yard buckets. The last 5900 was the last stripping shovel to be built by any manufacturer.

Although the giant stripping shovels served their owners handsomely and uncovered huge amounts of coal to meet the hungry appetites of the coal-fired generating stations, they have worked their way to obsolescence. The main reason for their demise is that during the 1980s, the United States saw the rapid rise in coal output from the West, particularly from Wyoming. Coal there is found in very thick seams and under very shallow overburden. Cheaper to mine, and low in sulfur, this Western coal has captured markets traditionally supplied by coal mines in the Midwest, especially in the Illinois Basin, domain of the big stripping shovels. Today, only a handful of stripping shovels still operate, but the coal-fired plants still run at maximum capacity burning coal shipped from the West.

Marion 271. Marion Steam Shovel Company put to work its first stripping shovel in 1911 at Mission Field near Danville, Illinois. Known as the Model 250 and built on solid, heavy-duty designs, it was a steam-powered, rail-mounted machine, having a working weight of 150 tons. It carried a 3.5-cubic-yard dipper on a 65-foot boom. Even at that early date, Marion had pioneered the concept of utilizing a hydraulic cylinder under each corner for equalizing stresses and leveling the machine. It was a resounding success, and set the stage for large-scale mechanized stripping of minerals by surface mining methods. In 1913, Marion brought out the 5-cubic-yard Model 271 with similar design features to the 250. The 271 briefly held the title of the world's largest operating shovel. *Keith Haddock collection*

Marion 5560. Marion introduced the 5560 in 1932 as its biggest shovel yet. Like the large Bucyrus-Erie shovels of the day, the 5560 had a counterbalanced hoist system. But Marion opted for a rack-and-pinion system to raise and lower the counterweight instead of the full-rope system used by the competition. The machine in the picture handles a 20-cubic-yard dipper on a 95-foot boom. It is one of the first Series 5560s, of which four were built. Soon after Bucyrus-Erie came out with their record-breaking 950-B in 1935, Marion upgraded the 5560 to compete. Its capacity was boosted to 32 cubic yards, made possible by using high-tensile steel in the front end and more efficient electric motors. Its weight was increased to 1,550 tons, some 345 tons heavier than the previous 5560. *Keith Haddock collection*

Marion 360. In 1923, Marion broke the world size record again with the huge Model 350 stripping shovel. Weighing no less than 560 tons, this giant swung an 8-cubic-yard dipper on a 90-foot boom. Initially rail-mounted, the 350s were equipped with crawler tracks after 1925. The same machine was also offered as a dragline, designated as Model 360 and available with steam or electric power. Drive to the crawler tracks was transmitted from the main hoist motor in the revolving frame through the center pintle and out to each of the four crawler assemblies through a series of shafts and gears. The 350 Series machines were a great success, with 47 units sold before production ended in 1929. The last to operate is shown preserved at the Diplomat Mine Museum near Forestburg, Alberta, Canada. *Keith Haddock*

Marion 5760. The Hanna Coal Company (now Consolidation Coal Company) ordered a shovel of record proportions for its coal mining operations in eastern Ohio. Christened the Mountaineer, the Marion-built 2,750-ton monster, wielded a dipper rated at 65 cubic yards on a boom 150 feet long. The single feature that most fascinated visitors was the three-passenger elevator installed in the 6-foot-diameter center pin. The machine also featured Marion's patent knee-action crowd, which first appeared on the 35-cubic-yard 5561 shovel of 1940. Knee-action takes the weight and bending off the boom because the dipper stick is mounted on a moveable and independent stiff leg, and the crowd mechanism is located in the gantry. The Mountaineer worked until 1979 and was scrapped in 1988. *Keith Haddock*

Marion 5761. After the Mountaineer went to work, four more 5760s were built before Marion upgraded it to the 5761 in 1959. Although keeping the same dipper capacity at 65 cubic yards, the new machine boasted more power, greater digging range, and almost 1,000 tons extra weight over its predecessor. With its 170-foot boom, the first 5761 captured the title of the world's largest shovel. It soon established itself as the standard stripping machine in many Midwestern U.S. coal mines. The 5761 illustrated started work in 1968 at the Mecco Mine near Lafayette, Illinois. It was one of 16 shipped from the factory from 1959 to 1970. *Keith Haddock*

Marion 5323. Not classed as a super stripper, the smaller-sized 5323 found a niche in certain quarries and mines with relatively low overburden depth. Although only nine 5323s were built, they were shipped over a 20-year period beginning in 1941. This model was derived from the earlier stripping shovel Models 5320, 5321, and 5322 of the 1930s. The 5323 shovels operated with boom lengths and dipper sizes tailor-made for each application. They ranged from 11 cubic yards on a 160-foot boom, to 20 cubic yards on a 105-foot boom. The 5323 in the picture was the last one shipped (1961), and carried a 17-cubic-yard dipper on a 145-foot boom. It worked in an ironstone quarry in central England for the United Steel Companies, Ltd. *Keith Haddock*

Marion 6360. The race for the largest stripping shovel ended in 1965 when Marion broke the final record for shovel size. The incredible Marion 6360, named The Captain, was purchased by the Southwestern Illinois Coal Corporation (now Arch Coal, Inc.) to work at their Captain Mine near Percy, Illinois. The 6360's dipper was rated at 180 cubic yards, and its boom length of 215 feet provided an operating radius of 220 feet. If scales could have weighed this behemoth, they would have read around 15,000 tons, making this the heaviest single machine of any type ever to move under its own power on land. Its eight-crawler undercarriage, with 15-foot-high crawlers, was the same design Marion used when it built two giant transporters still used today for moving rockets to their launch pads at Cape Canaveral, Florida. *Keith Haddock*

Marion 5860. Getting up there in size is this 80-cubic-yard stripping shovel. Marion built only two 5860s and shipped them in 1965 and 1966. They were both owned by Consolidation Coal Company (Consol), and worked at the Norris and Burning Star #3 mines in Illinois. Weighing some 5,175 tons, the 5860s were built at the peak of the super stripping shovel era. They did the job they were designed to do and made money for their owners, but they have long since met the cutting torch. The Norris machine was actually dismantled and the lower works used to mount the Bucyrus-Erie 5872-WX bucket-wheel excavator at the Captain Mine, Illinois (see chapter 17). *Keith Haddock*

Ruston No. 300. Ruston & Hornsby, Ltd. of Lincoln, England, built large stripping shovels prior to merging with Bucyrus-Erie Company to form Ruston-Bucyrus, Ltd. in 1930. The No. 300 was one of the world's largest when introduced in 1923, and in the same 8-cubic-yard size class as the Marion 350 and Bucyrus 320-B. The picture shows an electric rail-mounted version undergoing tests at the Lincoln factory. Boom length is 90 feet and machine-operating weight is 468 tons. Dragline versions were also offered for this machine with steam or electric power options. *Keith Haddock collection*

Rapier 5367. Going to work in 1943, the 5367 was the last stripping shovel Ransomes & Rapier built. The demands of World War II had brought stripping shovel production to an end. Over an eight-year period, Rapier had built 13 of these giant stripping shovels as well as some smaller ones. The Rapier 5360 Series machines were somewhat larger than the former Marion 350s on which they were based. Most had booms 104 feet long, and dippers from 9 to 11 cubic yards. They were all rail-mounted on twin rail tracks, and electrically operated. The Rapier-Marion agreement ended in 1936, and after that Rapier incorporated its own design features in subsequent models. *Keith Haddock*

Wilson Crane Navvy. Here's where it all began: John H. Wilson & Co. in England built the world's first fully revolving stripping shovel in 1900. Operated by Lloyds Ironstone Company to uncover iron ore, it carried a dipper of 1.5-cubic-yard capacity on a boom 70 feet long, providing a 60-foot dumping radius. The 78-ton unit was mounted on rail tracks and had a wire rope swing system. It was regarded as a marvel for its day when most excavation work was done by hand. This first stripper was so successful that it had a working life of 54 years! *Keith Haddock collection*

Rapier 5360. The long-established firm of Ransomes & Rapier, Ltd. of Ipswich, England, sold its first steam shovel in 1914. Then, in 1924, the company entered into an agreement with Marion Steam Shovel Company to build certain Marion-designed excavators under license in the United Kingdom. The first Rapier stripping shovel was based on the Marion 350 shovel, and designated the Model 5360. It went to work in 1934 stripping iron ore in central England. The machine in the picture is another 5360 working for Park Gate Iron & Steel Company in central England with an 8-cubic-yard dipper on a 105-foot boom. *Keith Haddock*

CHAPTER 14

WALKING DRAGLINES

Walking draglines belong to a family of excavators that includes some of the most massive machines ever to move on land. These monster machines work in surface mines where they move vast quantities of earth to uncover coal and other valuable minerals. Where the excavated material is to be deposited within the range of the machine, and where the geology of a site permits, a dragline is usually found to be the most efficient machine for bulk excavation.

A walking dragline looks like a large crane, but instead of carrying a hook to lift loads, it carries a digging bucket suspended on the end of its boom by

Bucyrus-Monighan 7-W. During the early 1930s, Bucyrus-Erie Company (now Bucyrus International, Inc.) entered the walking dragline market by purchasing a controlling interest in the Monighan Manufacturing Corporation of Chicago, Illinois, the first company to build a walking dragline. Although under Bucyrus control, the Monighan plant and its management remained an independent unit, and new machines were designed and produced under the Bucyrus-Monighan banner until 1946. One such machine was the 7-W, the first of which left the Chicago plant in 1942. The one in the picture utilizes a 7-cubic-yard bucket on a 140-foot boom to uncover coal for Sunnyhill Coal Company at New Lexington, Ohio. Most 7-Ws were electric powered, but a diesel version was available with a Cooper-Bessemer 440-horsepower diesel running at 525 rpm. The 7-W remained current as a Bucyrus-Erie machine until the last one was shipped in 1971. *Keith Haddock collection*

hoist ropes. In action, the bucket is dragged toward the machine by another set of ropes, called drag ropes, as it collects its load. When full, the bucket is hoisted, the machine swings, and dumps the load in a pile to the side. To swing, the machine revolves on a large roller bearing placed between the upper revolving frame and the circular base on which the machine sits while digging. In surface mining operations, the material is usually dumped into the empty cut alongside where the mineral has already been extracted.

Chapter 11 mentioned the versatility of a crawler-mounted universal (convertible) excavator with several different front-end attachments, including a dragline. These machines were ideally adapted to all kinds of excavation work where mobility and flexibility were key. But today, crawler draglines are only found in the larger sizes (over 6 cubic yards), and hydraulic excavators have largely superseded the small crawler draglines. With the exception of a few large crawler machines (see chapter 11), draglines over 10-cubic-yard capacity are normally of the walking type. This is because a walking dragline usually works on top of the excavation, on relatively soft ground. Here, a crawler machine of equivalent size would require tracks in multiple numbers, and in unmanageable widths, to support the machine's tremendous weight. This would be a costly alternative to the simple walking system found on walking draglines.

Dragline booms are suspended in several different ways, depending on their length and manufacturer's preference. Smaller walking draglines use multiple-part ropes passing back and forth from the boom point to the gantry. The rope is wound on an independently powered boom hoist drum on the machinery deck. This "live boom" feature is not usually found on the larger draglines. Boom cable suspension usually includes a secondary safety rope, which is tied in place at the boom's working angle. This rope is capable of supporting the boom in case the main rope or the boom hoist mechanism fails.

On larger draglines, no boom hoist mechanism is provided. The main hoist drum raises the boom on these machines. The boom hoist rope is temporarily wrapped around the hoist drum, and weaved through several parts to an intermediate mast that supports the

Bucyrus-Erie 650-B. Bucyrus-Erie (B-E) shipped the first 650-B in 1946. Its standard boom of 275 feet in length could handle a bucket carrying 15 cubic yards. Some machines were shipped with booms up to 235 feet for greater reach in certain applications, but in this configuration bucket size was limited to 10 cubic yards. The 800-ton 650-B was based on the earlier Monighan machines, retaining the same walking system, but significantly modified with B-E content to cater for this size of machine—larger than anything Monighan had produced. It was available only as a straight electric machine. The 650-B in the picture is uncovering limestone for the Carbon Limestone Company (now Essroc) at Lowellville, Ohio. *Keith Haddock collection*

Bucyrus-Erie 2550-W. The 1960s was regarded as the decade of the giants, a time when the two leading manufactures of walking draglines (Bucyrus and Marion) vied with each other to produce the biggest machines ever to roam on the earth. At the forefront of Bucyrus-Erie's dragline lineup in 1964 was the 2550-W, the largest dragline yet built by the company. Swinging a 75-cubic-yard bucket on a 275-foot boom, the 2550-W weighed 4,410 tons in operating condition. Bucyrus-Erie engineers used the huge proportions and powerful design of the 2550-W as a blueprint to design even larger draglines. The 2550-W was upgraded to the 85-cubic-yard 2560-W in 1969, and then to the first 2570-W in 1971, which carried a 100-cubic-yard bucket. *Bucyrus International, Inc.*

boom. The mast supports the boom by fixed-length bridge-strand cables, so that the mast and boom are raised in unison. When the boom reaches its predetermined working angle, it is tied back to the A-frame or gantry with further bridge-strand cables, or pinned to a solid connecting structure, depending on the machine design. Once the boom is in place, the hoist rope can be dispensed with, since a dragline does not normally change its boom angle during operation. The boom angle is set to provide a certain dumping radius complying with the original machine specification, along with the boom length and bucket capacity. The mine's engineer determines the machine's specification based on the mine's production requirements, site geology, and geotechnical conditions.

Raising and lowering a large dragline boom is a major task, and may occur only two or three times in a 20-year period. It is usual to have a dragline manufacturer's representative on site to oversee the raising and lowering of the boom, since the job is not routine for mine maintenance staff. Most dragline booms are equipped with a red light at the top to warn low-flying aircraft to keep clear. The drag ropes are guided through a fairlead consisting of a series of sheaves, which move to accommodate the constantly changing rope angle between the bucket and the machine as it swings. The fairlead also accommodates the changing fleet angle of the rope as it winds on its drum.

The drag and hoist machinery are termed the "draw works" and may have two or more DC motors to power each motion. The motors work together, and are geared directly through intermediate shafts to the main "bull" gear on the hoist or drag shaft. No clutches or brakes are needed during digging, as the DC motors allow control of speed and direction through the operator's levers in the cab. However, the hoist, drag, and swing motions are provided with independent air-operated brakes, which are applied when at rest.

Some intermediate-sized draglines (up to 20 cubic yards) use only one DC electric motor to power both the hoist and drag winding drums. In this arrangement, the drums are connected to their drive shafts through air-operated clutches. When released, individual air-operated hand brakes control rotation of each drum. The hoist and drag cables are wound on their drums so that when both drums are engaged to turn, one winds its rope in, while the other unwinds its rope. This system is called "synchronous control." Its big advantage, apart from the lower cost of utilizing only one motor, is that when both drums are engaged,

Bucyrus-Erie 4250-W; Big Muskie. Nearing completion after a four-year design-and-erection period, the Bucyrus-Erie 4250-W Big Muskie would break all records in dragline size. At 220 cubic yards, its bucket was the largest ever suspended from a boom, and its working weight was calculated to be around 14,500 tons. No wonder this monster became the most famous of the large stripping machines used in the surface mining industry. The house measured 150 feet 6 inches long, and the machine measured overall 151 feet wide by 487 feet in length, almost 1.5 times the length of a football field. Notice the two fairlead assemblies. Each will carry the two 5-inch-diameter drag ropes, the biggest ever manufactured at that time. Another four will hoist the bucket. In the picture the boom is not yet attached to the machine, but the mast legs are in place. *Bucyrus International, Inc.*

Bucyrus-Erie 4250-W. Big Muskie, the world's largest walking dragline is shown swinging a 220-cubic-yard bucket on a 310-foot boom at the Central Ohio Coal Company's Muskingum Mine soon after it first went to work in 1969. Ten 1,000-horsepower DC electric motors powered the hoist, eight 1,000-horsepower motors powered the drag motion, and another ten 625-horsepower motors powered the swing. Unlike other walking draglines, the 4250-W employed a walking system utilizing four giant hydraulic jacks, which lifted the machine's base entirely off the ground to take a step. Big Muskie's work ended in 1991 because markets for the high-sulfur coal at the Muskingum Mine had diminished. In 1999, Big Muskie was cut up for scrap, but one of the 220-cubic-yard buckets was saved as an epitaph to one of the world's greatest engineering feats. *Bucyrus International, Inc.*

the force of the loaded bucket pulling on the drag rope when it pays out helps to hoist the bucket to its dumping position. Similarly, the weight of the empty bucket when being lowered back into the cut helps to wind in the drag rope. This arrangement also results in greatly reducing the amount of wear on the brakes.

The walking system on a dragline is a very simple operation. To take one step, the shoes are rotated in the direction of travel by the walk shaft and an eccentric drive, so they touch the ground simultaneously. Further rotation of the walk shaft lifts the leading edge of the dragline's circular base, or tub, off the ground. In this raised position, the machine is supported on three points: the two shoes and the tub trailing edge. Continued eccentric rotation slides the machine ahead one step (about 6 feet), and gently lowers the machine back on its base. The shoes continue to rotate, and the process is repeated for the next step. Steering the machine is just a matter of swinging the machine to point in the desired direction when the shoes are off the ground. On the smaller draglines, the shoes are powered by a single large shaft running across the width of the machine, and driven by gearing from the propel motor. Separate walk shafts, one on each side of the machine, are utilized on larger draglines. An electronic timing device synchronizes the two shoes so they rotate in unison. Walking draglines always walk backwards, because they must walk away from the hole or pit being excavated.

An important advantage of the walking dragline is the very low ground pressure exerted by the machine's large-diameter base on which the machine sits while digging. When walking, only about 80 percent of the machine's weight is transferred to the shoes, which can also be made with large dimensions to reduce ground pressure. The tub carries the other 20 percent of the weight as it drags along the ground.

The first dragline machine was home-built by Page & Schnable, a contractor working on the Chicago Drainage Canal in 1904. Following its success, Page and others started building the new type of excavator. These early machines were mounted on rails or on skids and rollers, and pulled themselves along by means of their bucket, a very slow and clumsy

Bucyrus-Erie 380-W. Not all dragline innovations of the past three decades were of large size. With the rapid increase in the production of surface-mined coal in the 1970s, operators needed a machine that could be dismantled quickly and moved to a new location. Draglines taking many months to move and erect were not viable for small pockets of coal and short-term contracts. So, the modular dragline was born. Bucyrus-Erie was first with its 380-W in 1978, a machine in the 10- to 16-cubic-yard size. It was offered with diesel or electric power, and designed in modular units that were bolted together instead of welded. Thus, these machines could be dismantled and re-erected in a matter of a few weeks, and the diesel versions did not have to wait for a power source to be installed. *Bucyrus International, Inc.*

Bucyrus-Erie 680-W. Following its success with the 380-W, Bucyrus-Erie expanded the modular dragline concept into larger machines. The first 680-W dragline went to work in 1982, and five were sold up to 1988. Their booms varied from 190 to 260 feet, and buckets from 18 to 26 cubic yards. Although based on the proven modular concept, the 680-W represented a clean sheet design incorporating several new features and the latest technology, including a state-of-the-art controlled-frequency AC electric-drive system. This utilized independent AC electric motors for drag, swing, and propel. The 680-W in the picture carries a 25-cubic-yard bucket on a 225-foot boom and has an operating weight of 1,125 tons. It works for the Oxford Mining Company in Ohio. *Keith Haddock*

method. Starting in 1911, some draglines became self-propelling when fitted with crawler tracks. Then in 1913 Oscar Martinson, of the Monighan Machine Company, invented the radical idea of attaching two moveable shoes, one on each side of the dragline's revolving frame. This idea forever changed the way draglines move. In 1932, Monighan, with its patented propel system, was taken over by Bucyrus-Erie Company (now Bucyrus International, Inc.), which soon designed larger draglines incorporating Monighan patents.

The British firm of Ransomes & Rapier, Ltd. designed its first dragline in 1938. This was the W170, carrying a 4-cubic-yard bucket on a 135-foot boom. Larger machines followed, and by 1951 the Rapier W1400, at 1,880-tons operating weight with 282-foot boom, claimed the title of the world's largest dragline. The "world's largest" title was claimed once again by Rapier in 1961 when it launched its W1800, this time weighing 2,000 tons and carrying a bucket of 40 cubic yards. Bucyrus International purchased the patents and manufacturing rights of Ransomes & Rapier walking draglines in 1988.

The Marion Steam Shovel Company entered the walking dragline market in 1939 with the Model 7200, handling a 5-cubic-yard bucket on a 120-foot boom. Three short years later, Marion unveiled the world's largest walking dragline. A huge machine for its day, the 7800 could carry 30 cubic yards on a 185-foot boom. Marion, along with archrival Bucyrus, went on to produce several world-record-breaking super draglines during the 1960s, the decade of the big strippers. Marion startled the dragline world when it launched the 85-cubic-yard Model 8800 in 1963, then followed up with 130-cubic-yard and 145-cubic-yard machines in 1966 and 1967.

As far as draglines are concerned, the 1960s ended with a bang. Big Muskie (Model 4250-W), the most famous of all draglines, took its first steps in 1969. It earned Bucyrus-Erie Company the distinction of the largest bucket ever to swing from an excavator. Big Muskie, with its massive 220-cubic-yard capacity, 310-foot boom, and operating weight of 14,500 tons, walked away with the "biggest ever" title. None larger has ever been built.

Bucyrus-Erie 1570-W. In the 70-cubic-yard class, the 1570-W is regarded today as a mid-sized machine when it comes to walking draglines. The one in the picture works at Estevan, Saskatchewan, uncovering coal for Luscar, Ltd. It has a 320-foot boom and an operating weight of 3,745 tons. The 1570-W was a best-seller for Bucyrus, who shipped some 46 units from 1973 to 1991. Typical of all large electric excavators, the 1570-W dragline utilizes the Ward-Leonard system of speed control. With this system, AC-powered motor-generator sets provide variable voltage to the DC motors for the various machine functions. With Ward-Leonard control, maximum pull is available at stall speed, and a motor will not burn out when overloaded. *Keith Haddock*

As with the stripping shovels, described in chapter 13, Bucyrus and Marion dominated the large walking dragline industry over many decades until 1997. Then, the rivalry ended when Bucyrus International, Inc., purchased the Marion Power Shovel Company. The Marion plant in Ohio closed, and the manufacturing rights to the Marion machines transferred to the Bucyrus plant in Milwaukee, Wisconsin.

After inventing the dragline bucket in 1904, John W. Page continued to build draglines in moderate numbers and incorporated the Page Engineering Company in 1912. Most of Page's draglines up to 1935 were rail-mounted, although some were equipped with a crude walking system from about 1923. In 1924, Page developed the first diesel engine exclusively designed for dragline use. Then in 1935, Page unveiled the first of its 600 Series walkers, featuring a vastly improved walking system that was utilized right up to the demise of the company in 1988. Page modernized its draglines in the mid-1950s with the 700 Series. This included the Model 762, a 64-cubic-yard machine shipped in 1969 to British Columbia and, the company's largest, the 75-cubic-yard Model 757 delivered to a coal mine in Alberta, Canada, in 1983.

In 1988, Harnischfeger Corporation (P&H) purchased Page Engineering Company, which provided

Bucyrus-Erie 2570-WS. The world's largest draglines operating in 2002 are the two Bucyrus-Erie 2570-WS machines. These are a super version of the 2570-W dragline, but bear little resemblance to the earlier machines both in design and capacity. One has worked since 1993 at the Black Thunder Mine in Wyoming, swinging a 160-cubic-yard bucket on a 360-foot boom. The other, an 8,000-ton machine, started in 2000 at BHP Coal's Peak Downs mine in Australia. There are 34 main electric motors on board: 8 hoist, 8 drag, 14 swing, and 4 to power the walking shoes. The Peak Downs machine is equipped with a 360-foot boom and designed to carry buckets in the 140- to 160-cubic-yard range. *Bucyrus International, Inc.*

Marion 7200. Having built some of the world's largest crawler draglines for over two decades, the Marion Steam Shovel Company (Marion Power Shovel Company from 1946) decided in the 1930s to design a line of walking draglines. The first machine, an electrically powered Model 7200, went to work in 1939 with a 5-cubic-yard bucket on a 120-foot boom. It enjoyed instant success, and many more were shipped over the next 20 years, most with buckets of 6- or 7-cubic-yard capacity. In addition to the electric machine utilizing Ward-Leonard drive, some machines were diesel driven. The diesel 7200s were equipped with two engines: a Fairbanks-Morse 31A 300-horsepower diesel to power the hoist and drag drums through clutches and brakes, and a 144-horsepower Cummins engine to drive a DC generator for the electric swing motors. *Keith Haddock collection*

Marion 7400. When Marion launched the Model 7200 in 1939, the company had another larger dragline waiting in the wings. This was the famous Model 7400 that debuted the following year. In the 10- to 14-yard class, the Marion 7400 became one of the most successful and respected walking draglines ever built. Depending on bucket size, boom lengths from 160 to 235 feet were offered, and the machine's operating weight was approximately 650 tons. Like its smaller sibling, the 7400 was also available as a Ward-Leonard straight electric machine, or diesel powered. The latter was driven by a Cooper-Bessemer JS-8 900-horsepower engine of 13x16-inch bore and stroke running at 500 rpm. The Marion 7400 achieved an incredible 34-year manufacturing life, with 93 units shipped all over the world until the last in 1974. *Keith Haddock collection*

P&H with a line of draglines to add to its popular shovels. The first P&H dragline was sold to a coal mine in England. Commissioned in 1991, it was an updated version of the Model 757. Since then, P&H has redesigned its draglines and assembled several of its new 100-cubic-yard-class Model 9020 machines in Australia and Canada.

The world's largest draglines currently operating are the two Bucyrus-Erie 2570-WS machines. These are a "super" version of the 2570-W dragline, but bear little resemblance to the earlier machines in design or capacity. One has worked since 1993 at the Black Thunder Mine in Wyoming, swinging a 160-cubic-yard bucket on a 360-foot boom. The other, an 8,000-ton machine, started in 2000 at BHP Coal's Peak Downs mine in Australia. This modern-day monster has a rated suspended load of 800,000 pounds, ranking it high on the dragline size scale.

Except for machines built in the former Soviet Union, some in China, and one or two prototype machines, only four manufacturers have supplied the entire world market for walking draglines. These are: (1) Bucyrus International, Inc. (formerly Bucyrus-Erie), who purchased the rights to the Monighan machines in 1932, (2) Harnischfeger Corporation (P&H), who purchased Page Engineering Company, the dragline originator, in 1988, (3) Ransomes & Rapier, Ltd. of England, whose manufacturing rights were acquired by Bucyrus in 1988, and (4) the Marion Power Shovel Company, which was purchased by Bucyrus International, Inc., in 1997. With Bucyrus purchasing the rights to the former Marion and Rapier machines, the number of dragline suppliers reduced to just two, with the exception of those still built in the former Soviet Union.

Marion 7800. In 1942, Marion introduced the world's largest dragline, capable of swinging a 30-cubic-yard bucket on a 185-foot boom, and weighing a massive 1,250 tons. Launching the 7800 was an impressive achievement for Marion, who had only been in the dragline business for three years. Along with the 7200 and 7400, the 7800 enjoyed much success in the field, and a long production run. In fact, these three models were the only walking draglines produced by Marion over the next 20 years until the 40-cubic-yard Model 7900 was unveiled in 1962. The walking system employed on these first Marion walkers was a simple crank mechanism that can be seen on a Marion 7800 in this picture. Rotation of the walking shaft provided a circular motion to the two shoes, which were simultaneously lowered to the ground for each 6-foot step. *Keith Haddock collection*

Marion 8800. In 1963, Marion put to work a dragline more than double the size of any in existence at that time. Known as the 8800, it was ordered by Peabody Coal Company for work at its Homestead Mine in Kentucky. The dragline was designed with a boom 275 feet long to swing an 85-cubic-yard bucket, but was later approved to work with a 100-cubic-yard bucket. The total width of the machine was 116 feet, as wide as a six-lane highway. On the 8800, Marion had to redesign its traditional single-crank walking system to a two-crank system needed to support the massive 6,285-ton operating weight. This behemoth required 24 main DC electric motors to operate. The eight hoist, six drag, six swing, and four propel motors totaled 12,250 horsepower. *Keith Haddock collection*

Marion 7500. Marion added this model to its dragline roster in 1970. More powerful than the 7400 that continued in production, the 7500 offered longer booms, larger buckets, and greater range. Weighing in at 850 tons, this Ward-Leonard-controlled electric machine offered a choice of two different motor arrangements: either a single hoist motor for the hoist and drag drives operated through clutches and brakes, or separate motors for the hoist and drag motions. Both versions utilized a pair of motors to power the swing drive. The 7500 in the picture is one of two owned by Blaschak-Fisher Mining, working at English Center, Pennsylvania. It operates with a 22-cubic-yard bucket on a 200-foot boom. The last 7500 was shipped in 1981. *Keith Haddock*

Marion 7450. With the rapid expansion of coal markets in the 1970s, the need arose for a smaller dragline that could be moved relatively quickly from job to job. Like its competitors Bucyrus and Rapier, Marion designed a dragline consisting of modules that were bolted together instead of welded. The machine could be broken down into roadable components, and then quickly assembled in a matter of weeks instead of months. Marion shipped its first modular dragline in 1979, and another six were built up to 1985. Available as a diesel-electric or straight electric machine, the 7450 utilized independent motors for its hoist, drag, and swing motions. The drag motor was also used to propel the machine. The diesel version was furnished with a GM-EMD engine of 2,300 horsepower running at 900 rpm. *Keith Haddock*

Marion 8200. Another in Marion's 8000 Series walking draglines is the 8200, first shipped in 1973. This well-proportioned and reliable dragline proved to be one of Marion's most successful, with 34 sold up to 1996. Designed on similar lines to the larger 8750, the 8200 featured a tri-structure boom suspension. That's the large triangular structure at the front of the house. It served as a mast to support the boom, a support for the hoist sheaves, and as a fairlead for the drag ropes. The walking device on the 8000 Series draglines featured a single-cam system incorporating an eccentric cam with an outboard bearing support. This meant that both ends of the walk shaft on each side of the machine were supported by the dragline's frame. The 8200 Brutus drops another 75 yards from the end of its 325-foot boom at the Paintearth Mine of Luscar, Ltd. near Forestburg, Alberta. *Keith Haddock*

Marion 8750. In 1970, Marion announced the first of a redesigned line of draglines utilizing state-of-the-art electronics and structural design. The 8750, first shipped in 1971, carried a 110-cubic-yard bucket on a 300-foot boom. This model turned out to be one of Marion's most successful large draglines, with 24 sold up to 1993. Although identified with the same 8750 model designation, the later machines bore almost no resemblance to the early 8750s. As each new machine was commissioned, Marion incorporated design changes and improvements. The last 8750 shipped swings a 106-cubic-yard bucket on a boom 420 feet long, the longest ever installed on a dragline. The 8750 shown works for Luscar, Ltd. at its Boundary Dam Mine, Estevan, Saskatchewan. It has a 335-foot boom, 98-cubic-yard bucket, and 6,300-ton operating weight. *Keith Haddock*

Marion 8950. In 1973, Amax Coal Company purchased Marion's largest-ever dragline, the 8950. It swung a 150-cubic-yard bucket on a 310-foot-long boom. If scales could have weighed this monster, they would have shown 7,300 tons. A veritable powerhouse, the 8950 ran with ten 1,300-horsepower hoist motors, eight 1,300-horsepower drag motors, six 1,300-horsepower swing motors, and four 1,045-horsepower propel motors. The only 8950 built worked for some 20 years stripping coal at the Ayrshire Mine in Indiana. In 1997, Marion Power Shovel Company was purchased by archrival Bucyrus International, Inc. (formerly Bucyrus-Erie Company), including the Marion patents and designs. This takeover ended a competitive rivalry between these two companies lasting some 113 years. *Eric C. Orlemann*

Monighan 1-T. Monighan's Machine Works of Chicago, established in 1884, became interested in manufacturing draglines in 1907, when local contractor John W. Page placed an order for hoisting machinery to install in a dragline. Page had built the world's first dragline in 1904. The dragline's success prompted more machines to be built jointly by the two companies. In 1908, Monighan changed its name to the Monighan Machine Company. In 1913, a Monighan engineer named Oscar Martinson invented the first walking mechanism for a dragline. The device, known as the Martinson Tractor, is shown installed on a Monighan 1-T walking dragline. When digging, the chains carry the shoes. When it's time to move, the cam rotates, lowering the shoes to the ground. The cam makes contact with the shoes, tilting the whole machine and moving back one step. *Keith Haddock collection*

Monighan 6-W. With the invention of Martinson's walking device in 1913, Monighan's draglines gained a significant advantage over all others in the field. Consequently, the Monighan Machine Company prospered. In 1925, Martinson improved his walking system by eliminating the suspension chains, and substituting a cam wheel running in an oval track in a frame pivoted to the shoes. The first of the new models was the 3-W of 3-cubic-yard capacity. In 1926, Monighan launched five more models, the 1-W, 1.5-W, 2-W, 4-W, and 6-W, with capacities denoted by model numbers. The 316-ton 6-W was available in either diesel or electric versions. The diesel 6-W in the picture, employed in canal excavation for W.E. Callahan Construction Company, has a 280-horsepower Fairbanks-Morse 14x17-inch bore and stroke diesel engine running at 300 rpm. *Bucyrus International, Inc.*

Monighan 6150. Between 1929 and 1931, Monighan introduced three new walking draglines in a different model series, the 6150, the 6160, and the 8160. The first digit indicated the standard bucket capacity, and the last three digits indicated the boom length. The 6150 in the picture is doing its part to construct a river embankment at Newellton, Louisiana, for R.E. Cotton Company. Its power comes from a Fairbanks-Morse five-cylinder diesel engine developing 300 horsepower. Overall machine-operating weight is 375 tons. In the early 1930s, Bucyrus-Erie Company commenced purchasing blocks of Monighan shares with the latter's approval, and over the next three years Bucyrus-Erie took a controlling interest in the company. The machines became known by the name Bucyrus-Monighan until the formal merger of the two companies in 1946. *Keith Haddock collection*

Page 430. John W. Page is acknowledged as the builder of the world's first dragline machine in 1904. He was a partner in the contracting firm Page & Schnable, which needed a machine to dig below grade level. Eventually, Page realized that building draglines was more lucrative than contracting, so, in 1912, he incorporated Page Engineering Company in Chicago, Illinois, builder of draglines. Page draglines began to appear with a crude walking system about 1923. The 8-cubic-yard Model 430 was one of the first. The Page system consisted of three vertical legs, two in front and one at the rear, operated by rack and pinion. The legs were attached to an independent frame structure running on rollers. To walk, the dragline's three legs were extended downward, raising the entire machine off the ground. Once raised, the machine was pulled by chains along a horizontal roller path inside the frame, to complete one step. *Keith Haddock collection*

Page 615. In 1935, Page unveiled two models of a new line of walking draglines, the 4-cubic-yard 615, and the 8-cubic-yard 620. They featured a vastly improved walking system utilizing an eccentric drive to the shoes, which were attached to the machine by walking spuds or legs. The lower end of the spud connected to a crank on the end of the walk shaft via a slotted bearing. The crank also connected to a hanger that carried the weight of the machine during the walking step. The top end of the spud was guided by a roller fixed to the machine house and running in a vertical slot in the spud. As the crank rotated, the shoes moved in an elliptical path, necessary for a smooth walking motion. Page used this walking system on all its draglines until the demise of the company in 1988. *Keith Haddock collection*

Page 631. Page Engineering Company never produced a super-sized record-breaking machine, but its draglines in the small- and medium-sized ranges found a respectable market share. Specializing only in draglines and dragline buckets, Page produced a steady stream of walking draglines in its Chicago plant. Only one electric-powered Model 631 was built (1946). It is shown stripping anthracite in eastern Pennsylvania with an 8-cubic-yard bucket on a 200-foot boom. Electrical equipment included DC hoist and drag motors of 300 horsepower each, and two DC swing motors of 90 horsepower each. These were driven by two AC motor-generator sets totaling 800 horsepower. The 631 had an operating weight of 638 tons. *Keith Haddock collection*

Page 726. In 1924, Page developed the first diesel engines exclusively for dragline application. They were of the four-cycle, horizontal "V" type, or horizontal inline type, and mostly built with V-6, V-8, and V-10 configurations and a cylinder bore of 12.5 inches. These engines ranged up to 1,100 horsepower, and all ran at a constant speed of 450 rpm. Many of the Page diesel-powered draglines built in the 1940s and 1950s were equipped with two diesel engines and an electric swing system. The 726 of 1954, shown stripping coal in West Virginia, is one example. It has a 660-horsepower six-cylinder engine on the main deck driving the hoist and drag drums through clutches, and a 330-horsepower three-cylinder engine mounted on an upper deck to drive a generator for the electric swing motors. *Keith Haddock collection*

Page 752. Page Engineering's most popular 700 Series dragline was the Model 752. The first was built in 1965, and with its 42-cubic-yard bucket on a 220-foot boom, it was the largest dragline yet built by the company. In 1974, Page shipped the first 752LR, a long-range variation offering booms up to 255 feet long, while still supporting a 42-cubic-yard bucket. Electrical equipment included two hoist motors, two drag motors, and a propel motor, all of 625-horsepower each, plus four swing motors of 187.5-horsepower each. Page shipped a total of 27 Model 752s between 1965 and 1986. The 752LR illustrated works for Hopkins County Coal Company in Kentucky. The last Page draglines built were a pair of 752LRs shipped to Turkey in 1986. *Keith Haddock*

Page 723. Page modernized its draglines beginning in 1954, when the first of the 700 Series appeared. The first of these was the small 721 of 6- to 7-cubic-yard capacity. This proved a good seller for Page, with 21 units shipped until 1970. Page built two Model 723 diesel draglines in 1955 and 1956. Both were used in Kentucky on surface coal mining operations. The one illustrated carries a bucket of 9.5 cubic yards on a 160-foot boom. It is furnished with a single Page diesel engine of 12.5x16-inch bore and stroke, the same 660-horsepower diesel engine functioning as the main engine in the 726. Operating weight is 355 tons. *Keith Haddock*

Page 757. The largest dragline ever built by Page is the Model 757 delivered in 1983 to the Obed Mine near Hinton, Alberta. Owned by Luscar, Ltd., it swings a 75-cubic-yard bucket on a 298-foot boom. The 757 in the picture uncovers phosphate rock in Florida. It has a special long boom (333 feet), and consequently its bucket is reduced to 61 cubic yards. Operating weight is approximately 4,500 tons. In 1988, Harnischfeger Corporation (P&H) purchased Page Engineering Company and closed the Chicago plant. Harnischfeger modified the Page designs and continued producing walking draglines, a valuable addition to Harnischfeger's popular line of electric mining shovels. *Keith Haddock collection*

P&H 9020. After taking over Page Engineering Company in 1988, Harnischfeger Corporation (P&H) commenced marketing the draglines. It sold an updated version of the former Page 757 dragline to British Coal Opencast for work in the United Kingdom. Commissioned in 1991, the machine included a new walking system employing a cam-and-roller bearing, similar to that used on Marion and Rapier machines. P&H went on to assemble four of its new 9020 draglines in Australia. These ranged in capacity from 85 to 115 cubic yards on booms from 320 to 390 feet long. The 9020 in the picture is the newest at the time of writing. Starting work in 2000 at Luscar's Boundary Dam Mine, Estevan, Saskatchewan, the 9020 carries a 98-cubic-yard bucket on a 350-foot boom. Operating weight is 6,260 tons. *Keith Haddock*

Rapier W1800. Ransomes & Rapier Ltd. claimed title to the world's largest dragline when its W1400 went to work in 1951. Although its 20-yard bucket had been exceeded earlier, the Rapier W1400's 282-foot long boom and its operating weight of 1,880 tons were greater than any dragline built up to that time. In 1961, Rapier unveiled an even larger machine, the W1800, re-establishing the company as the builder of the world's largest dragline. Weighing over 2,000 tons and carrying a bucket of 40 cubic yards, this W1800 is stripping coal at Luscar's Boundary Dam Mine, Estevan, Saskatchewan, in 2002. *Keith Haddock*

Rapier W80. The British firm of Ransomes & Rapier, Ltd., established in 1869, designed its first dragline in 1938, the Rapier W170. It carried a 4-cubic-yard bucket on a 135-foot boom, and featured the patented Cameron & Heath walking system, where the shoes were attached to an eccentric cam running in a roller bearing. The 2-cubic-yard W-80 followed in 1940, then the 2.5-cubic-yard W-90 in 1943. These draglines utilized a single motor to drive the hoist, drag, and propel motions through clutches. The rope reeving and gearing on the hoist and drag drums was arranged so that when both clutches were engaged, one drum wound the rope in, while the other unwound. Thus, during hoisting, the pull on the drag rope assisted the hoisting action, and the bucket could be paid out without using the drag brake. *Keith Haddock*

Rapier W700. In 1981, Rapier launched its first modular walking dragline, the W700. At that time, manufacturers were designing draglines to fill the need for relatively small machines that could be erected in a short space of time. Ranging in size from 10 to 16 cubic yards, these machines could be broken down into roadable components, and then quickly assembled by bolting the modules together instead of welding. The Rapier W700 was built in both diesel- or electric-powered versions. The diesel W700 in the picture dumps 14 cubic yards of overburden from its 165-foot boom at C&K Coal Company's coal mine near Clarion, Pennsylvania. Two big Caterpillar diesels, a D399 V16 and a D398 V12, provided a total of 1,800 horsepower. *Bucyrus Europe, Ltd.*

Rapier W2000. The boom in coal mining in the 1970s prompted Ransomes & Rapier, Ltd. to design a new line of walking draglines. The new line represented a big change for Rapier in that a cable-supported conventional boom was utilized instead of the earlier cantilever type. Several of these new Rapier models went to work in the United Kingdom, the United States, and India. The largest Rapier dragline is the W2000, an example of which is shown uncovering coal near Leeds, England, for Miller Mining. It carries a 36-cubic-yard bucket on a 314-foot boom; its operating weight is 1,975 tons. In 1987, Bucyrus Europe, an offshoot of Bucyrus International, purchased the manufacturing rights to Rapier walking draglines, and the W2000 continued to be offered. At the time of writing, 14 W2000s are operating in India, and another is under erection. *Keith Haddock*

Ruston-Bucyrus 5-W. The 5-W was one of the most popular walking draglines ever in terms of numbers sold. Originating on the drawing boards of the Bucyrus-Monighan Company in Chicago, Illinois, the first was shipped in 1935. Available with either diesel or electric power, the 5-W carried a standard 5-cubic-yard bucket on a 120-foot boom. It still holds the all-time best-selling record for a walking dragline. A total of 79 were built in the Chicago plant and a further 62 in the Ruston-Bucyrus plant at Lincoln, England, over a production life that lasted until 1971. The picture shows the very last 5-W built. It was shipped from the Lincoln factory in 1971, and now sits idle waiting for the scrapper's torch. *David R. Wootton*

Ruston-Bucyrus 1260-W. To cope with the swelling order books for draglines during the late 1970s and early 1980s, Ruston-Bucyrus built several of the Bucyrus-Erie-designed walking draglines with some components sourced from Bucyrus-Erie in the United States. These included six Model 1260-Ws, two of which were exported to the United States. Most of the 1260-Ws operated in the 30- to 40-cubic-yard range with booms up to 285 feet. Working weight was approximately 1,750 tons depending on boom configuration. The example shown has a 32-cubic-yard bucket on a 260-foot boom. It was shipped to a British Coal Opencast site in central England in 1976. *R-B International, Ltd.*

CHAPTER 15

CONTINUOUS EXCAVATORS

Continuous excavators, as the name implies, move earth and other material in one continuous stream. Other types of earthmoving machines operate in cycles: excavators dig, swing and dump; bulldozers must back up after each push; and haulers must return empty after each load. In the right conditions, continuous excavators operate at a high level of efficiency. They come in many varieties, from the small ditching machines seen on sub-division projects to the giant bucket-wheel excavators that comprise some of the largest self-propelled machines ever constructed (see chapter 17). This chapter is dedicated to the other types of continuous excavators: elevating graders, surface miners, bucket chain excavators, and some unusual types for special applications. Trenching machines, also classed as continuous excavators, are covered in chapter 16.

Elevating graders were an early form of continuous excavator that found their most popular use in road construction. Most of the grader manufacturers, such as Russell (later Caterpillar), Austin-Western, and Adams produced these machines. Initially pulled by teams of horses and later by steam traction engine or crawler tractor, the elevating grader consisted of a cutting blade or disk, which directed the material onto a moving belt suspended laterally from the frame. The conveyor was powered by chain or gear drive from the wheels, or in later versions, a separate power unit was fitted. The discharged material could be loaded into wagons running alongside, or formed into windrows for compaction into a road base.

Probably the earliest elevating grader was the machine built by the New Era Manufacturing Company in 1866. In 1887, the Austin Manufacturing Company purchased the New Era company, and by 1898 the former wood-constructed machine was redesigned in steel. Both the Austin Manufacturing Company and the Western Wheeled Scraper Company made a line of elevating graders, which continued after these two companies merged into the Austin-Western Company in 1934. The Russell Grader Manufacturing Company also made these elevating graders in several sizes later adopted as Caterpillar machines after the latter took over Russell in 1928. The J.D. Adams Company, having initially marketed the Stroud Elevating Graders built since 1904, produced its own machines from 1930 to 1946.

By the mid-1940s, most grader manufacturers had discontinued the elevating types in favor of nimble motor scrapers and regular graders with greater capability. Although their technology is obsolete today, elevating graders did build roads efficiently, as the dirt moved straight from ditch to embankment over the shortest distance.

Adams No. 11 Elevating Grader. One of the earliest forms of continuous excavators was the elevating grader. In the late 1920s, the J.D. Adams Company of Indianapolis, Indiana, famous for inventing the leaning-wheel grader (see chapter 8), marketed the Stroud Elevating Grader, which had been built since 1904. In 1930, Adams commenced building its own elevating graders. The No. 11, built between 1932 and 1946, boasted its own gasoline or diesel power unit to operate all grader motions. Notice the broader wheel on one side to support the loaded elevator. The complete unit weighed 17,840 pounds when equipped with a 68-horsepower diesel engine. Adams discontinued manufacturing elevating graders in 1946. *Keith Haddock*

Austin Improved Steel New Era Grader. The Austin Manufacturing Company of Chicago had its ancestry in the Chicago firm H.W. Austin & Co., formed by 1849. This elevating grader with the long title, introduced about 1905, was designed to be operated by teams of horses. All grader functions were operated by hand wheels, and the elevator was driven from the large rear wheel. The Western Wheeled Scraper Company purchased the Austin company in 1902, and the Austin-Western Road Machinery Company was organized. The product lines were marketed as Austin or Western machines until 1934, when all three companies were merged into the Austin-Western Company. *Keith Haddock*

Barber-Greene 522 Bucket Loader. The Barber-Greene Company of Aurora, Illinois, pioneer inventor of the asphalt paver, produced a variety of materials handling machines including bucket loaders. Designed for loading windrowed or stockpiled loose material into trucks, bucket elevators were popular with townships and municipalities. A snow-loading version was also offered. The traction wheels propelled the machine into the bank and material was loaded onto the bucket elevator by the spiral feeder. The Model 522 was produced from 1938 to 1952. *Keith Haddock*

A type of machine developed by several manufacturers is the surface miner, also known by various trade names. These self-propelled machines usually utilize a powered cutting wheel to excavate the material, which is then directed onto a conveyor belt for loading trucks traveling alongside. Capable of extremely high output, surface miners seldom work with enough trucks to achieve their maximum output! Their ability to peel off thin layers of material makes surface miners useful in mining thin coal seams, or separating partings from the mineral.

In 1940, Euclid experimented with its first BV Loader, one of the earliest continuous excavators. Not released until after World War II, the machine was very effective when it was used with high-speed wagons on mass earthmoving projects before the era of efficient motor scrapers. The BV loader was designed to be pulled by the largest crawler tractors of the day, and it consisted of a blade that simply cut the material and directed it onto its conveyor belt.

Except for the giant bucket wheels, continuous excavators took a back seat during the 1960s, the decade of the big scrapers. Then, with advancing technology and the need to lower unit costs of earthmoving, continuous excavators came back for an encore in the 1970s. The lure of uninterrupted action provided by continuous excavators prompted several manufacturers to enter the market. An interesting array of different machines resulted, each based on a different design principle and in widely differing sizes. They were all put to work, and all did the job, but none sold in any great numbers.

Some manufacturers, such as CMI Corporation and Germany's Wirtgen, developed continuous miners from pavement profilers with their milling action, while others such as Holland Loader Company, Barber-Greene, and Huron Manufacturing Corporation produced giant high-production earthmoving machines. Some of these machines could dig and load at rates of more than 2 cubic yards per second. But sales of these specialized machines dwindled in the 1980s, and few of the machines covered in this chapter are still available today. Holland, Wirtgen, and Vermeer are still active in this market, while a few others will build them only by special order.

Bucket chain and bucket-wheel excavators were probably the earliest types of excavating machines ever built. They first appeared in sketches by Leonardo da Vinci in the sixteenth century. Over the decades, many different types and designs have been recorded in drawings and sketches, but it is unclear if these were actually built. The earliest confirmed multibucket excavators were ladder types on water-borne dredgers in the eighteenth century. Used to lift mud

Barber-Greene WL-50. The Barber-Greene Company marketed the WL-50 continuous excavator beginning in 1971. Several worked on large earthmoving jobs filling bottom-dump wagons, or on salvaging soil in surface mining operations. The WL-50's digging action came from a 16-foot-diameter wheel with buckets around its circumference. The wheel was designed to cut material from a face on one side of the machine. The discharge conveyor was 31 feet long, enabling it to load large haul trucks. Powered by a Caterpillar 575 horsepower diesel engine, the WL-50 weighed 116 tons, and propelled on three hydrostatically powered crawler tracks. McNally-Pittsburg took over the rights of the WL-50 in the mid-1980s. Then, in 1990, the rights passed to Svedala Bulk Materials Handling. *Keith Haddock*

from shipping channels, they were driven by animals, manpower, or even windmills.

The advent of the steam engine permitted dredgers to be built of more substantial proportions, enabling them to attack tougher material. One of the earliest recorded was a steam dredge working in 1796 in the Port of Sunderland, England. Many present-day ports were initially constructed, and later dredged, by large ladder dredgers in the early 1800s.

The first documented application of a bucket chain excavator for use on land was by Alphonse Couvreux in 1859. A contractor from Paris, France, Couvreux applied some of his first excavators on the Ardennes railway. In the period from 1863 to 1868, seven Couvreux excavators moved almost 8 million cubic yards of earth in the construction of the Suez Canal. Bucket chain excavators by Couvreux and machines built by

Weyher & Richemond and Buette were also used on the Panama Canal during the unsuccessful French attempt by Ferdinand de Lesseps, beginning in 1879.

Lubecker-Maschinenbau-Gesellschaft (LMG) of Germany made its first bucket dredger in 1877, with an output of 40 cubic yards per hour. This company pioneered and developed a vast range of models that were used in canal excavation projects in Europe, and in surface mining operations by 1900. Over the decades, many large bucket chain excavators were built and shipped around the world. Although very few bucket chain excavators are built today, they still find application in open pits where differing strata in the excavated face must be blended for the final product, such as in brick making. Adapting these machines for stockpiling and reclaiming bulk materials has further extended their application.

Caterpillar No. 42 Elevating Grader. Caterpillar added elevating graders to its product line when it acquired the Russell Grader Manufacturing Company in 1928. The elevating graders, along with the former Russell pull-type, and motor graders, were retained by Caterpillar and modified to suit its requirements. The Caterpillar No. 42 elevating grader, in production from 1935 to 1942, was available with its own engine, or driven by power take-off from the towing tractor. The No. 42 in the picture carries a 40-horsepower engine and has an operating weight of 16,630 pounds. The restored machine is shown in 1985 working on a county road job in Alberta, Canada, and belongs to Graham Brothers Contracting Group. Caterpillar phased out its elevating graders after 1942. *Keith Haddock*

CMI PR1200. From its line of pavement profilers, CMI Corporation of Oklahoma City, Oklahoma, developed some surface miners for coal loading operations in the mid-1970s. The machines featured a centrally mounted cutting drum whose powerful milling action could dig hard coal without ripping or blasting. The machines were mounted on three crawler tracks, and steered by the pivoting single front track. The massive PR1200 was one of the most powerful machines of its type, having a 1,200-horsepower engine to drive the rotary cutter through a mechanical drive and the crawlers through hydrostatic drives. In 1985, Caterpillar, Inc. acquired the paving products from CMI, including the PR Series pavement profilers and surface miners. *CMI Corporation*

CMI Autovator 1000. This spectacular machine was driven by two 425-horsepower diesel engines, and propelled on eight hydrostatically driven crawler track assemblies. The 90-ton machine could dig at speeds up to 240 feet per minute and excavate at rates up to 6,000 cubic yards per hour. The Autovator sliced material from the face at one side of the machine and loaded it into trucks from a discharge conveyor at the other side. Two separate cutting edges fitted with teeth facing opposite directions allowed the machine to dig in both directions. This avoided having to turn the machine around at the end of the cut. Two cabs were installed to let the operator always face the travel direction. *CMI Corporation*

Euclid BV Loader. An early continuous excavator was the Euclid BV (BeltVeyor) Loader. The first version was produced in 1940, but development was hampered by the war effort. Then, in 1948, a unit was exhibited at the Chicago Road Show, where it attracted much attention. Designed to be pulled by the largest crawler tractors of the day, the BV loader consisted of a blade that simply cut the material and directed it onto its conveyor belt. The belt was driven by a Cummins 150-horsepower engine, or optional GM 190-horsepower engine, and the machine was mounted on a pair of non-powered crawler tracks. The BV Loader enjoyed considerable success on big dirt-moving jobs where one unit could keep a dozen or more Euclid bottom-dump haulers on the jump. *Keith Haddock collection*

Euclid Super BV Loader. The BV Loader just described found success in the early 1950s, but its popularity waned in the shadow of vastly improved motor scrapers entering the market, and Euclid chose to discontinue the BV loader in 1956. But the idea was not quite dead. While Euclid was under the ownership of the White Motor Corporation in 1969, it took another shot at the belt loader concept. The substantially larger Super BV had a 635-horsepower GM engine to drive the conveyor, and four non-powered crawlers to support the machine. While experiencing some success, including one machine that worked on the San Luis Dam in California, the Euclid loader concept once again lost ground to the more flexible and efficient motor scraper, and only two of the Super BVs were built. *Eric C. Orlemann*

Haiss Path-Digging Loader. George Haiss Manufacturing Company of New York began making elevator loaders in 1913. In 1918 the company originated power crowding (wheel drive) and force feeding (spiral propellers) on elevator loaders. The company produced a variety of both wheeled and crawler-mounted models, and by 1934 machines capable of loading up to 8 cubic yards a minute were being produced. The crawler-mounted Path-Digging Loader, originating in the 1920s, was powered by a 37-horsepower Waukesha gasoline engine, and operating weight was approximately 7.5 tons. The Haiss company became a division of Pettibone Milliken Corporation, and the elevating loaders were continued. *Keith Haddock collection*

Holland H1 Loader. The Holland Loader, with its 15-foot-high cutting blade and a 6-foot-wide main conveyor, is another machine that cuts a vertical slice of material. The entire machine is suspended on a frame, supported between two large crawler tractors that provide the cutting and propelling power. The frame can be raised or lowered hydraulically. The loader illustrated is coupled to two 410-horsepower Caterpillar D9H tractors. The sheer brute force of the tractors, combined with the 525 horsepower of the loader engine driving the conveyor, produce up to 7,000 cubic yards per hour. The Holland Construction Company of Billings, Montana, first built the loaders for its own use in 1971, then later began building them for sale. *Keith Haddock*

Holland 710 Loader. Holland Loaders are usually coupled between two of the largest crawler tractors available. Since Holland built its first loader in 1971, tractors increased in size from Caterpillar D9Gs, then D9Hs or Fiat-Allis 41s, to Caterpillar D11Ns. In the latter configuration, the two tractors and the conveyor engine combine to produce a massive 2,065 horsepower. In 1997, two of these units worked on the East Side Reservoir project in California. The Holland is offered in vertical or horizontal cut versions. The outfit in the picture making the dirt fly is a horizontal-cutting Holland Model 710 loader with a 700-horsepower Caterpillar D10 up front, and a 520-horsepower Caterpillar D10N pushing behind. Over 70 Holland Loaders have been built to date for use on major earthmoving jobs around the world. *Fred Thiessen*

Huron 475 Easi-Miner. The Huron Manufacturing Corporation of Huron, South Dakota, was established in 1963. Initially building curb and gutter machines, Huron developed a continuous coal loader called the Easi-Miner, and advertised it on the market in 1976. The Easi-Miner moved on four crawlers that supported a main frame carrying a cutting drum mounted centrally. The excavated material was fed onto a conveyor belt that could discharge to either side or the rear. The picture shows the smallest model, the 475. It could cut a 12-foot path and excavate a cut up to 16 inches deep. Power came from a 368-horsepower Detroit diesel engine, and its operating weight was 26 tons. *Keith Haddock*

Huron 1224 Easi-Miner. The big 1224 Easi-Miner found application in a number of coal mines where thin seams or partings had to be removed or separated from a larger block of coal. But the powerful 1224, largest of the Easi-Miners, was also capable of high-production loading from a 24-inch-deep cut while making a pass 13 feet wide. It could load at rates up to 2,800 tons per hour if enough trucks were available. The machine weighed 140 tons and was powered by a 1,200-horsepower Cummins engine. In 1985, Bucyrus-Erie Company took over the marketing of this machine, but low demand from the coal industry caused it to be soon discontinued. Bucyrus-Erie Company (now Bucyrus International, Inc.) took over marketing of this machine for a few years starting in 1985. *Huron Manufacturing Corporation*

Krupp KSM2000. The Surface Miners made by Krupp Fordertechnik GmbH of Germany, include the largest machines of their type yet produced. First available in 1988, these machines consist of a rotating wheel fitted with teeth at the front of the machine. Material discharge to the rear is via a conveyor that can swing through an arc of 200 degrees. Mounted on a pair of crawler tracks, the entire upper frame pivots at the rear so the digging wheel can be raised and lowered by two hydraulic cylinders attached to the front of the crawler frame. The KSM 2000 is outfitted with diesel power of 1,340 horsepower and tips the scales at 210 tons. In 1996, a KSM 2000 was delivered to the Taldinskij Mine in Russia. *Krupp Canada*

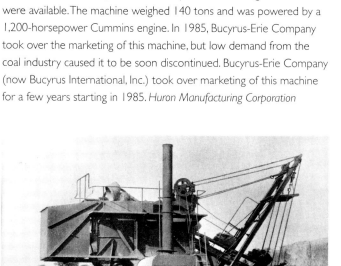

LMG 1882 Bucket Chain Excavator. The bucket chain excavator consists of a series of buckets attached to an endless chain, which can be raised and lowered over the working face. The buckets excavate the material, lifting it upward to dump into a hopper, which empties onto a conveyor or into rail wagons. In 1877, Lubecker-Maschinenbau-Gesellschaft (LMG) of Germany made its first bucket dredger, with an output of 40 cubic yards per hour. The picture shows LMG's bucket chain excavator of 1882, the first by the company for use on land. Steam-driven and rail-mounted, it was adaptable for digging above and below grade level. LMG made rapid progress in bringing out a vast range of improved models that were used for canal excavation in Europe, and for surface mining around 1900. *Orenstein & Koppel*

LMG 1909 Bucket Chain Excavator. LMG was a leader in bucket chain excavators in the early part of the twentieth century. As early as 1909, LMG built this large 335-horsepower steam-powered machine with a digging depth of 72 feet and an output of 1,300 cubic yards per hour. LMG machines were very successful, proved by the fact that two of the Type B bucket chain excavators built in 1887 were still operating in Germany as late as 1957. In 1911, Orenstein & Koppel (O&K), founded in 1876, bought the majority interest in LMG and continued the bucket chain excavators under the O&K banner. *Orenstein & Koppel*

P&H C-30A. Excavator builder Harnischfeger Corporation (P&H) offered its Model C-30A EL Loader in the late 1950s. Designed to be pulled by a crawler tractor of 150 horsepower or more, it was controlled by the single tractor operator. Raising and lowering both the cutting disc and conveyor assembly were controlled by the double-drum winch on the tractor. The conveyor was driven by a P&H 120-horsepower diesel engine through an air-operated clutch controlled by a small lever within reach of the operator. Furnished with a 30-foot-long, 48-inch-wide conveyor, the C-30A weighed about 17 tons. Depending on the material being excavated, the makers claimed it could cut up to 36 inches in one pass. *P&H Mining Equipment*

RAHCO CME-12. RAHCO International, formerly R.A. Hanson Company, of Spokane, Washington, introduced a Continuous Coal Excavator in 1987 known as the CME-12. This twin-crawler machine utilized a rotating cutter head to excavate a 12-foot-wide path at rates up to 1,000 tons per hour. It could excavate thin coal seams with the cutting head at ground level, but since the cutting head was mounted on a boom, it could be raised to cut up to 14 feet high. Excavated material was discharged to the rear via a swinging conveyor. The operator's cab was a modified Caterpillar 973 crawler loader cab. Overall machine weight was 50 tons, and a 475-horsepower Caterpillar diesel engine provided the power. *RAHCO International*

RAHCO Full-Section Canal Excavator. This strange-looking machine is one of many continuous excavating machines designed by RAHCO International to fulfill a special need. Mounted on two long crawler assemblies and supported on four parallelogram legs, the machine was capable of hydraulically lowering itself below grade as it excavated to a specified depth. With the adjustable side cutters and augers, the machine excavated and trimmed the canal bottom and sides to a perfect smooth profile. The material was discharged to the surface by conveyors. Shown ready for shipment in 1987, the Full-Section Canal Excavator was equipped with two diesel engines (250 and 165 horsepower), and could cut canals up to 9 feet deep with a 10-foot bottom width. *RAHCO International*

RAHCO Mobile Stacking Conveyor. Another special-purpose machine from the many innovative designs of RAHCO International is this mobile conveyor unit. One of many installed by the company around the world, the one in the picture was commissioned in 1996 at the El Abra Copper Mine in Chile. Its job is to stockpile copper ore for leaching. The tripper assembly with operator's cab travels the full length of the conveyor bridge, picking up the ore and depositing it onto the stockpile. The mobile conveyor bridge is 1,300 feet long and travels on 11 hydrostatically driven crawler assemblies. The machine has a theoretical capacity of 8,600 tons per hour. *RAHCO International*

Ruston Shale Cutter. The shale cutter or shale planer is a specialized continuous excavator. It was developed in the early 1920s by Ruston & Hornsby Ltd. of Lincoln, England. Many of these machines found homes in the rich shale beds around Peterborough, England, where large brick plants are located. The shale planer worked from the pit floor and ran on rails running parallel to the working face. Its excavating boom with a chain of cutters, and mounted on a revolving frame, could be crowded into the face. Shale planers were designed to tackle faces up to 52 feet in height. Machine weight ranged from 50 to 70 tons. The shale planer is particularly efficient because it does not have to hoist the excavated material. It cuts downward, thereby making full use of gravity. The last of the shale planers at Peterborough was shut down in 2002 after a working life of some 74 years! *David R. Wootton*

Stothert & Pitt Bucket Chain Excavator. Over the decades since they were invented in the nineteenth century, bucket chain excavators have been employed in special applications where geological conditions make their use most efficient. They have been popular in clay pits, where the full face of material must be blended for brick making and other applications. They are also used in the German coalfields to mine lignite, and at the vast Yallourn open-pit coal mine in Victoria, Australia. The British-built machine in the picture was designed and built by Stothert & Pitt, Ltd. It mined clay for cement manufacture at the Hope Works in England, a property of Blue Circle Industries (now Lafarge Cement, U.K.). This application lends itself to a bucket chain excavation because a full face of clay can be blended to improve the product sent to the processing plant. *Keith Haddock*

Steenbrugge Bucket Chain Excavator. Another type of bucket chain excavator was the Steenbrugge machine built in Belgium. Instead of transporting the excavated material by the usual method of conveyor, this machine pulverized the clay and, with the addition of water, pumped the material in the form of a slurry to the processing plant. The machine illustrated worked at the Hope Works in England. Although the machine and its builder are long since defunct, the technology of slurry transportation is very much alive when solids must be transported long distances in slurry form. *Keith Haddock*

Vermeer T1055 Terrain Leveler. The Terrain Leveler is basically an attachment for the T1055 trencher made by Vermeer Manufacturing Company of Pella, Iowa. The Caterpillar-powered T1055 has a 400-horsepower engine, features hydrostatically driven counter-rotating crawlers, and weighs 58 tons in operation. When equipped with the Terrain Leveler, it functions as a continuous excavator. It features a hydrostatically powered cutting drum 11 feet wide that can mill through rock, or mine minerals such as gypsum. A high-technology control system monitors the digging conditions and automatically adjusts traction speed accordingly. Vermeer also offers a larger Terrain Leveler as an attachment to its 600-horsepower T1255 trencher with an operating weight of 91 tons. *Vermeer Manufacturing Company*

Unit Rig Unimatic Continuous Excavator. Another continuous coal excavator was offered for a short time by Unit Rig of Tulsa, Oklahoma, now a division of Terex Corporation. Unit Rig purchased the manufacturing rights from Satterwhite International, Inc., and tested it in 1975. Called the Unimatic, the machine utilized a 12-foot-diameter cutting drum fitted with buckets and teeth, and driven electrically by AC motors. Mounted on four large steerable, hydrostatically driven rubber tires, the Unimatic weighed 125 tons and could cut a path 15 feet wide. Optional diesel engines in the 1,200-horsepower range drove generators to power the electric wheel motors and pumps for the hydraulic motions. The Unimatic in the picture is ready for work at the Navajo Mine in New Mexico in 1975. *Keith Haddock*

Wirtgen 3700SM. In 1980, Wirtgen GmbH of Bonn, Germany, began producing a line of continuous excavators known as Surface Miners. These machines were based on the company's already well-established line of road milling machines. Propelled on four crawler assemblies, the machine consists of a centrally mounted drum with cutting teeth, and a rear-mounted conveyor, which can swing through 180 degrees. The milling action of the cutting drum enables it to cut through hard material. The present range of Wirtgen Surface Miners consists of four models from the 800-horsepower 2200SM at 56 tons, to the massive 4200SM at 1,600 horsepower weighing 210 tons. The 3700SM illustrated also has a 750-horsepower engine but less weight at 194 tons. *Wirtgen GmbH*

CHAPTER 16

TRENCHING MACHINES

Trenching machines, also known as trenchers or ditchers, belong to the family of continuous excavators—machines that excavate and move material in one continuous stream. Trenching machines are categorized separately because they are single-purpose machines designed for digging trenches. In fact, in the right geological conditions, no other trenching method can come close to the trencher's output. And they really shine on cross-country pipelines where, free of obstructions, they can dig ditches at phenomenal rates of speed.

Trenching machines are either of the wheel or ladder type. The wheel ditcher carries a wheel with a series of buckets fixed to its circumference. The rotating wheel is lowered into the ground, and the action of the buckets digs the trench. As each loaded bucket reaches its highest point on the wheel, the material empties onto a conveyor via a chute. The conveyor, running laterally through the wheel, can run in either direction so that the excavated material can be dumped at either side. The machine is propelled on its crawler tracks, forcing the rotating wheel into the earth to carve the trench. In recent years, powerful ditchers fitted with special teeth have been developed to mill through hard, rocky material without blasting.

Ladder ditchers are similar to wheel ditchers except that the buckets are attached to an endless chain called a ladder. The ladder assembly is lowered into the ditch using a hoisting arrangement, and the buckets discharge onto a lateral conveyor in the same way as the wheel ditcher. The ladder ditcher is capable of digging a deeper trench than a wheel type, but has more moving parts, resulting in a higher operating cost. The early ditchers of both types were entirely mechanically driven, involving many drive shafts, couplings, and gearboxes. As hydraulics came to the fore in the late 1940s, more and more manufacturers dispensed with complicated drive trains and substituted hydraulic motors and rams to actuate the trencher's many motions.

James B. Hill claimed to have built the first mechanical ditching machine in 1893 while he was working at the Bowling Green Foundry and Machine Company in Bowling Green, Ohio. After persevering with

Austin 105. In the 1920s and 1930s, the Austin Machinery Corporation of Muskegon, Michigan, produced an array of construction machinery. This company descended from the former F.C. Austin Machinery Company, with roots going back to 1849. The company's products included diesel locomotives, elevator loaders, concrete mixers and pavers, crawler cranes and excavators, as well as trenching machines. The picture shows a 1929 Model 105 ladder ditcher, powered by a Waukesha diesel engine. All operations were mechanical, and the boom carrying the ladder was raised and lowered by pinions running in dual curved racks at the top of the main frame. *Keith Haddock*

Badger M302. Established in 1945, the Badger Machine Company of Winona, Minnesota, started to produce trenching machines toward the end of the 1940s. The Model M302 shown here was available mounted on wheels or crawler tracks and had a digging depth of over 10 feet. The company is known today as the Badger Equipment Company, and since the 1970s had manufactured specialized earthmoving, railroad, and materials-handling equipment encompassing familiar crane and excavator brand names such as Burro, Cullen-Friestedt, Hopto, Insley, and Little Giant. Badger trenchers were made up to 1958. *Keith Haddock*

Banister 710. Sometimes there just isn't a commercially made ditcher large enough to satisfy specialized pipeline contractors' demands, so they build their own machines. Here is the Banister 710 wheel ditcher, designed and built by Banister Equipment Co. of Edmonton, Alberta. Designed for digging through frost in northern Canada, the first Model 710 was tested in 1972. It weighs 115 tons, and is capable of digging a ditch 7 feet wide and 10 feet deep. The 710 wheel has 18 buckets, each of 1-cubic-yard capacity. Two Caterpillar diesel engines provide 1,120 horsepower. Banister Pipelines operates five of these giant ditchers built by the company's equipment arm. *Banister Equipment*

his machine and building several more at various locations, he was instrumental in founding the Van Buren, Heck & Marvin Company in 1902 at Findlay, Ohio, to manufacture the ditching machines. In 1906, the company name was changed to Buckeye Traction Ditcher Company to reflect the popularity of the machine. Buckeye became a pioneer in the trencher field, and developed many sizes and types of ditching machines throughout the 1920s and 1930s.

Another prominent ditcher manufacture is Cleveland Trencher Company, which still makes ditchers in Cleveland, Ohio. The company originated in 1921 when the A.J. Penote Company of Cleveland built a small wheel ditcher for its own use in Detroit. Following many inquiries about this successful machine, the company decided to manufacture and sell it. The Cleveland Trencher Company was established in 1923.

The Parsons Company of Newton, Iowa, was also a leading force in the ditcher business. George W. Parsons made his first production model, a ladder ditcher, in 1905. As early as 1906, a ladder ditcher capable of digging a ditch 12 feet deep and 2 feet wide was in production. Over the next quarter-century, Parsons not only became famous for its large ladder machines; but also made a line of wheel ditchers from the smallest to the largest then built.

The Barber-Greene Company of Aurora, Illinois, famous for its paving machines, also started to build ditchers at an early date. Co-founded by Harry Barber and William B. Greene in 1916, Barber-Greene invented many machines for the road builder in the 1920s and 1930s. Its ditchers enjoyed great popularity, and, as early as 1926, the company claimed more sales than any other make of trenching machine. Barber-Greene developed hydrostatic drive on its crawler models, permitting infinite crowding speeds (propel), and allowing crowding to precisely match the speed of the digging wheel.

In the 1970s and 1980s, some of the large specialist pipeline contractors couldn't find a trencher on the market big enough for the projects they were tackling, so they built their own machines. Those built by Banister Pipelines and Henuset Pipeline Services in Alberta, Canada, are some of the largest trenching machines ever built. Banister built its first wheel ditcher in 1965, the Model 508, designed to cut through frozen ground, and developed technology used later in its super ditchers. In 1972, the Banister 710 appeared, a monster machine weighing 115 tons. With 1,120 horsepower installed, it could dig well in frozen ground, but in unfrozen conditions it could dig a trench at 20 feet per minute! In 1978, Banister built an even larger ditcher, known as the Model 812, almost twice the size of the 710. Designed to dig 12 feet deep, this monster weighed 240 tons, measured 76 feet long, and was over two stories high. However, after successful field trials, it was dismantled when the project for which it was designed was canceled.

Barber-Greene 44. In 1923, Barber-Greene unveiled one of the first vertical-boom ladder ditchers, the Model 44. Able to dig a trench 18 inches wide and up to 5 feet deep with its standard boom, the machine had the obvious advantage of cutting a clean vertical trench from start to finish, minimizing hand work at each end. The following year, the 44A appeared with a patented automatic spring release drive sprocket, to protect the machinery when it hit an obstacle in the trench. Booms to dig ditches 7 feet deep were also available. The 44 Series ditchers were so successful that, with upgrades, they remained in production until 1957. Shown here is an early 1950s version with its boom in the raised position. *Keith Haddock collection*

Another giant ditcher was the Polar Bear, which was designed and built by Henuset Pipeline Services, Ltd. of Calgary, Alberta, in 1982. The 2,000-horsepower ditcher tipped the scales at 168 tons.

At the opposite end of the scale, there are many manufacturers that make small ditching machines; some are so small that the operator walks behind them. The first of these machines, which have become known as compact trenchers, was designed and built by Edwin Malzahn in 1949. He went on to establish the Charles Machine Works and the famous Ditch Witch line. Other pioneers in this field include ARPS Corporation of New Holstein, Wisconsin, who made a chain ditcher attached to a farm tractor and later built self-propelled machines; the Davis Manufacturing Company of Wichita, Kansas, who made its Task Force line of small crawler machines that were acquired by Case in 1968; and the Vermeer Manufacturing Company of Pella, Iowa, who built its first ditcher in 1951, and made its name in the compact ditcher industry.

In the past, ditchers were a common sight on all sewer and pipe jobs, as well as on housing and subdivision projects. Although they are not seen as frequently today, manufacturers who have specialized in this kind of equipment are still making them. Many ditcher projects have been taken over by the nimble tractor backhoe, which is a much cheaper machine to purchase. The increasing practice of plowing in pipelines using powerful crawler tractors with cable plowing equipment has also eroded applications for the traditional trenching machine. But for the serious pipeline contractor, faced with many miles of big ditch to dig, the trenching machine remains unbeatable.

Barber-Greene 705. A smaller machine for utility work was this Barber-Greene 705 mounted on an International wheeled tractor. It could dig trenches from 5.5 to 10.5 inches wide, and up to 4 feet deep. The first series, introduced in 1948, is shown. In 1950 this was upgraded to the 705A, which featured hydraulic crowd (wheel drive). Further upgrades brought the 705B in 1952, which remained in production until 1965. It was a favorite with utility contractors who took advantage of its wheeled mobility to supply sewer and water connections on housing projects. *Keith Haddock*

Barber-Greene 710. The Barber-Greene Company was co-founded by Harry Barber and William B. Greene in 1916 and became famous for inventing the asphalt paver. As well as building some of the largest commercially available trenching machines, the company also manufactured machines for special work, such as conduit and cable laying. One such machine was this Model 710 vertical boom ditcher produced from 1946 to 1950. Note the parallelogram boom arrangement utilized on Barber-Greene vertical trenchers. Although making a trench only 5.5 inches wide, it was able to cut through rock with its chain of teeth providing rock-sawing action. The 710 was powered by a 50-horsepower Buda diesel engine. *Keith Haddock*

Barber-Greene 777. Barber-Greene claimed its Model 777 wheel ditcher was the world's largest, fastest, and most powerful commercially available pipeline ditcher. Powered by a 144-horsepower diesel engine, it could dig trenches up to 54 inches wide and up to 8 feet 6 inches deep. The 33-ton machine featured the patented Hydra-Crowd, which provided independent, full hydraulic drive to each track, giving the operator an infinite range of speeds from 0 to 44 feet per minute. The 777 was made from 1960 to 1966, when it was replaced by the similar-sized but upgraded TA-77. *Keith Haddock*

Barber-Greene TA-65. The 22-ton TA-65 was introduced in 1967. It could dig up to 7 feet, 6 inches deep, and was powered by a Caterpillar 160-horsepower diesel engine. In 1987, Barber-Greene became a division of Astec Industries, Inc., which in turn sold the rights to Barber-Greene's paving products to Caterpillar, Inc., in 1991. But Astec retained the ditchers, since it already owned another trencher company, Trencor-Jetco, Inc. (now Trencor, Inc.). The Barber-Greene ditchers continue to be manufactured as the BG Series in the Trencor line. *Keith Haddock*

Buckeye No. 88. James B. Hill claimed to have built the world's first ditching machine in 1893 at Bowling Green, Ohio. After building several more machines, he became associated with Van Buren Foundry and Machine Company, who built his ditchers on a royalty basis. In 1902 a new partnership, Van Buren, Heck & Marvin Company, was founded in Findlay, Ohio, to build steam-powered ditchers. The machine illustrated was built that year. Four years later, the company changed its name to the Buckeye Traction Ditcher Company. The No. 88 is now preserved at the Hancock Historical Museum, Findlay, Ohio. *Mae Huston Local History Resource Center, Hancock Historical Museum*

Buckeye Model O. The Buckeye Traction Ditcher Company built some giant ditchers in the early part of the last century. In 1906, steam-driven monsters capable of digging a trench 54 inches wide by 12 feet deep were leaving the factory. By 1919, even bigger giants were built, some weighing more than 70 tons, measuring 55 feet in length and propelled on massive 8-foot-wide crawlers. At the other end of the scale, here is a product dating from 1913 being demonstrated during a convention of the Historical Construction Equipment Association, Bowling Green, Ohio, in 1995. The machine is a 10-horsepower Model O wheel ditcher. *Keith Haddock*

Buckeye 301. Buckeye developed many sizes and types of ditching machines throughout the 1920s and 1930s. By 1943, the range included 10 wheel ditchers and 6 ladder ditchers. The largest wheel could dig a trench 4 feet wide by 8 feet deep at rates of up to 10 feet per minute, depending on the material. Some of Buckeye's large wheel ditchers retained rather archaic design features up to the 1950s. This Model 301, built in 1949, employed hand-powered tiller-wheel steering reminiscent of an old traction engine. *Keith Haddock*

Buckeye 306. In 1947, Gar Wood Industries purchased the Buckeye Traction Ditcher Company, but Gar Wood continued the Buckeye products. In 1971, Gar Wood became a division of Sargent Industries, and ditcher production was transferred from Findlay to Wayne, Michigan. However, by this time ditcher sales were diminishing, and the machines were produced only a short time under Sargent's control. The Wayne plant closed down in 1972 when production ended. The Model 306 wheel ditcher shown here was built from 1950 to 1954. The 306 could dig trenches 5 feet, 6 inches deep, and up to 20 inches wide. *Keith Haddock*

Buckeye 120. This big Buckeye ladder ditcher, dating from the early 1940s, was fitted with a 60-horsepower diesel engine and had an operating weight of 11.5 tons. It boasted a digging depth of 11.5 feet and could turn out trenches up to 36 inches wide. The 120 featured a telescoping boom to minimize time needed to change boom lengths or for readying the machine for transportation. Also, its boom could be offset left or right for digging trenches against walls or other obstructions. Starting out as a Buckeye machine in the early 1940s, the 120 was continued as a Gar Wood product after that company took over Buckeye in 1947. *Keith Haddock*

Bucyrus Class 72. The Bucyrus Company, founded as the Bucyrus Foundry and Manufacturing Company in 1880 and known today as Bucyrus International, Inc., added steam-powered ditchers to its well-established line of steam shovels in 1915. The big Class 72 shown here weighs 40 tons and is digging a trench 17 feet deep with a standard ladder. An extension was offered to dig down to 20 feet. The machine could be fitted with various buckets to produce trenches from 24 to 72 inches wide. The latter number is indicated in the Class 72 model number. The conveyor was driven by an independent reversible steam engine so the excavated material could be discharged on either side of the trench. *Bucyrus International*

Bucyrus-Ruth HU. This unique machine was initially designed and built in 1906 by the Ruth Dredger Manufacturing Corporation of Los Angeles, California. In 1939, Bucyrus-Erie Company acquired the rights to manufacture and sell the machine but only did so for four years. The distinguishing feature of the Bucyrus-Ruth machine was that its boom carrying the buckets could be swung laterally through 180 degrees, so the ditcher's most useful application was trimming river or canal banks on either side of the machine while it traveled along the top. The Model HU shown carries a Caterpillar D4400 engine of 32 flywheel-horsepower, but gasoline power was also available. Machine operating weight was 18 tons. *Bucyrus International*

Capitol 1050. Capitol Trencher Corporation of San Dimas, California, made an extensive range of machines from the Model 450 at 7.5 tons weight and digging depth to 4 feet, to the top-of-the-line Model 1050 wheel ditcher (illustrated) weighing up to 90 tons and with a depth capability to 10 feet. This machine is equipped with a Caterpillar 3408TA diesel engine. Capitol Trenchers featured hydrostatic crawler drive, and the machines could be equipped with either ladder, wheel, or trapezoidal ditch digging attachments. The Capitol trencher designs are now incorporated in the line offered by Trencor, Inc. of Grapevine, Texas, who purchased Capitol in 1994. *Trencor, Inc.*

Cleveland Baby Digger. Another prominent ditcher manufacture is Cleveland Trencher Company, who still manufactures ditchers at their Cleveland, Ohio, factory. The company originated in 1921 when A.J. Penote Company of Cleveland built a small wheel ditcher for its own use in Detroit. Following many inquiries, in 1923 the company formed the Cleveland Trencher Company to manufacture and market this successful machine. One of the first ditching machines produced was this Baby Digger of 1924, which helped to establish the company's reputation for tough, reliable machines. *Cleveland Trencher Company*

Cleveland 95. Over the years, Cleveland produced a wide range of wheel ditchers, including many to the armed forces in World War II for grueling overseas work. An outgrowth of the original Baby Digger was the Model 95 wheel ditcher, a popular machine in the 1940s and 1950s. This maneuverable and versatile compact ditcher was advertised as capable of "more trench in more places at less cost." It could dig trenches from 17 to 24 inches wide to a maximum depth of 5 feet, 6 inches. Power came from either a gasoline of diesel engine of 50 horsepower, and the machine tipped the scales at 11,000 pounds. *Cleveland Trencher Company*

Cleveland 7036 SD. From 1968 to 1984, Cleveland Trencher was owned by American Hoist & Derrick Co. of St. Paul, Minnesota, and then by a management buyout team until 1986. Because of American's dominant crane lines and the depressed market for ditching machines in the 1980s, Cleveland trencher sales diminished. In 1987, the company was rescued and purchased by Metin Aydin, Cleveland distributor for the Middle East and Far East. The 7036 SD was a mid-sized machine marketed by the new owners in the late 1980s. It featured a hydrostatic vari-crowd (propel) with two speed ranges, and a Detroit 102-horsepower diesel engine. It could dig 7 feet deep in widths up to 36 inches. *Cleveland Trencher Company*

Cleveland 9624. In 2002, Cleveland trenching machines continue to be built in the original Cleveland, Ohio, plant. The line consists of seven sizes of wheel ditchers ranging from the small Model 9624 to the big cross-country 400W-HD that can dig 9 feet deep in widths from 36 to 72 inches. The fully hydraulic Model 9624 features a hydrostatic drive and carries a 140-horsepower engine. Machine weight is 17,000 pounds, and trenches up to 6 feet can be excavated in widths up to 24 inches. *Cleveland Trencher Company*

Eagle 8300 Trapezoidal. The Eagle Trencher Company of Ontario, California, built a range of wheel, ladder, and chainsaw trenchers from 9- to 45-ton operating weights and digging depths to 12 feet. After the company went out of business in the early 1990s, Guntert & Zimmerman, the well-known concrete slip-form paver builder, acquired the drawings and manufacturing rights. The new owners at Ripon, California, resurrected the Eagle trenchers and manufacturing recommenced in 1998. In 2002 the line consisted of five wheeled trenchers from 11- to 48-ton weights, including two special trapezoidal models. The top-of-the-line 8300 Trapezoidal ditcher digs a ditch 8 feet deep with a bottom width of 6 feet. It features a laser-guided automatic steering and grade control system, and a Caterpillar 400-horsepower engine. *Guntert & Zimmerman*

Ditch Witch RT115. In 1949, Edwin Malzahn produced the world's first service line ditching machine, the Ditch Witch®, while he worked with his father, Charlie Malzahn, at Charlie's Machine Shop in Perry, Oklahoma. Over the next few years, the machine revolutionized the utility trenching industry and virtually put an end to the hand-excavated trenches that were still common in the 1950s. The Malzahns established The Charles Machine Works, Inc. in 1958, and developed a full line of Ditch Witch® machines. The model RT115 is the largest model of the new generation of rubber-tired trenchers. It features a turbocharged John Deere diesel engine with 115 horsepower, fully hydrostatic propel, and interchangeable attachments. The RT115 can trench 94 inches deep and up to 24 inches wide. *The Charles Machine Works, Inc.*

Henuset Polar Bear. Pipeline contractor Henuset Pipeline Services, Ltd. of Calgary, Alberta, built one of the world's largest trenches. When nothing on the market would satisfy its needs, this innovative contractor built a machine called the Polar Bear in 1982. Based on Caterpillar D9H undercarriage components and equipped with a turbocharged 16V Detroit diesel engine developing 2,000 horsepower, the outfit tipped the scales at 168 tons. This giant ditcher could dig a trench 7 feet wide by 11 feet deep at high speed. The spotlight shone on this machine in the 1980s when it worked on a 23-mile, 42-inch water pipe job in central Alberta. *Henuset Pipelines*

Parsons 31. George W. Parsons founded the Parsons Company of Newton, Iowa. He made his first production model, a ladder ditcher, in 1905. Over the next quarter century, Parsons not only found fame for its large ladder machines, but also its many varieties of wheel ditchers from the smallest to the largest then built. The Parsons Company became a division of Koehring Company in 1929. Making the dirt fly was this Model 31 ladder trencher produced from 1927 until 1941. For this application, its rack-and-pinion conveyor adjustment was wound to its limit to enable the conveyor to load trucks. The 31 could put down a trench 15 feet deep in widths from 18 to 51 inches. *Kukla Trenchers*

Parsons 355. Billed as the world's largest-capacity ladder trencher of its time, the Parsons 355, made between 1964 and 1974, could dig a trench 25 feet deep and up to 6 feet wide. A 164-horsepower GM 6-71 diesel powered the 355, which had an operating weight of 28 tons. The ladder boom on this machine, shown working in Lubbock, Texas, was equipped with longitudinal rotating picks to trim the trench to wider than normal dimensions. Note also the parallel discharge conveyor for filling trucks ahead of the machine, minimizing disruption to the street. *Kukla Trenchers*

Allen-Parsons 12-18. From 1930, Parsons ditchers were made under license in the United Kingdom by John Allen & Sons (Oxford), Ltd. The picture shows an Allen 12-18 ditcher in use by the British Army in the early 1950s. The ladder chain is fitted with wide cutting teeth enabling the standard 12-inch buckets to dig a trench 18 inches wide to a maximum depth of 6 feet. In 1956, the 12-18 was superseded by the 12-21 with similar dimensions, and diesel power coming from either Dorman or Gardner engines. Other trenchers in the Allen-Parsons range included the 14-30 and 16-60. The model numbers denote the trench widths in inches. *Keith Haddock collection*

Parsons 155A Trenchliner. Requiring a two-man labor force to clean the top of the trench, this Parsons 155A Trenchliner is cutting a trench for drain pipes in sticky clay. The 155A could dig 11 feet deep, and carried an 80-horsepower engine. In 1976, Koehring divested its trencher interests, selling its small rubber-tired line of compact machines to the Seaman Company, today sold by Seaman-Maxon, Inc., of Milwaukee, Wisconsin; and the large Parsons wheel and ladder ditchers to Trenchliner in Austin, Texas. Trenchliner only survived until 1980, then Michael Kukla International acquired the large-machine line. Today, Kukla continues to build a line of cable plows and rubber-tired chain trenchers, but the last of the big Parsons trenchers left the factory in 1984. *Kukla Trenchers*

Tesmec TRS 1000. Founded in Curno, Italy, in 1951, the Tesmec Group today specializes in trenchers for hard rock applications and stringing equipment for power lines and fiber-optic cables. Its subsidiary company, Tesmec USA, Inc., established in 1984, now builds trenchers at a modern factory at Alvarado, Texas. The 28-ton Model TRS 1000 was one of the first Tesmec machines to be built in the United States. Designed for cutting through solid rock, it can be fitted with either a cutting wheel as shown, able to dig 4 feet deep, or a heavy-duty digging chain for increased depth to 10 feet. A Caterpillar 300-horsepower engine provides the power. *Tesmec*

Tesmec TRS 1675. Tesmec's largest trenching machine to date, the heavyweight TRS 1675 carries a Caterpillar 3412 engine of 750 horsepower and weighs in at 115 tons. Tesmec's rock-cutting design incorporates hydrostatic drive to the crawlers, with special automatic hydraulic vibration dampers to minimize shock on machine components and increase operator comfort. The machine can also be fitted with a high discharge conveyor for loading the excavated material into trucks. The big TRS 1675 is designed to be broken down into three major components for transportation. *Tesmec*

Trench-Tech 2500C. This company was founded in 2000 to manufacture heavy-duty ladder chain-type trenchers. Its predecessor company was a dealer for Trencor trenchers. The line, known as the 2000 Series, consists of four models ranging in weight from 25 to 115 tons, and in horsepower from 240 to 750. They are designed to mill through rock, and boast heavy-duty crawlers with independent drive and a mechanically driven digging chain. The Model 2500C shown has a maximum digging depth of 16 feet, with power provided by a Caterpillar C-15 diesel engine developing 525 horsepower. *Trench-Tech*

Trencor 660C. Trencor was established in 1981 as the Trencher Corporation of America (Trencor). In 1984 it purchased wheel trencher builder Dallas Jetco, a company originating as the Jiffy Excavator Tooth Company (Jetco) in 1945 at Alhambra, California. The merger of the two companies as Trencor-Jetco was a natural fit, as Jetco specialized in wheel trenchers, and Trencor designed and built the chain types for rock excavation. The 660C is a mid-sized hydrostatically driven model built on a Caterpillar-type undercarriage. Digging depths to 8 feet and trench widths to 28 inches are possible. The machine in the picture sports a parallel conveyor with rotating-head discharge so that only one lane is obstructed during highway trenching. *Trencor, Inc.*

Trencor 1660HD. The massive 1660HD can be fitted with a digging chain that digs 25 feet deep and up to 5 feet wide in solid rock. All machine functions operate through hydraulic or hydrostatic drives powered by a Caterpillar 3412 engine of 750 horsepower. Machine weight is approximately 120 tons. Astec Industries, Inc., purchased Trencor-Jetco in 1988, and merged the line with the Barber-Greene ditchers purchased a year earlier. Capitol Trenchers were added in 1994, providing Trencor with an even wider range of wheel and chain trenchers. That same year, the company, still owned by Astec, changed its name to Trencor, Inc. *Trencor, Inc.*

Trencor 1860HD. King of the Ditches is this top-of-the-line Trencor 1860HD, claimed to be the world's largest production model trenching machine. This 265-ton brute needs two engines to master its capabilities! A 1,200-horsepower Caterpillar 3512 engine has the exclusive job of driving the digging chain, while a 300-horsepower Caterpillar 3306B engine keeps the crawler tracks and the conveyors running. The digging chain is driven through a torque converter and a four-speed transmission. Five double-acting hydraulic cylinders provide boom hoist and positive down pressure on the cutting teeth. *Tim Twichell collection*

Trencor 1860HD. Another view showing the giant proportions of the 1860HD. In the late 1990s the machine shown earned its keep for Key Enterprises at Odessa, Texas, by digging a trench 5 feet wide, 7 miles long, and up to 32 feet deep in solid rock for a sewer outfall. For this job, the contractor built a special primary boom for the 1860HD, enabling it to dig 20 feet, plus an extension that allowed the 265-ton monster to reach down 32 feet. The digging chain consisted of four strands, each equivalent in size to Caterpillar D10 crawler track. *Tim Twichell collection*

Vermeer 12 Pow-R-Ditcher. One of Gary Vermeer's first inventions was a modified farm wagon with a mechanical hoist. Its success motivated him to establish the Vermeer Manufacturing Company in Pella, Iowa, in 1948. Recognizing the need for a trenching machine geared for farming applications, Vermeer developed a small rubber-tired ditcher in 1951, the Model 12 Pow-R-Ditcher. Towed behind a farm tractor, this first ditcher built by Vermeer Manufacturing Company boasted hydraulic motions and a lateral conveyor, just like the big ditchers. Two years after producing its first trenching machine, Vermeer built its first crawler-mounted ditcher, the Model 24T Pow-R-Ditcher. *Vermeer Manufacturing Company*

Vermeer T-755. The Vermeer company made its name in the compact ditcher industry, but machines leaving the Pella, Iowa, factory have gradually increased in size over the past two decades. The company has recently taken a substantial share of the large ditcher market, and offers an extensive line of rubber-tired and crawler-mounted ladder-type ditchers. These are all hydrostatically driven, and most models offer an optional oscillating track frame ensuring a vertical trench on slopes of up to 10 degrees. One of the larger machines is this T-755 with an operating weight of 33 tons and a 250-horsepower Caterpillar 3306 engine. As the advertisements say, the Diggin' Dutchman is very busy these days. *Keith Haddock*

Vermeer T1255 Commander. This is the largest production crawler trencher available from Vermeer Manufacturing Company. Suited to large-scale trenching applications, the T1255 features hydrostatic transmission with independent drive to each crawler track. Power is provided by a Caterpillar 600-horsepower diesel engine, and the machine tips the scales at 91 tons. The adjustable boom allows the machine to dig up to 18 feet deep in widths to 30 inches. The hydrostatically driven conveyor is 36 inches wide and can operate at speeds from 0 to 812 feet per minute. *Vermeer Manufacturing Company*

CHAPTER 17

BUCKET-WHEEL EXCAVATORS

Bucket-wheel excavators (BWEs) represent some of the very largest excavating machines working today. They are found in surface mines and occasionally on large construction projects where vast amounts of material must be moved. BWEs excavate in a continuous manner, utilizing a rotating wheel mounted at the end of a boom. The wheel is fitted with digging buckets around its circumference, and the buckets are filled by thrusting the rotating wheel into the working face while the boom swings from side to side. The excavated material falls onto a conveyor mounted within the boom structure, which transports the material in a continuous stream on further conveyors to the discharge point. BWEs are usually connected to an elaborate system of conveyors, which can transport the material a considerable distance. BWEs can also be arranged to load trucks, but keeping enough trucks on the haul road to take advantage of the BWEs full potential is the most challenging aspect of this method.

Geological conditions have to be just right to employ a BWE. Boulders are the machine's worst enemy, and when a breakage occurs, the entire earthmoving system grinds to a halt until the problem is fixed. This can be the major drawback of BWE systems when compared with discontinuous excavation systems such as a shovel and truck spread. But in the right conditions, nothing can match the tremendous output of a bucket-wheel excavator when used to its full capacity.

The continuous excavation method was developed in Europe when early water-borne dredgers took to land in the form of bucket chain excavators in the mid-nineteenth century (see chapter 15). The first documented bucket-wheel excavator was designed by British engineer A.R. Grossmith in 1908, and put to work in the ironstone fields near Corby, England. Although earlier attempts to build a BWE had been made, it is surprising to find that this first BWE did not appear until some 50 years after the first bucket chain excavator. Several earlier BWE patents were taken out, and some experiments were conducted, but apparently the technology of the day did not support a reliable machine. Even the Grossmith machine was unsuccessful, and was soon converted to a shovel.

After the initial attempts, BWE development continued in Germany, with one of the first machines built by

Humboldt in 1919. The first successful BWE appeared in 1925 at the Luise Mine of Braunkohlenwerke, in Germany, where it was used in reclaiming stockpiles. In 1926, ATG Leipzig purchased manufacturing rights to the Humboldt machines and expanded the BWE program. By 1938, ATG had delivered its 50th machine.

Orenstein & Koppel (O&K) and its associate firm since 1911, Lubecker-Maschinenbau-Gesellschaft (LMG), built its first BWE in 1934. LMG had been building bucket chain excavators since 1882. In 1935, O&K unveiled a machine with an output of 3,500 cubic yards per hour, and in 1937, O&K's first crawler-mounted BWE appeared. In 1955, O&K made news when it erected the first giant BWEs at the vast open-pit coal mine of Rheinische Braunkohlenwerke AG (now RWE Rheinbraun) in Cologne, Germany. Billed as the

Bucyrus-Erie 954-WX. In 1954, Bucyrus-Erie Company began manufacturing cross-pit bucket-wheel excavators under license from the United Electric Coal Companies (now Freeman Energy Company), who had been building BWEs for their own use. Designed under the direction of Frank Kolbe, these machines had been used successfully by United Electric to uncover coal in the Illinois basin since 1944. The picture shows the digging end of one of Bucyrus-Erie's first bucket-wheel excavators, the 954-WX. The sticky material required buckets with chain backs to dislodge the contents. There were nine buckets, each holding 1 cubic yard. The 954-WX was built on the base of a retired Bucyrus-Erie 950-B stripping shovel and estimated to weigh 1,300 tons. *Bucyrus International, Inc.*

Bucyrus-Erie 1054-WX. Built on a retired Bucyrus-Erie 1050-B stripping shovel base, the 1054-WX weighed approximately 1,600 tons. As with all cross-pit bucket-wheel machines, its function was to remove the top layer of glacial till material while the lower, harder material was cast aside by the stripping shovel seen in the background. The massive 1054-WX could cut a face 100 feet high, and the material traveled over 350 feet from wheel teeth via conveyors to the spoil pile. Two 1,000-horsepower AC motor-generator sets powered DC motors for the machine's various functions. The machine shown started work in 1960 at Peabody Coal Company's River King Mine, Illinois. *Bucyrus International, Inc.*

Bucyrus-Erie 684-WX. Bucyrus-Erie built this wheel excavator for the contractors' joint venture for the 40-million-cubic-yard San Luis Dam project in California. Starting work in 1964, the six-story-high machine was designed to load trucks at 4,500 cubic yards per hour using it 30-foot-diameter wheel carrying 10 2.5-cubic-yard buckets. After successful completion of the dam job, the 812-ton 684-WX was dismantled and shipped to Alberta, Canada, where it spent over 20 years excavating in the Suncor oil sands operation. Now retired, the 684-WX is shown preserved at the Oil Sands Interpretive Center at Fort McMurray, Alberta. *Keith Haddock*

Bucyrus-Erie 1060-WX. Unlike other cross-pit wheel excavators, the 1060-WX was built from scratch as a totally new machine, its eight-crawler base was equipped with hydraulic leveling cylinders like the stripping shovels. The Bucyrus-Erie cross-pit bucket wheels incorporated a crowding action where the wheel boom could extend into the bank under power. Crowding of 51 feet was possible on the 1060-WX. The various electric motors on this machine totaled 2,775 horsepower. Overall length from bucket teeth to top of discharge conveyor was 454 feet, or one-and-a-half football fields! Commissioned in 1967, this monster weighed 1,735 tons. *Keith Haddock*

largest mobile land machine in the world, this monster weighed 6,120 tons and could excavate more than 5,000 cubic yards per hour. Over the subsequent two decades, this same mining company ordered many more BWEs, several claiming title as the world's largest. In 2002, RWE Rheinbraun operates at least six BWEs with rated outputs of 314,000 cubic yards per hour.

Because of the extensive expertise and technology required to build large bucket wheels, two of the leading German manufacturers formed a joint arrangement in the 1960s called the Bucket Wheel Export Union. This group, consisting of Krupp and O&K, combined their forces and expertise to build giant machines for export around the world. Krupp had delivered its first BWE in 1948, and by 1972 it had sold more than 100 machines.

Other German companies building BWEs included Buckau-Wolf AG, established in 1928, who built its first crawler-mounted BWE in 1938. By the 1950s this firm had expanded its range to include many sizes and types of BWEs and bucket chain excavators sold worldwide. After World War II, Demag-Lauchhammer continued pre-war bucket-wheel technology and produced many varieties of BWEs over the years. Hermann Surken built BWEs for special purposes from 1956 to 1971. Weserhütte AG also built a large variety of smaller machines. In 1980,

Bucyrus-Erie 5872-WX. The largest-ever bucket-wheel excavator built by Bucyrus-Erie, and the largest in North America, was this behemoth installed at the Captain Mine of Arch Coal, Inc. in Illinois in 1986. This cross-pit machine had a 40-foot diameter wheel and moved excavated material from the digging face to the spoil pile, a distance of more than 700 feet! Using 12 buckets, each of 2.14-cubic-yards capacity, its operating weight was approximately 5,380 tons, and its highest point above ground measured 25 stories (250 feet). It was built on the lower works of a retired 80-cubic-yard Marion 5860 stripping shovel. When the Captain Mine closed, the 5872-WX was cut up for scrap in 1999. *Eric Orlemann*

Demag-Lauchhammer SchRs 1000/3 25. After World War II, German firm Demag-Lauchhammer continued the bucket wheel technology pioneered by Mitteldeutsche Stahlwerke AG, and former companies ATG Leipzig and Maschinenbau-Anstalt Humbolt. In 1916, Maschinenbau-Anstalt Humbolt had produced the first rail-mounted BWE for excavating overburden above track level. McDowell-Wellman Engineering Company erected the Demag-Lauchhammer machines in North America. In 1964, Consolidation Coal Company purchased the 3000-ton cross-pit BWE shown here. It featured an independently slewable discharge conveyor, unlike the fixed types of Kolbe and Bucyrus-Erie. Beginning life at the Glen Harold Mine in North Dakota, it was moved to the company's Norris Mine in Illinois in 1969. During its rebuild, the BWE received the 21-foot-high cylindrical base extension for added digging height, and a longer boom for greater range. *Keith Haddock*

Weserhütte became a member of the PWH Group, and was known as PHB Weserhütte, another group heavily involved with BWE manufacture. PHB Weserhütte was associated with O&K in the 1980s, and following the merger with Krupp in 1993, became part of Krupp Fordertechnik.

Several other European countries also developed BWEs, such as the former German Democratic Republic (East Germany), now part of the Federal Republic of Germany (MAN Takraf); Czechoslovakia (Unex); and those made in the former Soviet Union. In Scotland, Mavor & Coulson, Ltd. launched the Mavor E10 diesel-powered bucket-wheel excavator in 1967. Voest-Alpine Bergtechnik of Austria broke away from its more traditional underground mining machines and made a name for itself in open-pit mining equipment, including BWEs.

Successful BWEs were not confined to those designed in Europe. In the United States, the United Electric Coal Companies (now Freeman Energy Company) designed its own BWEs for its mines in Illinois. Under the guidance of its president, Frank Kolbe, a series of six cross-pit BWEs was built beginning in 1944. All were built on old stripping shovel bases, utilizing four two-crawler assemblies to propel, level, and steer the machine. The resulting BWEs turned out to be five times as productive as the shovels they replaced! The machine known as the W3A, rebuilt in 1981, is still operating in 2002.

In the 1950s, Bucyrus-Erie Company commenced building BWEs to the designs of the Kolbe machines under license, and later designed and built machines to its own design. These included the 810-ton Model 684-WX built in 1964 for contractors working on the 40-million-yard San Luis Dam job in California, and culminated with the world's largest of this type, the 5872-WX, commissioned at the Captain Mine in Illinois in 1986. Built on the lower works of a retired 80-yard Marion stripping shovel, this monster BWE boasted a 259-foot cutting radius, 442-foot dumping radius, and calculated operating weight of 3,500 tons.

Demag-Lauchhammer SchRs 1900/5 28. One of the largest BWEs built by this company was this machine owned and operated by RWE Rheinbraun AG near Cologne, Germany. It started work in 1958, and its theoretical capacity was 117,000 cubic yards per day. It dug with 12 buckets, each holding 2.5 cubic yards, attached to a digging wheel measuring 46 feet across. The machine's highest point towered 148 feet in the air, and it could tackle a working face 92 feet high. Electric motors installed for all operations totaled 5,230 horsepower, and operating weight was listed at 3,300 tons. Even with this weight, its 12 crawler tracks, with 9-feet-wide shoes reduce the ground pressure to a mere 10.7 psi.

Grossmith Wheel. Bucket-wheel excavators were developed some 50 years after the first bucket chain excavators (see chapter 15). In 1908, British engineer A.R. Grossmith put to work one of the first bucket-wheel excavators in the ironstone fields near Corby, England. Although the principle was sound, the Grossmith wheel was only used for a short time, then converted to a shovel. Technology had just not advanced far enough to produce a reliable bucket-wheel machine. The difficulty of transferring the material from wheel to conveyor, and lack of reliable material with which to build a conveyor are reasons cited for its failure. The picture shows the Grossmith under repair with its digging wheel removed. *Keith Haddock collection*

Krupp 50. This baby of the bucket-wheel world weighed a mere 52 tons, and was designed for a maximum output of 275 cubic yards per hour. It was installed in 1958 by the German firm of Krupp at the Athabasca oil sands in Alberta, Canada, in a pioneering project that led to the vast oil sands operations of today. The machine is now preserved in the Heritage Park at Fort McMurray, Alberta. Krupp delivered its first bucket-wheel excavator in 1948, and gained much experience in this technology over the subsequent decades. *Keith Haddock*

Mechanical Excavators, Inc. (MX) of Los Angeles, who acquired the construction rights from Bill Mittry of Mittry Construction Company in 1960, built another American-designed line of BWEs. These machines were of the compact type, mounted on wheels or crawler tracks. This machine's claim to fame was its angled digging wheel, which allowed material to flow straight onto the belt, and eliminated the usual discharge chute. After placing many MX machines of different sizes in North America and several overseas countries, Mechanical Excavators, Inc., was sold to American Hoist & Derrick Co. in 1982.

The European BWE manufacturers have adopted a standard nomenclature for their models from which it is possible to obtain the size of the machine and its range. The prefix SchRs is short for German words meaning "slewable crawler-mounted bucket-wheel excavator." The first number after the prefix is the capacity of each bucket in liters, followed by a slash mark and a number representing the cutting depth below grade in meters. The last number is the excavator cutting height in meters. Thus, the O&K SchRs 3600/5 48 has a 3,600-liter bucket capacity and can cut 5 meters below grade or 48 meters above grade.

Kolbe W4. This is the largest of the cross-pit BWEs built by the United Electric Coal Companies. Known as the Kolbe W4, it started work at the Cuba Mine in Illinois in 1959. The W4 was built on the lower works of a retired Marion 5600 stripping shovel originally built in 1929, and could excavate at the tremendous rate of 2 million cubic yards of overburden per month. The digging wheel was 27 feet in diameter, and the machine measured 420 feet from end to end. Its highest point towered 150 feet above ground, and machine weight was 2,100 tons. The operator obtained a good view of the proceedings in his cab perched 90 feet above the ground! *Bucyrus International, Inc.*

Krupp SchRs 250/0.8 12.5. Installed in a surface coal mine in the north of England by Derek Crouch Contractors in 1960, this machine took the upper clay layer, up to 40 feet high, and fed it onto a round-the-pit conveyor system. Below, draglines removed the lower strata, exposing the coal up to 180 feet deep. The Krupp wheel was self-contained, with its transfer conveyor supported by the upper boom, which swung independently from the wheel boom and machinery house. This enabled the machine to load trucks when the conveyor system was not in use. Machine operating weight was 350 tons. *Keith Haddock*

Krupp Spreader. This is the discharge end of the conveyor system fed by the Krupp bucket-wheel excavator in the previous picture. A moveable tripper, traveling on rails, picked up the material from the main belt and transferred it to the crawler-mounted slewable spreader. The material from the spreader was dumped over the spoil piles left by draglines excavating the lower strata, leaving a relatively level surface and requiring only minimal grading before being covered with subsoil and topsoil for return to agriculture. This method also ensured that the top unconsolidated material taken by the bucket-wheel excavator remained on top after mining was completed. *Turners Photography, Ltd.*

Krupp SchRs 1500/5 30.5. Peabody Coal Company purchased this monster Krupp cross-pit bucket-wheel excavator in 1963 and installed it at its Northern Illinois Mine. There it attempted to excavate probably the hardest shale material ever encountered by a BWE, and tooth wear was excessive. The 3,600-ton machine was later moved to the company's River King Mine in Illinois. This Krupp BWE was designed with independently swinging discharge and digging booms. Its digging wheel measured 38 feet in diameter and carried 10 buckets, each holding 2 cubic yards. The excavated material traveled 468 feet from the bucket teeth to the end of the discharge conveyor. *Peabody Energy*

Krupp SchRs 6600/9 51. One of the largest open-pit coal mines in the world is the huge Hambach Mine in Germany, owned and operated by RWE Rheinbraun AG. A fleet of the very largest bucket-wheel excavators ever built carries out excavation here. One of these is machine No. 288 shown here in 2001 moving on a specially prepared road from Hambach to a new location some 14 miles distant. This machine had worked at Hambach since new in 1978. This larger-than-life monster towers 315 feet at its highest point, and excavates up to 314,000 cubic yards of earth per day. *Walter Baertsh*

Krupp SchRs 6600/9 51. With eight huge crawlers in front and another four behind, the monster bucket wheel slowly negotiates the 14-mile distance from the Hambach to the Garzweiler pit in 2001. Even though the 12 crawlers reduce the 14,500-ton machine's weight to a manageable ground pressure, special care was taken to prepare the road so the machine remained stable throughout its journey. On the open road, the machine achieved a top speed of .37 miles per hour! *Walter Baertsh*

Krupp C700. The leading bucket-wheel excavator manufacturers offer what they call compact excavators. Although quite large machines, their proportions are nowhere near those of the big brothers just described. Unlike the monster bucket wheels designed for a specific mine, these off-the-shelf machines are made to a standard specification. Krupp offers its C-700 model with a 25-foot-diameter wheel with 12 buckets of just under 1 cubic yard each. Incoming electric power runs motors totaling 1,310 horsepower, and operating weight is 404 tons. The machine can be dismantled into a few roadable sections for easy transportation. *Krupp Industries*

Krupp SchRs 6600/9 51. The monster bucket-wheel excavator digs with a 70-foot-diameter wheel around which are mounted 18 buckets, each holding 8.6 cubic yards. As the wheel rotates, 48 buckets empty every minute, resulting in an output unmatched by any other type of excavating machine on the planet. During the move from the Hambach pit to the Garzweiler pit depicted in these pictures, the giant Krupp BWE attracted much attention from the media and public. Visitors were welcome as long as they kept clear of the machine. RWE Rheinbraun even prepared and handed out a brochure with machine history and specifications, and a map showing the machine's route to its new home. *Walter Baertsh*

MAN Takraf No. 293. The newest giant bucket-wheel excavator operated by RWE Rheinbraun is this MAN Takraf machine, which went into service in late 1995. This manufacturer was established when the materials handling division of Germany's MAN GHH Group merged with Takraf in the former East Germany after the two political halves of Germany reunited. Like its sister machines built by O&K and Krupp, the MAN Takraf has a capacity of 314,000 cubic yards per hour, and weighs approximately 14,500 tons. These giant bucket-wheel machines propel on 12 crawler tracks, each measuring 49 feet long by 12 feet wide. Instead of separate swinging discharge booms found on cross-pit BWEs, the big diggers of RWE Rheinbraun employ a transfer conveyor and a single large revolving structure on which the digging wheel, support structures, and machinery house are mounted. *Yvon LeCadre*

MAN Takraf Spreader. A huge machine in its own right, the spreader accomplishes the final stage of overburden movement at the extensive German open-pit coal mining operations. The spreader shown handles the spoil excavated by the MAN Takraf No. 293. The crawler belt tripper picks up the material sent by the excavator some few miles distant, and discharges it on a rope-suspended conveyor boom which in turn feeds the big spreader. The revolving spreader is able to lay down the discharged material into a flat contour as a first step in the reclamation process. Note the freshly dumped subsoil at the right of the picture. The process ensures that the excavated layers of material are replaced in their original positions after mining. *Yvon LeCadre*

Mechanical Excavators MX 2000. Established in 1960, Mechanical Excavators of Los Angeles, California, designed and developed a line of mobile bucket-wheel excavators ranging from small wheel-mounted machines to the MX 3000 with a rated capacity of 3,500 cubic yards per hour. The machine shown is a Model MX 2000, located at the Captain Mine in Illinois in 1977. Its wheel carried 8 buckets of 1.5 cubic yards each. Diesel power was provided by a pair of GM 12V-71N engines. The unique feature of the MX machines was their straight-line digging capability. The wheel was mounted at an angle to the wheel boom axis, so material dropped from the buckets onto the conveyor did not change direction. After many successful installations, the company was sold to American Hoist & Derrick Company in 1982. *Keith Haddock*

Mavor C10. This mobile wheel-mounted excavator was launched in 1967 by underground mining equipment maker Mavor & Coulson, Ltd. Built at the company's Glasgow, Scotland, works, it found favor working gravel pits and stockpiles, and stripping overburden at surface mines. Later, a crawler-mounted version was offered, and its compact width of 10 to 12 feet allowed the machine to be transported from job to job in one piece. The wheeled excavator weighed 30 tons, while the crawler version weighed 42 tons. The Mavor excavators, including crawler versions, were marketed by Anderson Strathclyde, Ltd. throughout the 1970s. *Keith Haddock collection*

O&K/LMG SchRs 600/0.5 16.5. Bucket-wheel excavators built by Germany's Orenstein & Koppel AG (O&K) derive their heritage from Lubecker-Maschinenbau-Gesellschaft (LMG), in which O&K purchased the majority interest in 1911. LMG built a bucket chain excavator as early as 1882 and became a world leader in this type of equipment by 1900 (see chapter 15). Continuing with the well-respected name of LMG, O&K built its first bucket-wheel excavator in 1934. The picture shows an O&K/LMG machine from the late 1930s. It was one of the first crawler-mounted BWEs and had a nominal output of 1,300 cubic yards per hour. It worked in the German lignite coalfields near Cologne. *Keith Haddock collection*

O&K SchRs 3600/5 48. In 1955, O&K unveiled the first of the super wheels at the Fortuna open-pit coal mine in the Rheinland, Germany. Billed as the largest mobile land machine in the world when erected in 1955, it weighed approximately 6,100 tons. Including the attached belt wagon, the outfit measured 656 feet from bucket teeth to rear conveyor (longer than two football fields), and ran on 18 crawler tracks. Each of the 12 buckets held 4.7 cubic yards, and daily output averaged over 140,000 cubic yards. This record-breaking machine paved the way for even larger BWEs to work in the huge German coal mines.
Keith Haddock collection

O&K SchRs 6300/9 51. This is one of several similar-sized BWEs at work in the extensive Hambach open-pit coal mine of RWE Rheinbraun, Germany. The machines are capable of excavating 314,000 cubic yards each day, and are some of the largest mobile land machines ever created. After taking 2.5 years to erect, the O&K machine in the picture went to work in 1991. Towering to the height of a 30-story building, it can cut to a height of 167 feet. The wheel is 70 feet in diameter and each bucket holds 8.2 cubic yards. It takes 12 crawlers to carry the main BWE, with another six for the attached belt wagon. If scales could weigh this machine, they would show 14,900 tons! *Yvon LeCadre*

O&K SchRs 6300/9 51. The wheel of another largest-class BWEs that is operated by RWE Rheinbraun at its open pit coal operations in Germany. The 70-foot diameter digging wheel, so often dwarfed by the overall size of the excavator, is shown here in comparison with a mine supervisor and wheel dozer. The rotating wheel swings from side to side to pick up material within its reach, but it needs the wheel dozer to make sure the working pad is absolutely flat before the excavator's 12 crawlers move forward and carry the 14,000-ton monster digger. The operator has a front-row seat in the cab located at the end of the wheel boom. *Walter Baertsh*

O&K SchRs 70/0.5 6.5. Not all BWEs are built in the outsized proportions of the machines just described. This 70-ton, diesel-powered machine was purchased by John Laing & Son, Ltd. and shipped to their Wraysbury Reservoir construction site in Kent, England, in 1965. It excavated fill at production rates up to 415 cubic yards per hour from a borrow pit, and loaded a fleet of AEC haul trucks. The flexible pipes seen leading onto the machine carried water that was sprayed onto the clay as it filled the trucks. This ensured the fill material met the specified water content before it was compacted into the earth-fill dam. *Keith Haddock collection*

O&K SH630. In bucket-wheel language, a compact excavator means a machine built to a standard specification and supplied as an off-the-shelf machine, rather than designed for a specific operation like the large BWEs. Although compact does not always mean small. The O&K compact excavator Model SH-630 weighs 370 tons and has a maximum output of 3,900 cubic yards per hour. The machine shown here works in conjunction with a mobile transporter bridge to carry the overburden to the spoil pile. In 1993, O&K and Krupp merged, and the expertise of both companies combined to form Krupp Fordertechnik.

Voest-Alpine VABE 700. Austrian manufacturer Voest-Alpine Bergtechnik GmbH has been building BWEs since 1976. The company expanded into surface mining equipment from its basic line of underground boom-type miners produced since 1965. This VABE 700 was ordered in 1984 by GKB Mining Company for work in Austria. Its 24-feet, 6 inch-diameter wheel digs with 12 buckets, each holding just under one cubic yard, to provide a theoretical output of over 4,000 cubic yards per hour based on 80 bucket discharges per hour. Machine operating weight is 550 tons. *Voest-Alpine*

Voest-Alpine VABE 1500. Starting work in 1991, this mid-sized BWE forms part of a huge cross-pit excavator and spreader system employed by Texas Utilities Mining Company at its Winfield South coal mine in Texas. It carries a 40-foot-diameter digging wheel with 16 2-cubic-yard buckets. Its two larger crawlers, 80 inches wide, reduce the 1,375-ton machine weight to a manageable ground pressure of 15 psi. The BWE works in conjunction with a 1,100-foot-long cross-pit spreader with the world's longest freely suspended excavating boom at 834 feet long. The system is designed to move 20 million cubic yards per year. *Keith Haddock*

BWE operator's cab. Riding in the sky, the operator of a 314,000-cubic-yard-per-day BWE is positioned high above the ground in his cab near the business end of his giant machine. He has control of all machine functions, and indicators warn him of any malfunction, such as an overloaded conveyor, electrical short, or overheated bearing. He watches the 70-foot-diameter wheel go around hour after hour as it gouges into the overburden and sends it close by his cab to discharge onto the multiple conveyor system far behind him. Even farther away, sometimes several miles distant, the material the operator saw excavated perhaps 20 minutes earlier arrives at the spreader machine and drops on the spoil pile. Far behind and below his bird's-eye view, the 12 crawler tracks inch the 14,500-ton machine forward for its next slice of the bank. *Walter Baertsh*

BIBLIOGRAPHY

The following books were used as reference for this book, and are recommended for additional background information on earthmoving vehicles.

Giant Earthmovers an Illustrated History; Extreme Mining Machines
by Keith Haddock

Super Duty Earthmovers; Giant Earthmoving Equipment; Euclid and Terex Earthmoving Machines
by Eric C. Orlemann

Classic Caterpillar Crawlers
by Keith Haddock and Eric C. Orlemann

Allis-Chalmers Construction Machinery
by Norm Swinford

All the above were published by MBI Publishing Company, Osceola, Wisconsin.

The Amazing Story of Excavators
by Peter N. Grimshaw; published by KHL Group, Sussex, England.

History of Komatsu
by Arthur McNae; published by the author, Queensland, Australia.

INDEX